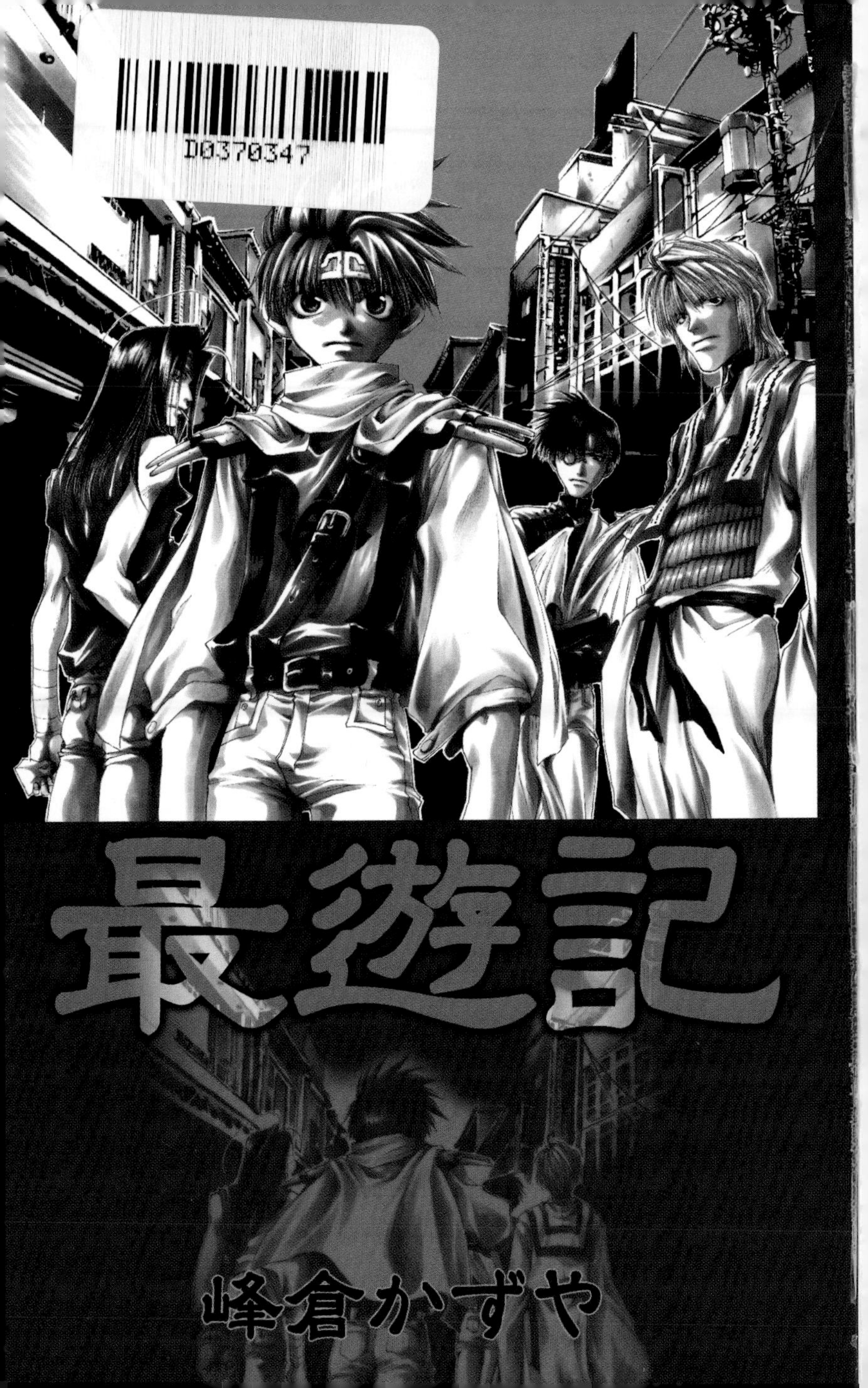

最遊記

峰倉かずや

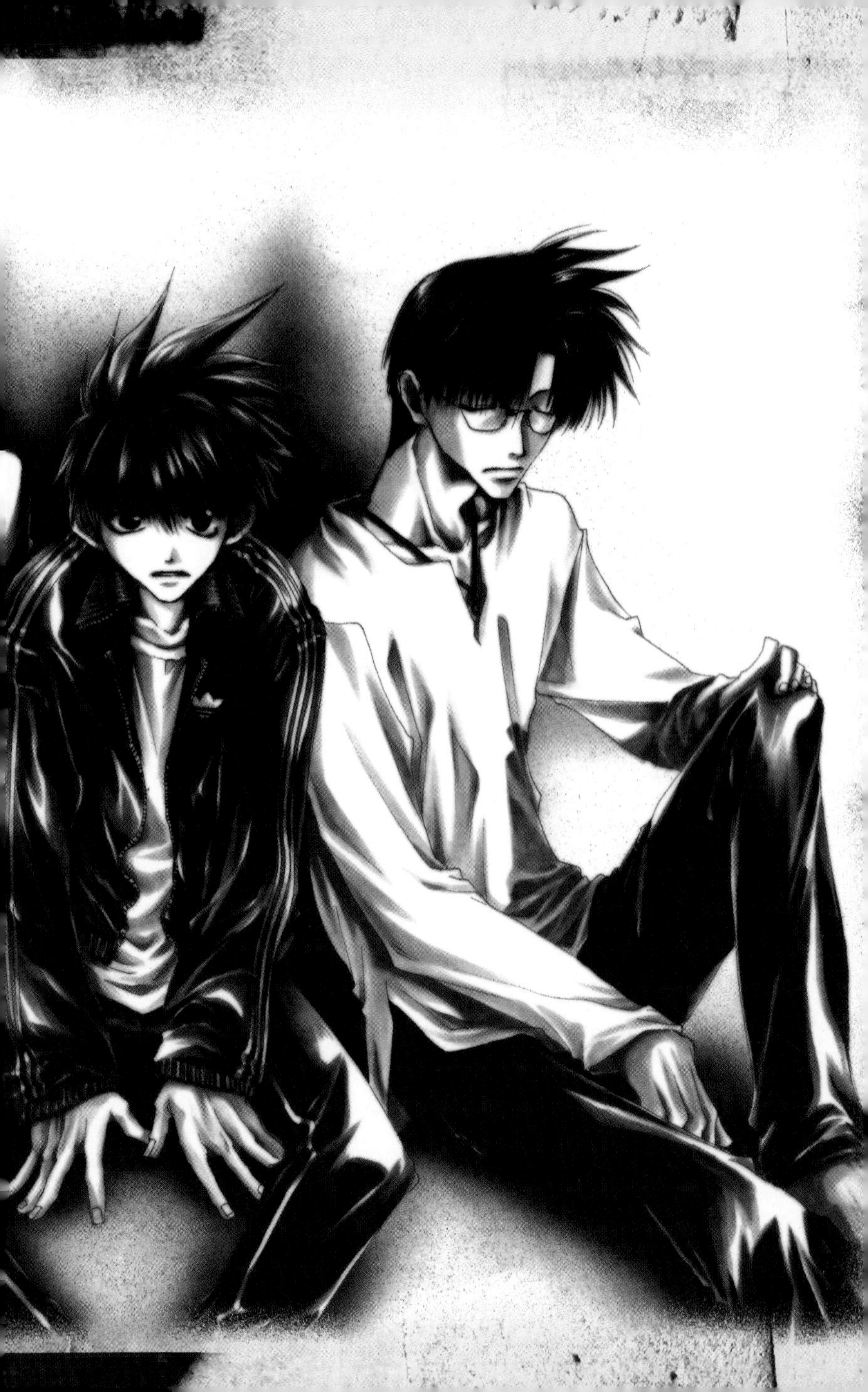

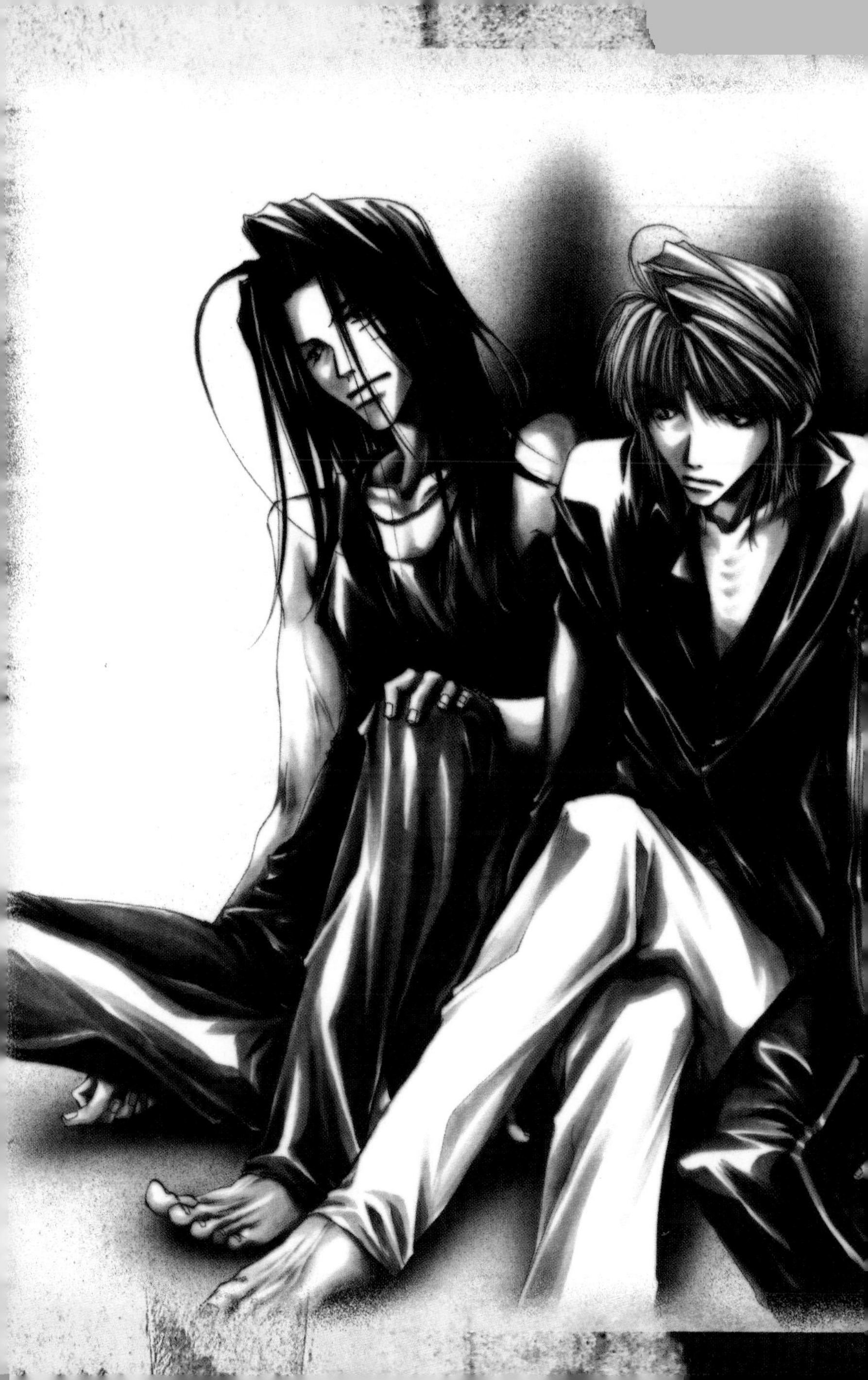

第参巻目次 CONTENTS

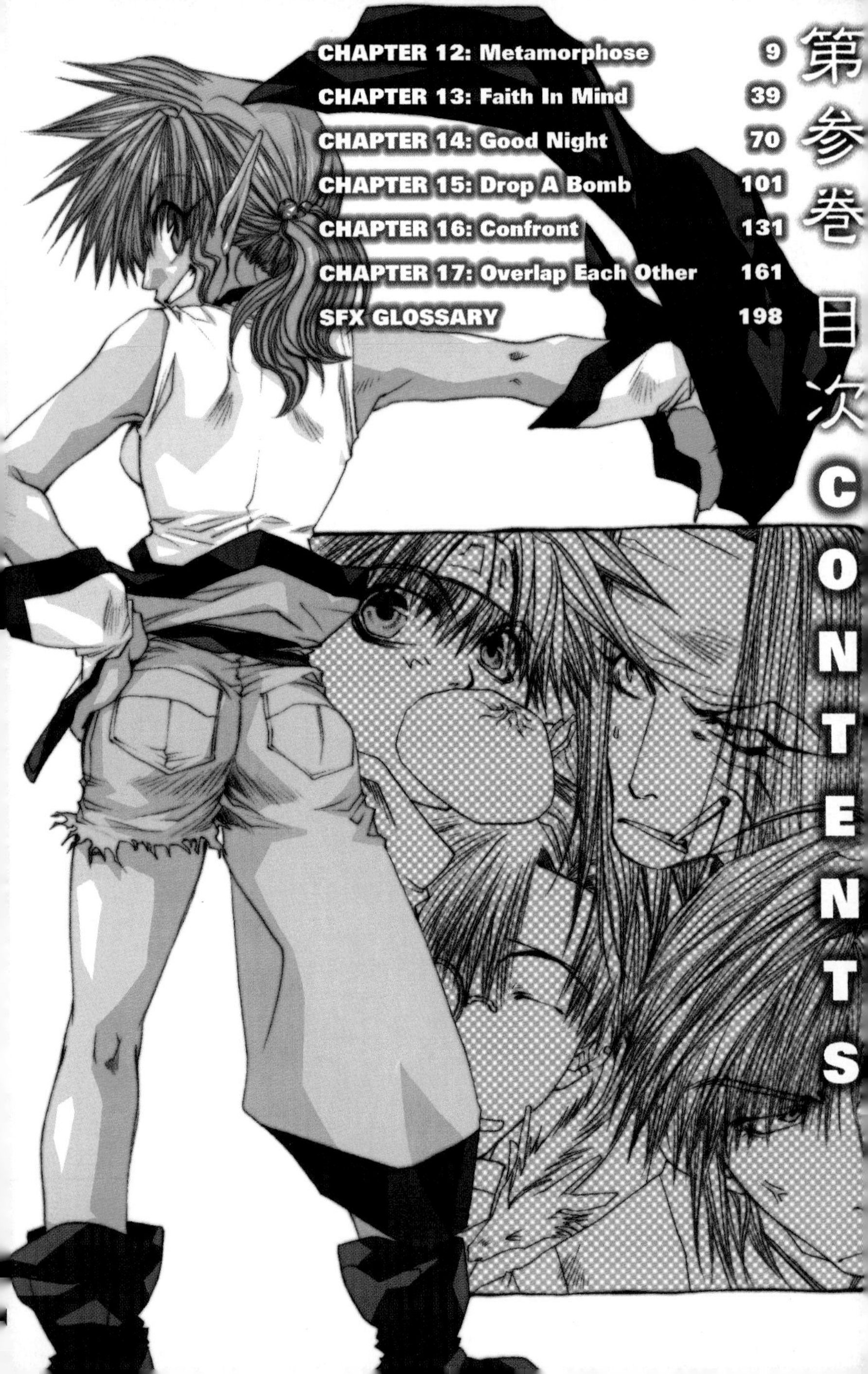

SAIYUKI

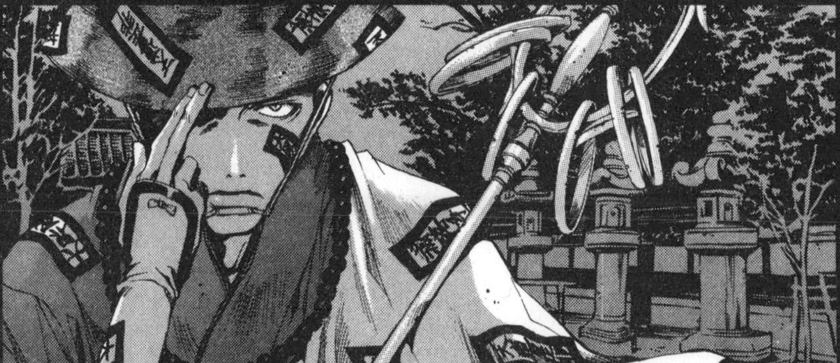

3

KAZUYA MINEKURA

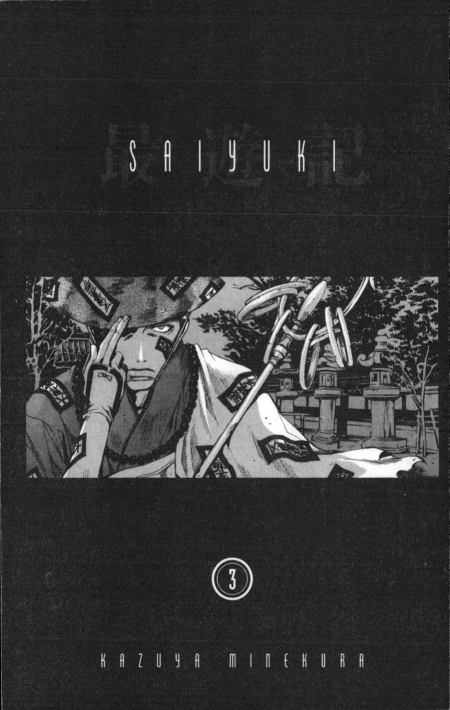

Translators - Alethea Nibley & Athena Nibley
Associate Editor - Lianne Sentar
Retouch and Lettering - Haruko Furukawa
Cover Layout - Anna Kernbaum
Graphic Designer - John Lo

Editor - Jake Forbes
Digital Imaging Manager - Chris Buford
Pre-Press Manager - Antonio DePietro
Production Managers - Jennifer Miller, Mutsumi Miyazaki
Art Director - Matt Alford
Managing Editor - Jill Freshney
VP of Production - Ron Klamert
President & C.O.O. - John Parker
Publisher & C.E.O. - Stuart Levy

Email: info@TOKYOPOP.com
Come visit us online at www.TOKYOPOP.com

A TOKYOPOP® Manga

TOKYOPOP Inc.
5900 Wilshire Blvd. Suite 2000
Los Angeles, CA 90036

SAIYUKI Vol. 3

SAIYUKI Volume 3 ©2003 by KAZUYA MINEKURA
All rights reserved.
First published in Japan in 2003 BY ISSAISHA, Tokyo.
English translation rights arranged with
ISSAISHA through Tuttle-Mori Agency, Inc., Tokyo.

English text copyright ©2004 TOKYOPOP Inc.

ISBN: 1-59182-653-5

First TOKYOPOP printing: July 2004

10 9 8 7 6 5 4 3 2 1
Printed in the USA

The Story So Far

The beautiful Shangri-La, pillar of civilization and religion in the East, has fallen into chaos. An experiment to revive the dreaded youkai Gyumaoh combined science and youkai magic against the laws of nature; the result was a Minus Wave that spread through the land and drove all once-peaceful youkai into a human-eating frenzy. As humans and youkai now fight to the death, Priest Genjyo Sanzo and three youkai with human blood--Son Goku, Cho Hakkai, and Sha Gojyo--travel West to India with the intention of halting the experiment and saving the land. If they don't throttle each other first.

During their journey, Gojyo revealed the existence of a youkai brother named Jien--a kind soul who saved Gojyo's life at the expense of a grave sin. Since Jien disappeared years earlier, Sanzo and co. now keep a look out for Gojyo's brother amidst the berserker youkai. They also faced their first attack from the team of Kougaiji, son of Gyumaoh, in the form of the beautiful alchemist Yaone. Hakkai managed to defeat her before her poisons and explosives did their work, but Kougaiji returned to retrieve his loyal underling and both parties avoided any loss.

Afterward, however, the Sanzo team met a youkai-slaughtering monk named Rikudo who is, in fact, a fellow monk from Sanzo's past now under a bloodthirsty curse. Despite Sanzo's discomfort with dwelling on his turbulent youth, he still defended Goku when Rikudo-once-Shuei attacked... and now Sanzo lies in the rain, drenched in raindrops and blood.

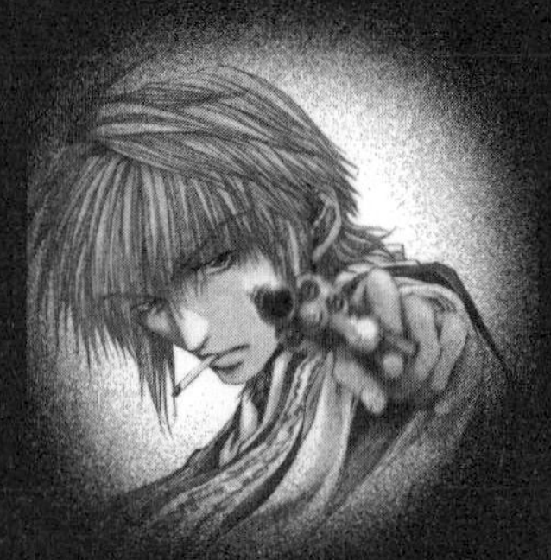

Genjyo Sanzo -

A very brutal, worldly priest. He drinks, smokes, gambles, and even carries a gun. He's looking for the sacred scripture of his late master, Sanzo Houshi. He's egotistical, haughty, and has zero sense of humor, but this handsome 23-year-old hero also has calm judgment and charisma. His favorite phrases are "Die," and "I'll kill you." His main weapons are the Maten Sutra, a handgun, and a paper fan for idiots. He's 177cm tall (approx. 5'10"), and is often noted for his drooping purple eyes.

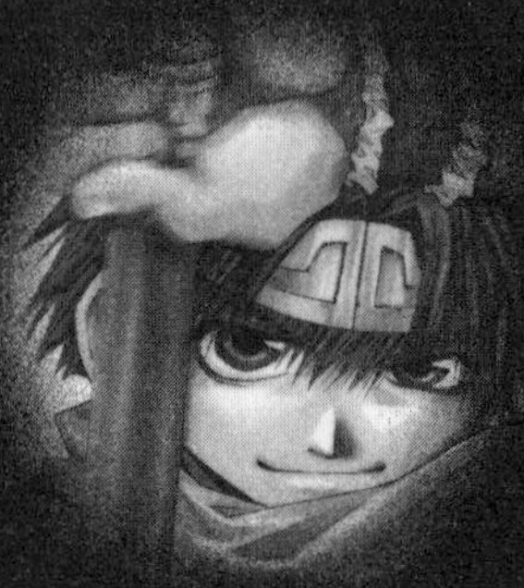

Son Goku -

The brave, cheerful Monkey King of legend; an unholy child born from the rocks where the aura of the Earth was gathered. His brain is full of thoughts of food and games. To pay for crimes he committed when he was young, he was imprisoned in the rocks for five hundred years without aging. Because of his optimistic personality, he's become the mascot character of the group; this 18-year-old of superior health is made fun of by Gojyo, yelled at by Sanzo and watched over by Hakkai. He's 162cm tall (approx. 5'4"). His main weapon is the Nyoi-Bo, a magical cudgel that can extend into a sansekkon staff.

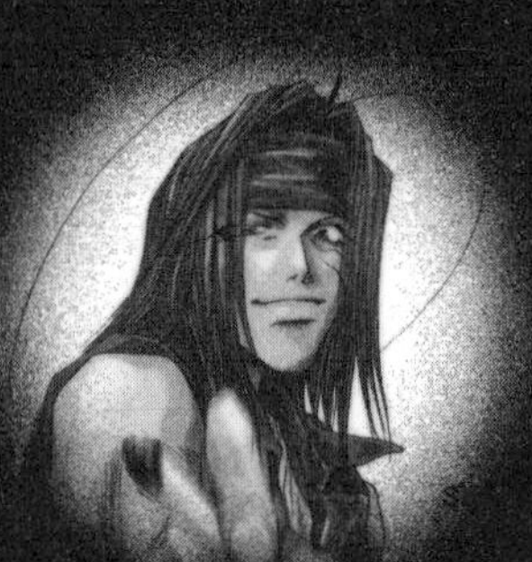

Sha Gojyo -

Gojyo is a lecherous kappa (water youkai). His behavior might seem vulgar and rough at first glance (and it is), but to his friends he's like a dependable older brother. He and Goku are sparring partners, he and Hakkai are best friends, and he and Sanzo are bad friends (ha ha!). Sometimes his love for the ladies gets him into trouble. Because of his unusual heritage, he doesn't need a limiter to blend in with the humans. His favorite way of fighting is to use a shakujou, a staff with a crescent-shaped blade connected by a chain; it's quite messy. He's 184cm tall, has scarlet hair and eyes, and is a 22-year-old chain smoker.

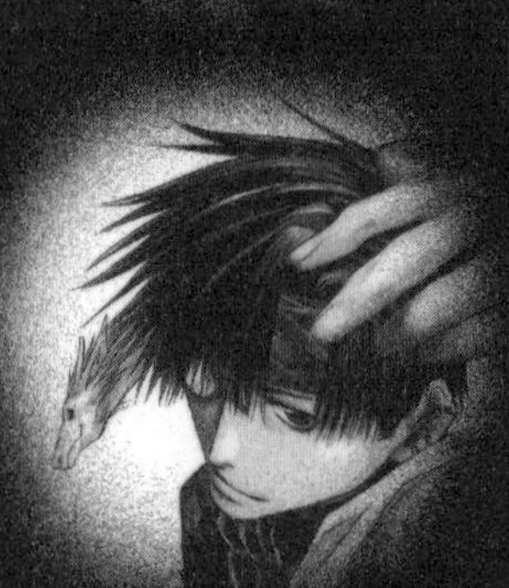

Cho Hakkai -

A pleasant, rather absent-minded young man with a kind smile that suits him nicely. It's sometimes hard to tell whether he's serious or laughing to himself at his friends' expense. His darker side comes through from time to time in the form of a sharp, penetrating gaze, a symbol of a dark past. As he's Hakuryu's (the white dragon) owner, he gets to drive the Jeep. Because he uses kikou jutsu (Chi manipulation) in battle, his "weapon" is his smile (ha ha!). He's 22 years old, 181cm tall (approx. 5'11") and his eyes are deep green (his right eye is nearly blind). The cuffs he wears on his left ear are Youkai power limiters.

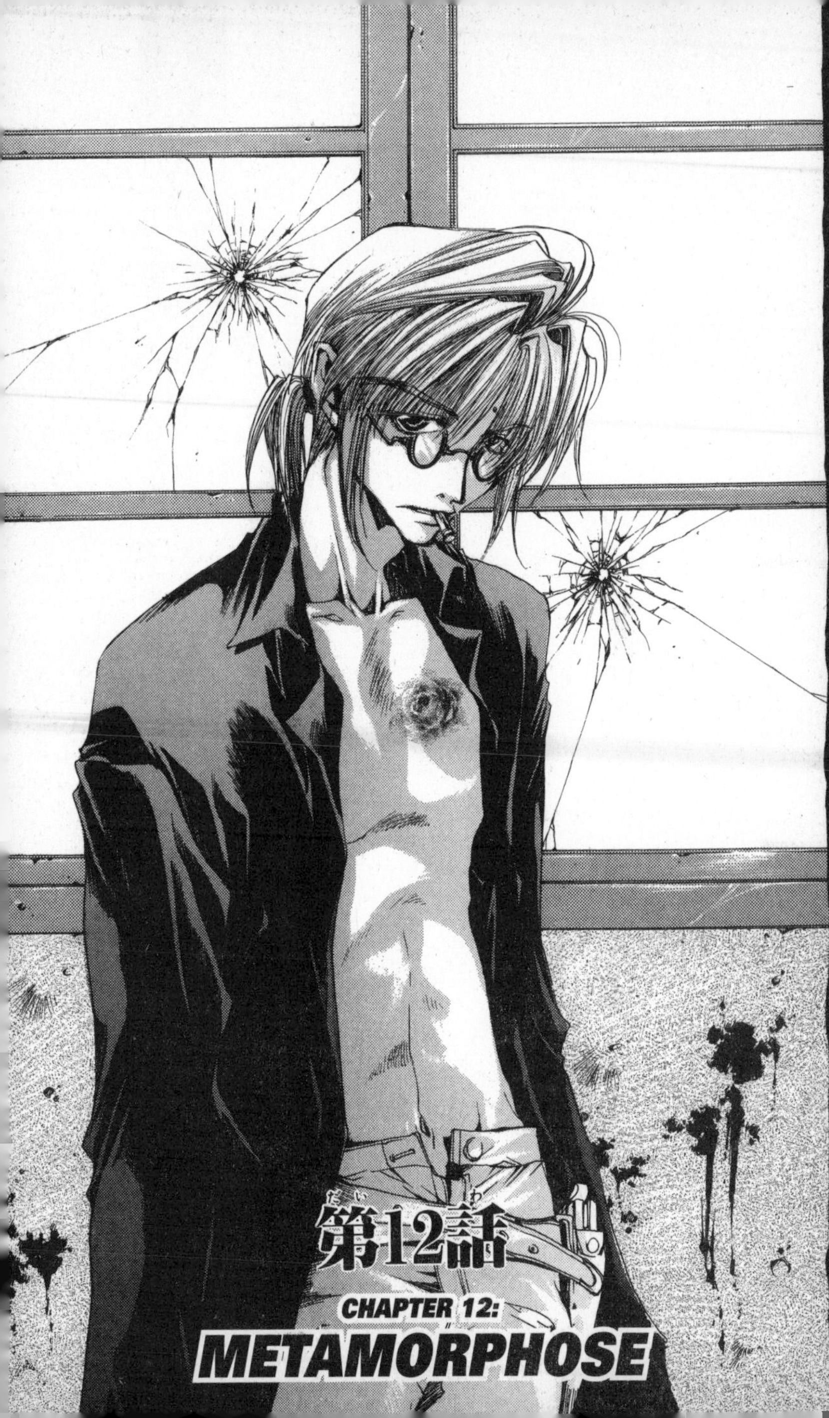
第12話
CHAPTER 12:
METAMORPHOSE

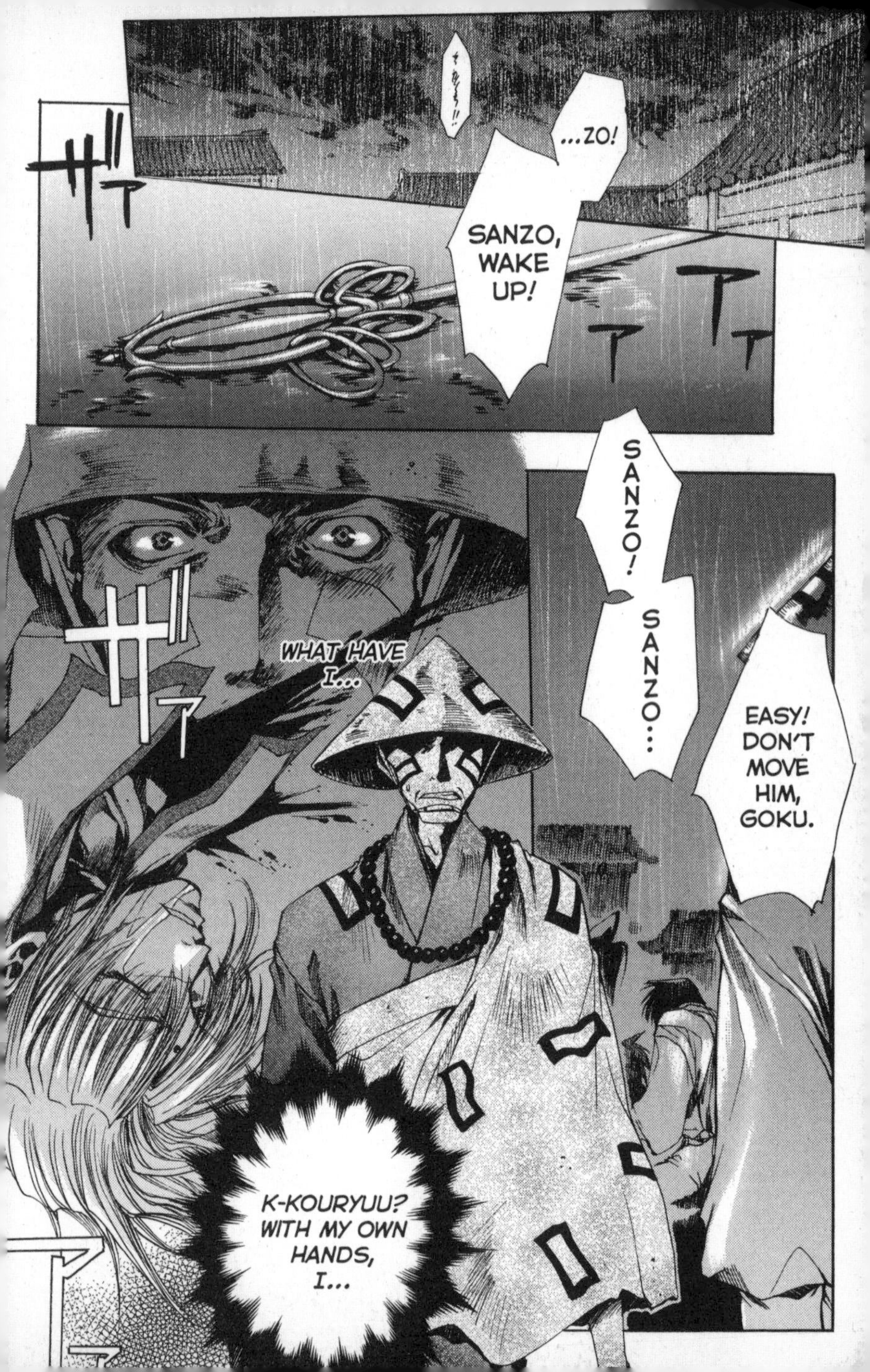
...ZO!
SANZO, WAKE UP!
SANZO! SANZO...
EASY! DON'T MOVE HIM, GOKU.
WHAT HAVE I...
K-KOURYUU? WITH MY OWN HANDS, I...

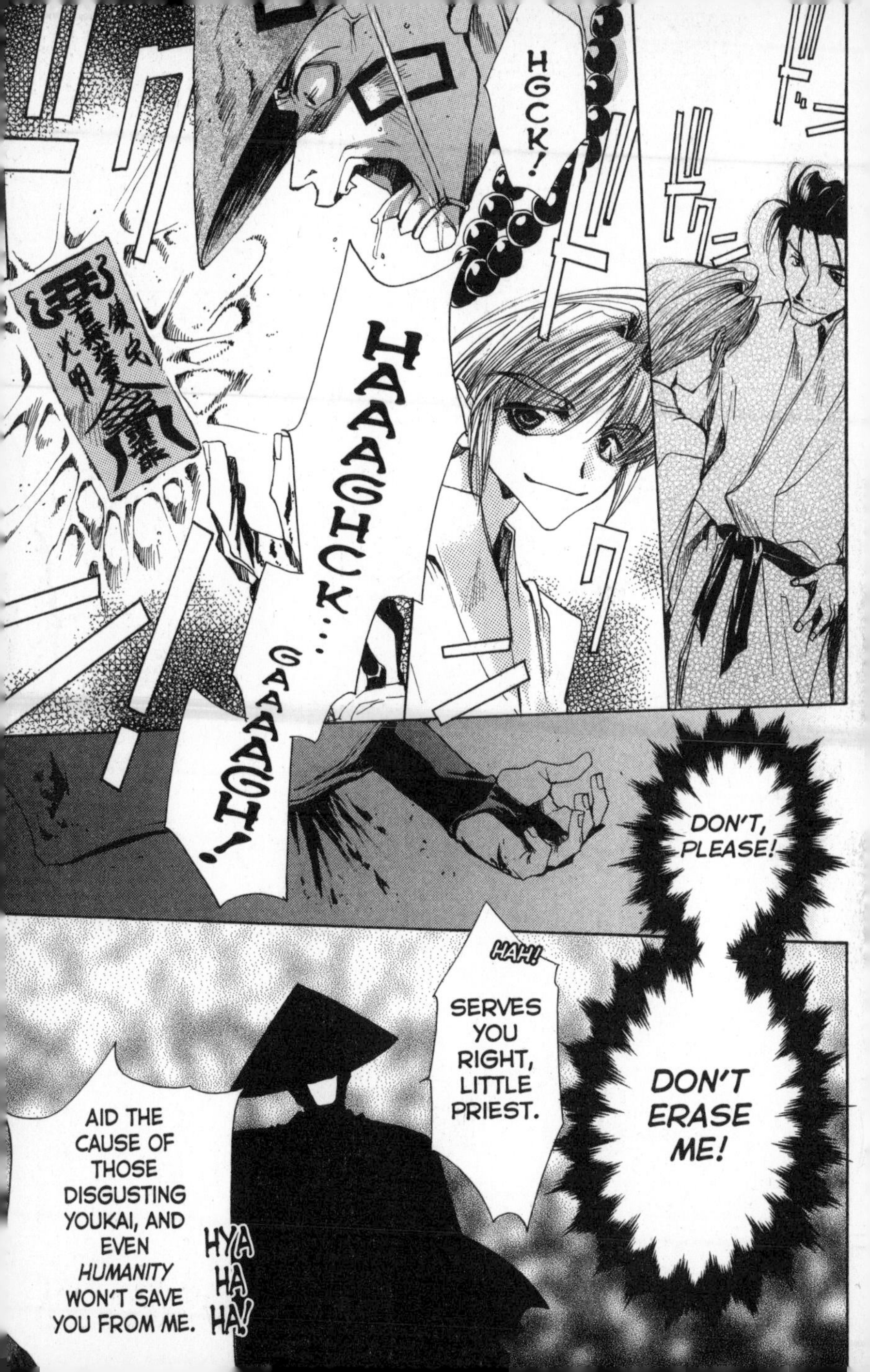
HGCK!
HAAAGHCK...
GAAAAAGH!
DON'T, PLEASE!
DON'T ERASE ME!
HAH!
SERVES YOU RIGHT, LITTLE PRIEST.
AID THE CAUSE OF THOSE DISGUSTING YOUKAI, AND EVEN *HUMANITY* WON'T SAVE YOU FROM ME.
HYA HA HA!

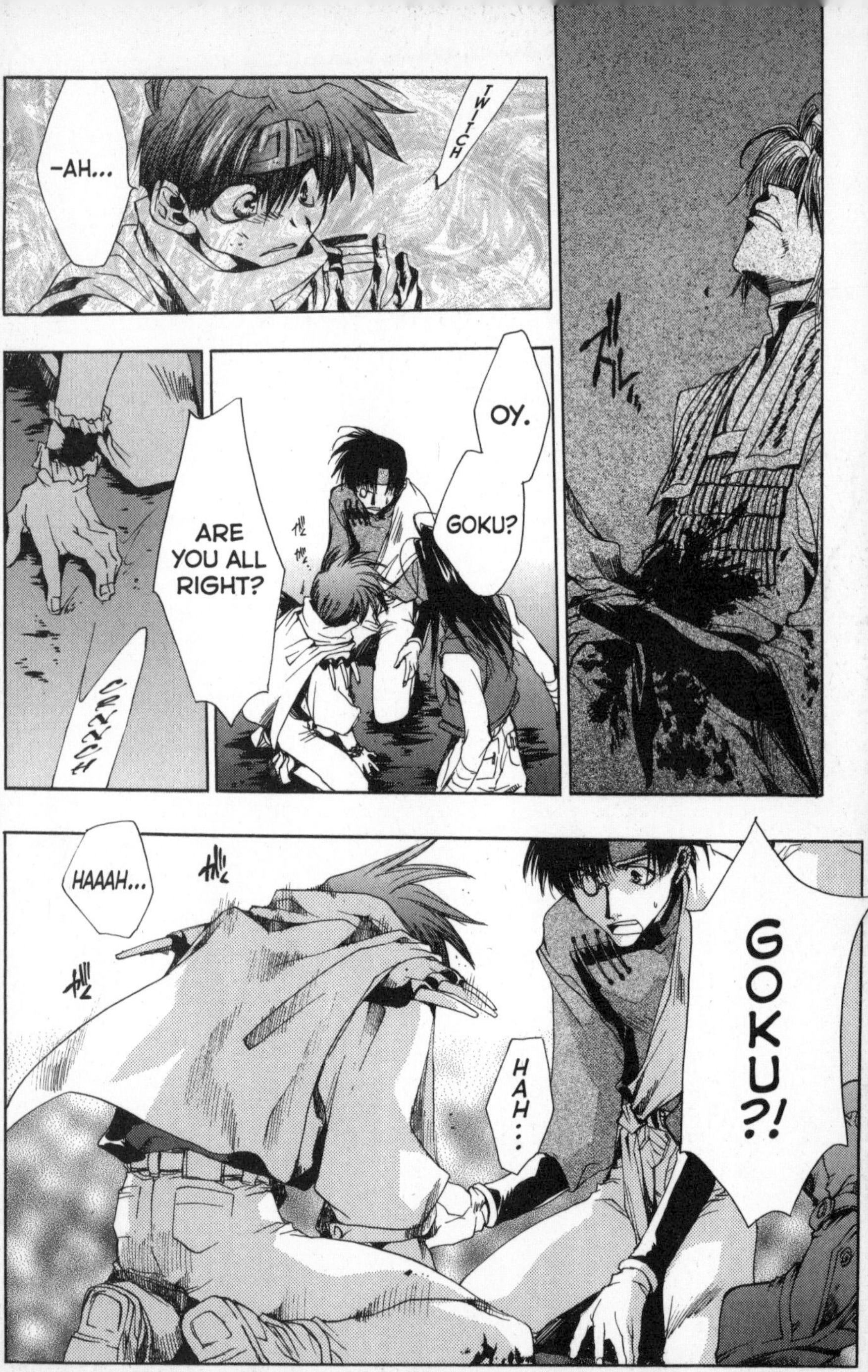
TWITCH
-AH...
OY.
GOKU?
ARE YOU ALL RIGHT?
CRUNCH
GOKU?!
HAH...
HAAAH...

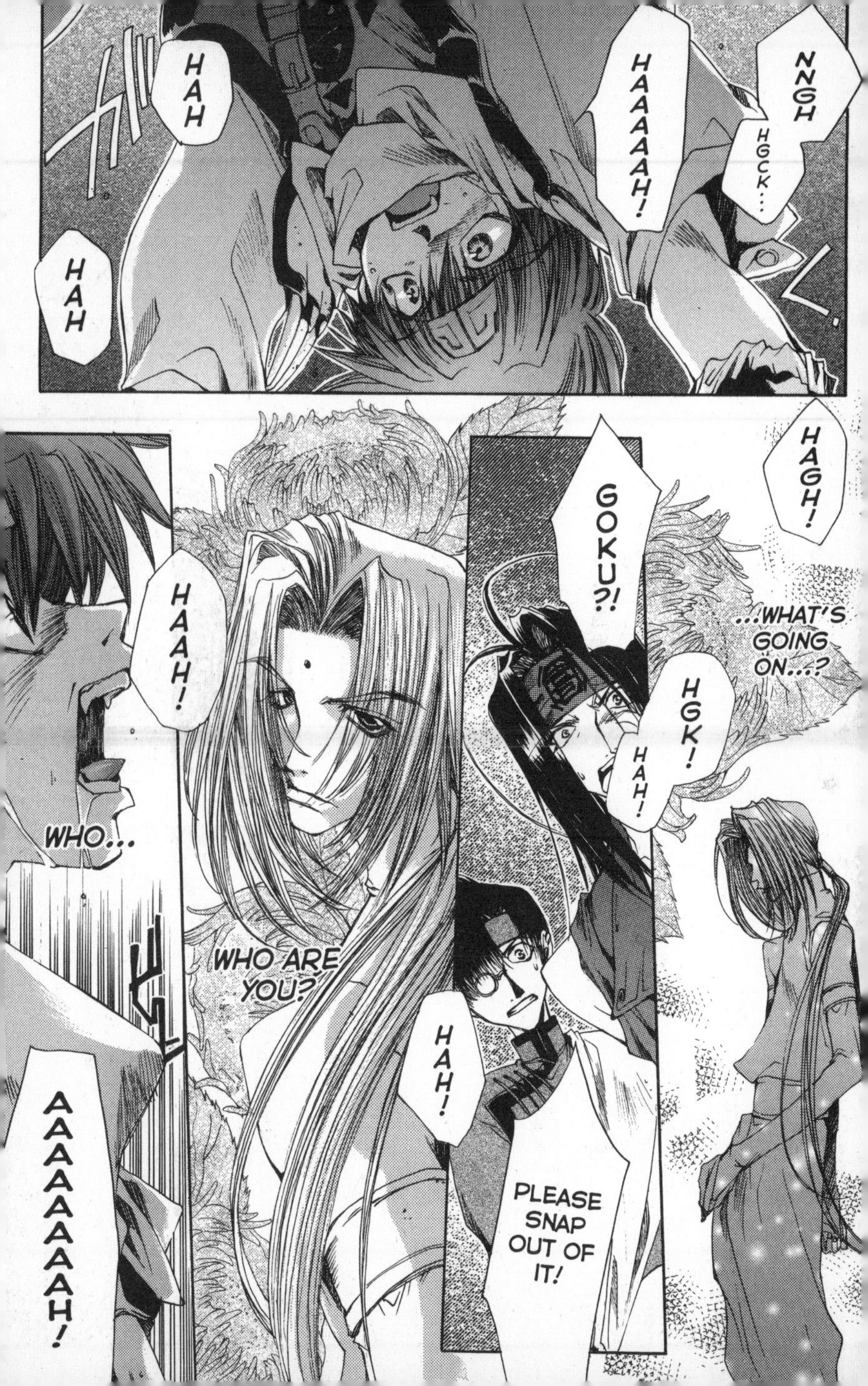
NNGH
HGCK...
HAAAAAAH!
HAH
HAH
HAGH!
...WHAT'S GOING ON...?
GOKU?!
HGK!
HAH!
HAH!
PLEASE SNAP OUT OF IT!
HAAAH!
WHO ARE YOU?
WHO...
AAAAAAAAAAH!

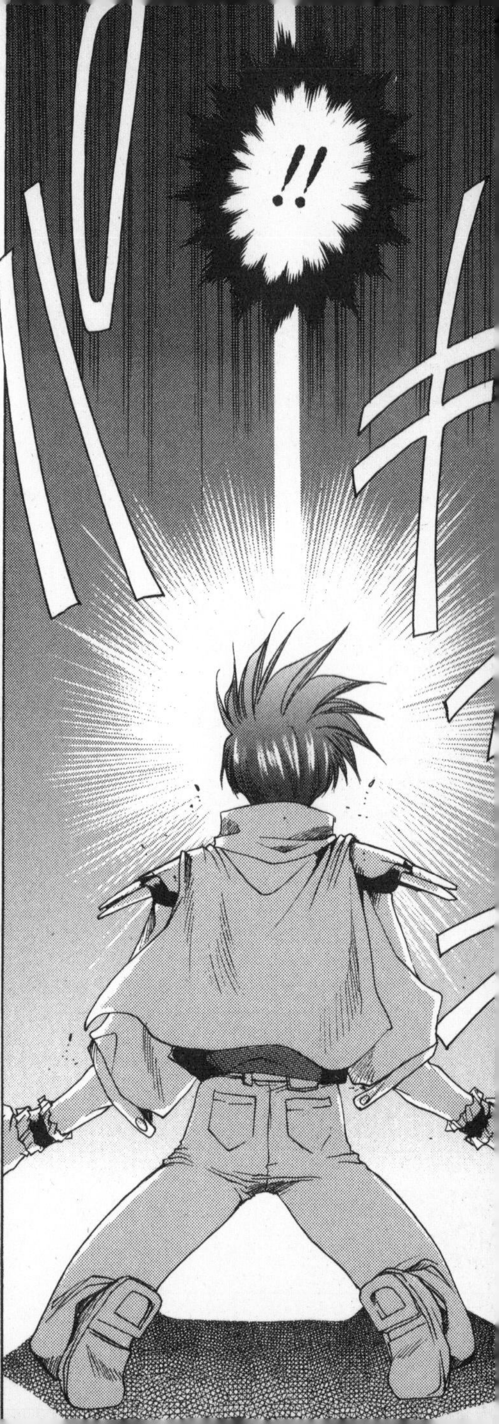
!!
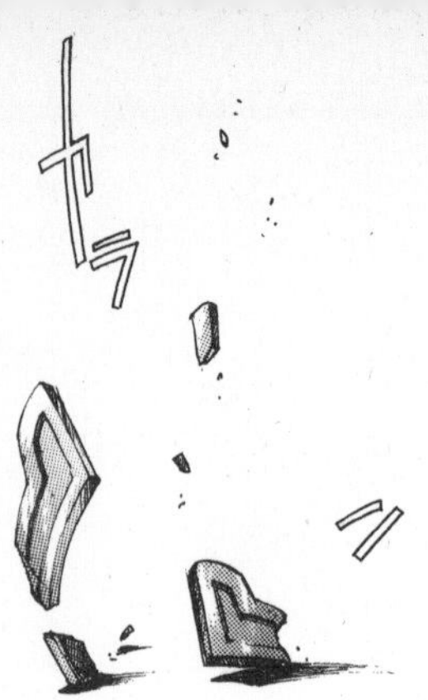
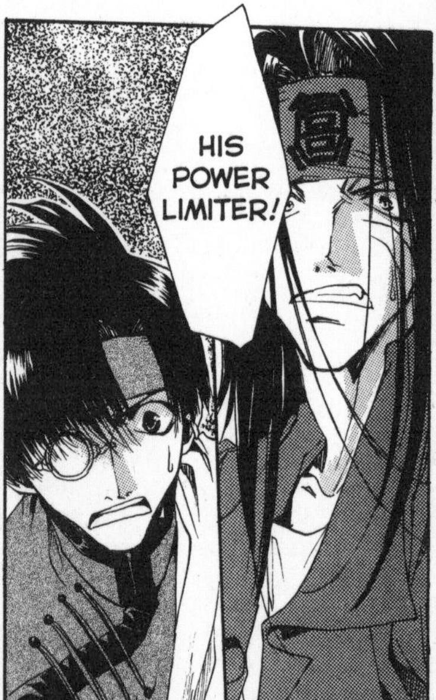
HIS POWER LIMITER!
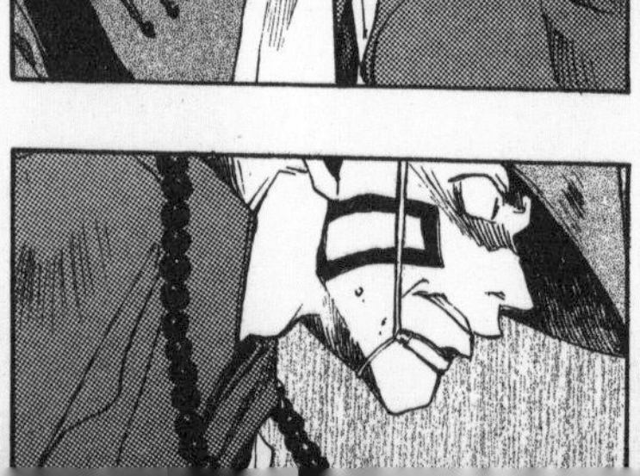

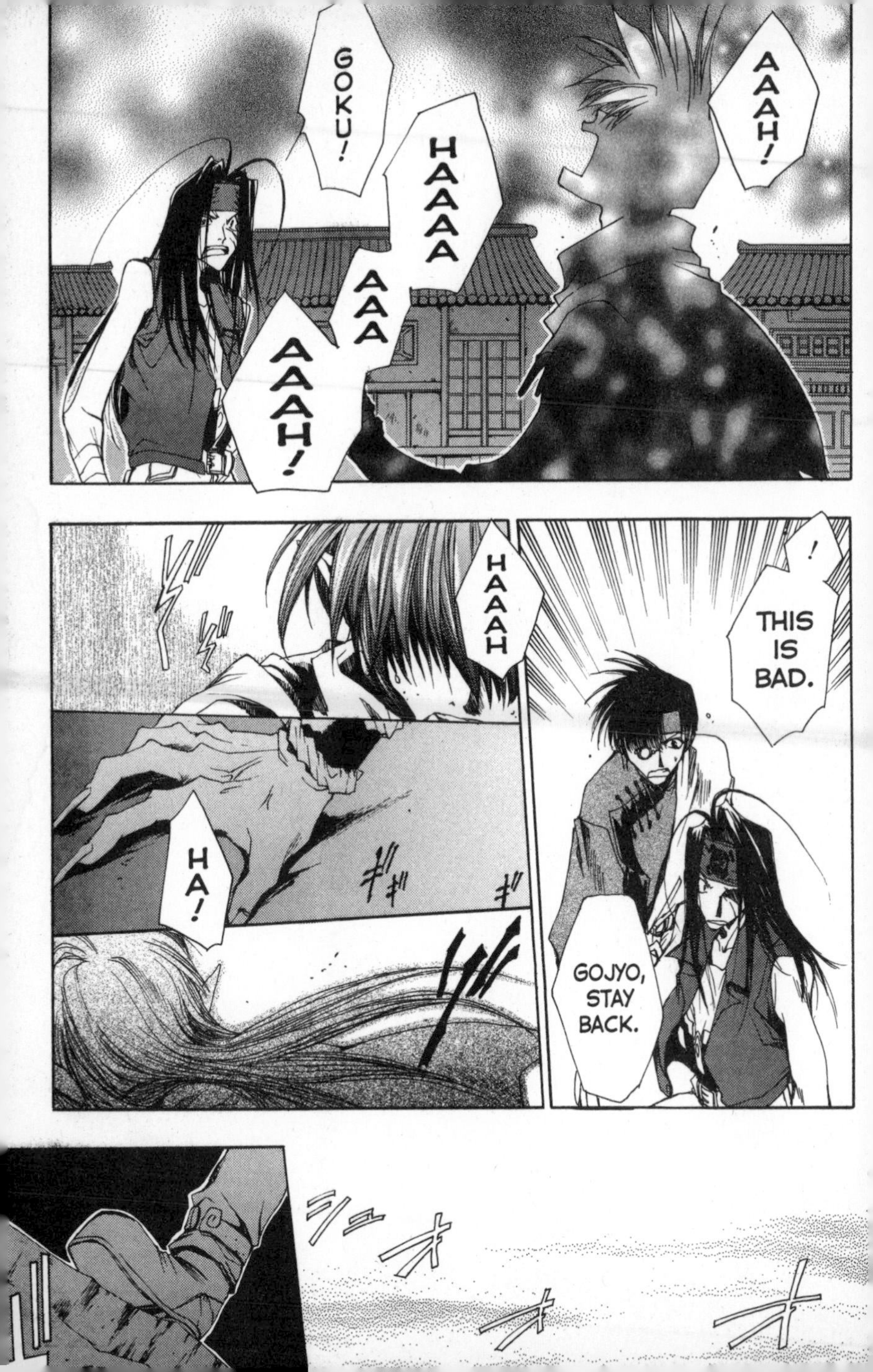
AAAH!
GOKU!
HAAAAA AAA AAAAH!
!
THIS IS BAD.
GOJYO, STAY BACK.
HAAAAH
HA!

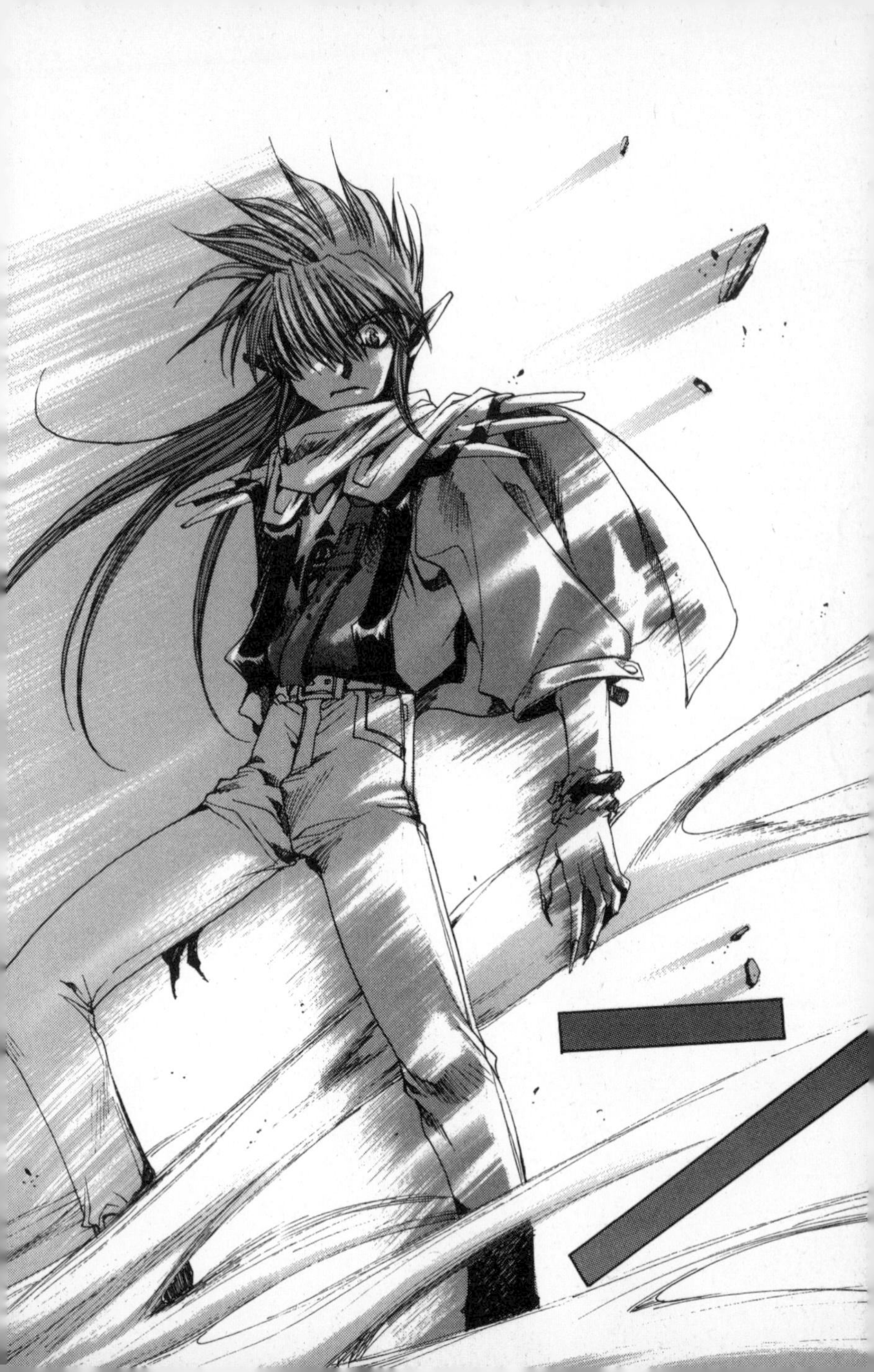

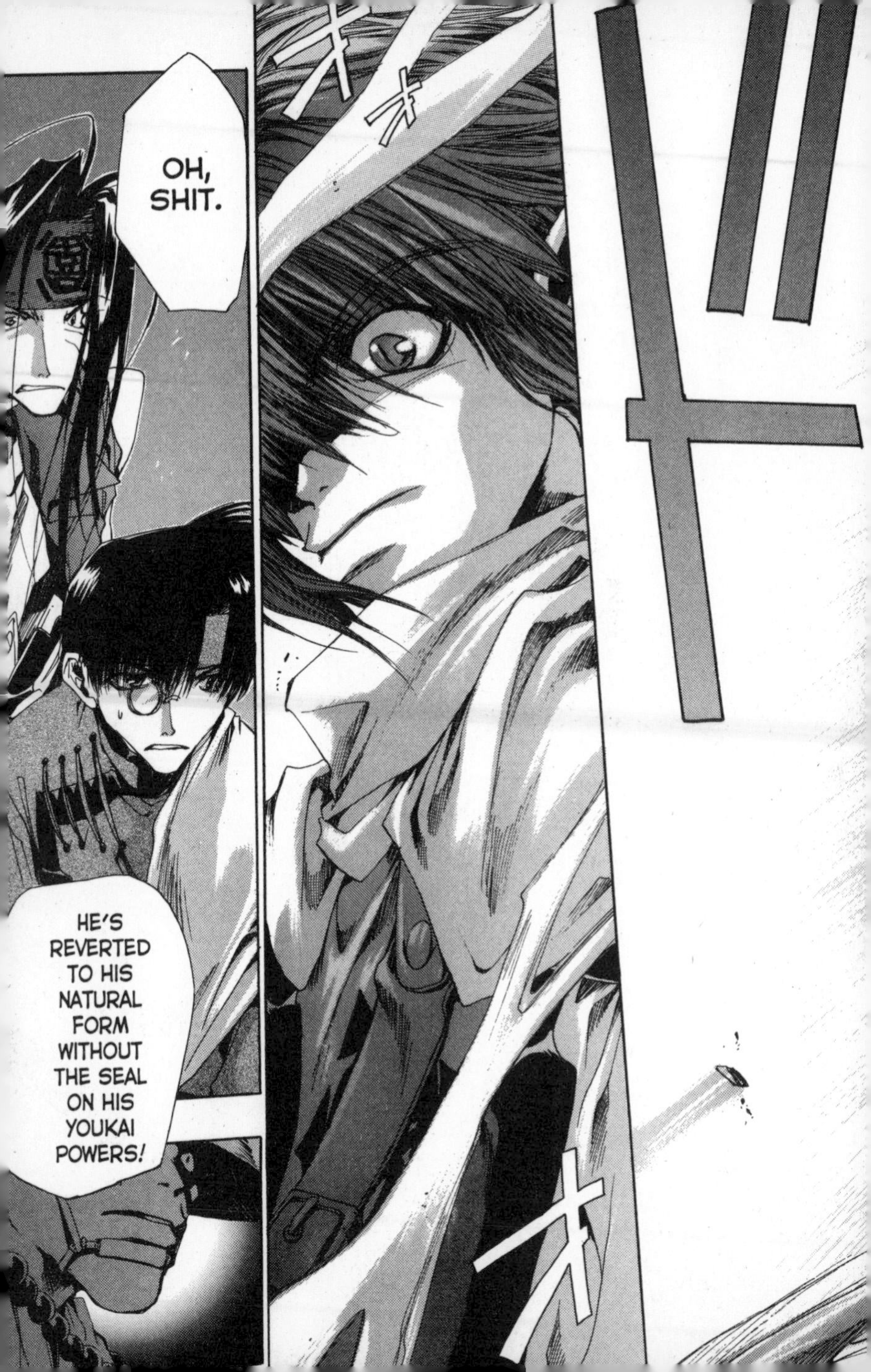
OH, SHIT.
HE'S REVERTED TO HIS NATURAL FORM WITHOUT THE SEAL ON HIS YOUKAI POWERS!

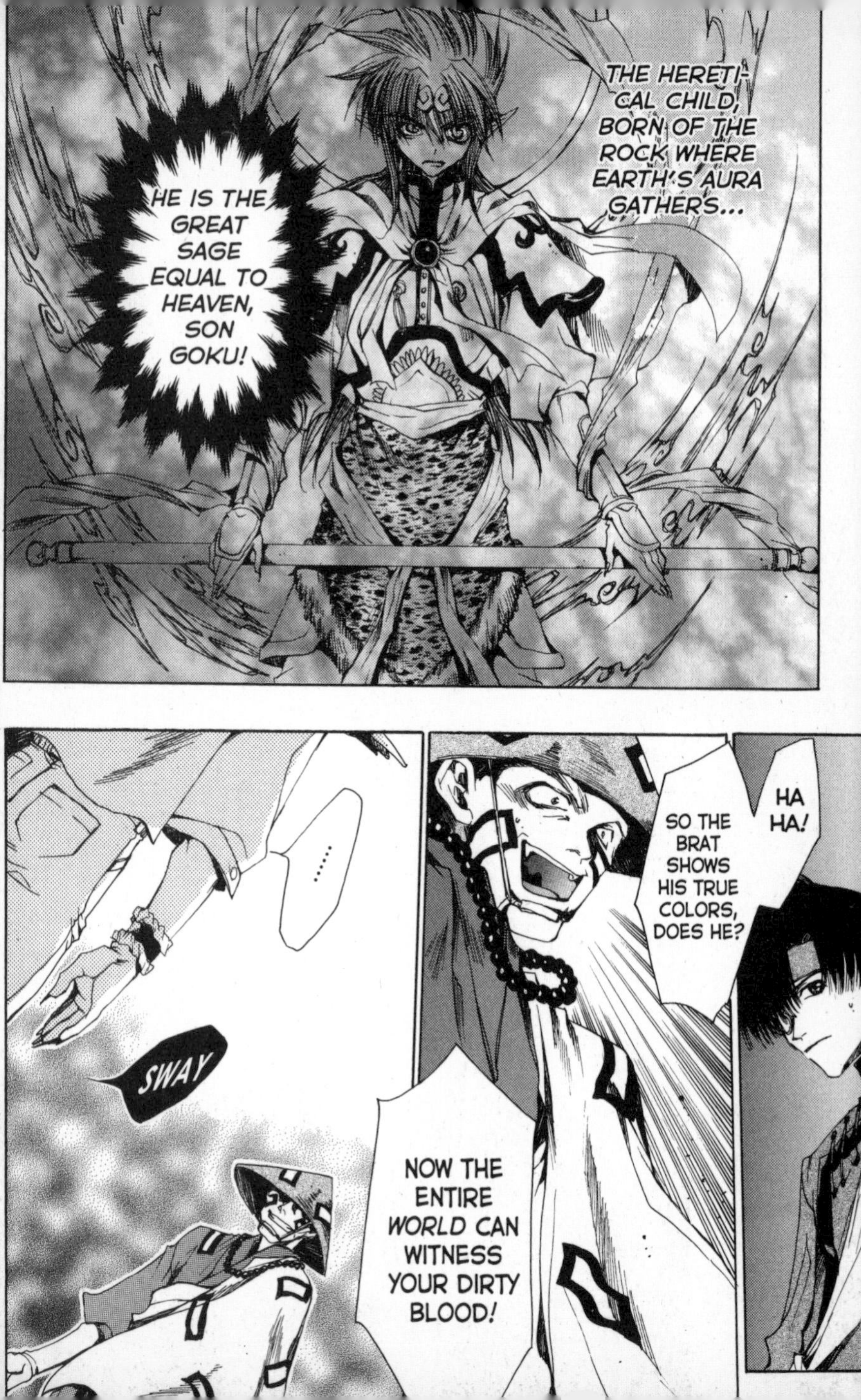
THE HERETICAL CHILD, BORN OF THE ROCK WHERE EARTH'S AURA GATHERS...
HE IS THE GREAT SAGE EQUAL TO HEAVEN, SON GOKU!
HA HA!
SO THE BRAT SHOWS HIS TRUE COLORS, DOES HE?
NOW THE ENTIRE *WORLD* CAN WITNESS YOUR DIRTY BLOOD!
......
SWAY

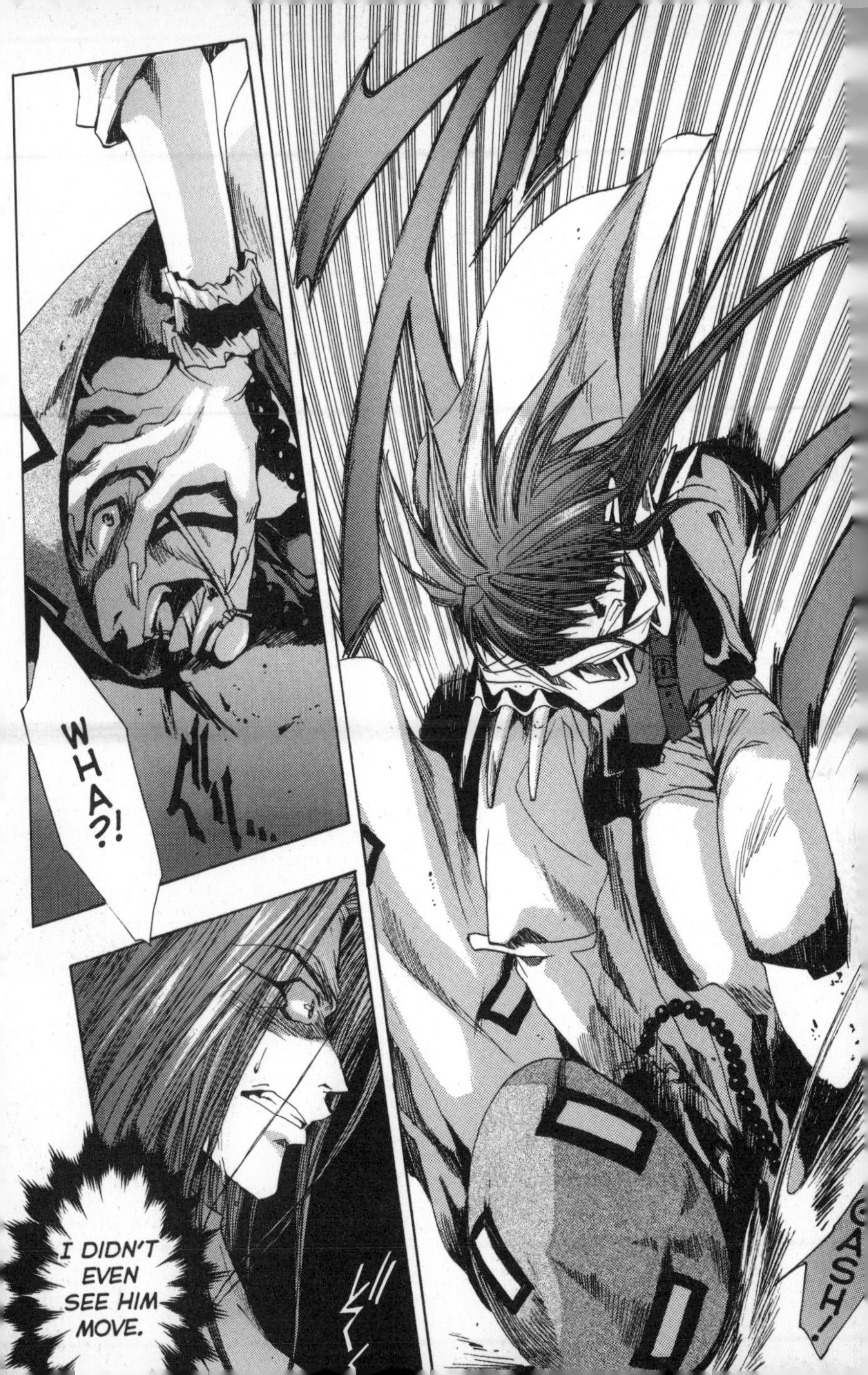
GASH!
WHA?!
I DIDN'T EVEN SEE HIM MOVE.

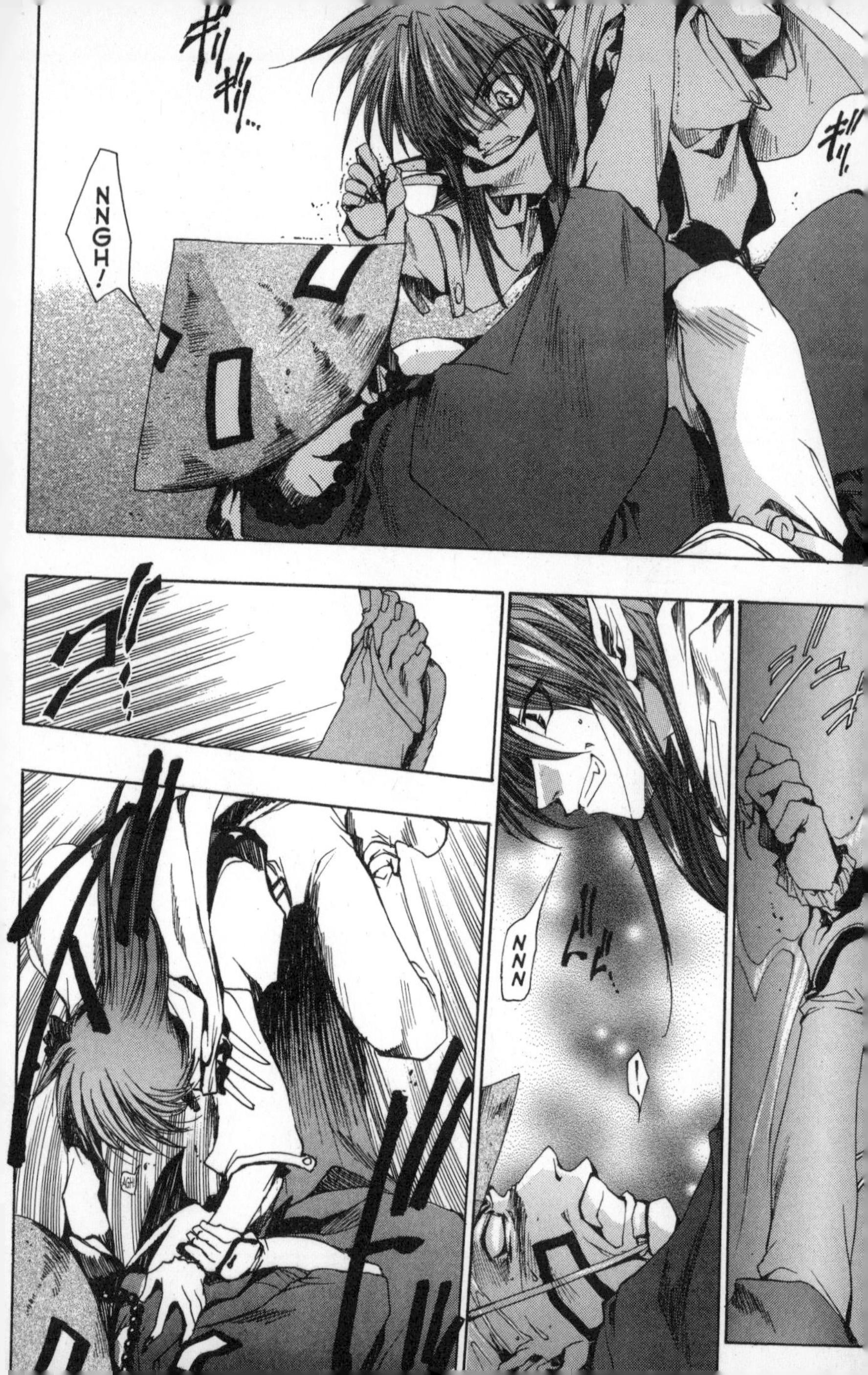
ギリ
ギリギリ...
NNGH!
NNN
!
AGH!

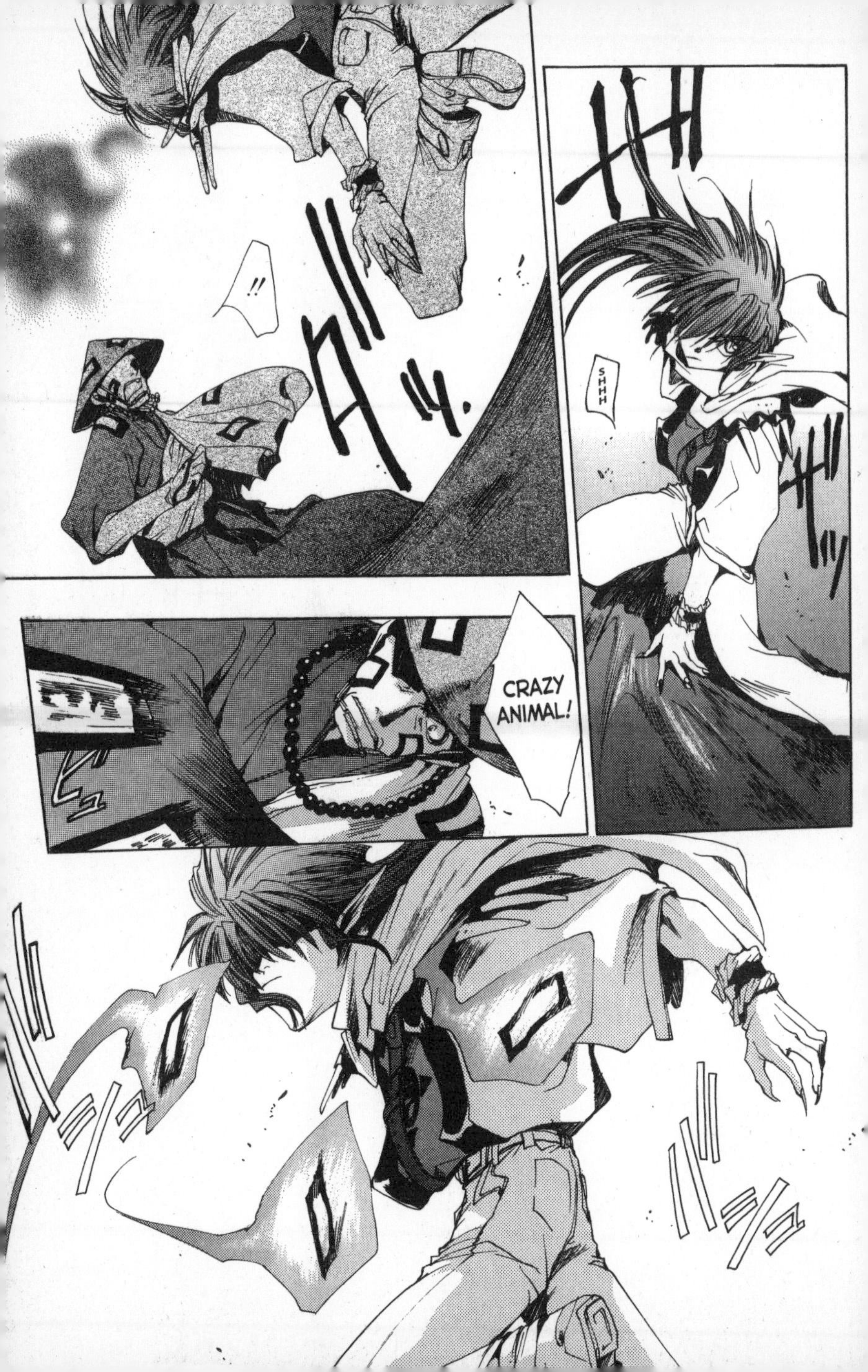
SHHH
!!
CRAZY ANIMAL!

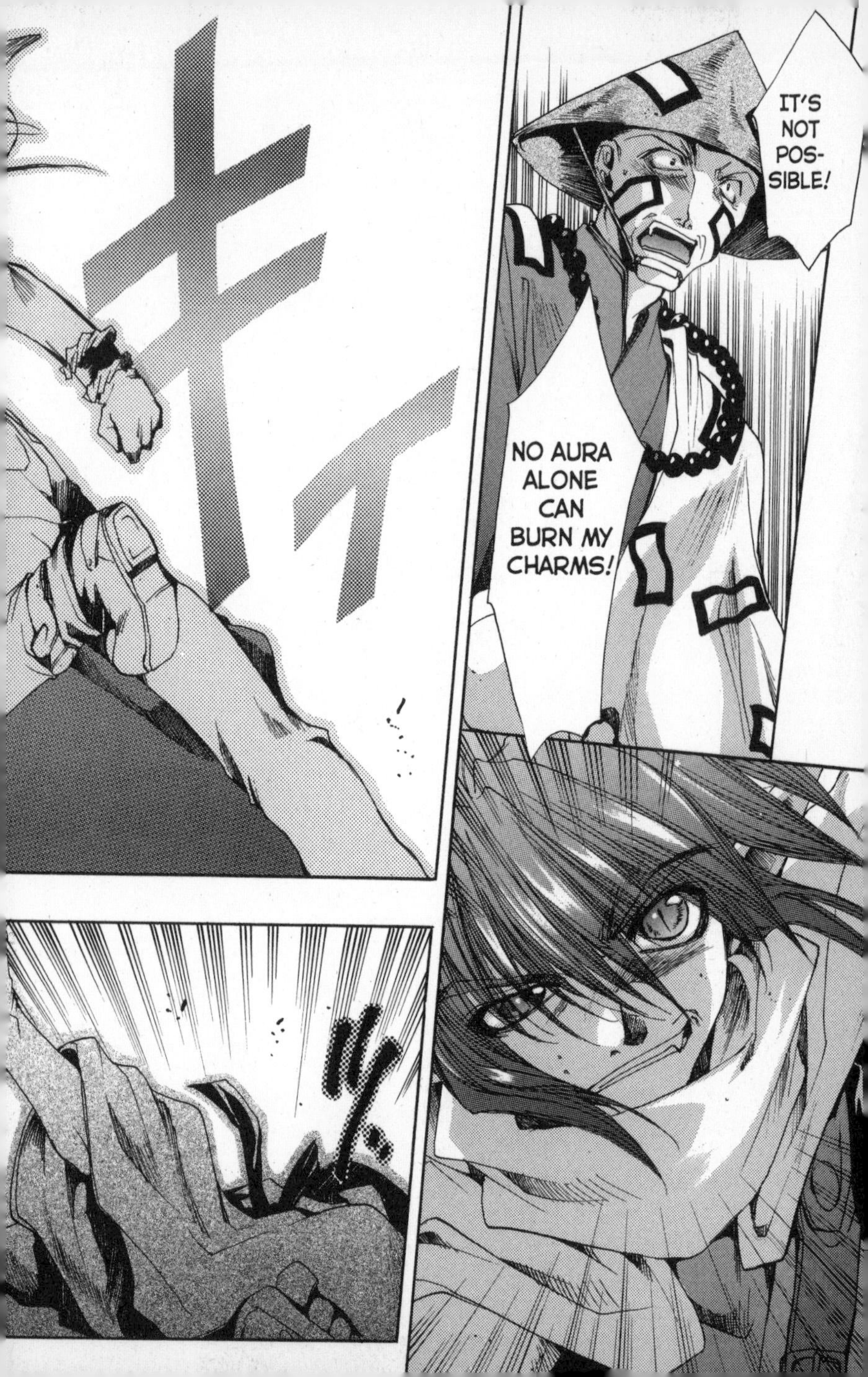
IT'S NOT POS-SIBLE!
NO AURA ALONE CAN BURN MY CHARMS!

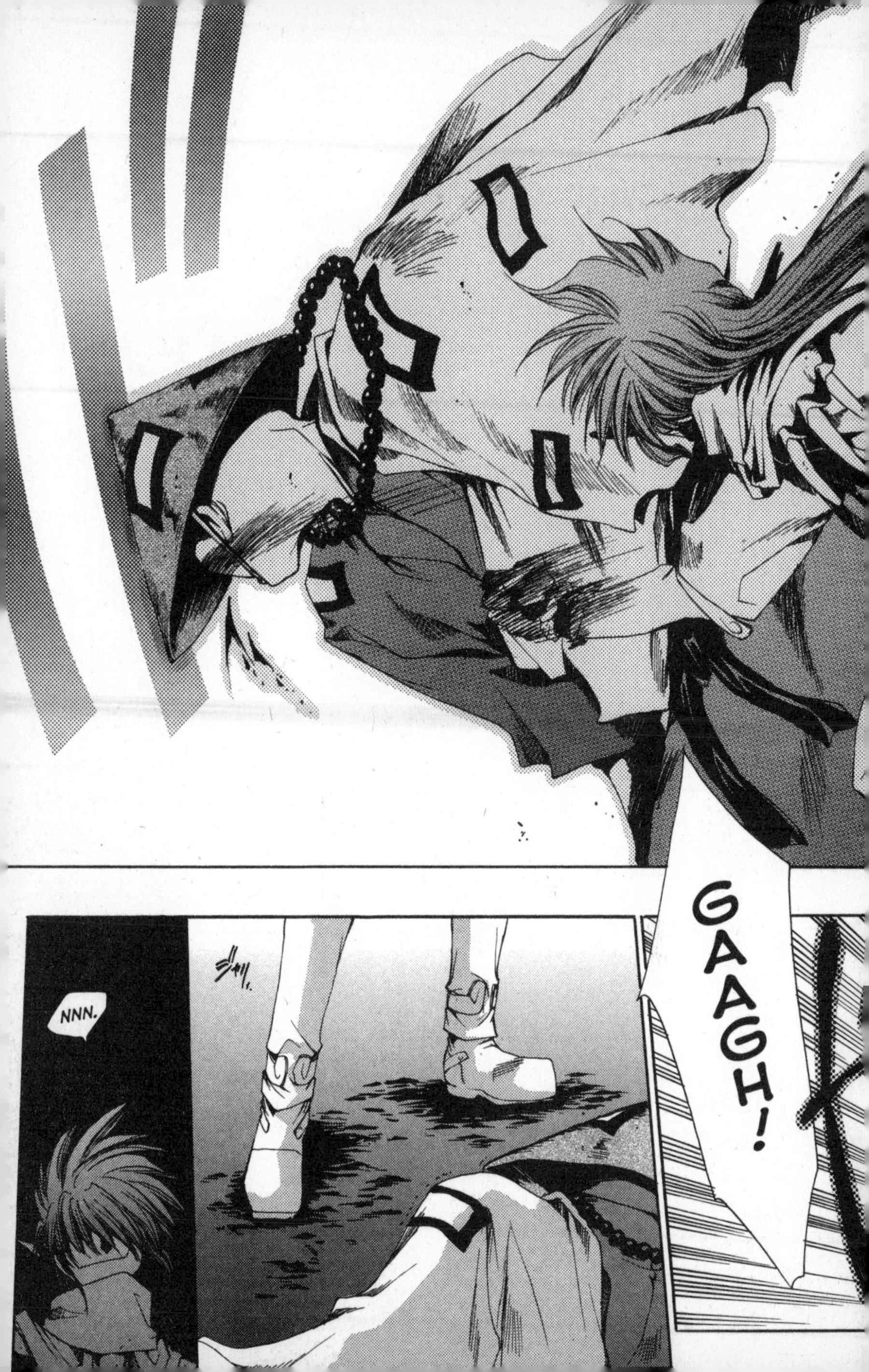
GAAGH!
ジャリ
NNN.

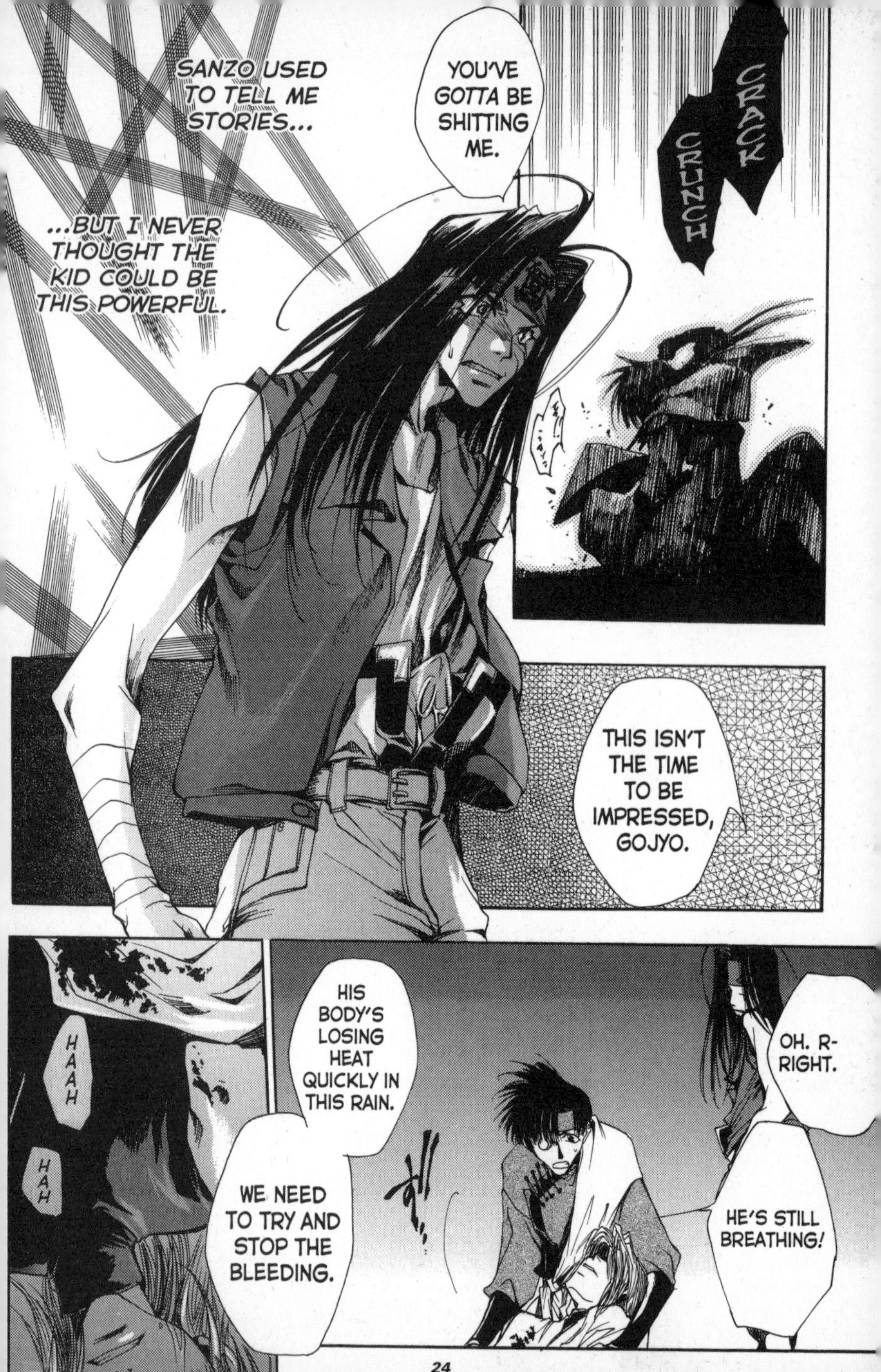
CRACK
CRUNCH
YOU'VE GOTTA BE SHITTING ME.
SANZO USED TO TELL ME STORIES...
...BUT I NEVER THOUGHT THE KID COULD BE THIS POWERFUL.
THIS ISN'T THE TIME TO BE IMPRESSED, GOJYO.
OH. R-RIGHT.
HE'S STILL BREATHING!
HIS BODY'S LOSING HEAT QUICKLY IN THIS RAIN.
WE NEED TO TRY AND STOP THE BLEEDING.
HAAAH
HAH

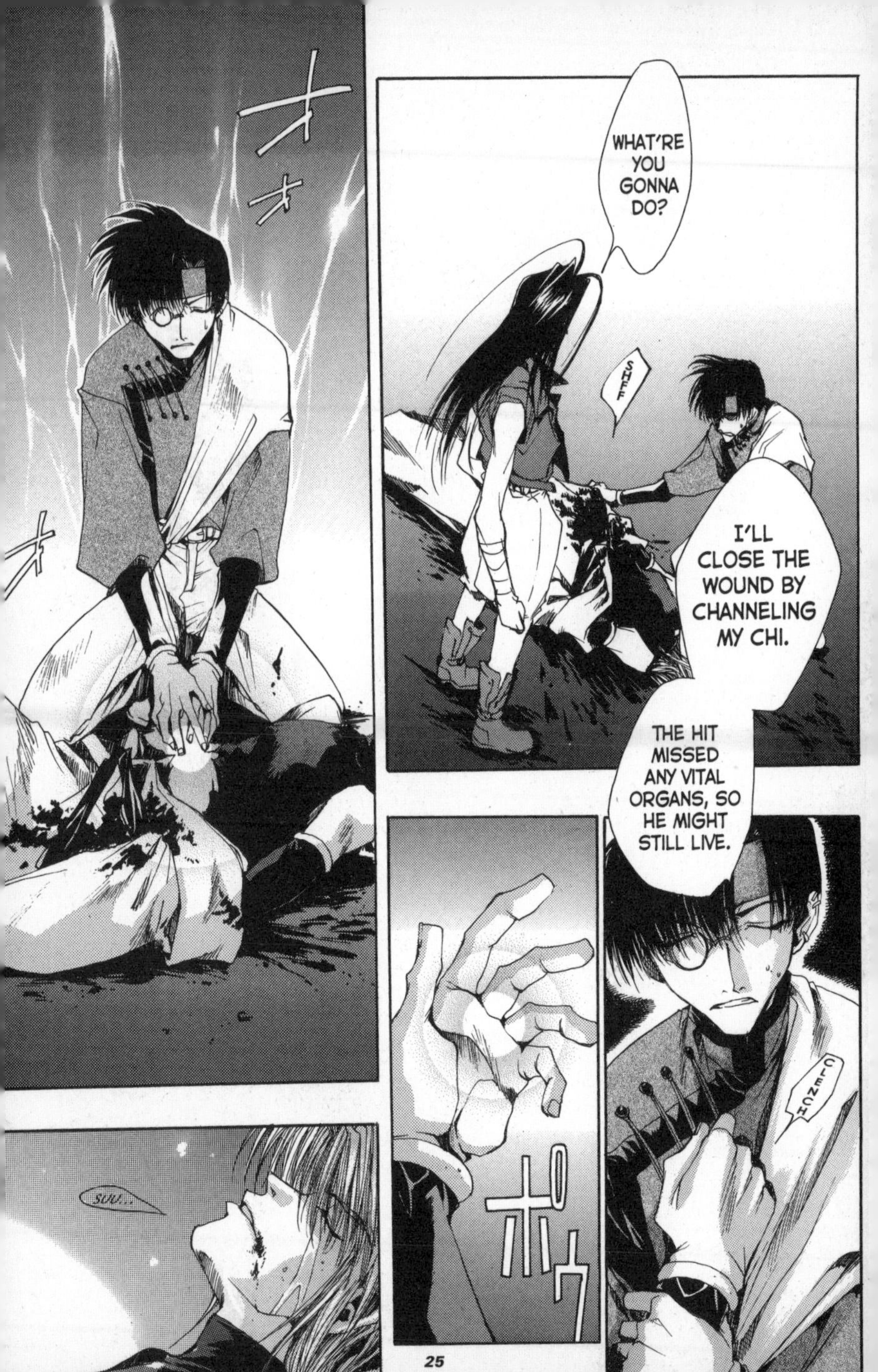

WHAT'RE YOU GONNA DO?
SHFF
I'LL CLOSE THE WOUND BY CHANNELING MY CHI.
THE HIT MISSED ANY VITAL ORGANS, SO HE MIGHT STILL LIVE.
CLENCH
SUU...

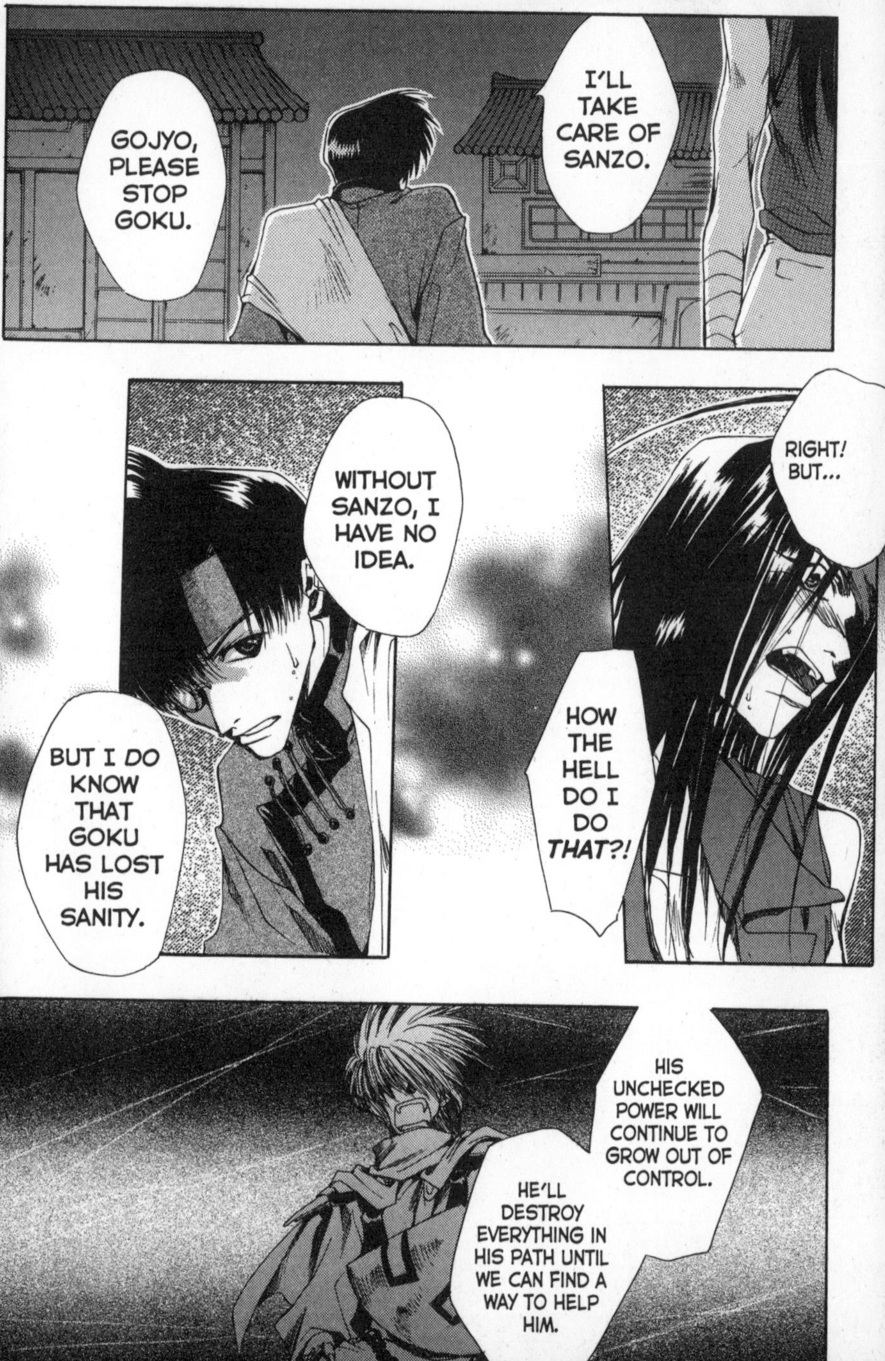
GOJYO, PLEASE STOP GOKU.
I'LL TAKE CARE OF SANZO.
WITHOUT SANZO, I HAVE NO IDEA.
BUT I *DO* KNOW THAT GOKU HAS LOST HIS SANITY.
RIGHT! BUT...
HOW THE HELL DO I DO *THAT?!*
HIS UNCHECKED POWER WILL CONTINUE TO GROW OUT OF CONTROL.
HE'LL DESTROY EVERYTHING IN HIS PATH UNTIL WE CAN FIND A WAY TO HELP HIM.

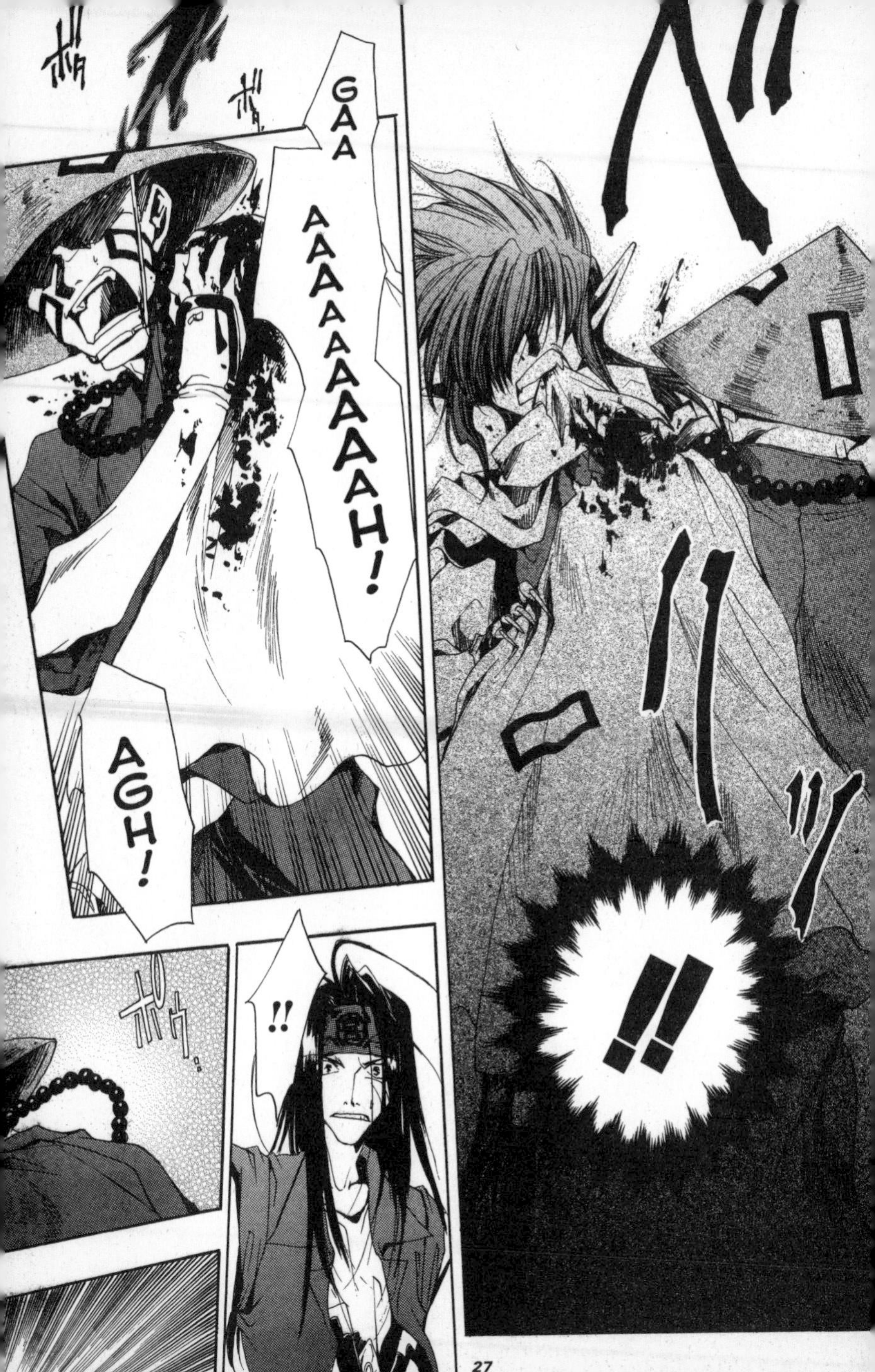
ベリッ
!!
GAA
AAAAAAAAAH!
AGH!
!!

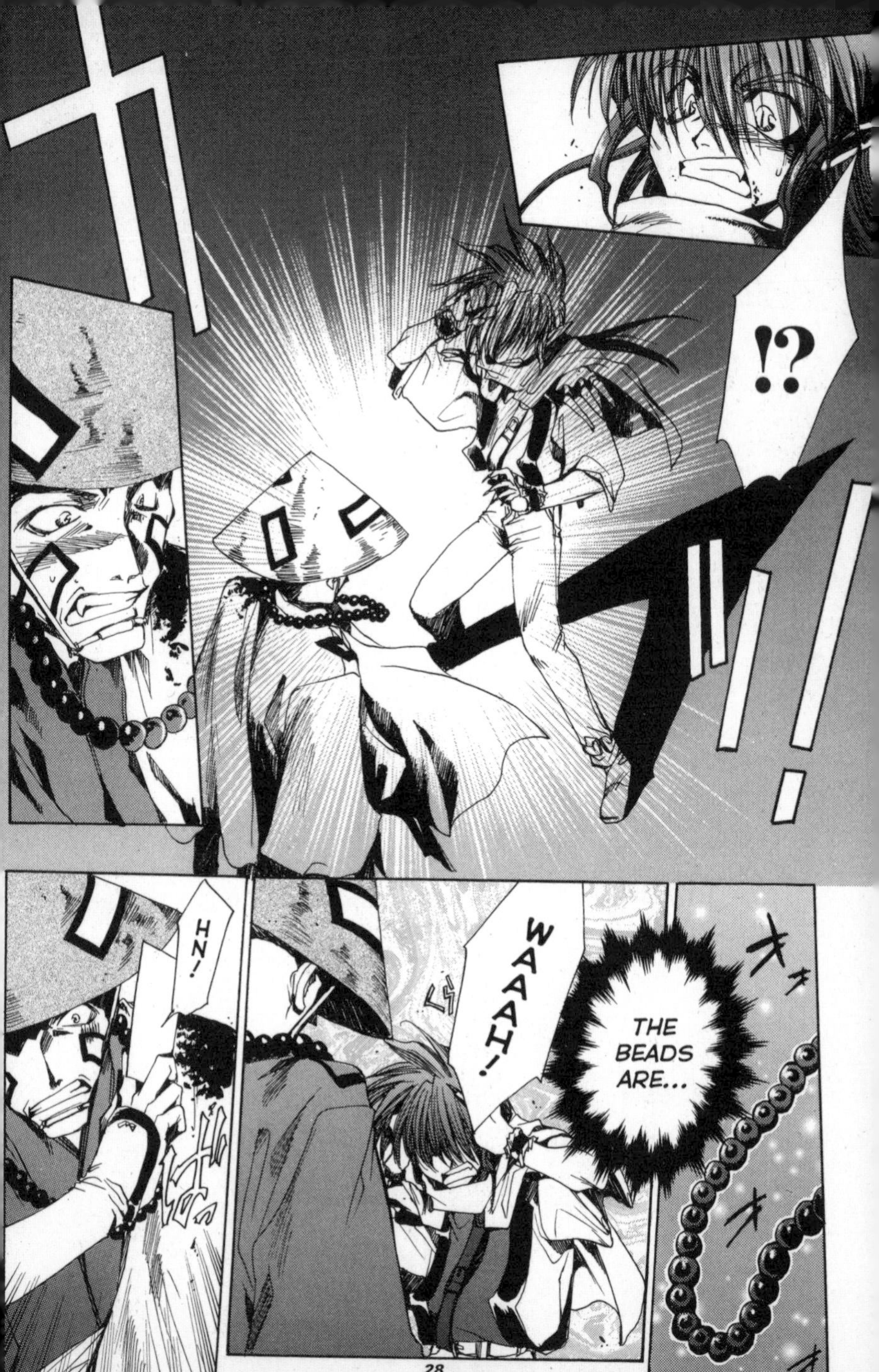
!?
THE BEADS ARE...
WAAAAH!
HN!

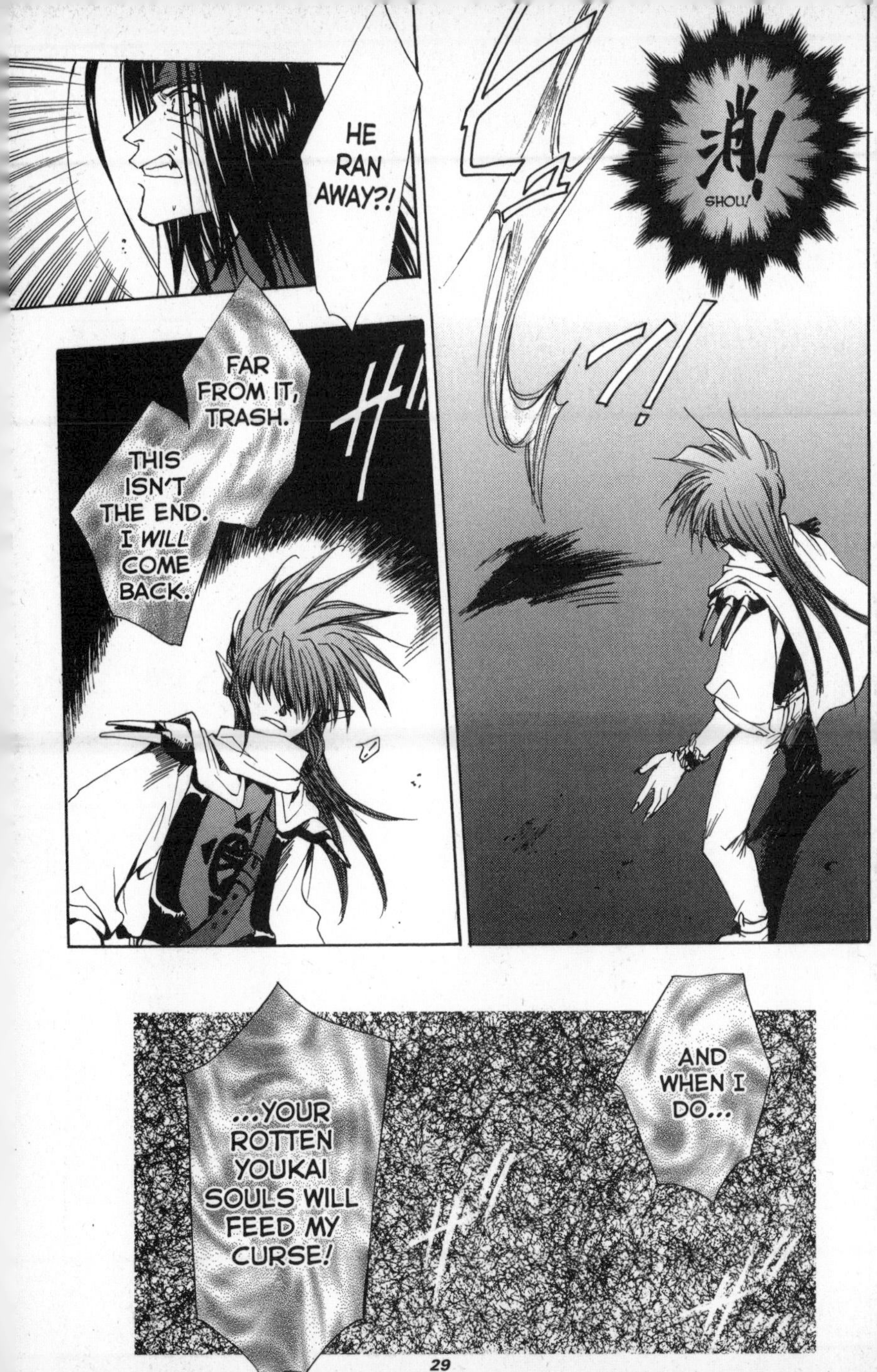
消!
SHOU!
HE RAN AWAY?!
FAR FROM IT, TRASH.
THIS ISN'T THE END. I *WILL* COME BACK.
AND WHEN I DO...
...YOUR ROTTEN YOUKAI SOULS WILL FEED MY CURSE!

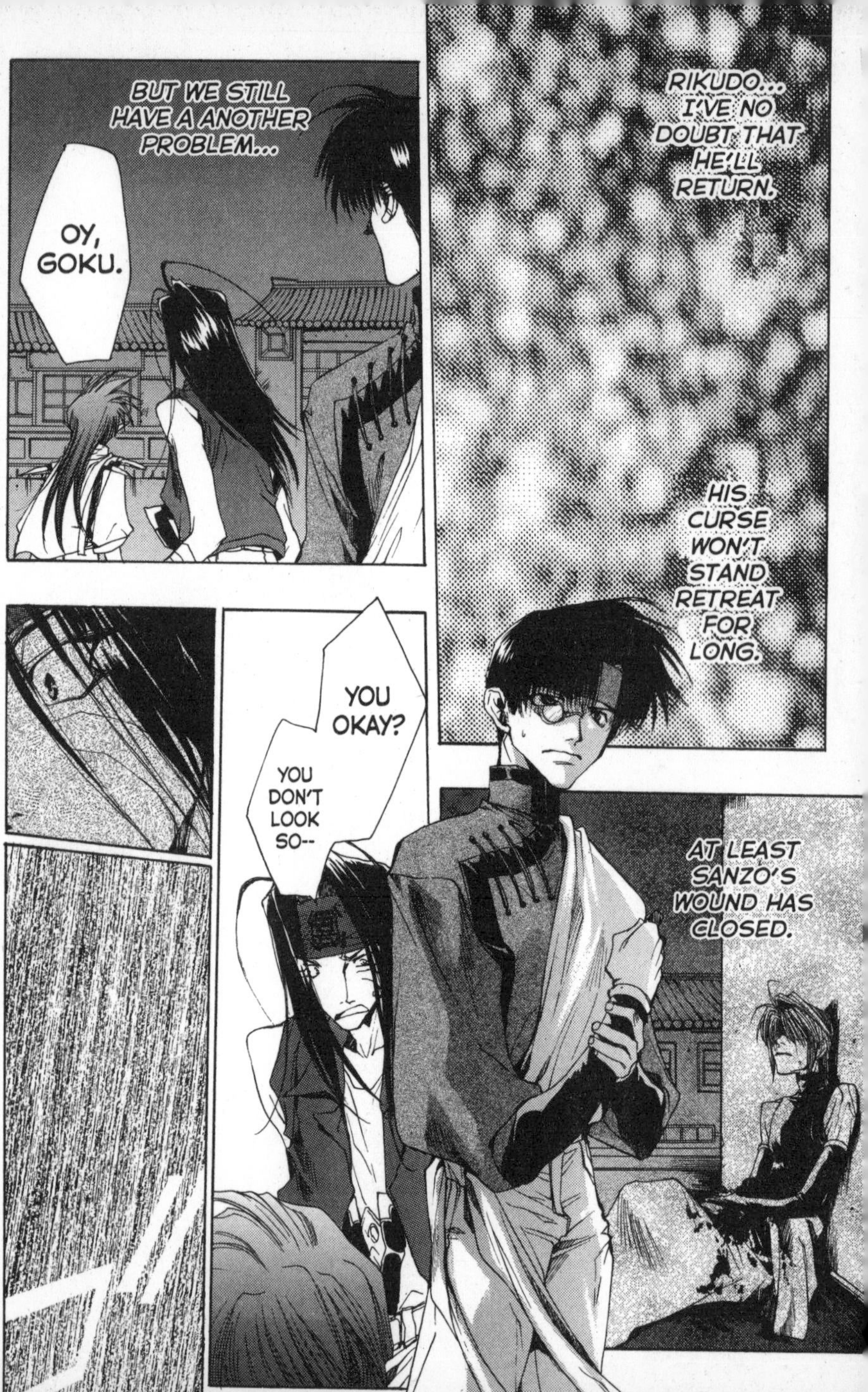
RIKUDO... I'VE NO DOUBT THAT HE'LL RETURN.
HIS CURSE WON'T STAND RETREAT FOR LONG.
AT LEAST SANZO'S WOUND HAS CLOSED.
BUT WE STILL HAVE A ANOTHER PROBLEM...
OY, GOKU.
YOU OKAY?
YOU DON'T LOOK SO--

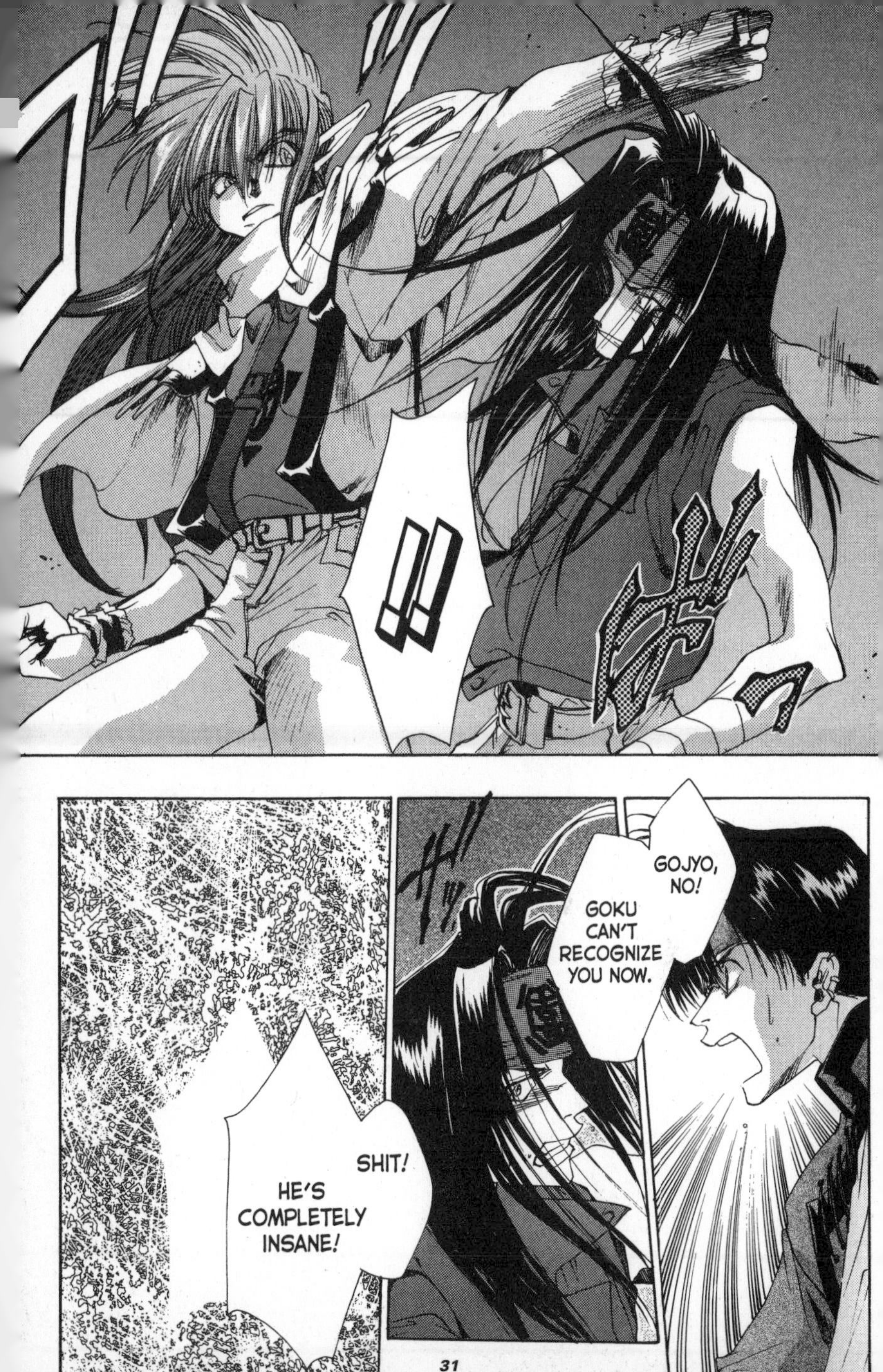
!!
GOJYO, NO!
GOKU CAN'T RECOGNIZE YOU NOW.
SHIT!
HE'S COMPLETELY INSANE!

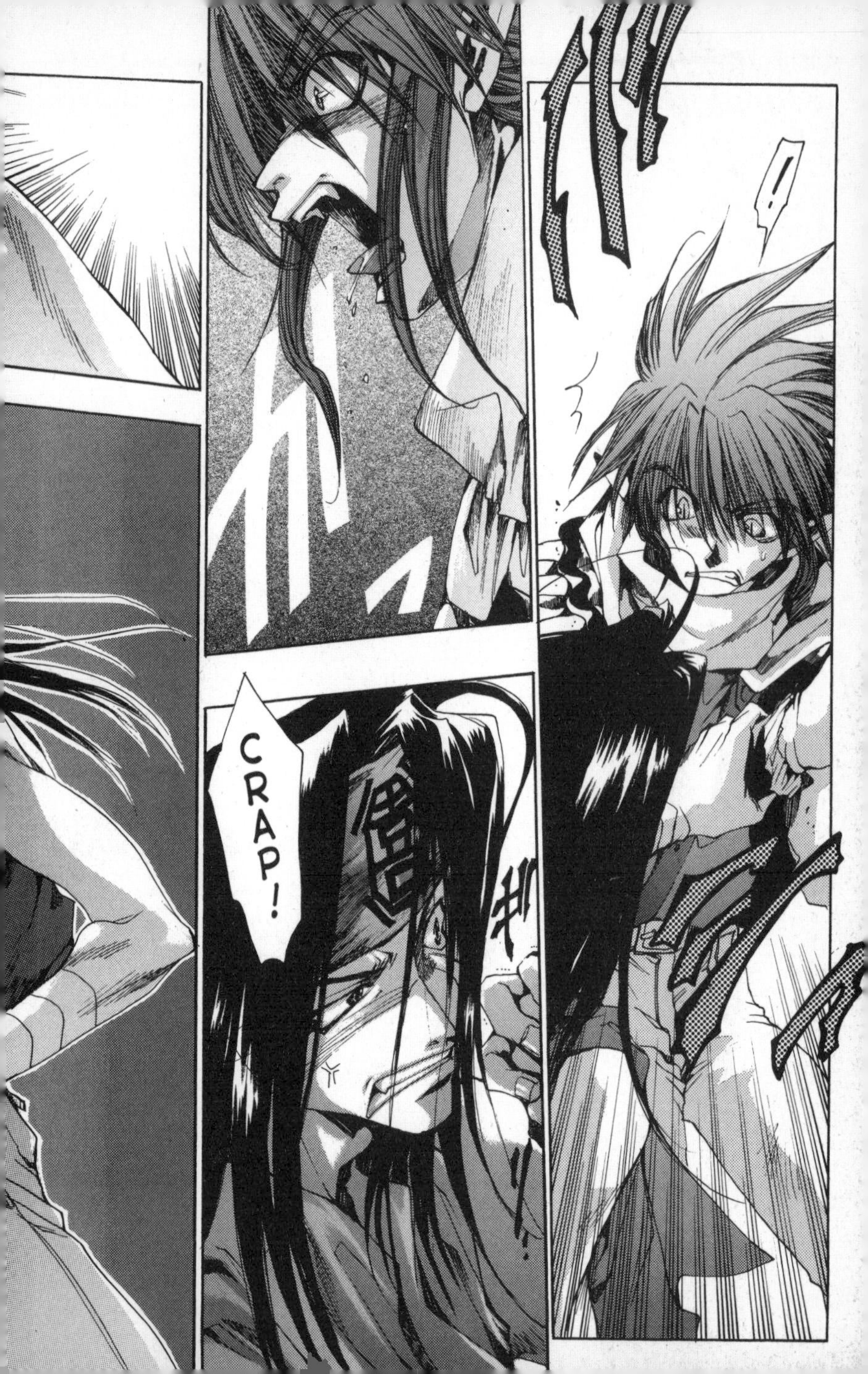
!
CRAP!

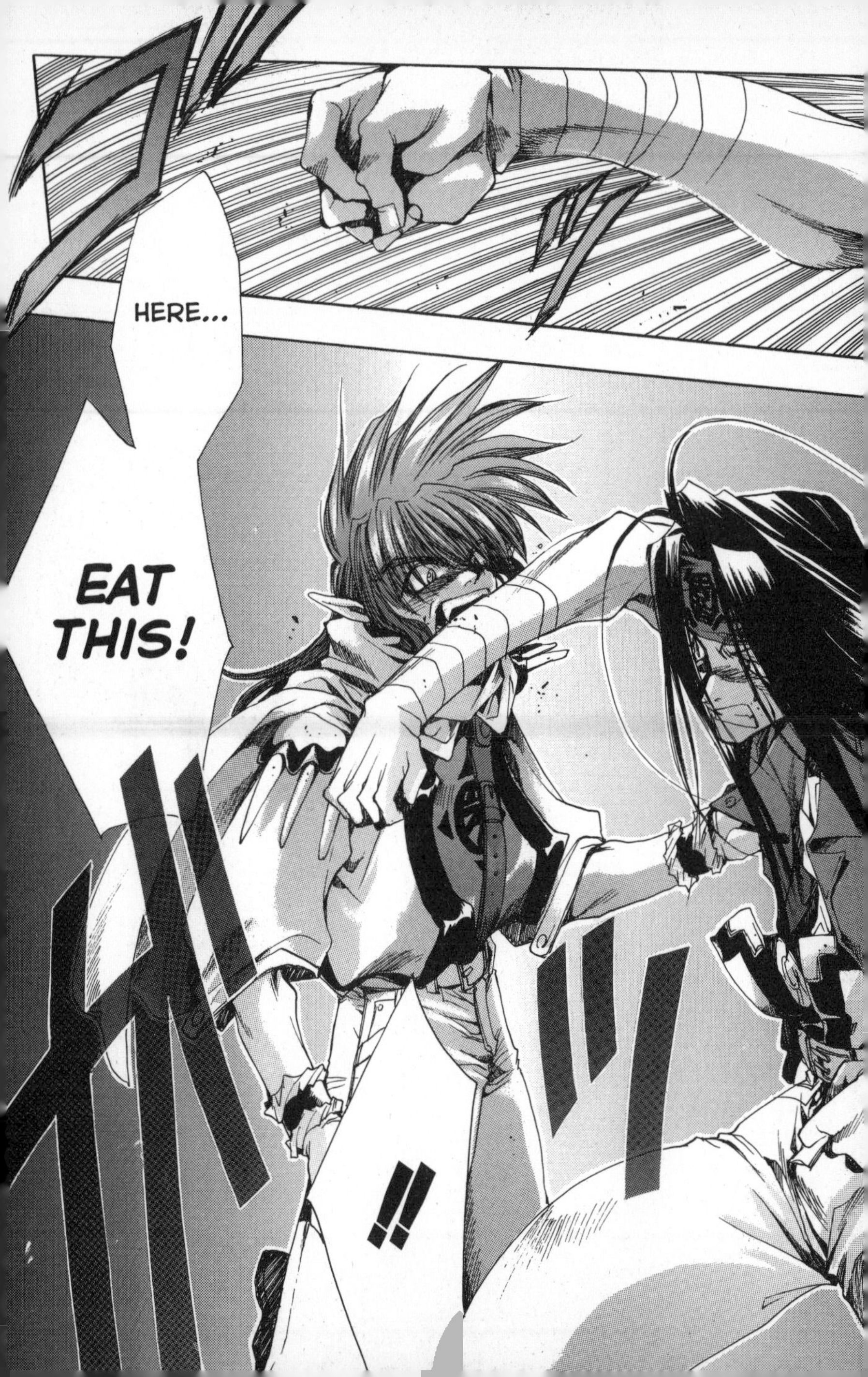
HERE...
EAT THIS!
!!

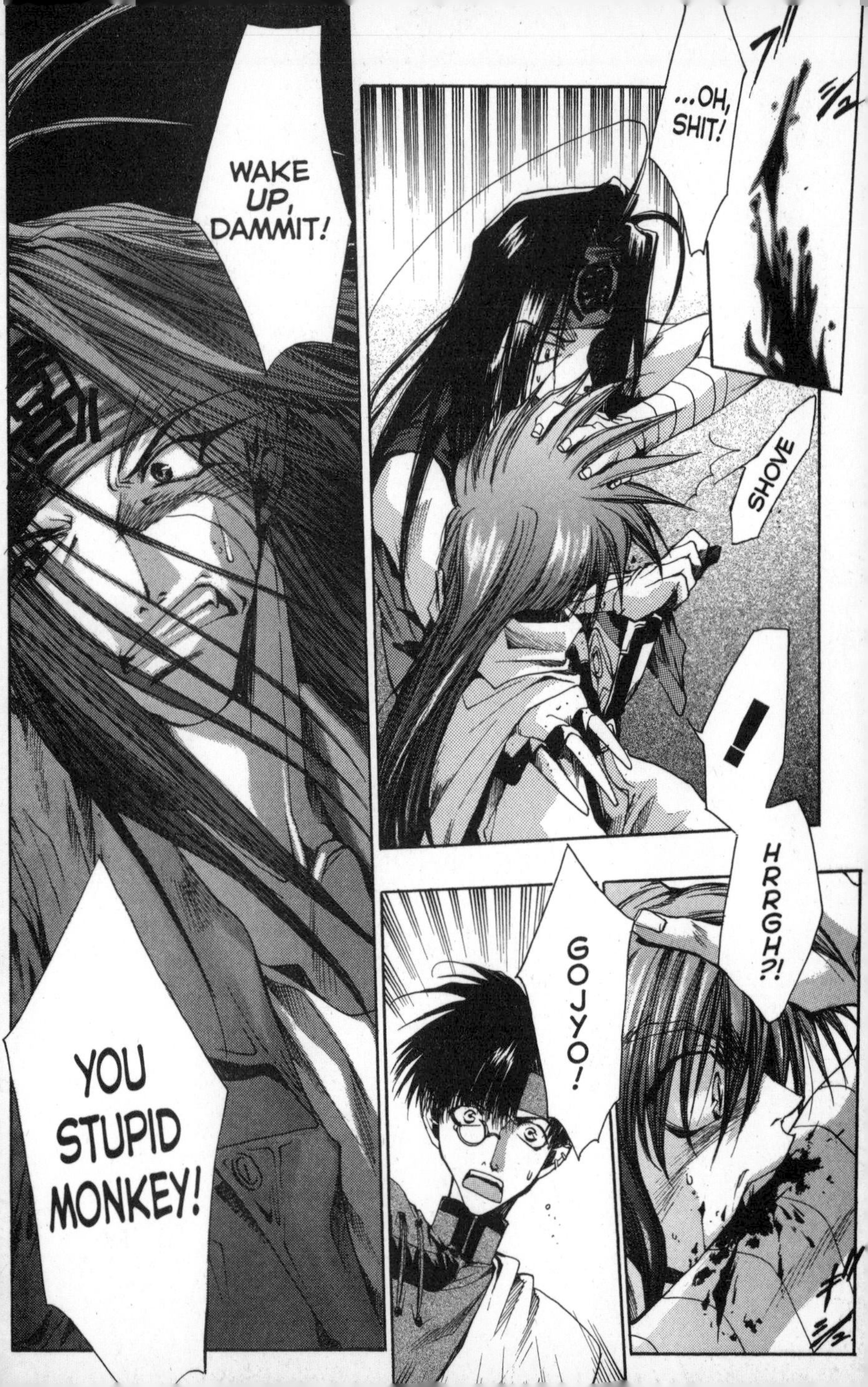
...OH, SHIT!
SHOVE
!
HRRGH?!
GOJYO!
WAKE UP, DAMMIT!
YOU STUPID MONKEY!

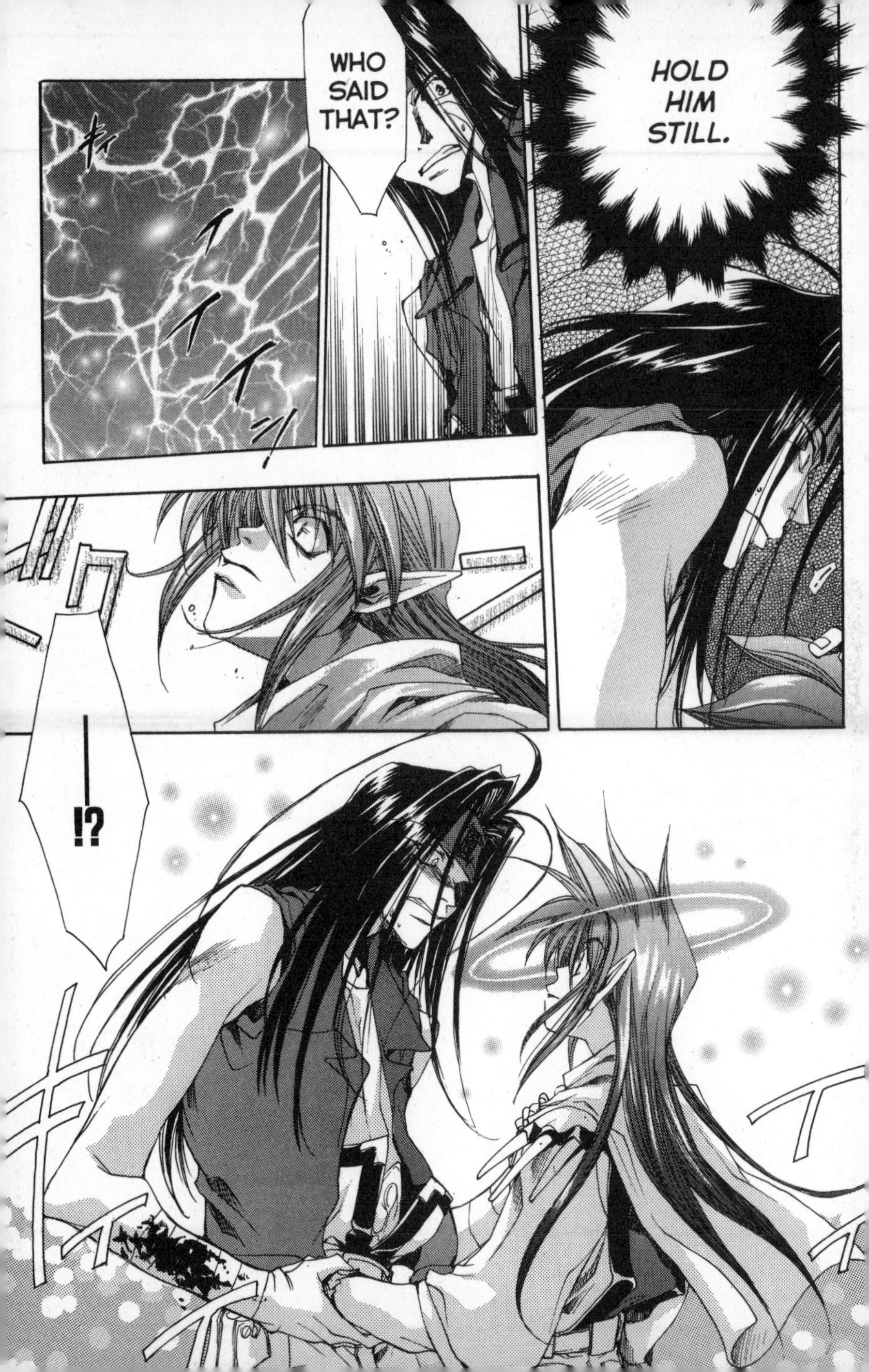
HOLD HIM STILL.
WHO SAID THAT?
——!?

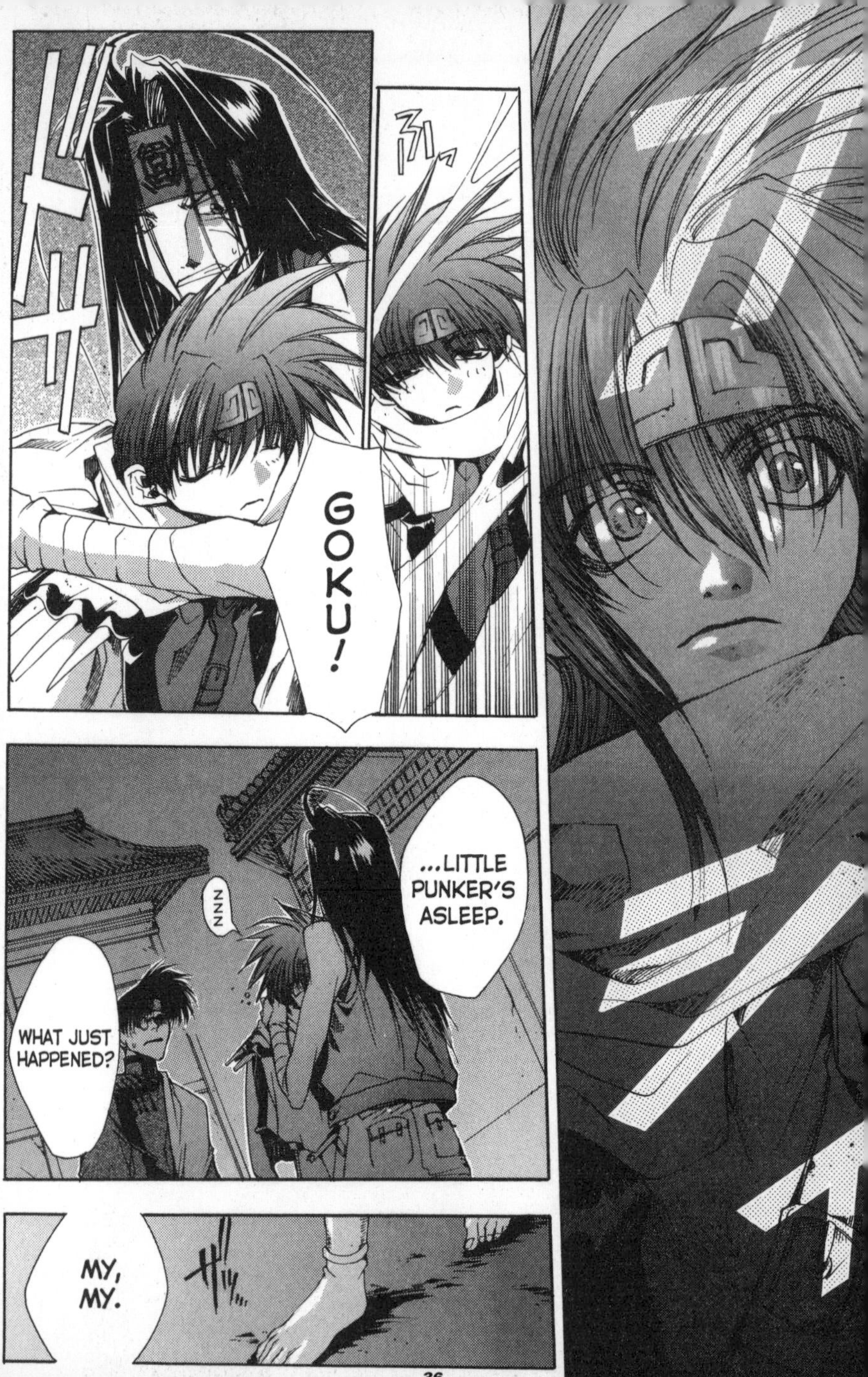
GOKU!
...LITTLE PUNKER'S ASLEEP.
ZZZ
WHAT JUST HAPPENED?
MY, MY.

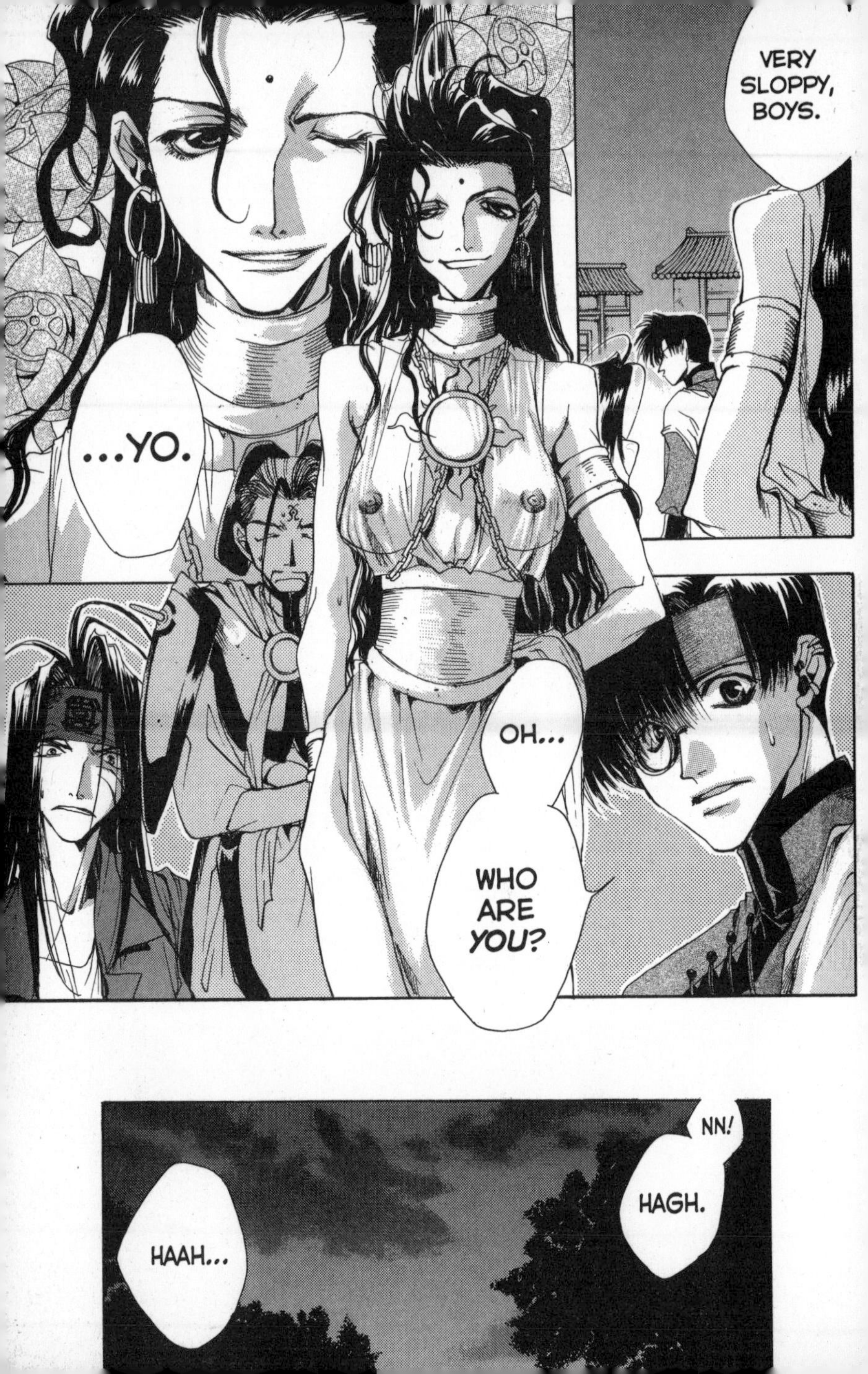
VERY SLOPPY, BOYS.
...YO.
OH...
WHO ARE YOU?
NN!
HAGH.
HAAH...

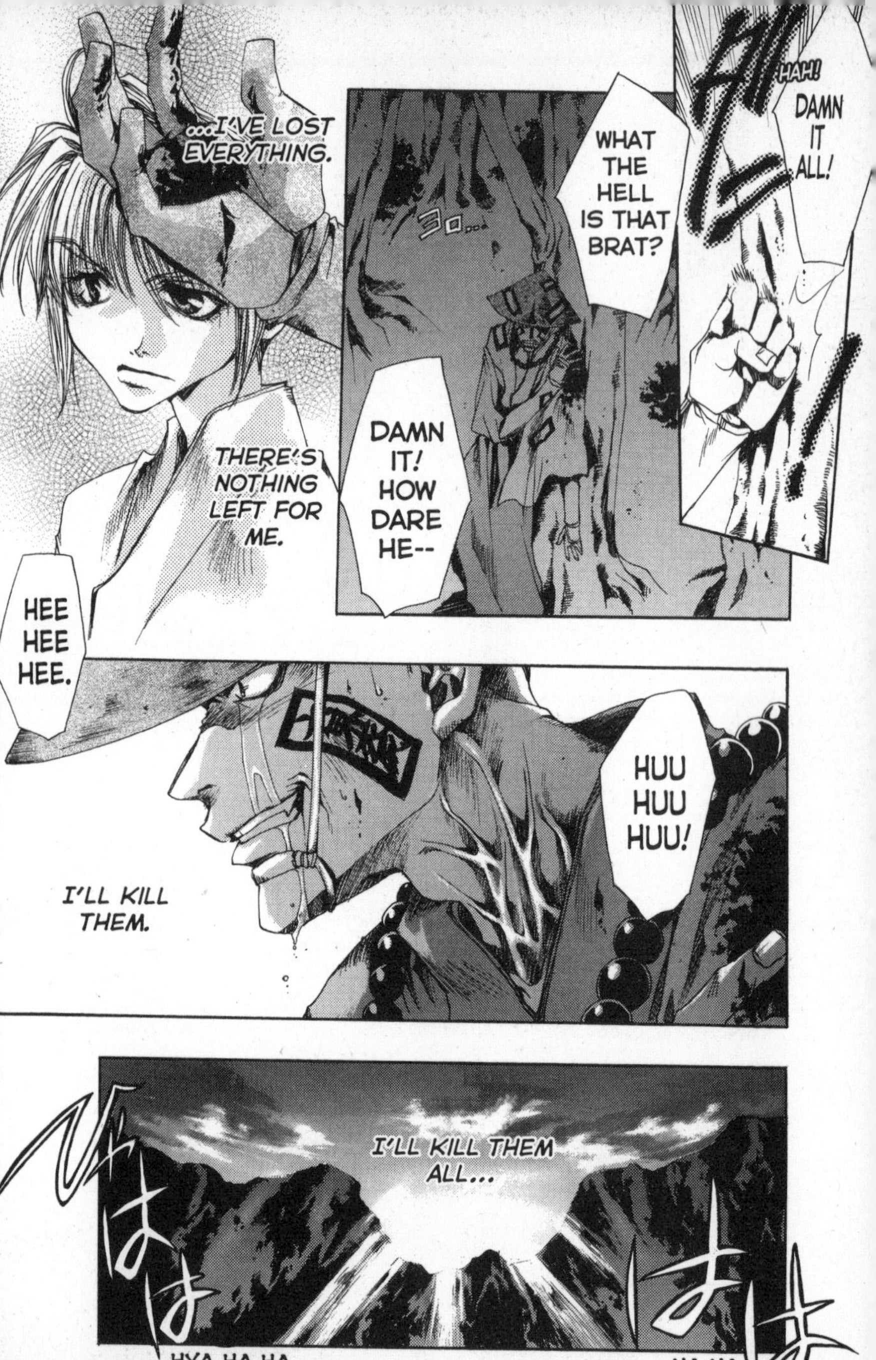
HAH! DAMN IT ALL!
WHAT THE HELL IS THAT BRAT?
DAMN IT! HOW DARE HE--
...I'VE LOST EVERYTHING.
THERE'S NOTHING LEFT FOR ME.
HEE HEE HEE.
HUU HUU HUU!
I'LL KILL THEM.
I'LL KILL THEM ALL...
HYA HA HA
HA HA

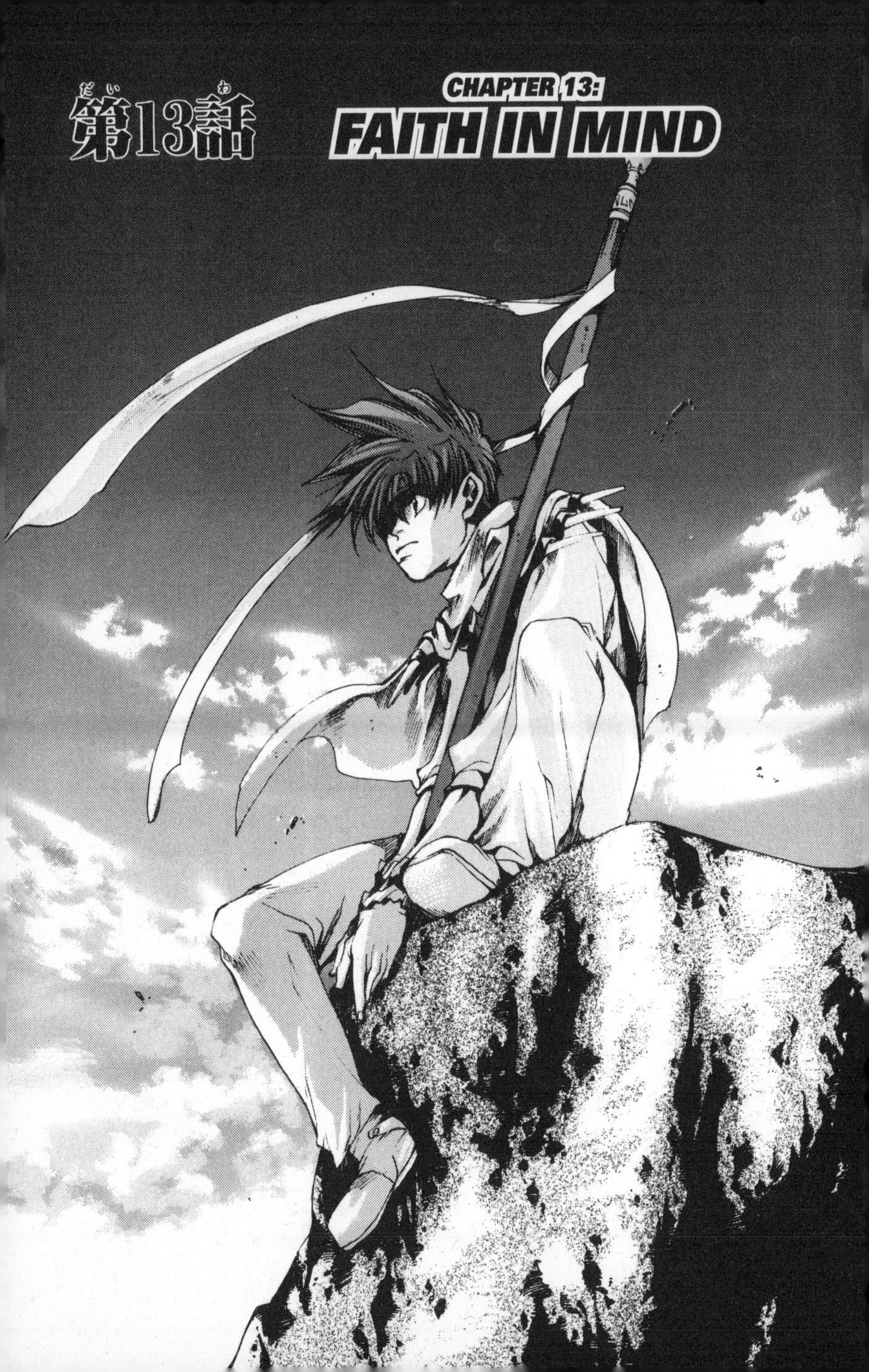
第13話
CHAPTER 13:
FAITH IN MIND

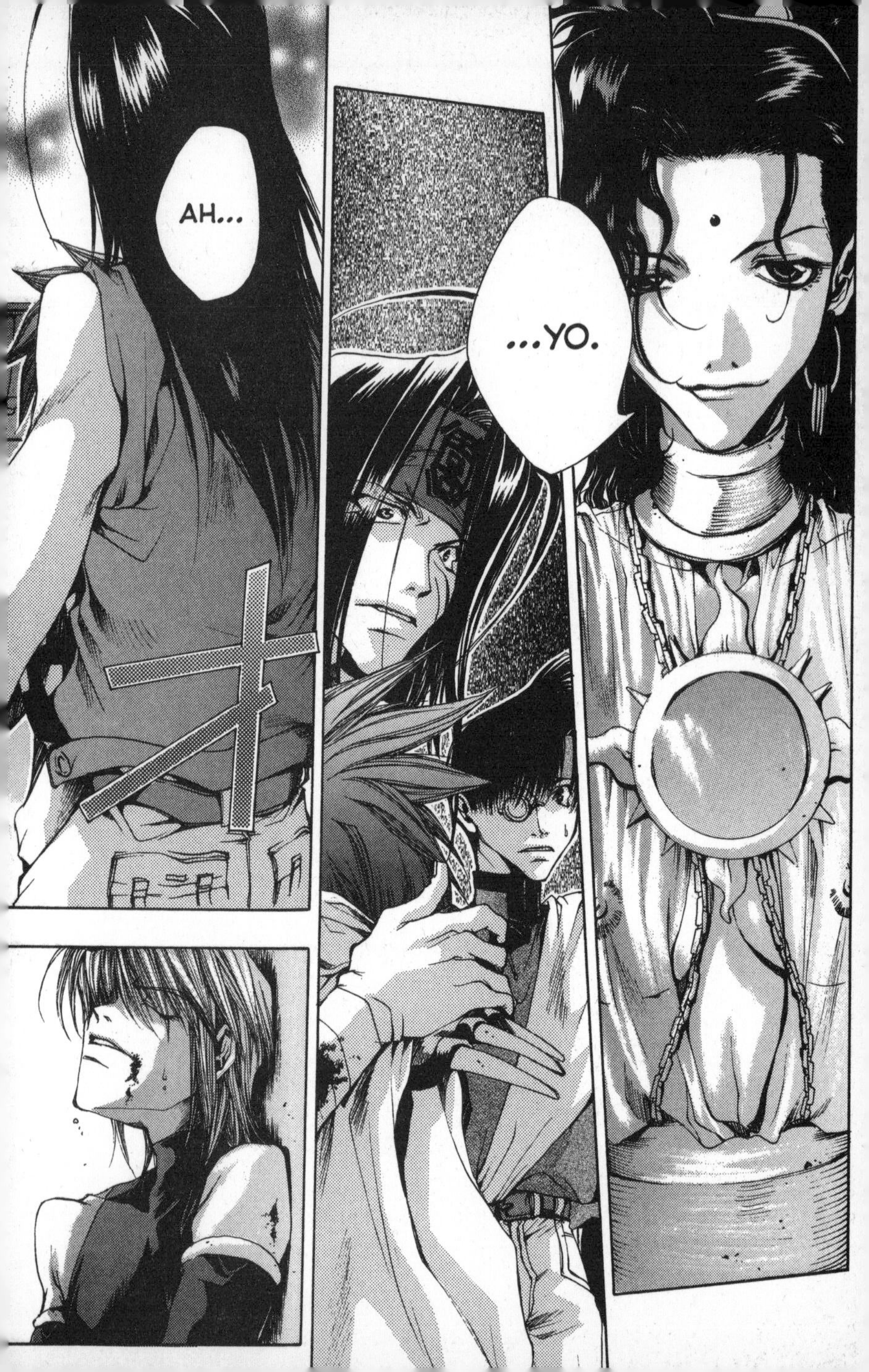
...YO.
AH...

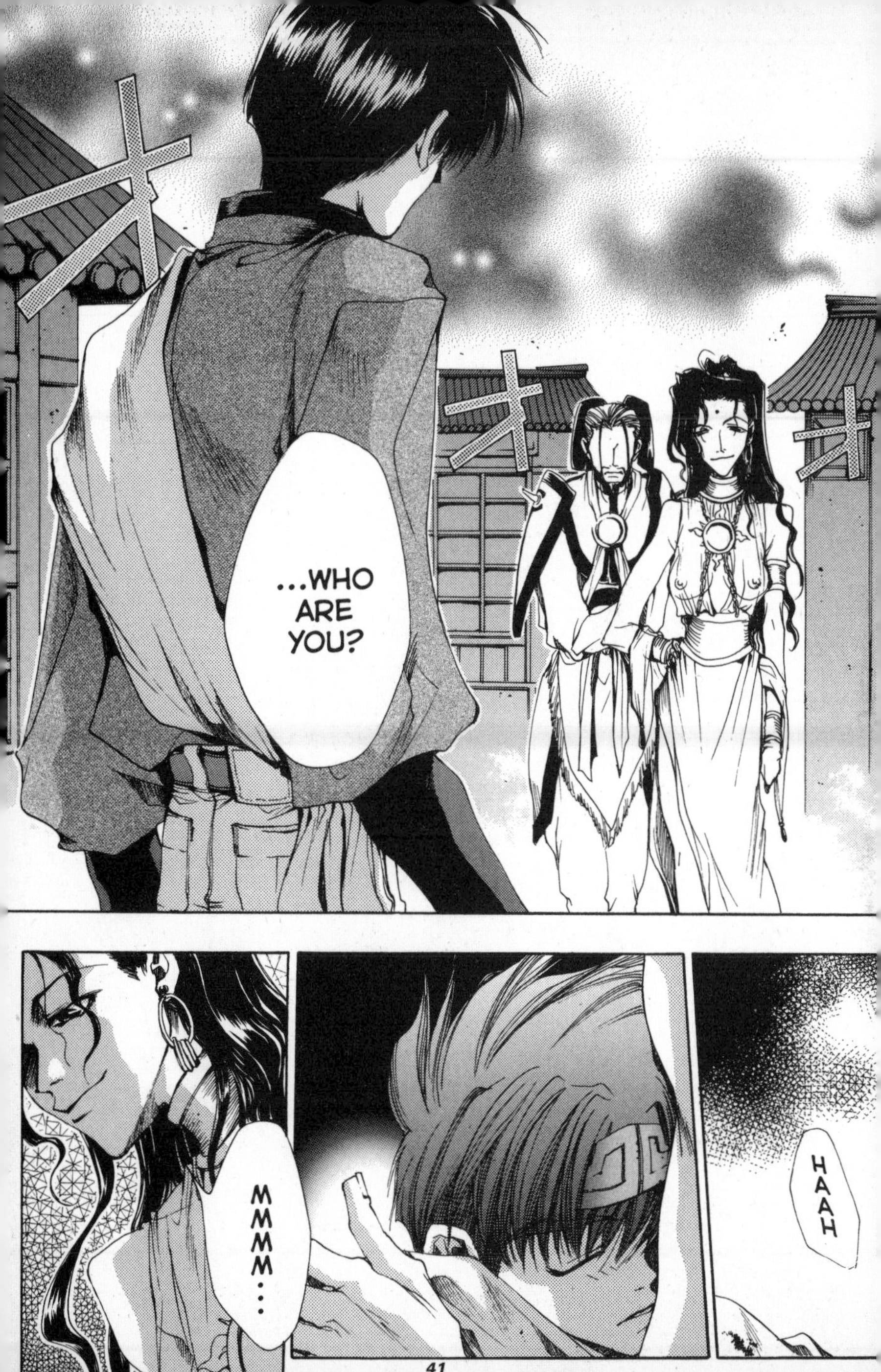
...WHO ARE YOU?
HAAH
MMMM...

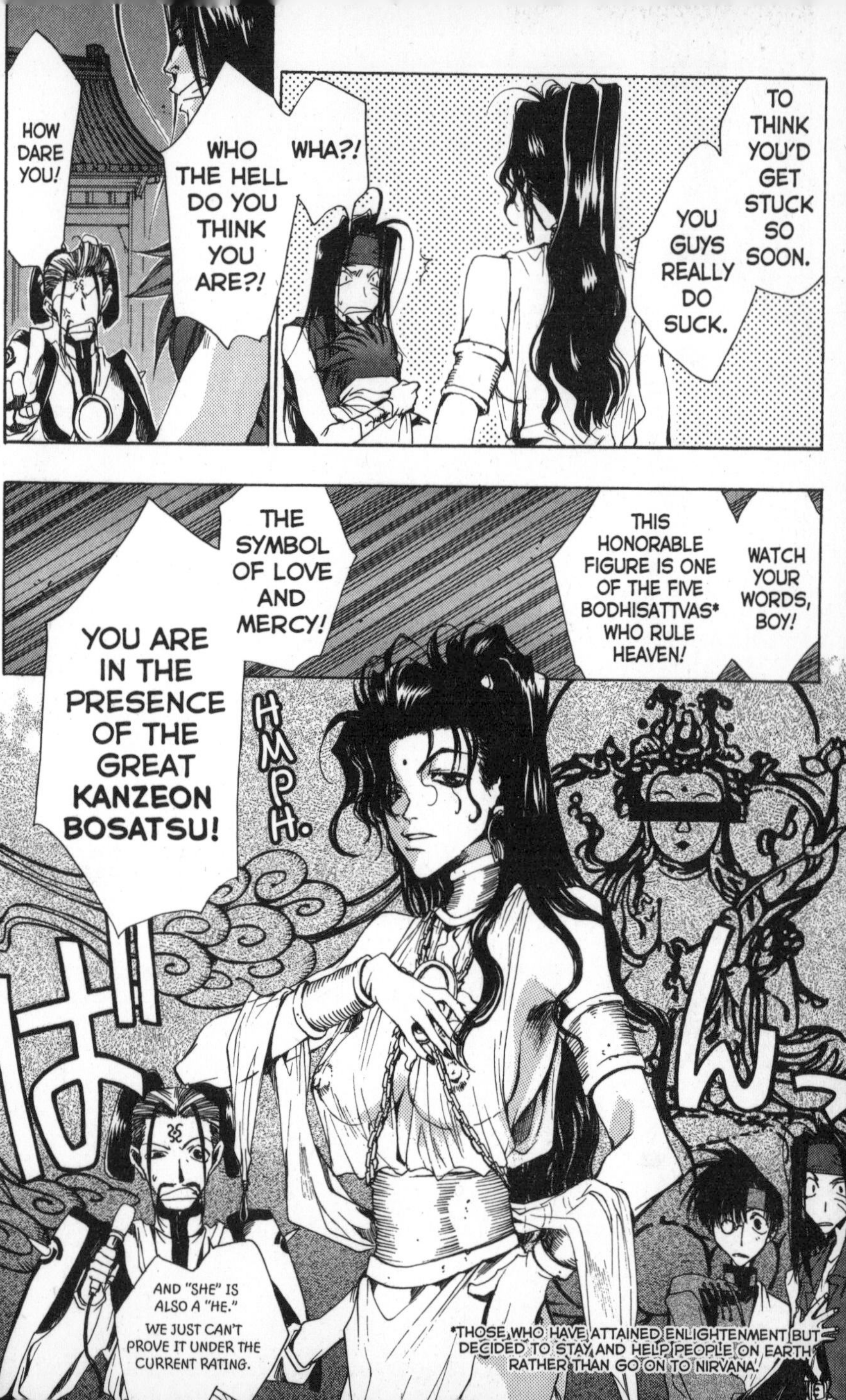
TO THINK YOU'D GET STUCK SO SOON.
YOU GUYS REALLY DO SUCK.
WHA?!
WHO THE HELL DO YOU THINK YOU ARE?!
HOW DARE YOU!
WATCH YOUR WORDS, BOY!
THIS HONORABLE FIGURE IS ONE OF THE FIVE BODHISATTVAS* WHO RULE HEAVEN!
THE SYMBOL OF LOVE AND MERCY!
YOU ARE IN THE PRESENCE OF THE GREAT KANZEON BOSATSU!
HMPH.
AND "SHE" IS ALSO A "HE." WE JUST CAN'T PROVE IT UNDER THE CURRENT RATING.

*THOSE WHO HAVE ATTAINED ENLIGHTENMENT BUT DECIDED TO STAY AND HELP PEOPLE ON EARTH RATHER THAN GO ON TO NIRVANA.

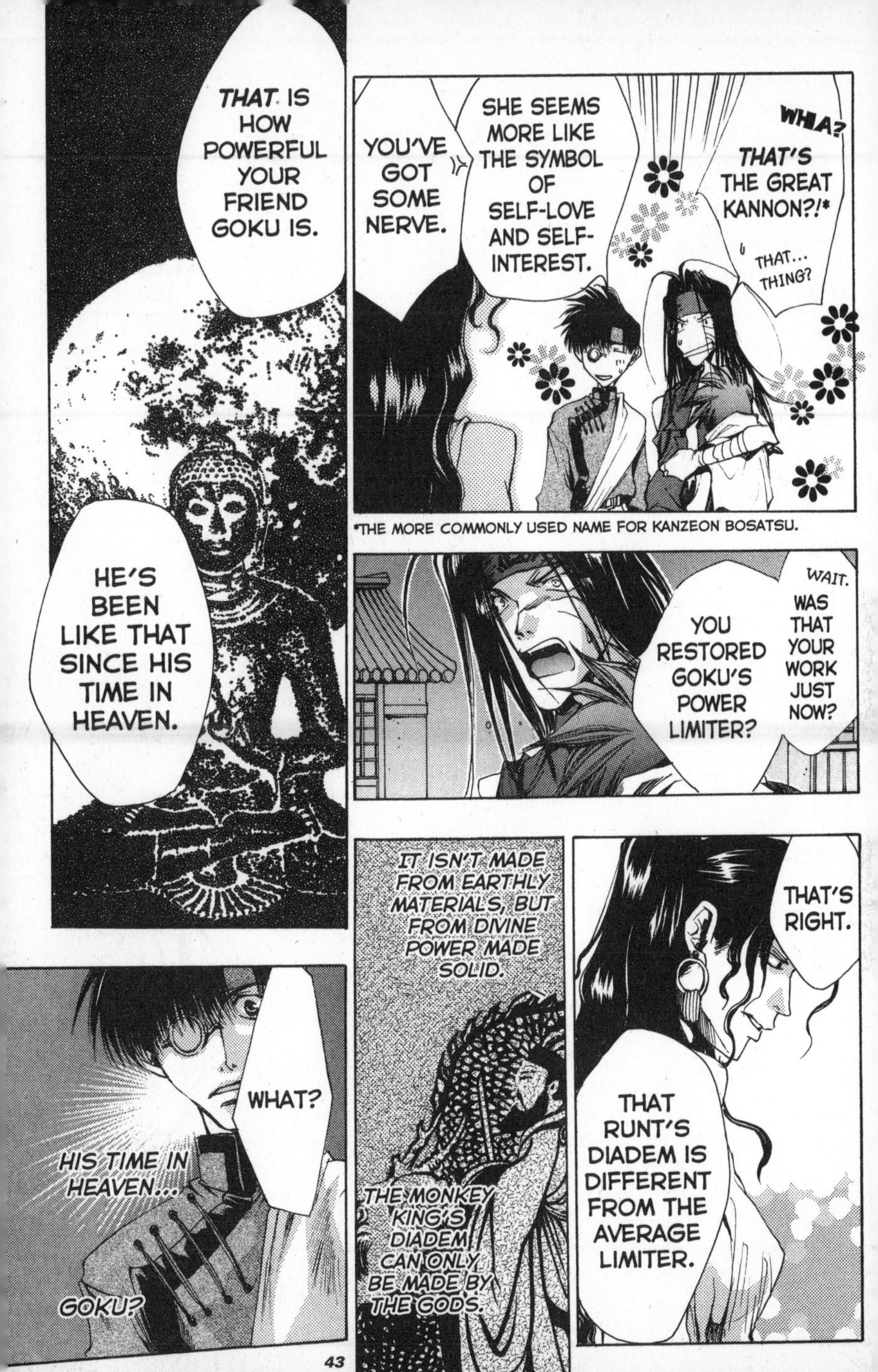
WHIA?
THAT'S THE GREAT KANNON?!*
THAT... THING?
SHE SEEMS MORE LIKE THE SYMBOL OF SELF-LOVE AND SELF-INTEREST.
YOU'VE GOT SOME NERVE.
*THE MORE COMMONLY USED NAME FOR KANZEON BOSATSU.
WAIT.
WAS THAT YOUR WORK JUST NOW?
YOU RESTORED GOKU'S POWER LIMITER?
THAT'S RIGHT.
THAT RUNT'S DIADEM IS DIFFERENT FROM THE AVERAGE LIMITER.
IT ISN'T MADE FROM EARTHLY MATERIALS, BUT FROM DIVINE POWER MADE SOLID.
THE MONKEY KING'S DIADEM CAN ONLY BE MADE BY THE GODS.
THAT IS HOW POWERFUL YOUR FRIEND GOKU IS.
HE'S BEEN LIKE THAT SINCE HIS TIME IN HEAVEN.
WHAT?
HIS TIME IN HEAVEN...
GOKU?

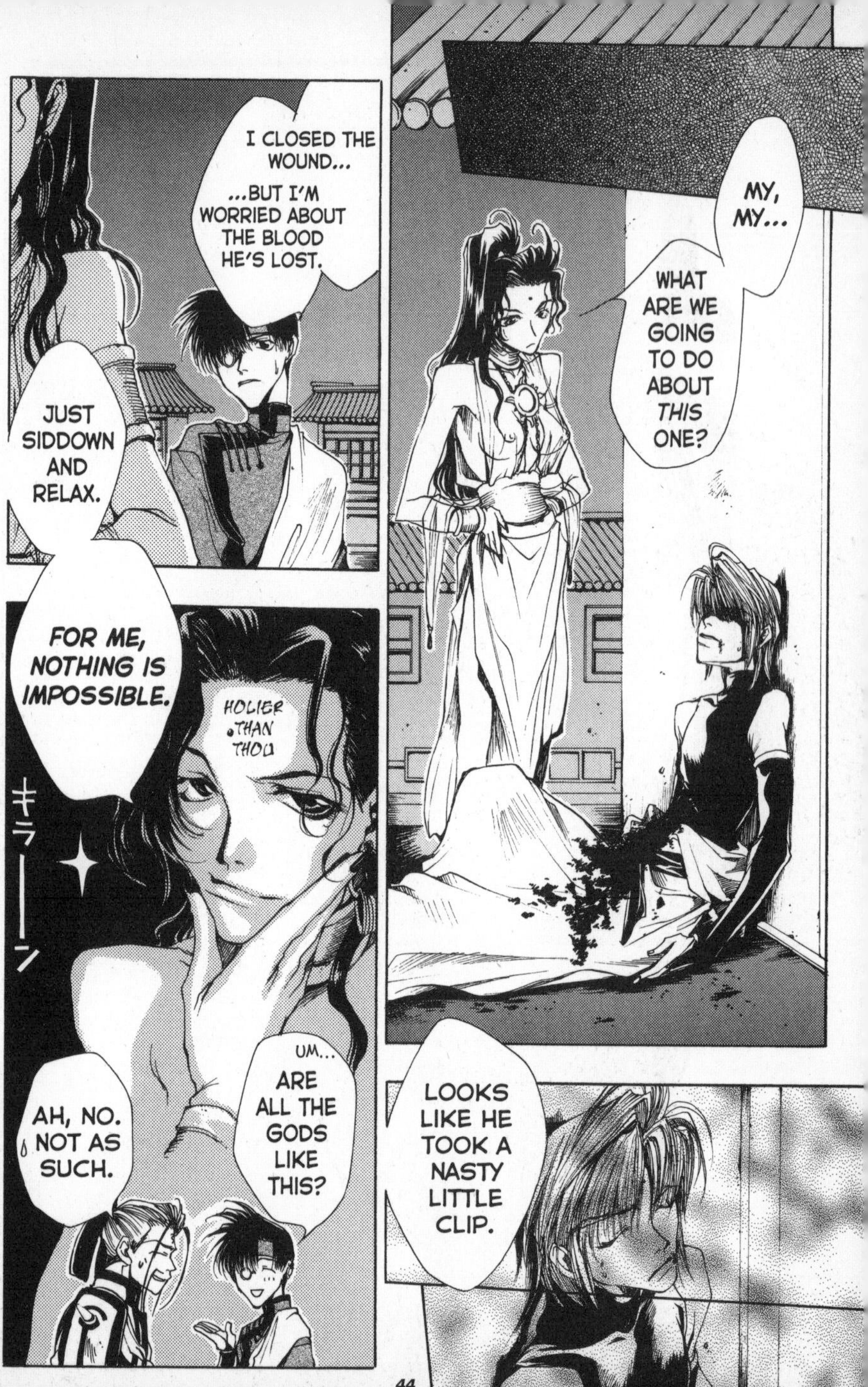
MY, MY...
WHAT ARE WE GOING TO DO ABOUT THIS ONE?
I CLOSED THE WOUND...
...BUT I'M WORRIED ABOUT THE BLOOD HE'S LOST.
JUST SIDDOWN AND RELAX.
FOR ME, NOTHING IS IMPOSSIBLE.
HOLIER THAN THOU
キラーン
UM...
ARE ALL THE GODS LIKE THIS?
AH, NO. NOT AS SUCH.
LOOKS LIKE HE TOOK A NASTY LITTLE CLIP.

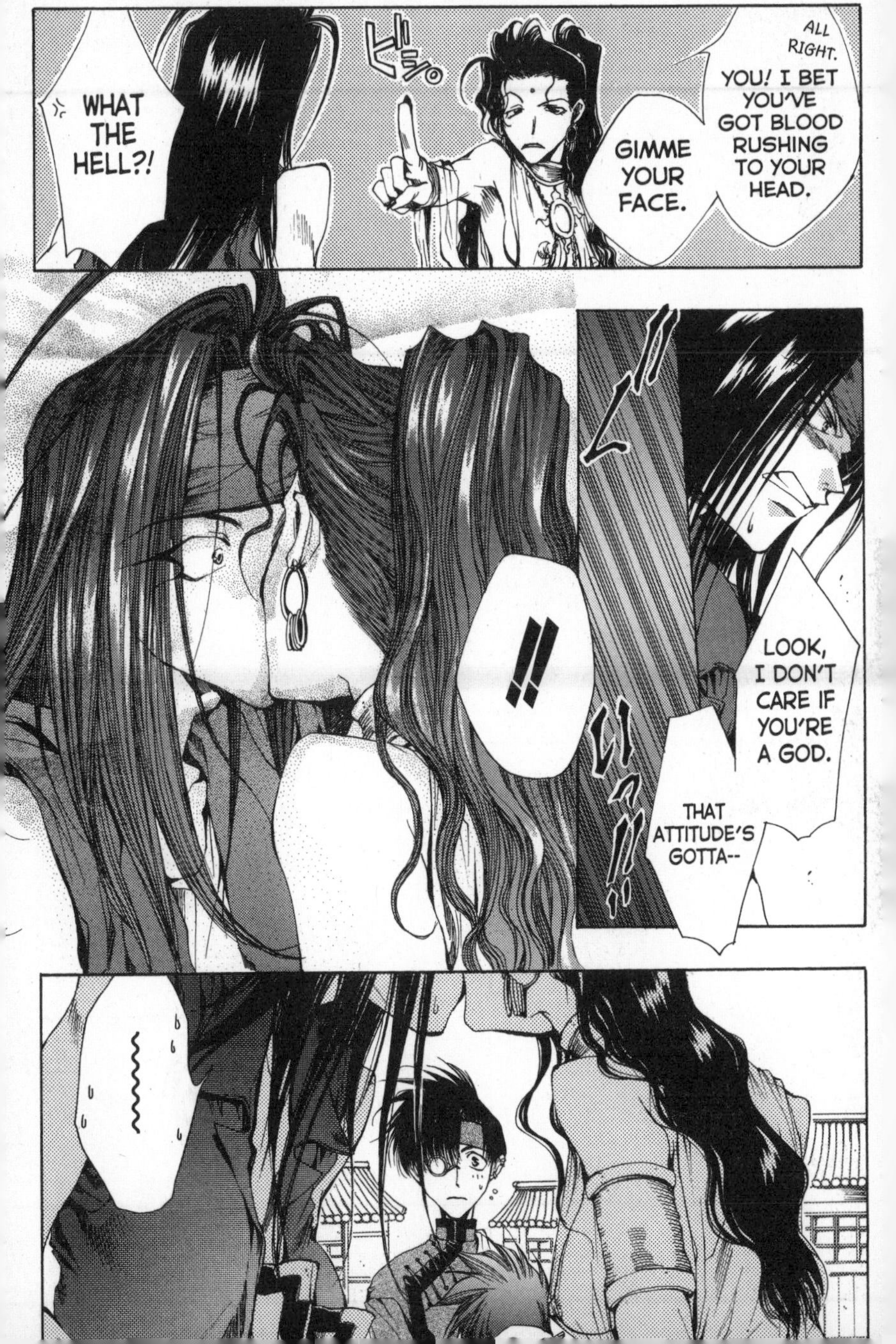
ALL RIGHT.
YOU! I BET YOU'VE GOT BLOOD RUSHING TO YOUR HEAD.
GIMME YOUR FACE.
WHAT THE HELL?!
LOOK, I DON'T CARE IF YOU'RE A GOD.
THAT ATTITUDE'S GOTTA--
!!

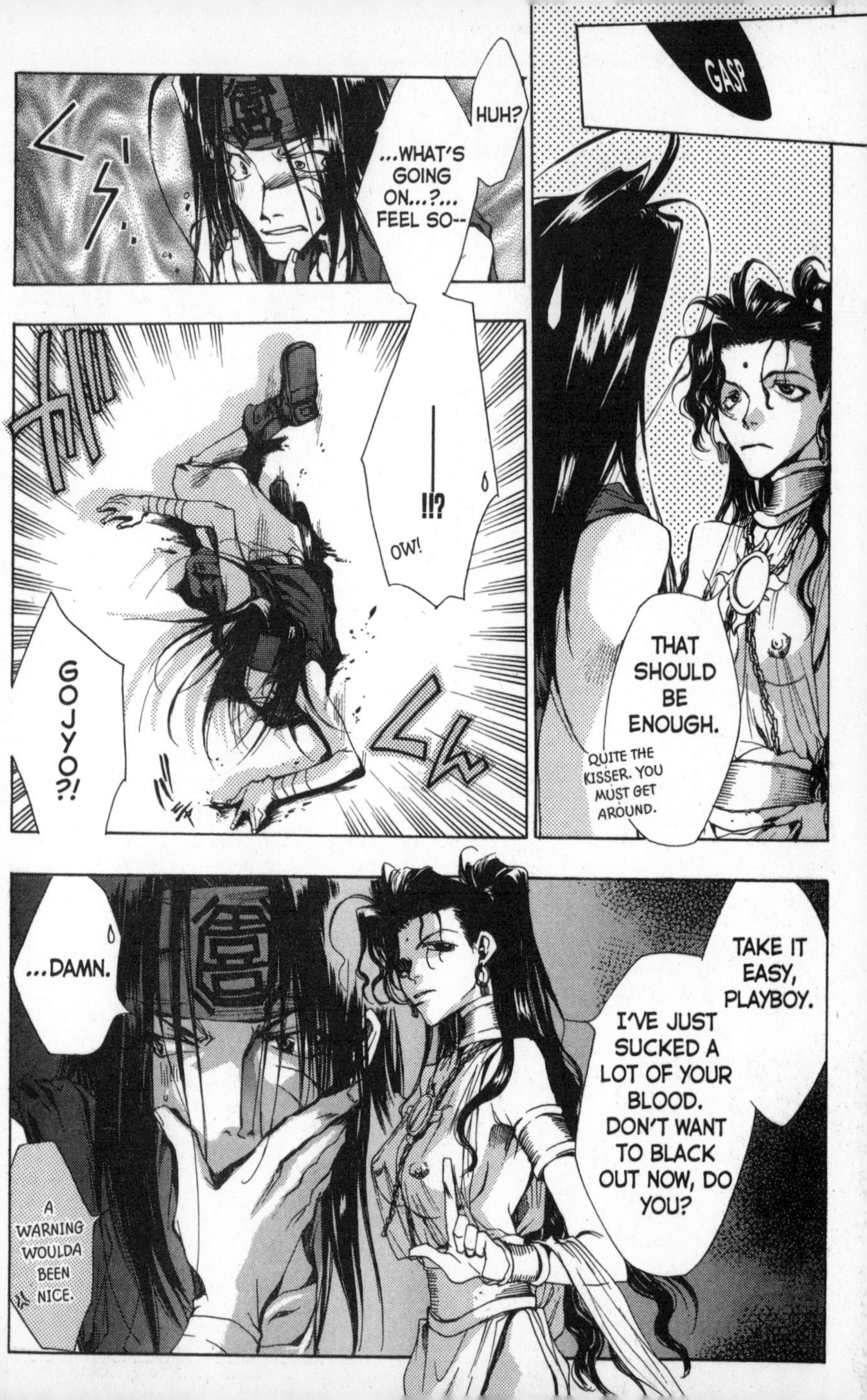
GASP
THAT SHOULD BE ENOUGH.
QUITE THE KISSER. YOU MUST GET AROUND.
HUH?
...WHAT'S GOING ON...?... FEEL SO--
—
!!?
OW!
GOJYO?!
TAKE IT EASY, PLAYBOY.
I'VE JUST SUCKED A LOT OF YOUR BLOOD. DON'T WANT TO BLACK OUT NOW, DO YOU?
...DAMN.
A WARNING WOULDA BEEN NICE.

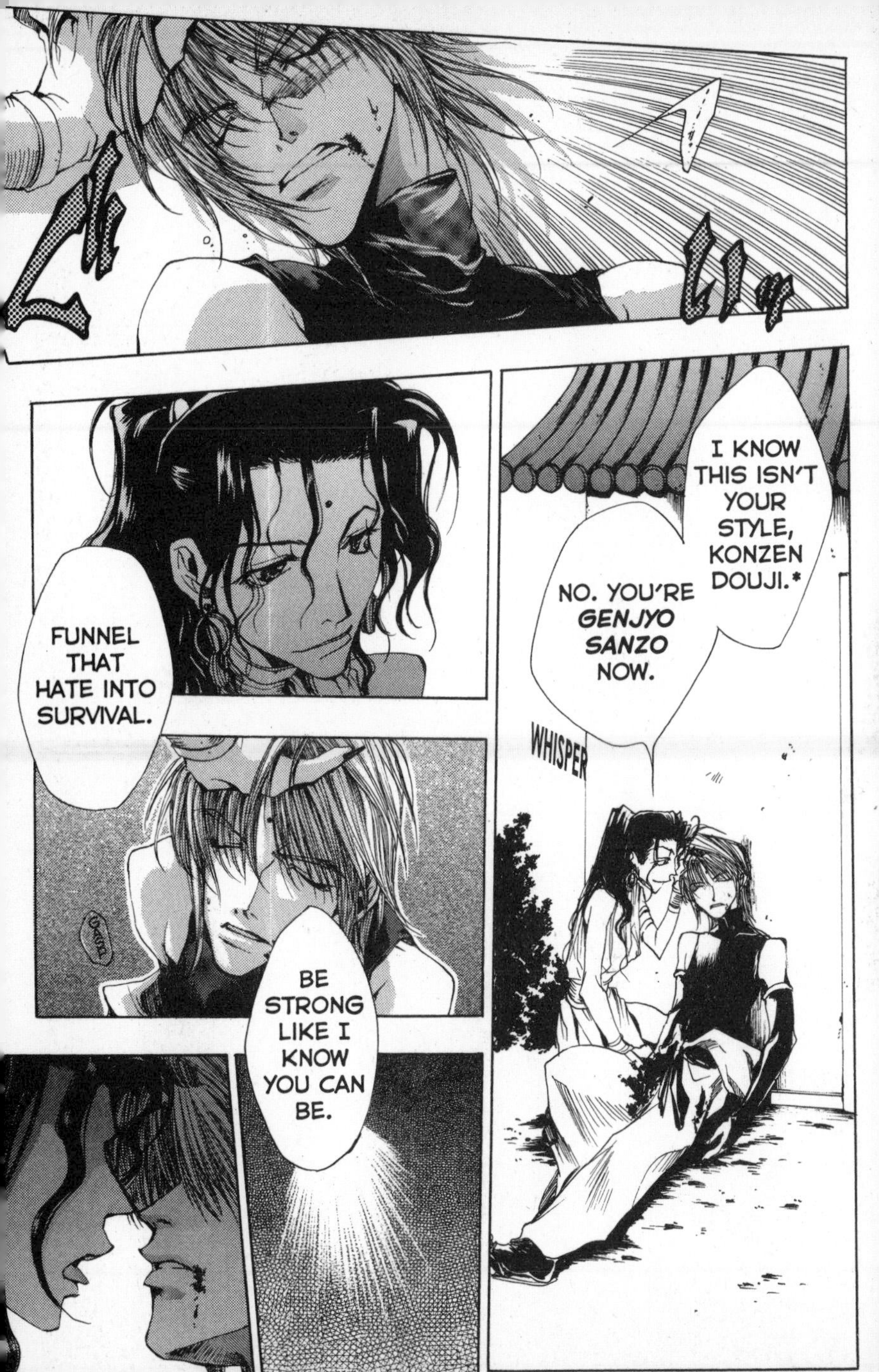
I KNOW THIS ISN'T YOUR STYLE, KONZEN DOUJI.*
NO. YOU'RE GENJYO SANZO NOW.
WHISPER
FUNNEL THAT HATE INTO SURVIVAL.
BE STRONG LIKE I KNOW YOU CAN BE.

*LITERALLY GOLDEN CICADA CHILD.

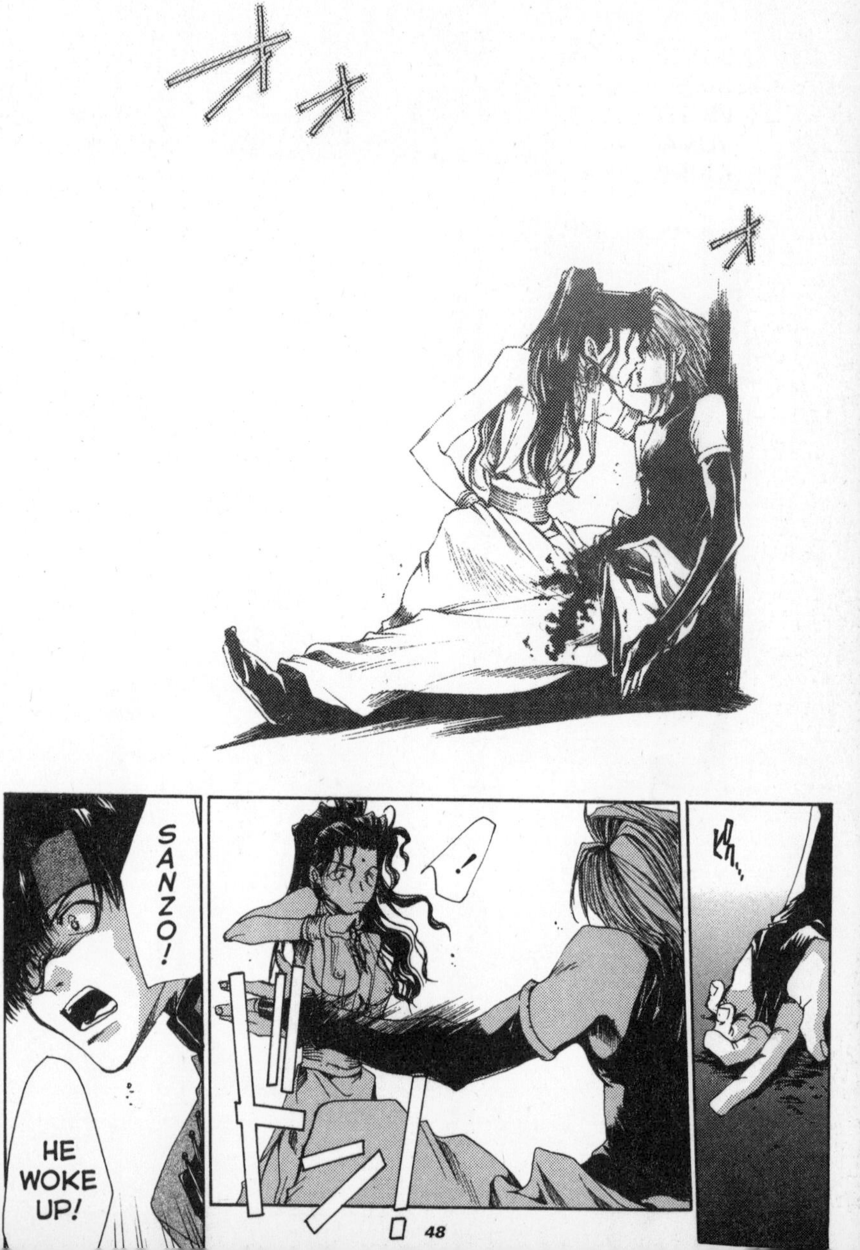
オオ
オ
!
SANZO!
HE WOKE UP!

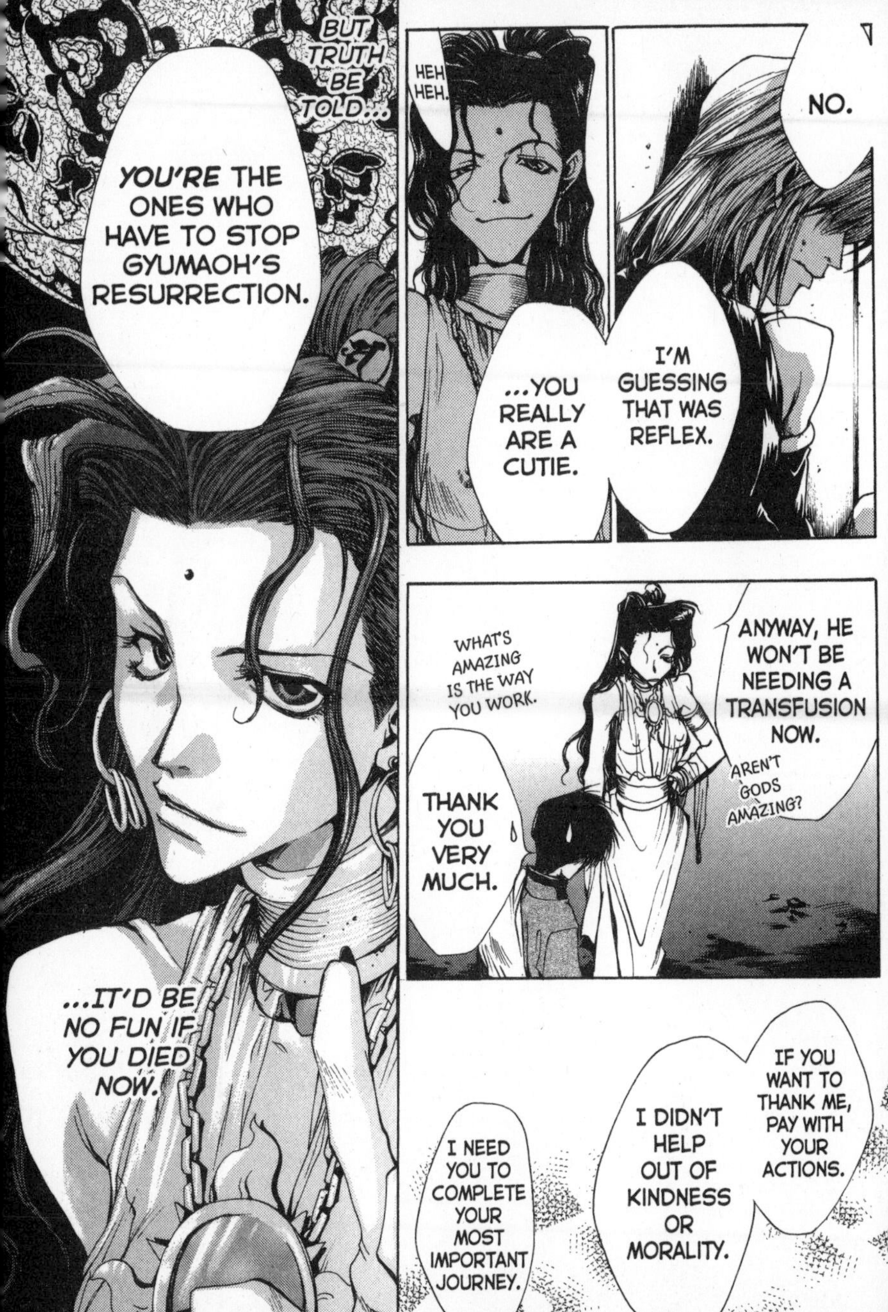
NO.
I'M GUESSING THAT WAS REFLEX.
HEH HEH.
...YOU REALLY ARE A CUTIE.
ANYWAY, HE WON'T BE NEEDING A TRANSFUSION NOW.
AREN'T GODS AMAZING?
WHAT'S AMAZING IS THE WAY YOU WORK.
THANK YOU VERY MUCH.
IF YOU WANT TO THANK ME, PAY WITH YOUR ACTIONS.
I DIDN'T HELP OUT OF KINDNESS OR MORALITY.
I NEED YOU TO COMPLETE YOUR MOST IMPORTANT JOURNEY.
BUT TRUTH BE TOLD...
YOU'RE THE ONES WHO HAVE TO STOP GYUMAOH'S RESURRECTION.
...IT'D BE NO FUN IF YOU DIED NOW.

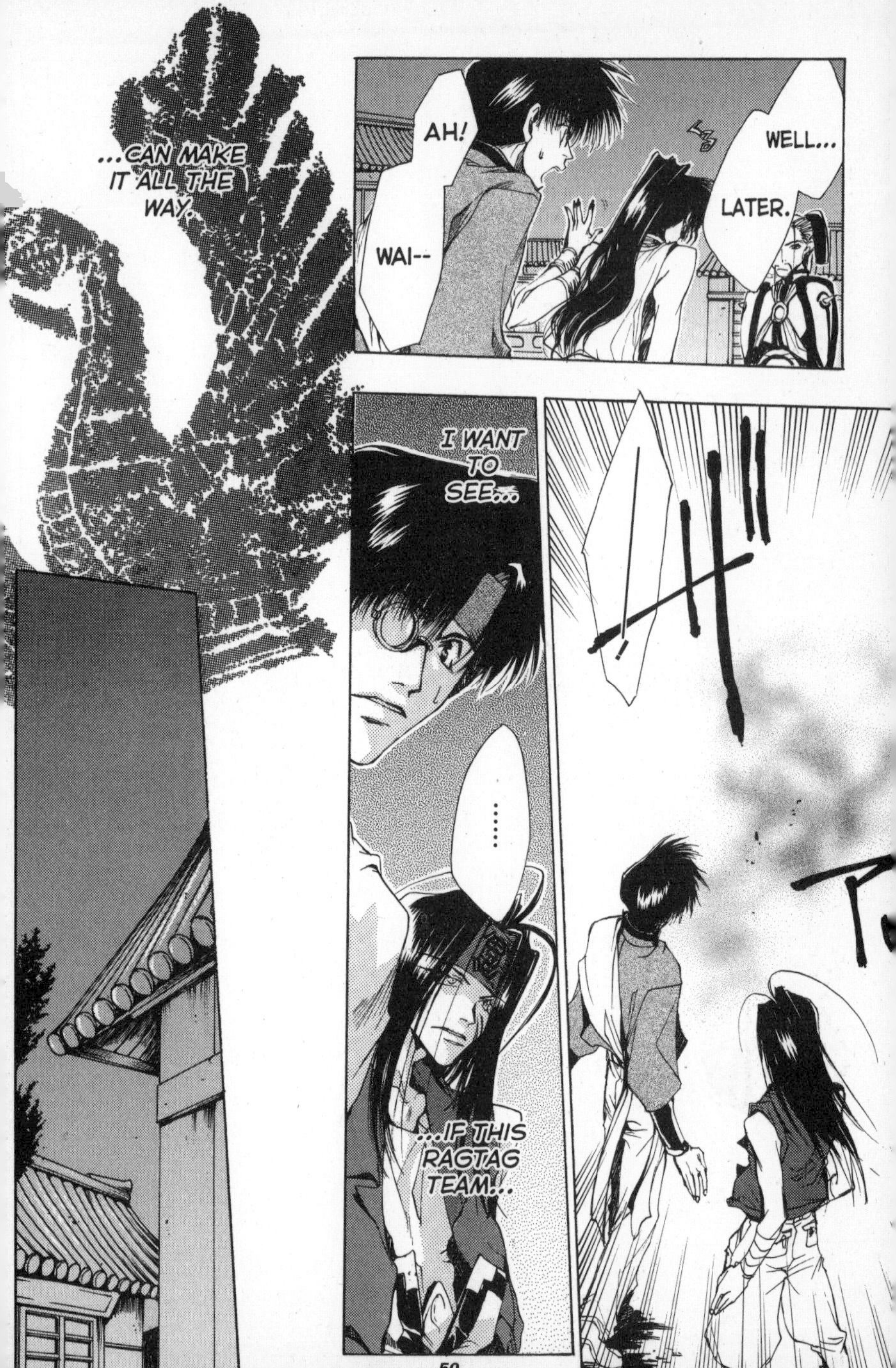
WELL...
LATER.
AH!
WAI--
I WANT TO SEE...
......
...IF THIS RAGTAG TEAM...
...CAN MAKE IT ALL THE WAY.

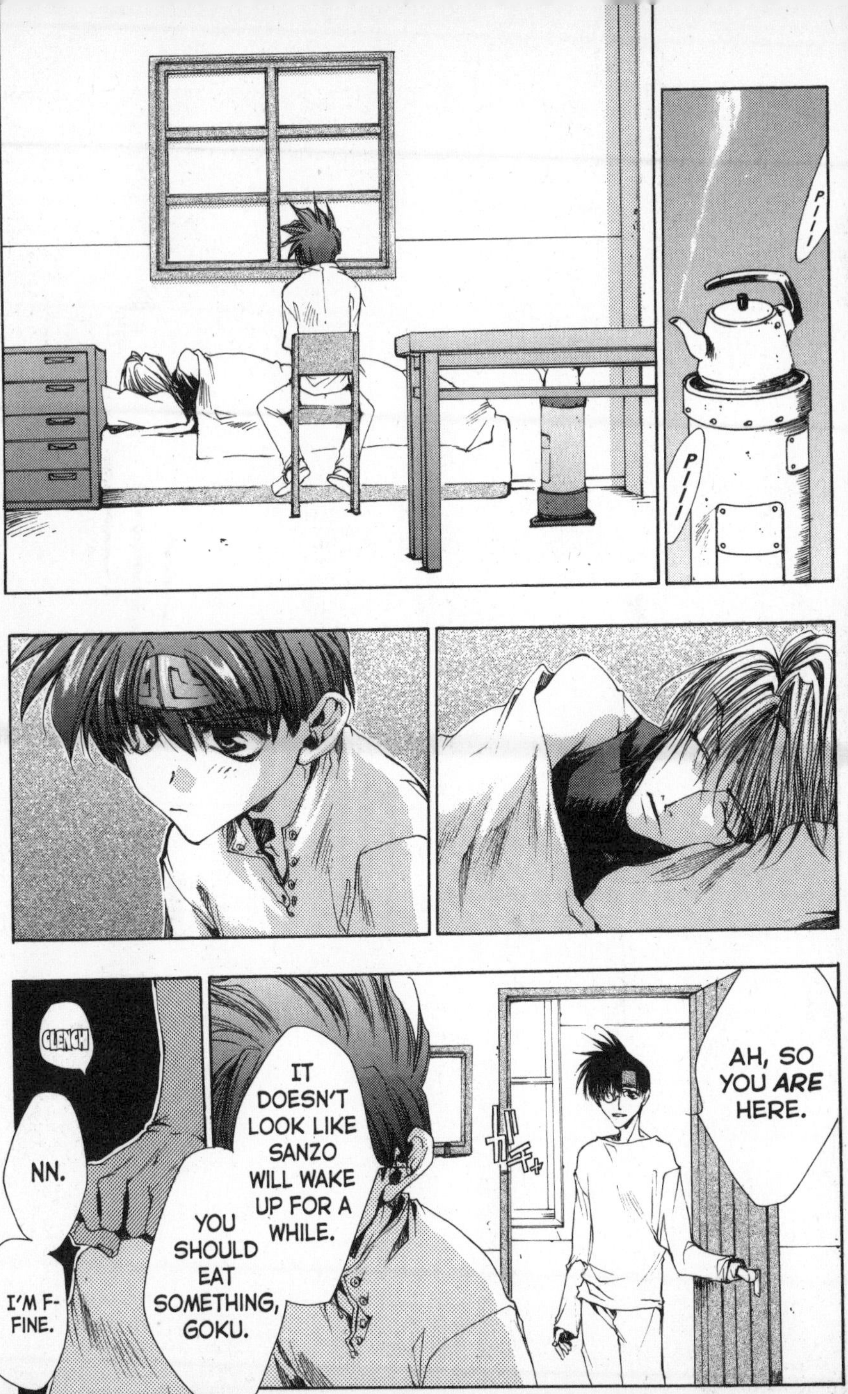
PIII
PIII
AH, SO YOU *ARE* HERE.
ガチャ
IT DOESN'T LOOK LIKE SANZO WILL WAKE UP FOR A WHILE.
YOU SHOULD EAT SOMETHING, GOKU.
CLENCH
NN.
I'M F-FINE.

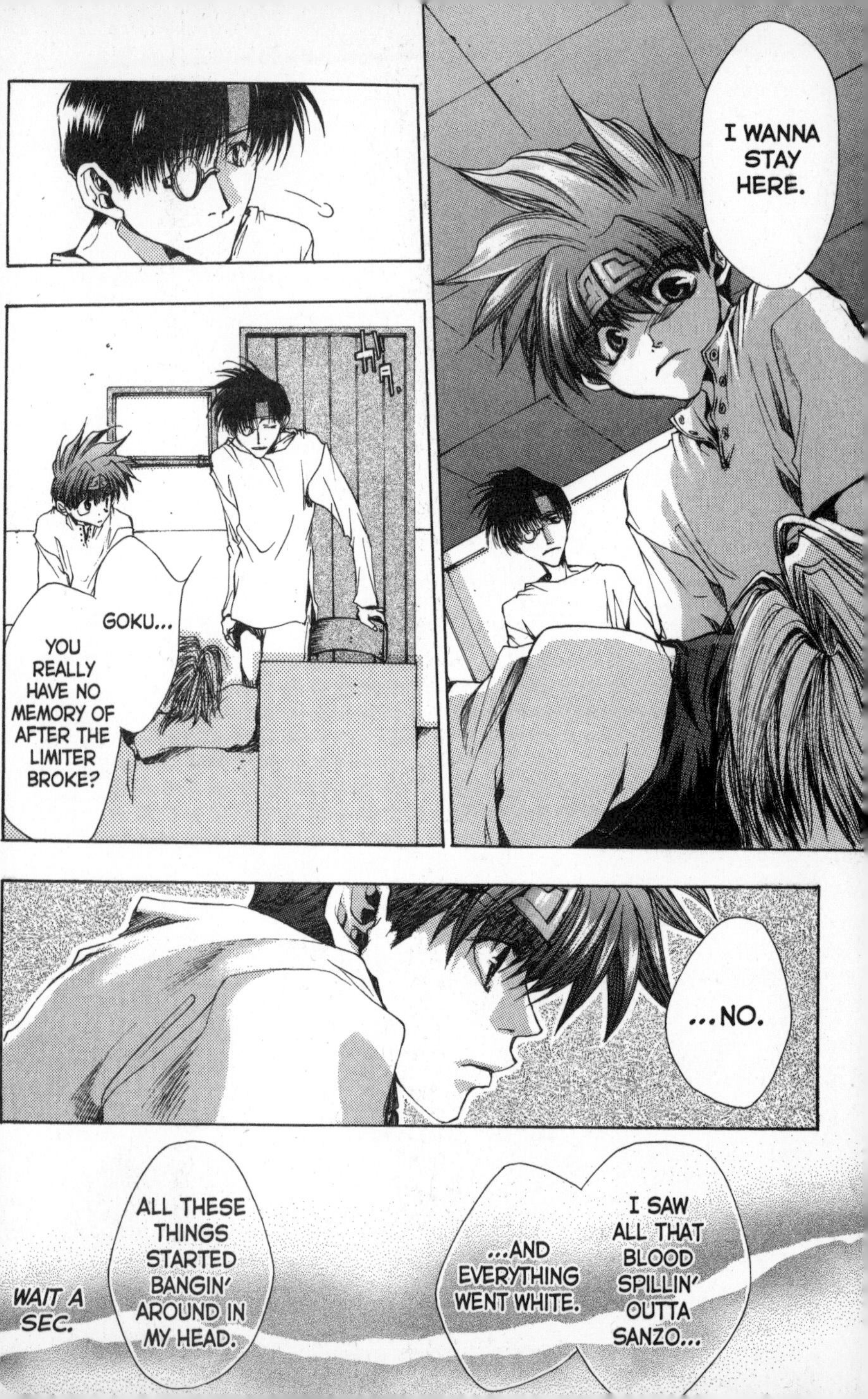
I WANNA STAY HERE.
GOKU...
YOU REALLY HAVE NO MEMORY OF AFTER THE LIMITER BROKE?
...NO.
I SAW ALL THAT BLOOD SPILLIN' OUTTA SANZO...
...AND EVERYTHING WENT WHITE.
ALL THESE THINGS STARTED BANGIN' AROUND IN MY HEAD.
WAIT A SEC.

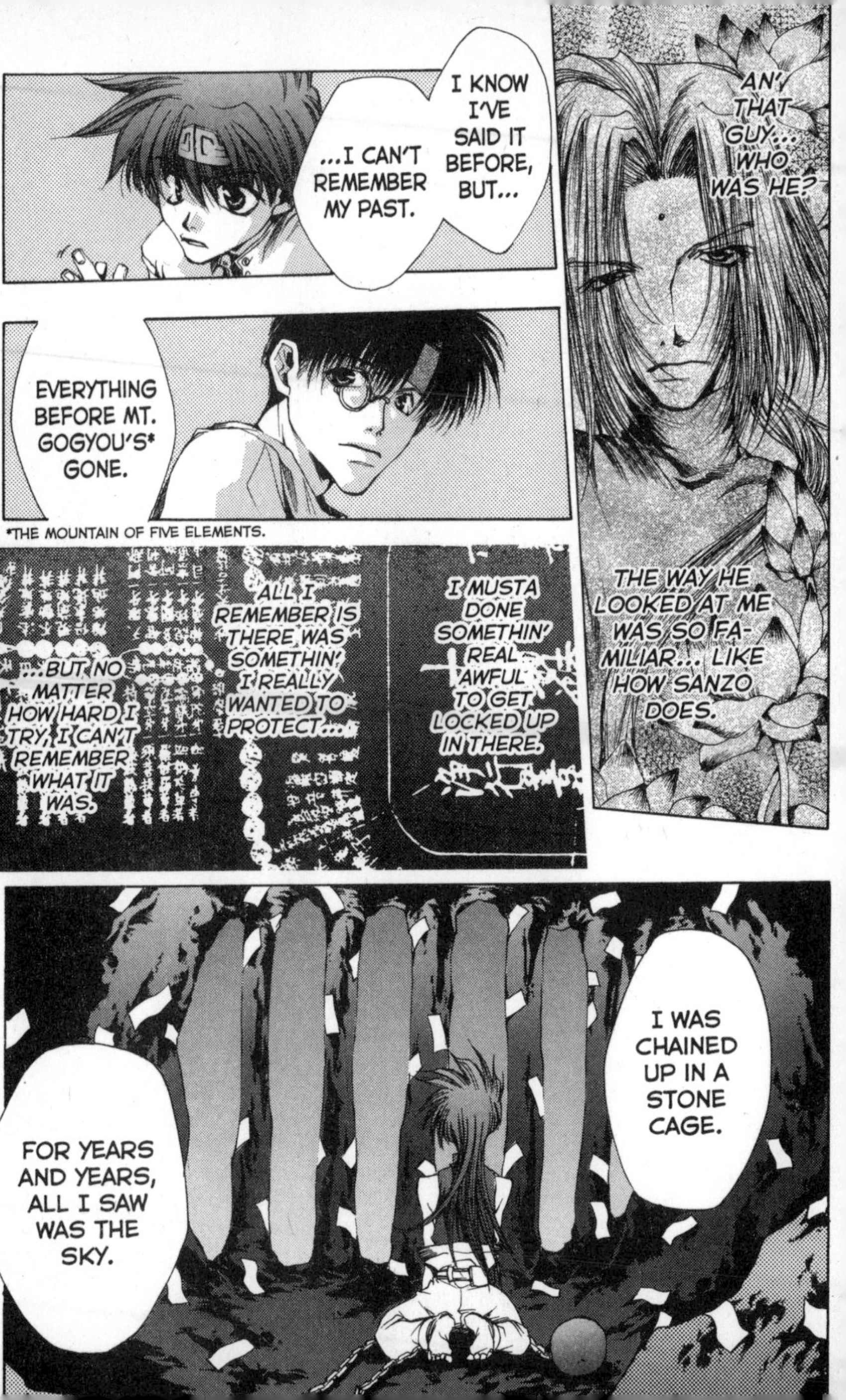
AN' THAT GUY... WHO WAS HE?
THE WAY HE LOOKED AT ME WAS SO FA-MILIAR... LIKE HOW SANZO DOES.
I KNOW I'VE SAID IT BEFORE, BUT...
...I CAN'T REMEMBER MY PAST.
EVERYTHING BEFORE MT. GOGYOU'S* GONE.
I MUSTA DONE SOMETHIN' REAL AWFUL TO GET LOCKED UP IN THERE.
ALL I REMEMBER IS THERE WAS SOMETHIN' I REALLY WANTED TO PROTECT...
...BUT NO MATTER HOW HARD I TRY, I CAN'T REMEMBER WHAT IT WAS.
I WAS CHAINED UP IN A STONE CAGE.
FOR YEARS AND YEARS, ALL I SAW WAS THE SKY.

*THE MOUNTAIN OF FIVE ELEMENTS.

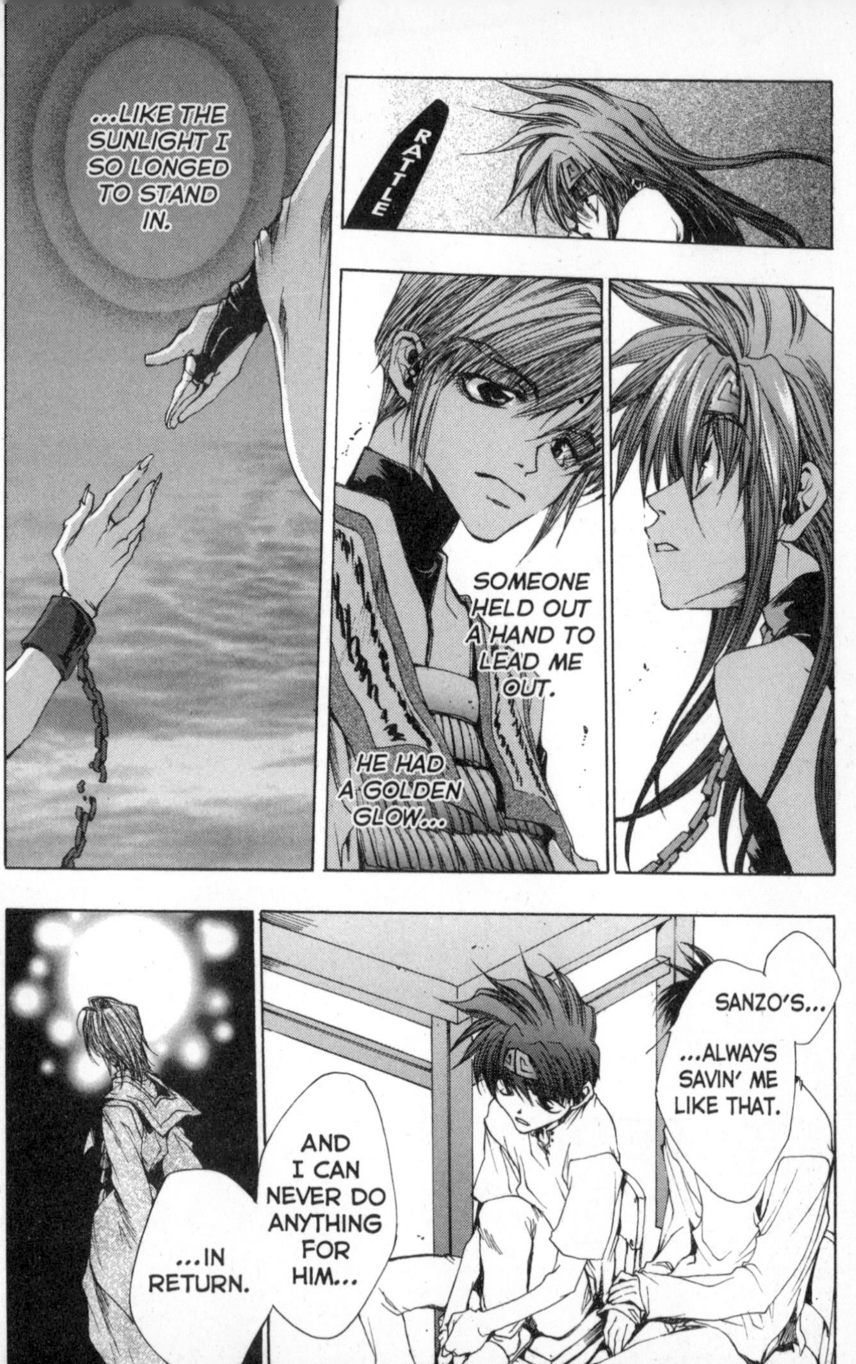
RATTLE
SOMEONE HELD OUT A HAND TO LEAD ME OUT.
HE HAD A GOLDEN GLOW...
...LIKE THE SUNLIGHT I SO LONGED TO STAND IN.
SANZO'S...
...ALWAYS SAVIN' ME LIKE THAT.
AND I CAN NEVER DO ANYTHING FOR HIM...
...IN RETURN.

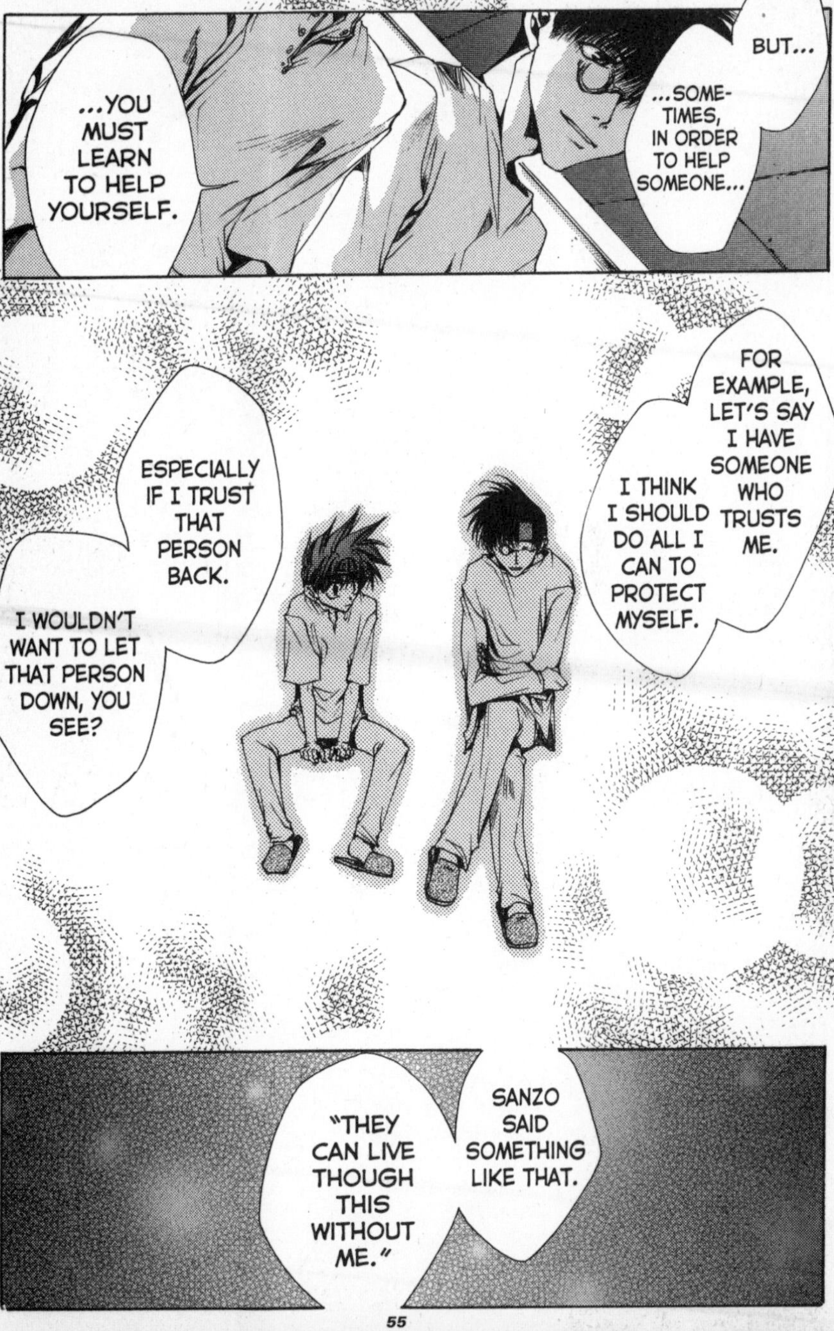
BUT...
...SOME-
TIMES,
IN ORDER
TO HELP
SOMEONE...
...YOU
MUST
LEARN
TO HELP
YOURSELF.
FOR
EXAMPLE,
LET'S SAY
I HAVE
SOMEONE
WHO
TRUSTS
ME.
I THINK
I SHOULD
DO ALL I
CAN TO
PROTECT
MYSELF.
ESPECIALLY
IF I TRUST
THAT
PERSON
BACK.
I WOULDN'T
WANT TO LET
THAT PERSON
DOWN, YOU
SEE?
SANZO
SAID
SOMETHING
LIKE THAT.
"THEY
CAN LIVE
THOUGH
THIS
WITHOUT
ME."

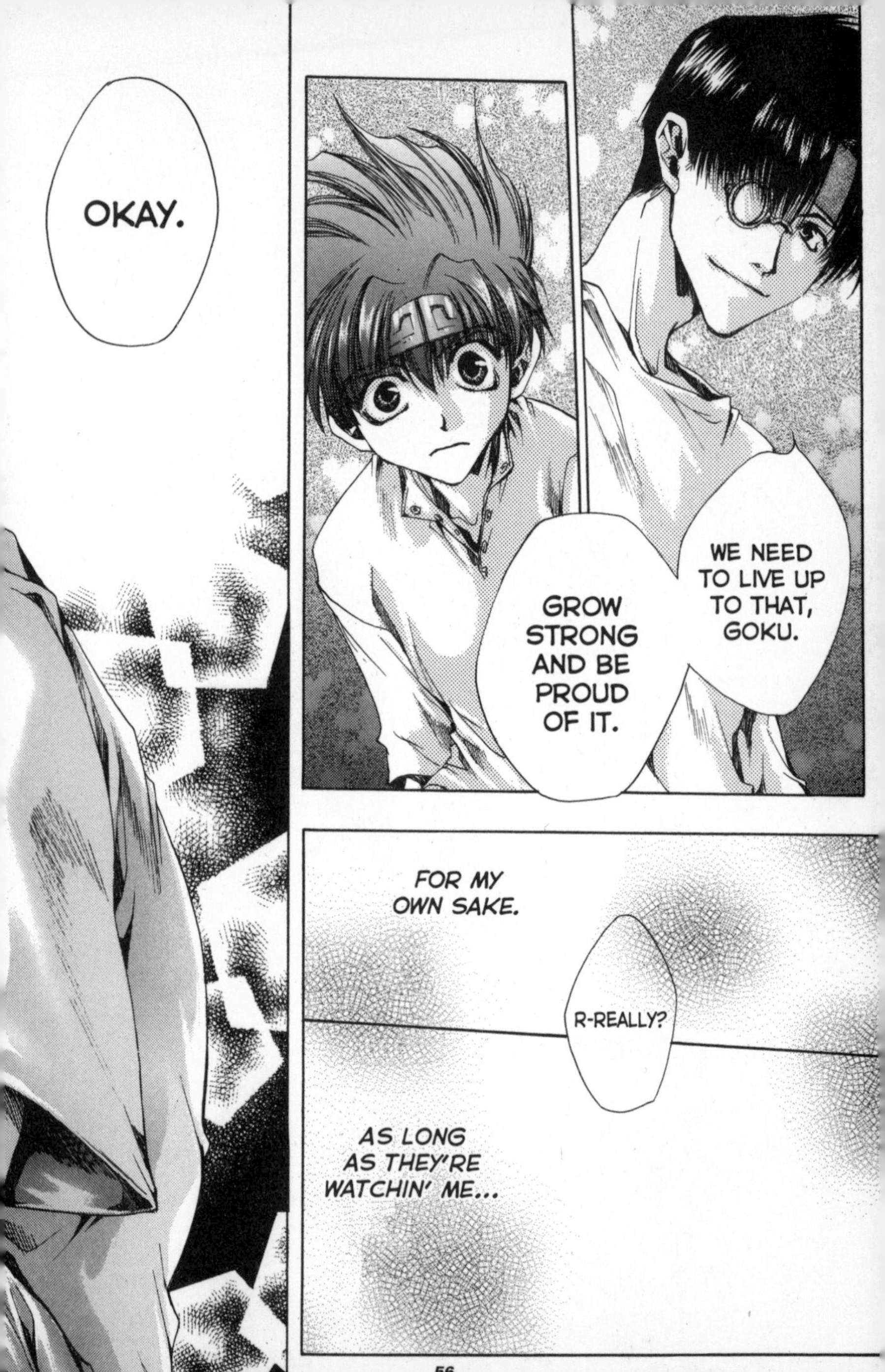

WE NEED TO LIVE UP TO THAT, GOKU.
GROW STRONG AND BE PROUD OF IT.
FOR MY OWN SAKE.
R-REALLY?
AS LONG AS THEY'RE WATCHIN' ME...
OKAY.

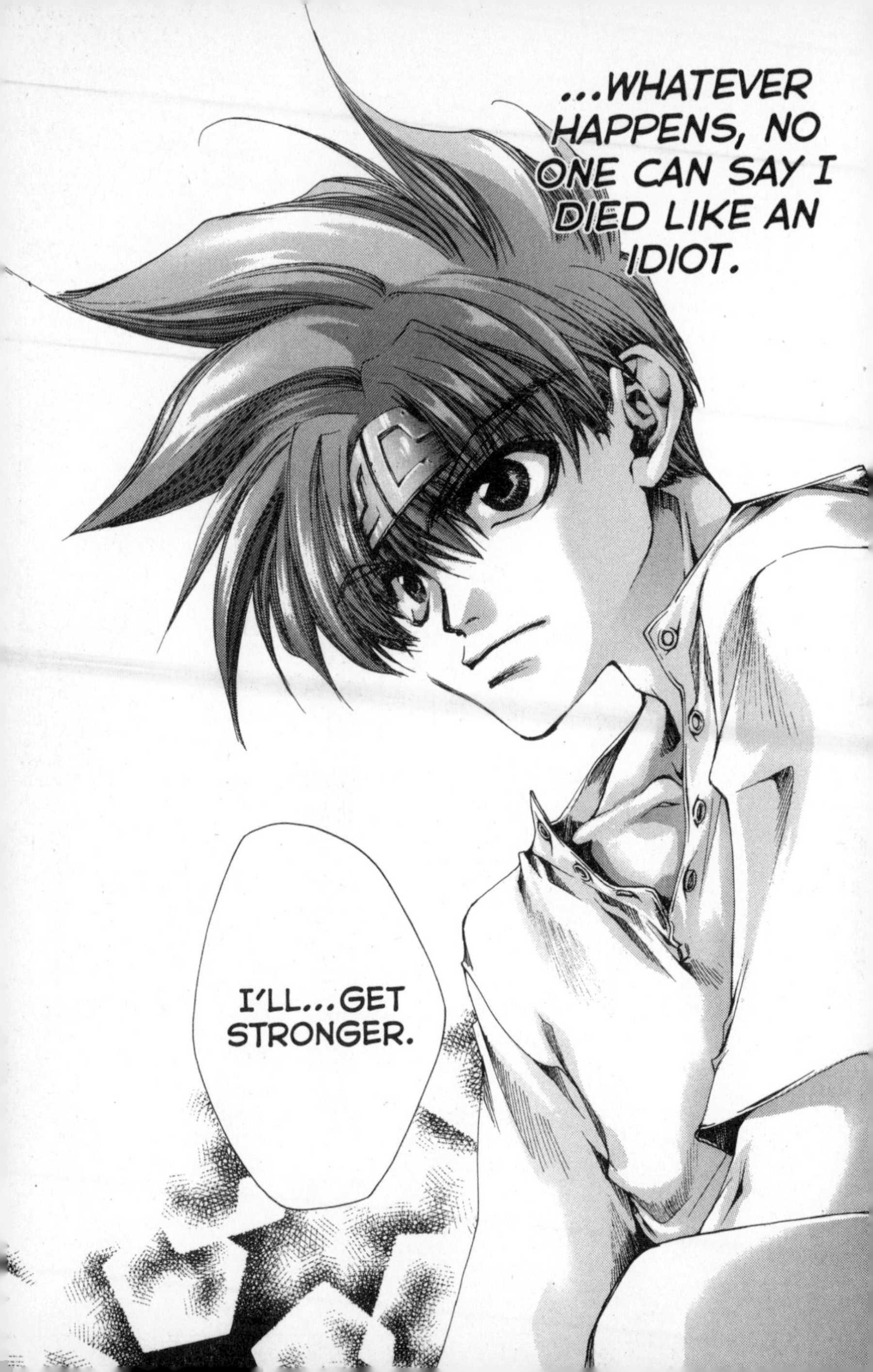
...WHATEVER HAPPENS, NO ONE CAN SAY I DIED LIKE AN IDIOT.
I'LL...GET STRONGER.

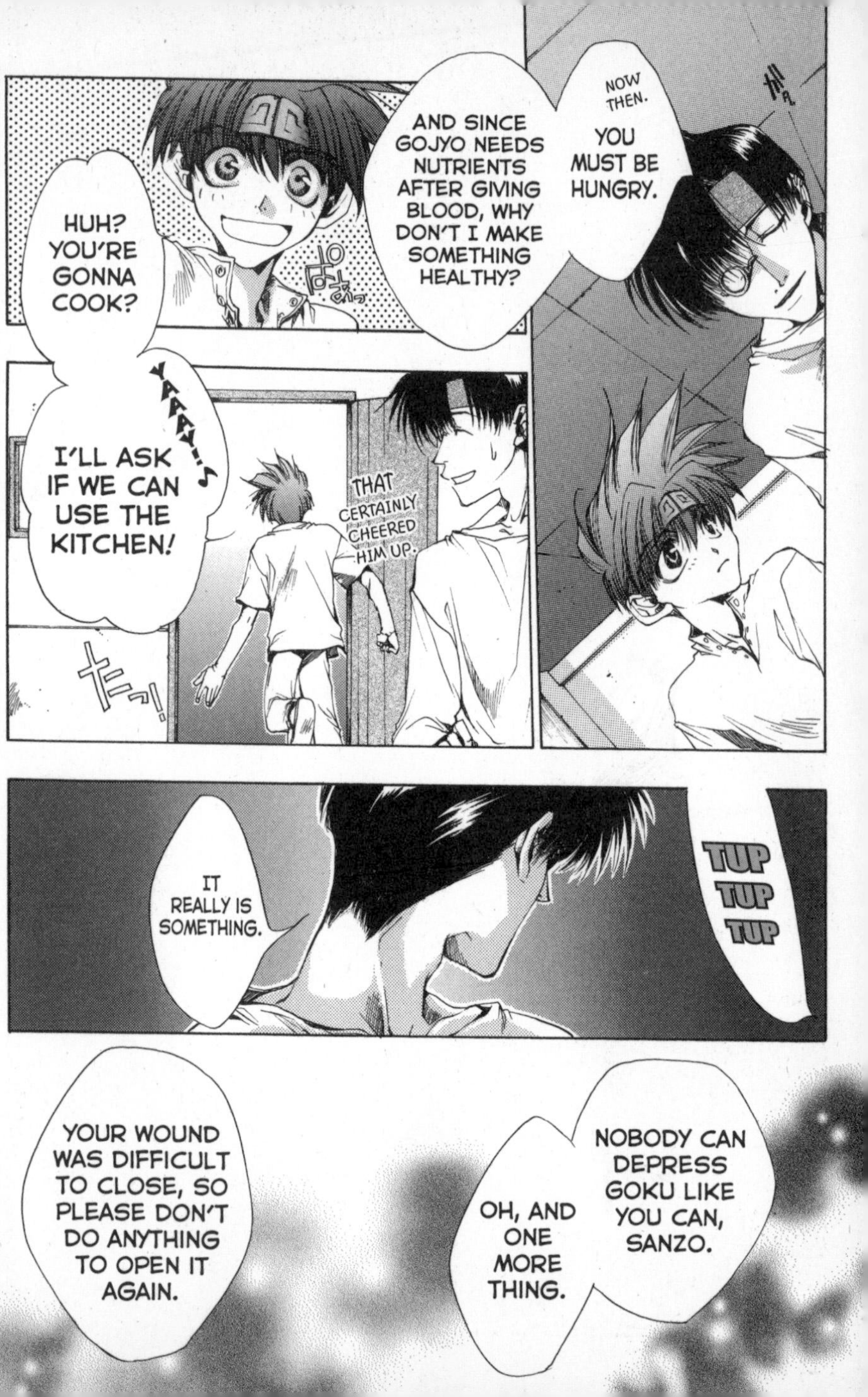
NOW THEN.
YOU MUST BE HUNGRY.
AND SINCE GOJYO NEEDS NUTRIENTS AFTER GIVING BLOOD, WHY DON'T I MAKE SOMETHING HEALTHY?
HUH? YOU'RE GONNA COOK?
YAAAY!♪
I'LL ASK IF WE CAN USE THE KITCHEN!
THAT CERTAINLY CHEERED HIM UP.
TUP TUP TUP
IT REALLY IS SOMETHING.
NOBODY CAN DEPRESS GOKU LIKE YOU CAN, SANZO.
OH, AND ONE MORE THING.
YOUR WOUND WAS DIFFICULT TO CLOSE, SO PLEASE DON'T DO ANYTHING TO OPEN IT AGAIN.

I'D RATHER
WE DIDN'T
ALL SUFFER
FURTHER.

THUNK

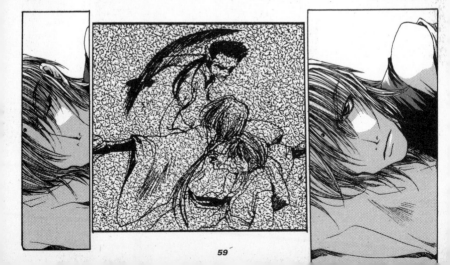

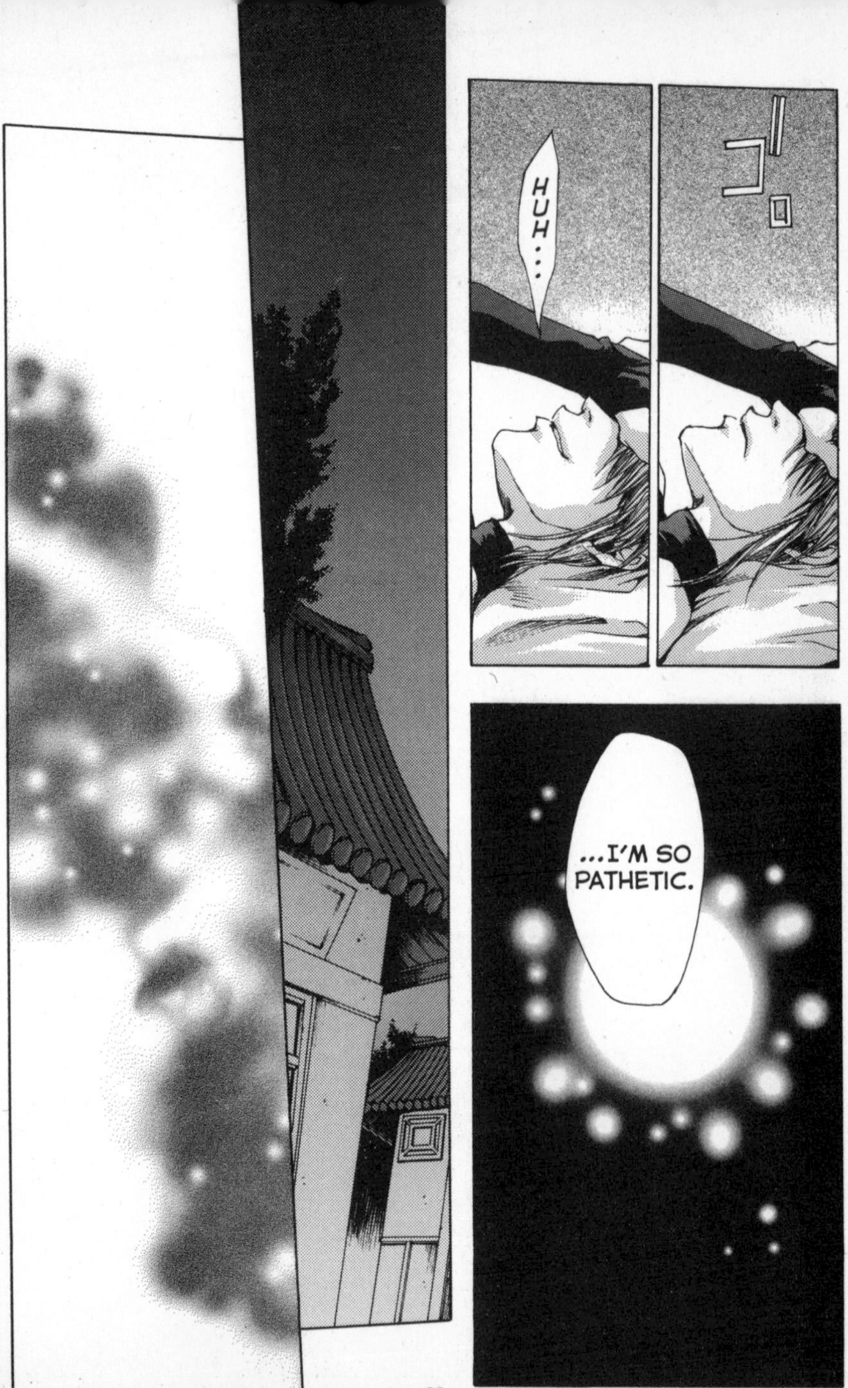
ゴロ
HUH...
...I'M SO PATHETIC.

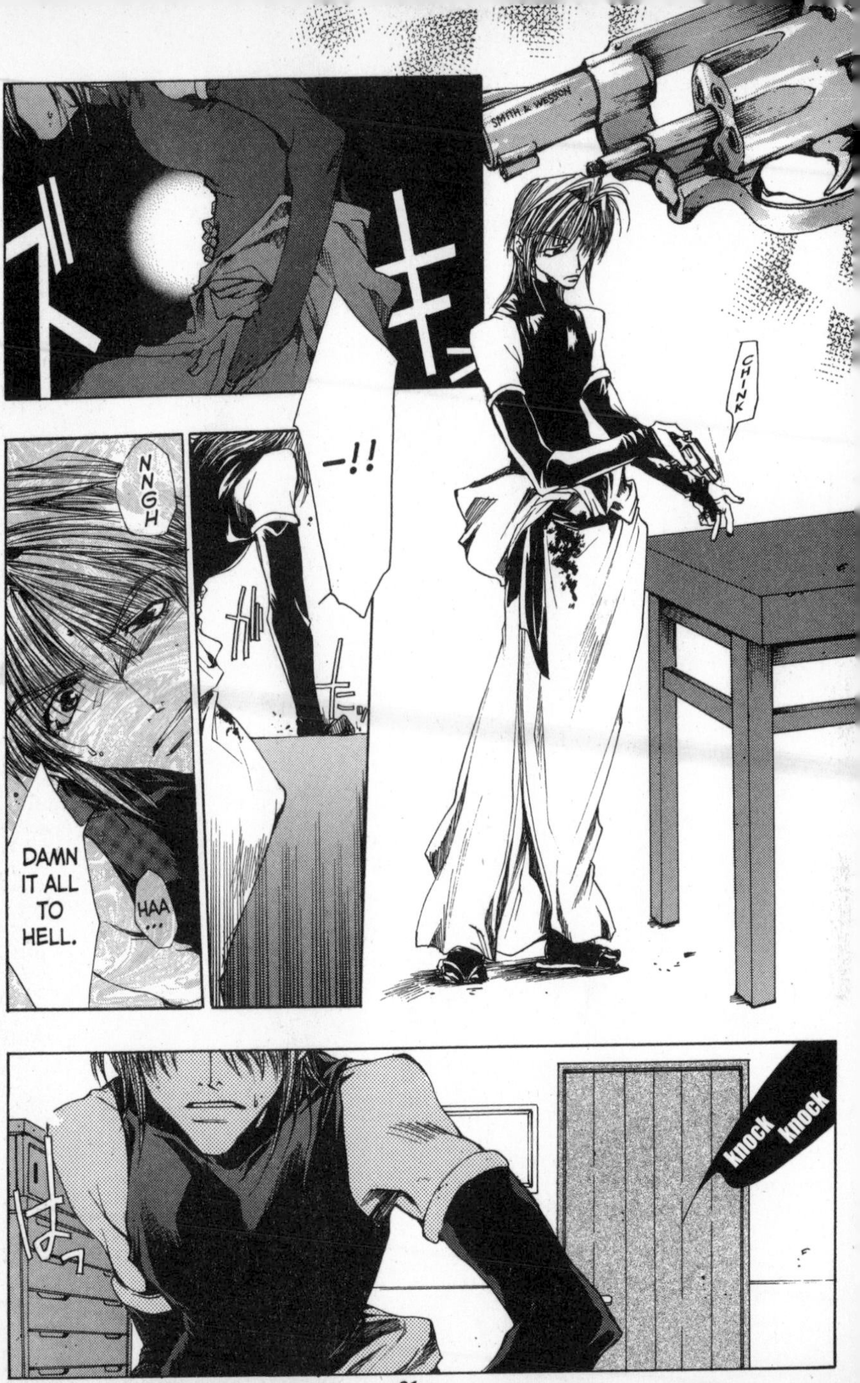
SMITH & WESSON
CHINK
—!!
NNGH
DAMN IT ALL TO HELL.
HAA...
knock knock

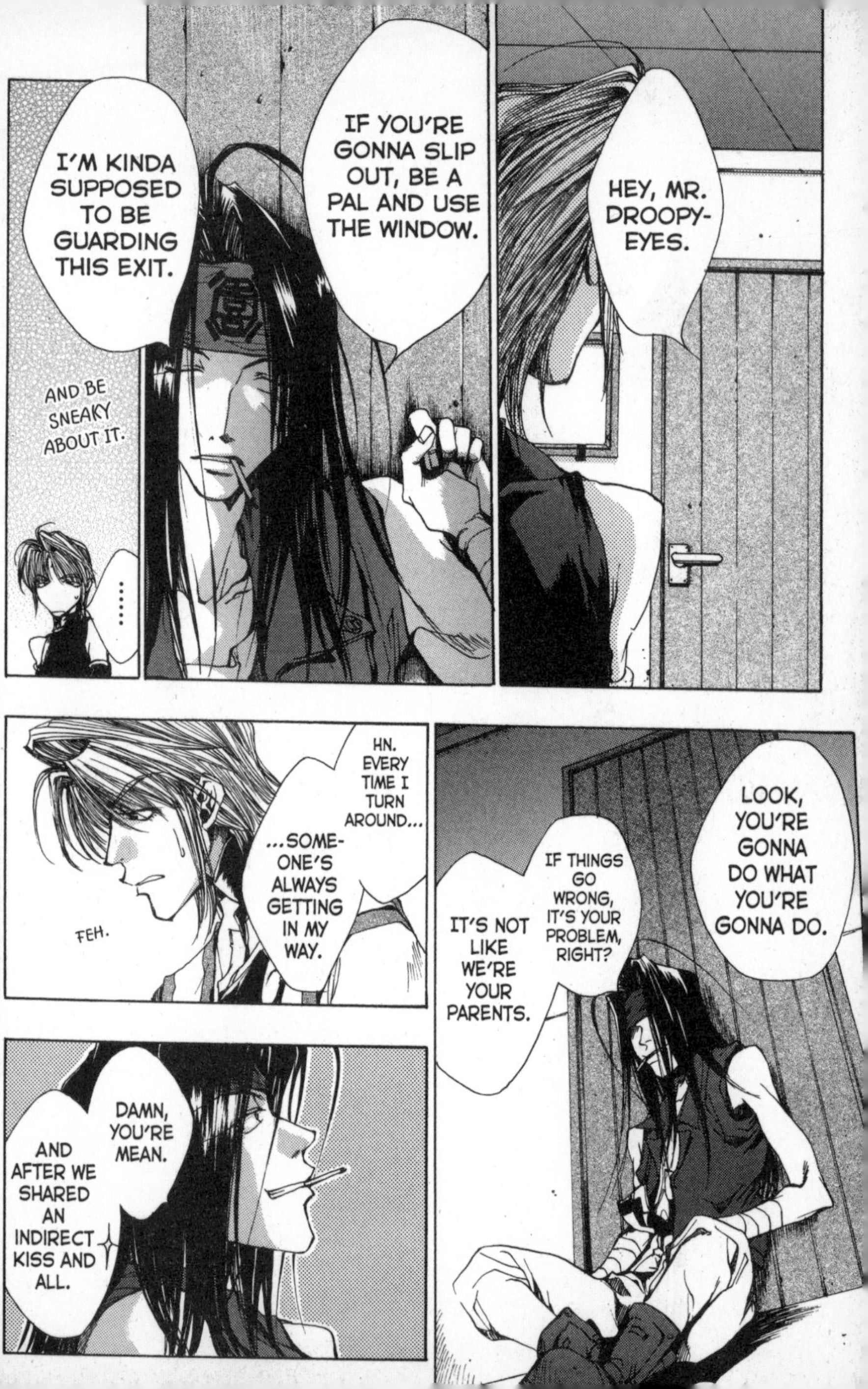
HEY, MR. DROOPY-EYES.
IF YOU'RE GONNA SLIP OUT, BE A PAL AND USE THE WINDOW.
I'M KINDA SUPPOSED TO BE GUARDING THIS EXIT.
AND BE SNEAKY ABOUT IT.
......
LOOK, YOU'RE GONNA DO WHAT YOU'RE GONNA DO.
IF THINGS GO WRONG, IT'S YOUR PROBLEM, RIGHT?
IT'S NOT LIKE WE'RE YOUR PARENTS.
HN. EVERY TIME I TURN AROUND...
...SOME-ONE'S ALWAYS GETTING IN MY WAY.
FEH.
DAMN, YOU'RE MEAN.
AND AFTER WE SHARED AN INDIRECT KISS AND ALL.

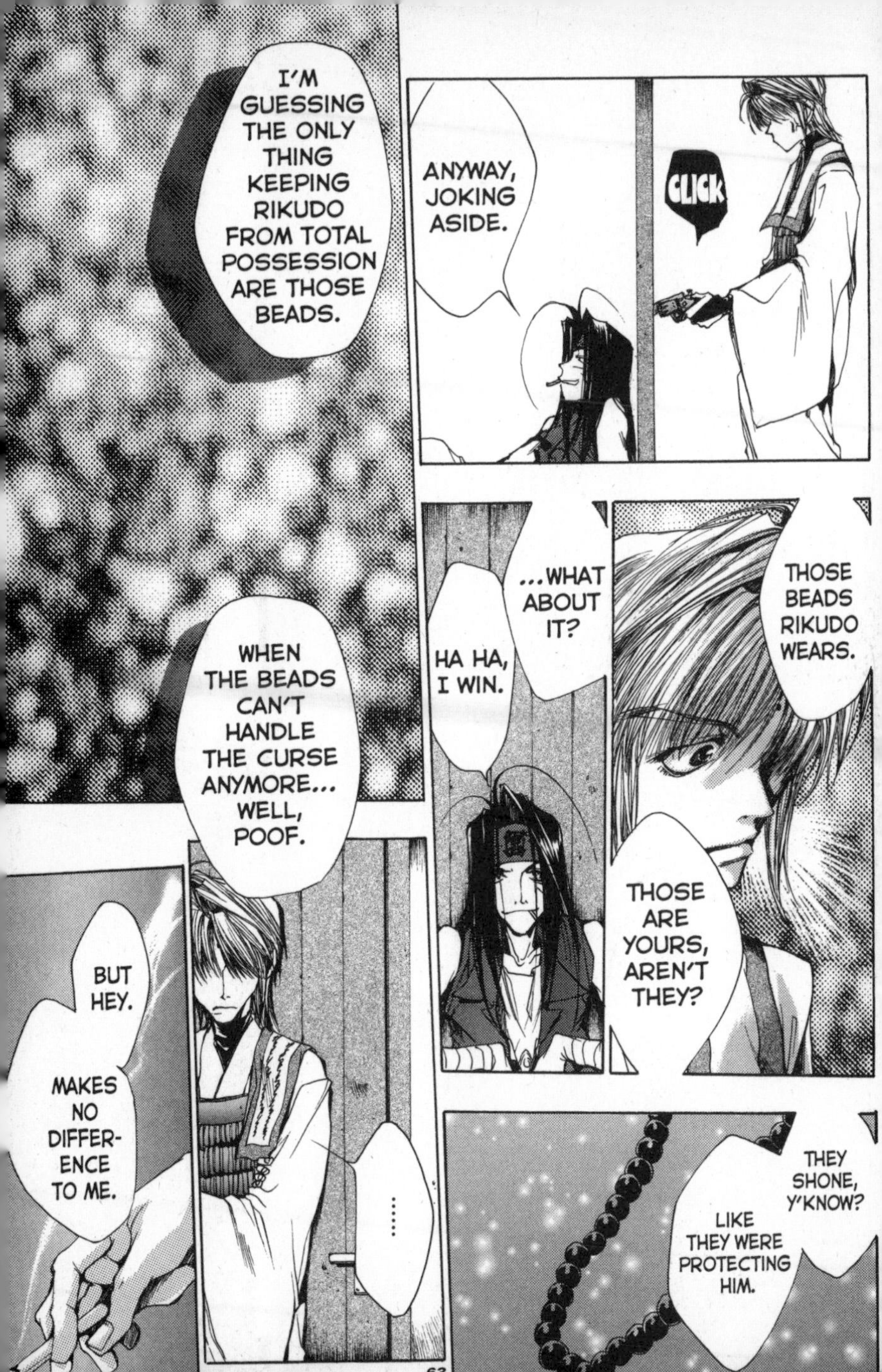
CLICK
ANYWAY, JOKING ASIDE.
THOSE BEADS RIKUDO WEARS.
THOSE ARE YOURS, AREN'T THEY?
...WHAT ABOUT IT?
HA HA, I WIN.
I'M GUESSING THE ONLY THING KEEPING RIKUDO FROM TOTAL POSSESSION ARE THOSE BEADS.
WHEN THE BEADS CAN'T HANDLE THE CURSE ANYMORE... WELL, POOF.
THEY SHONE, Y'KNOW?
LIKE THEY WERE PROTECTING HIM.
......
BUT HEY.
MAKES NO DIFFERENCE TO ME.

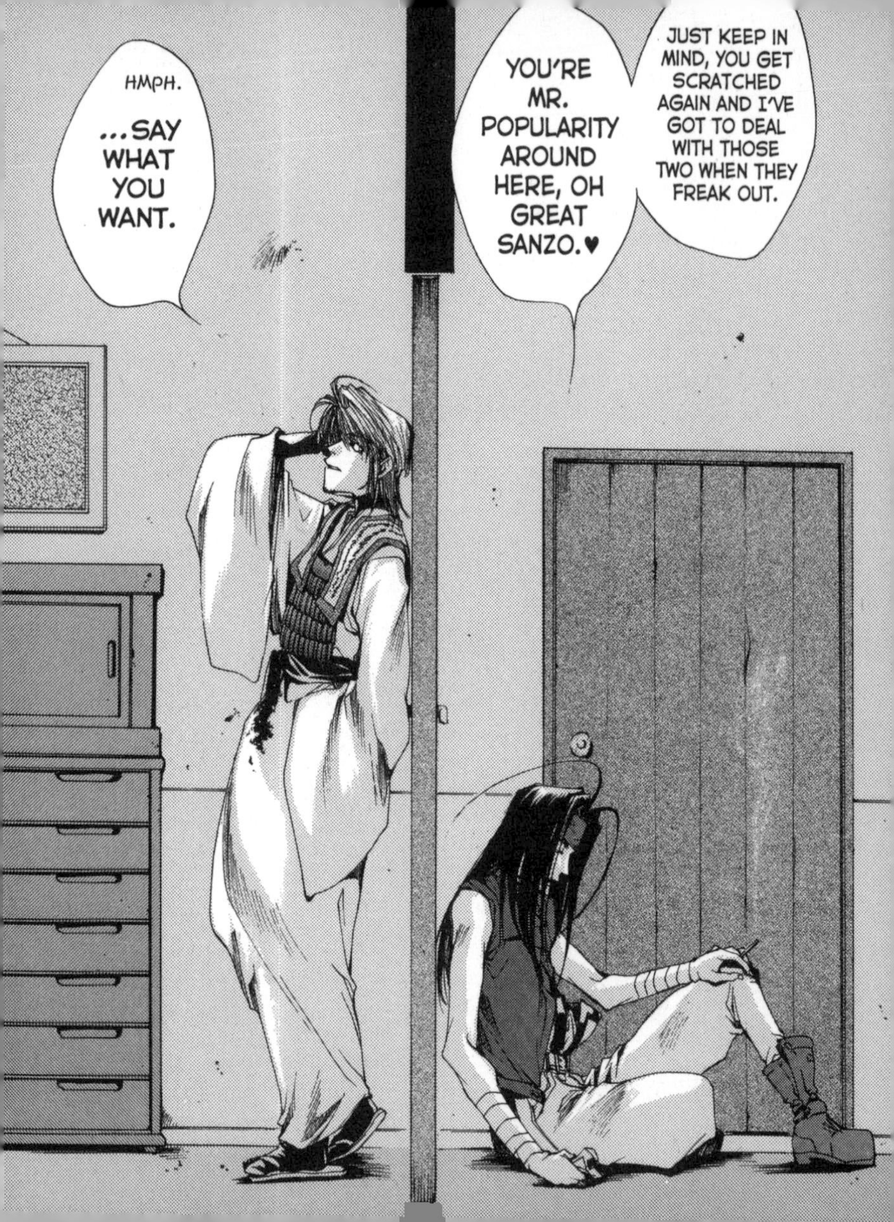
JUST KEEP IN MIND, YOU GET SCRATCHED AGAIN AND I'VE GOT TO DEAL WITH THOSE TWO WHEN THEY FREAK OUT.
YOU'RE MR. POPULARITY AROUND HERE, OH GREAT SANZO.♥
HMPH.
...SAY WHAT YOU WANT.

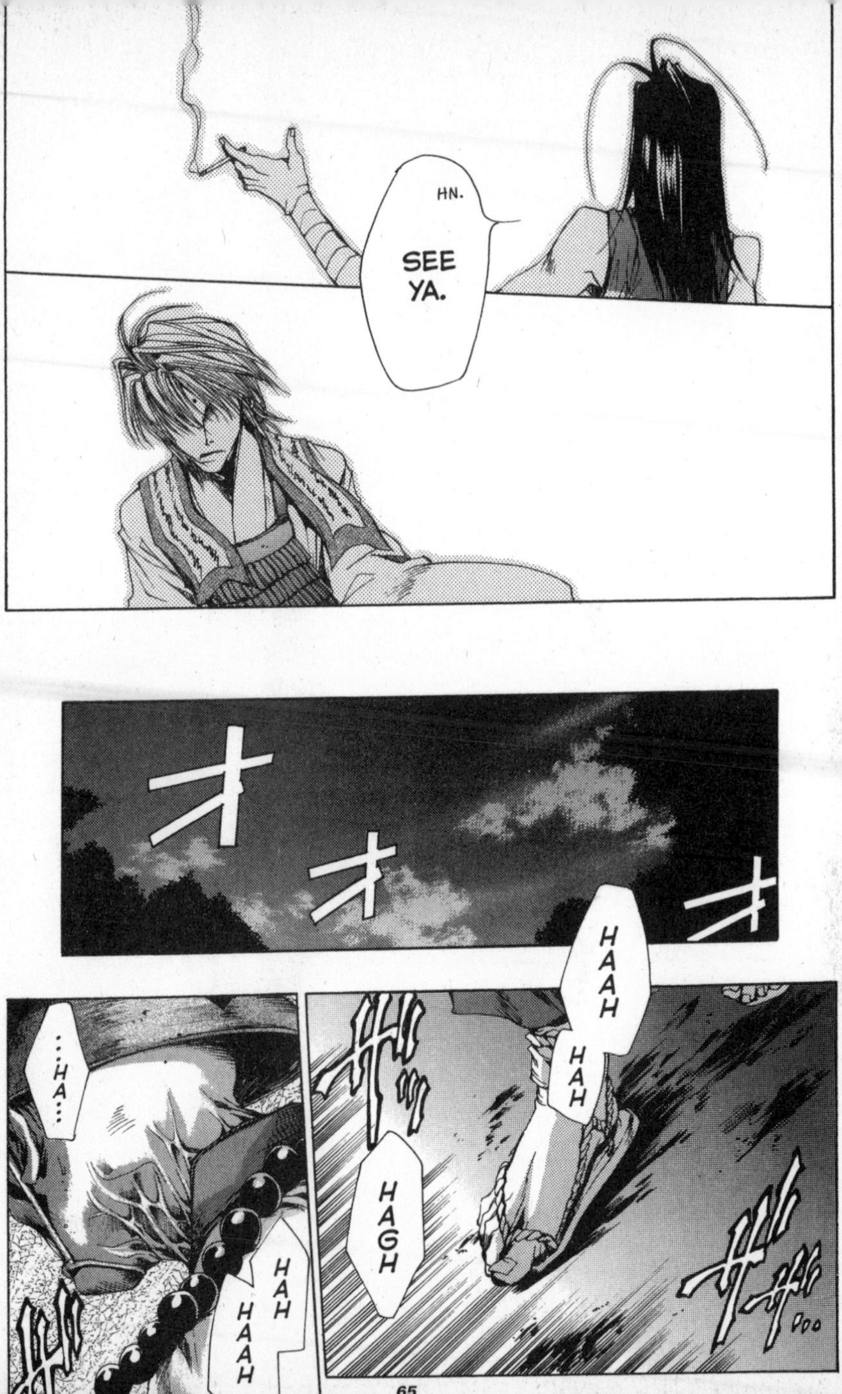
HN.
SEE YA.
HAAAH
HAH
HAGH
...HA...
HAH
HAAAH

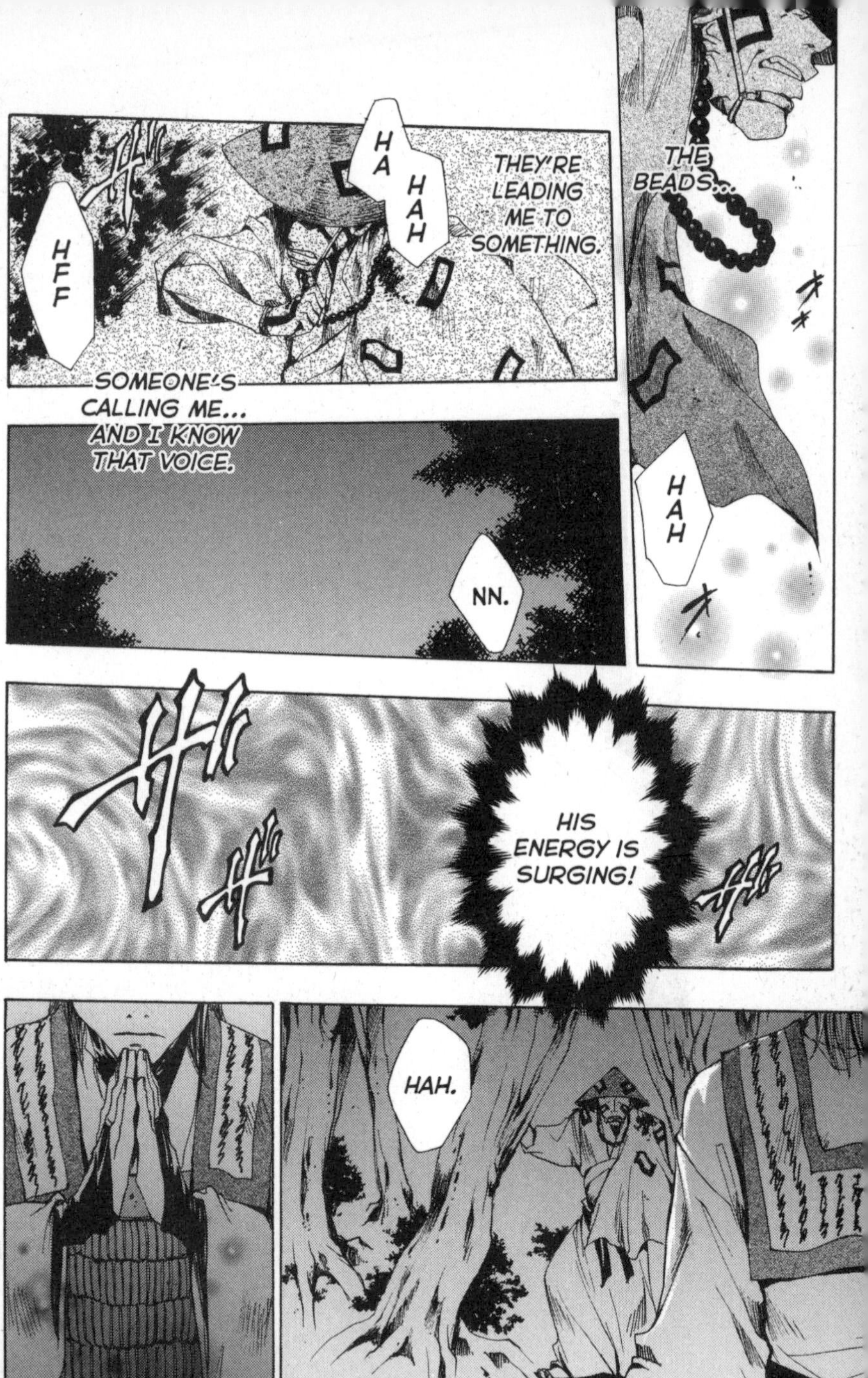
THE BEADS...
HAH HAH
HA HAH
THEY'RE LEADING ME TO SOMETHING.
HFF
SOMEONE'S CALLING ME...
AND I KNOW THAT VOICE.
NN.
HIS ENERGY IS SURGING!
HAH.

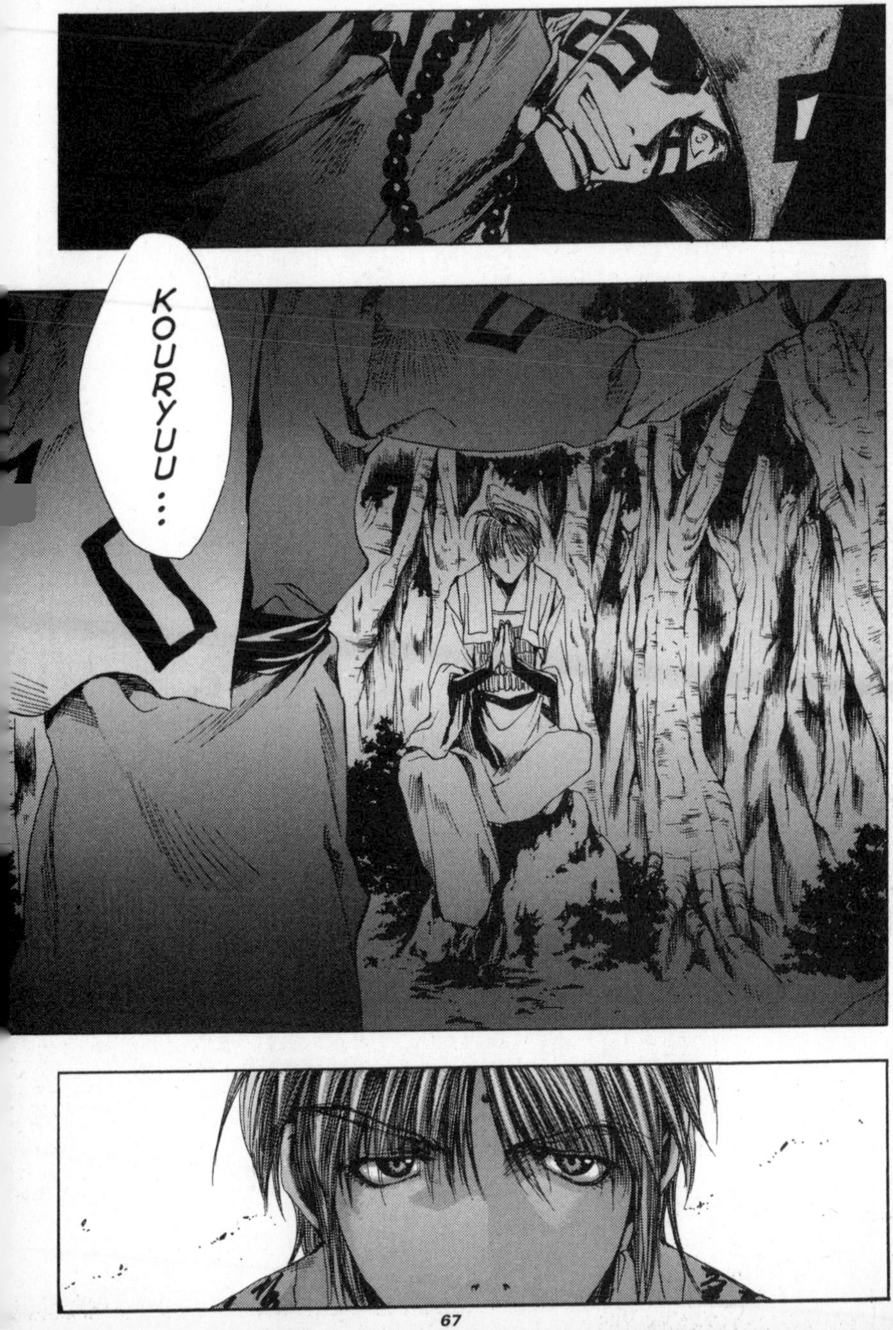
KOURYUU...

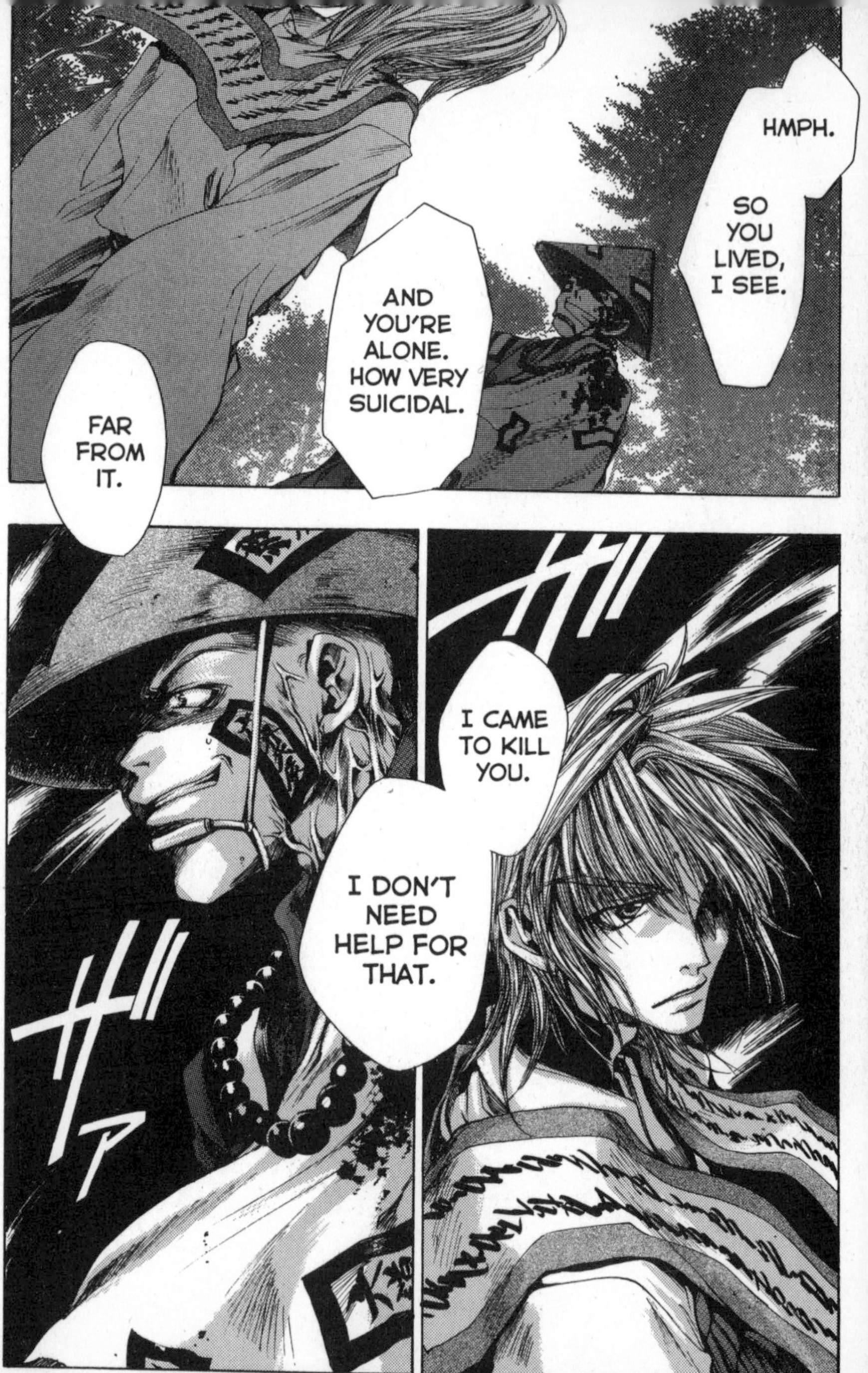
HMPH.
SO YOU LIVED, I SEE.
AND YOU'RE ALONE. HOW VERY SUICIDAL.
FAR FROM IT.
I CAME TO KILL YOU.
I DON'T NEED HELP FOR THAT.

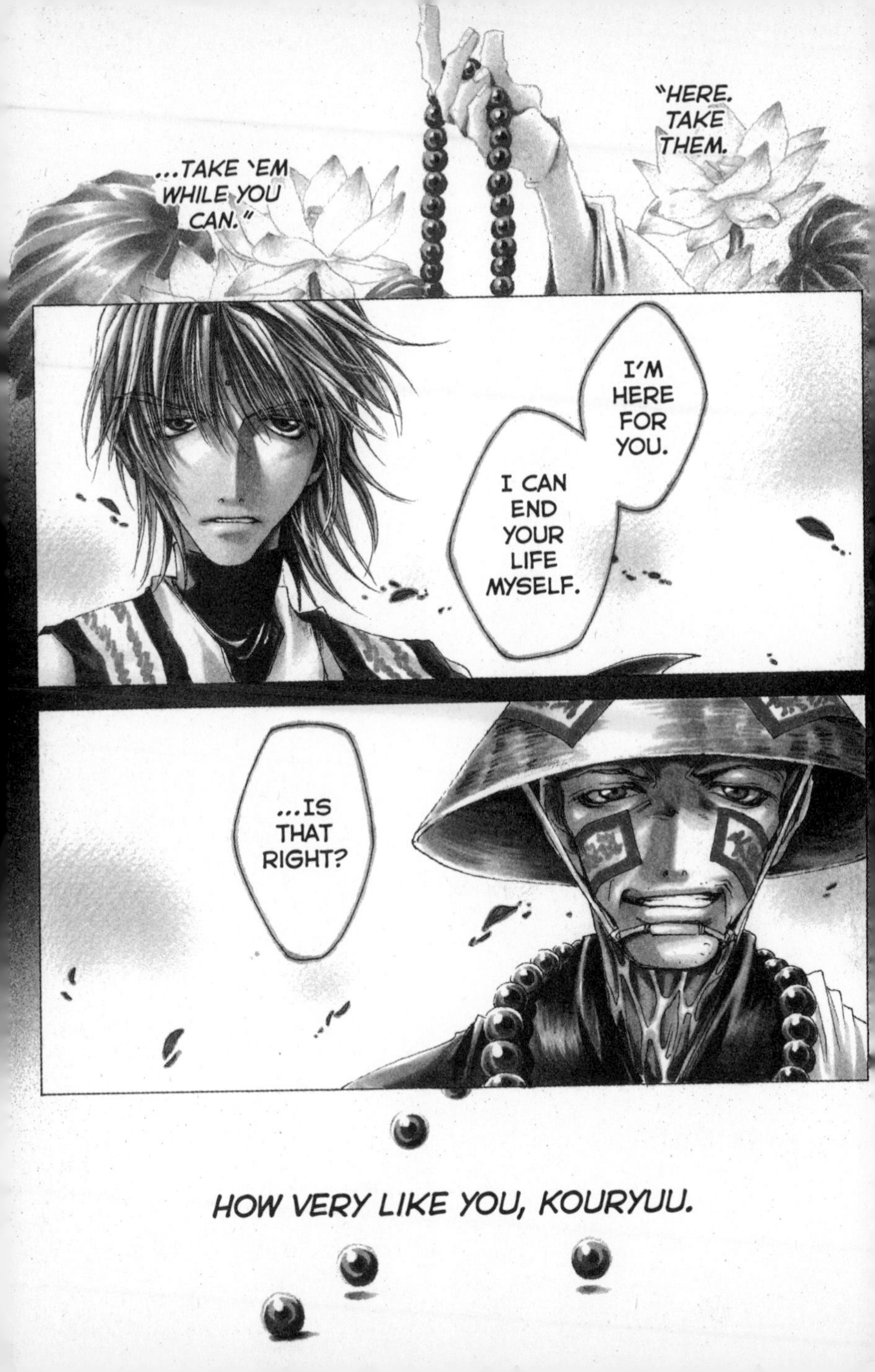
"HERE. TAKE THEM.
...TAKE 'EM WHILE YOU CAN."
I'M HERE FOR YOU.
I CAN END YOUR LIFE MYSELF.
...IS THAT RIGHT?
HOW VERY LIKE YOU, KOURYUU.

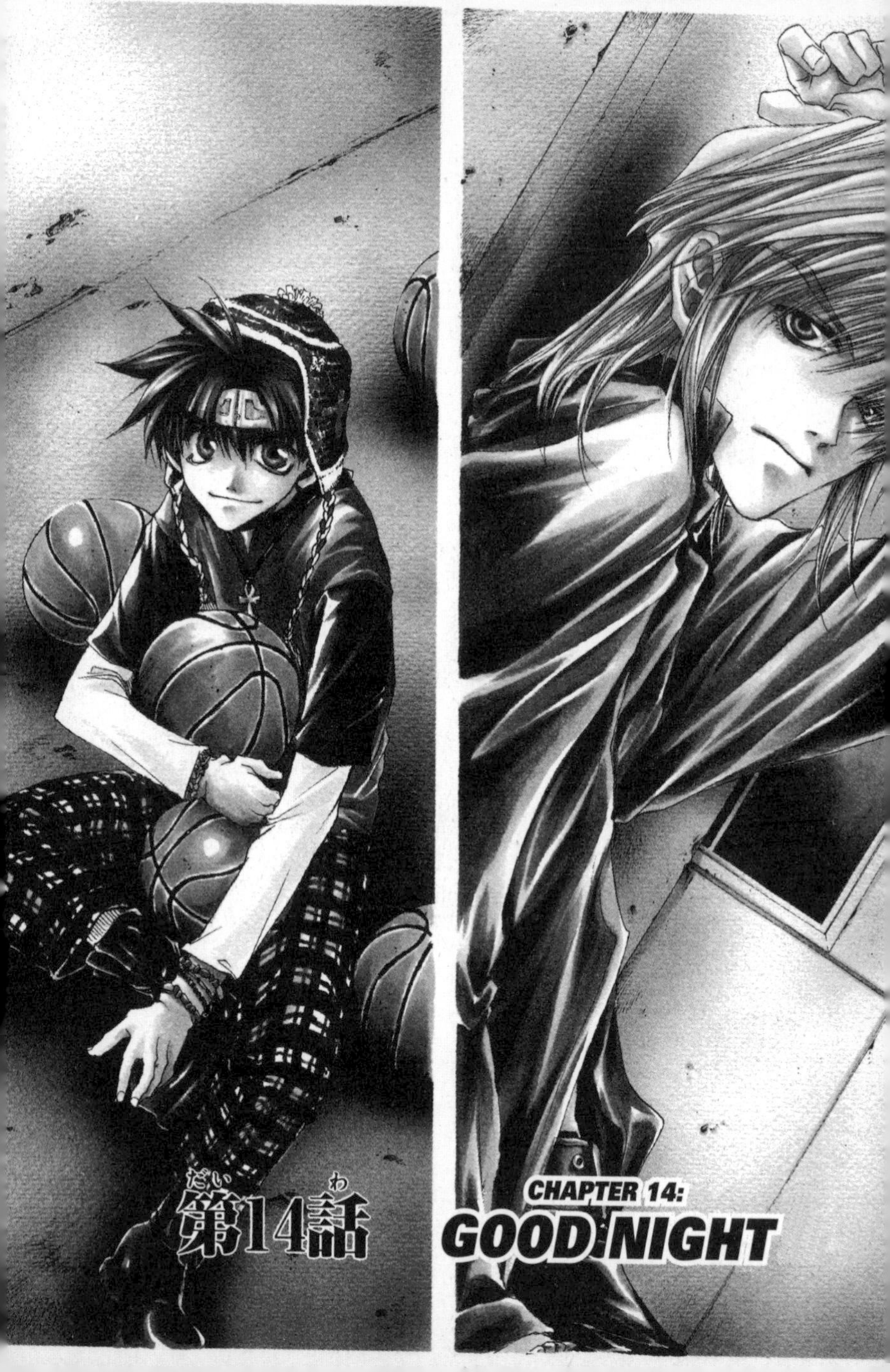
CHAPTER 14:
GOOD NIGHT
第14話

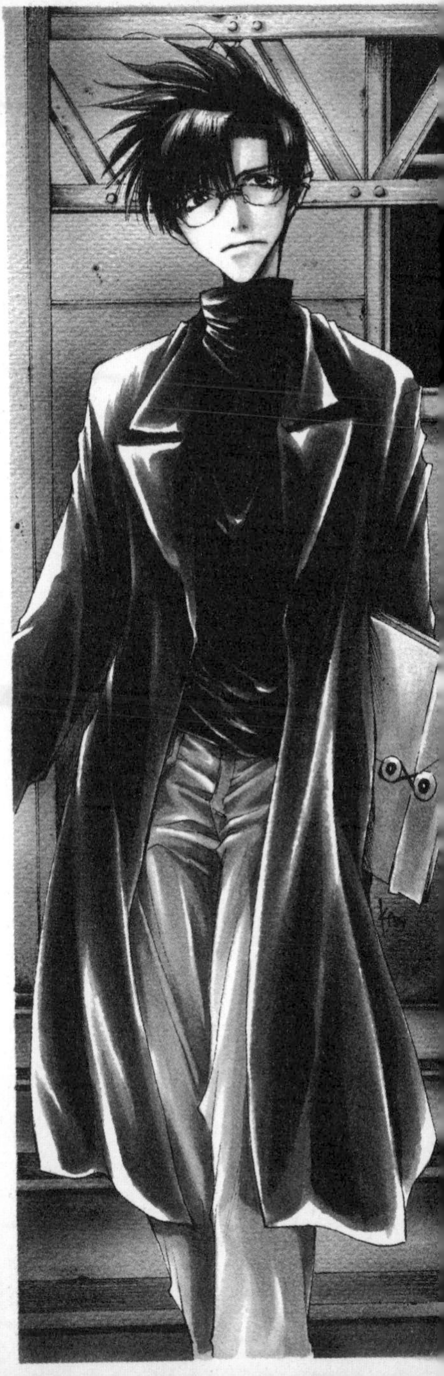
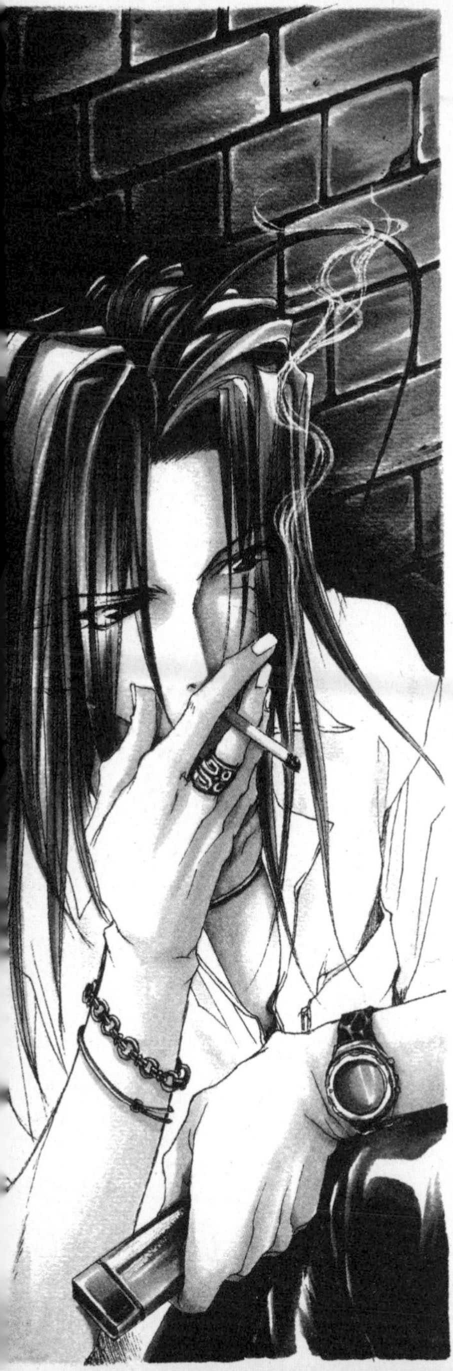

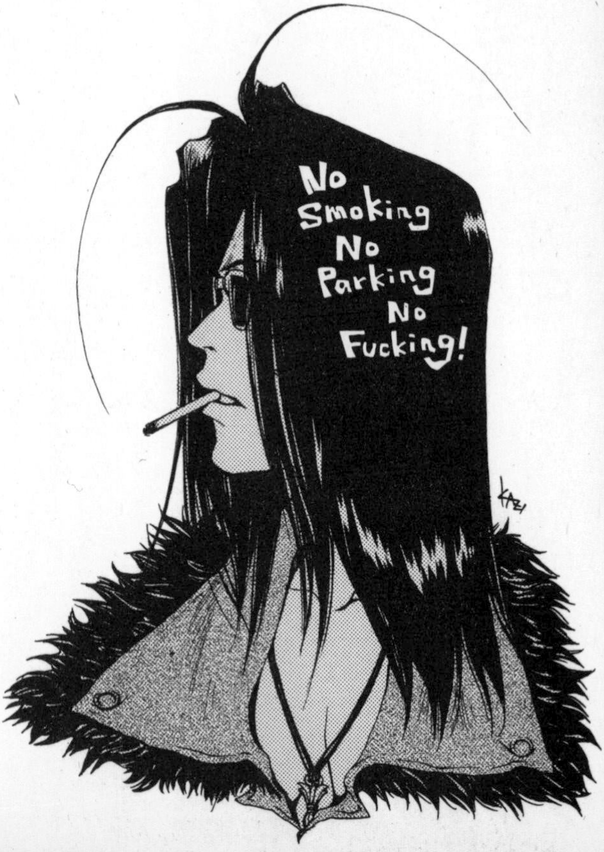
No Smoking No Parking No Fucking!
KAZU

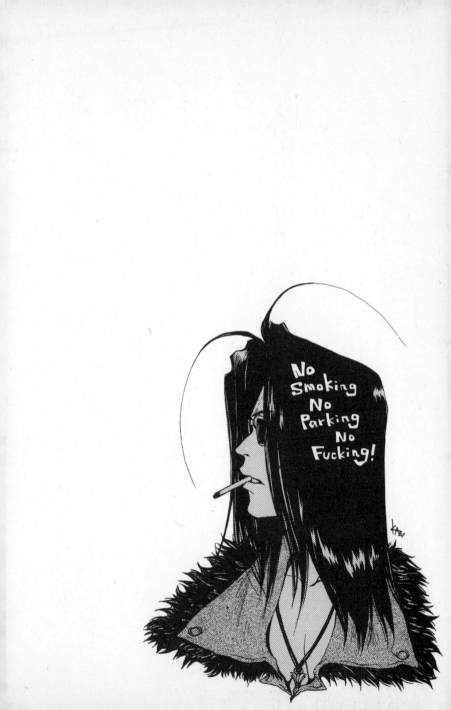

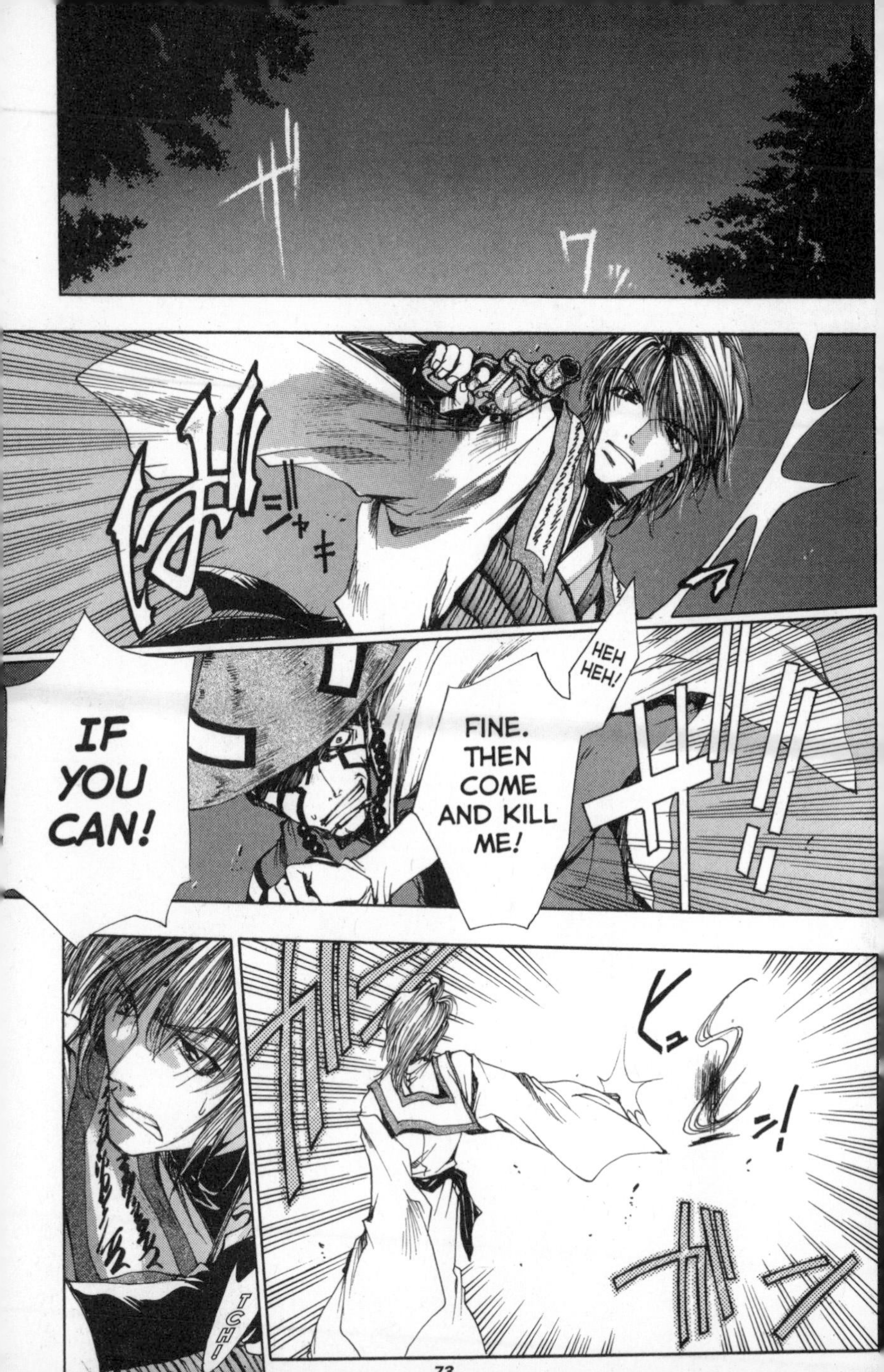
HEH HEH!
FINE. THEN COME AND KILL ME!
IF YOU CAN!
TCHI

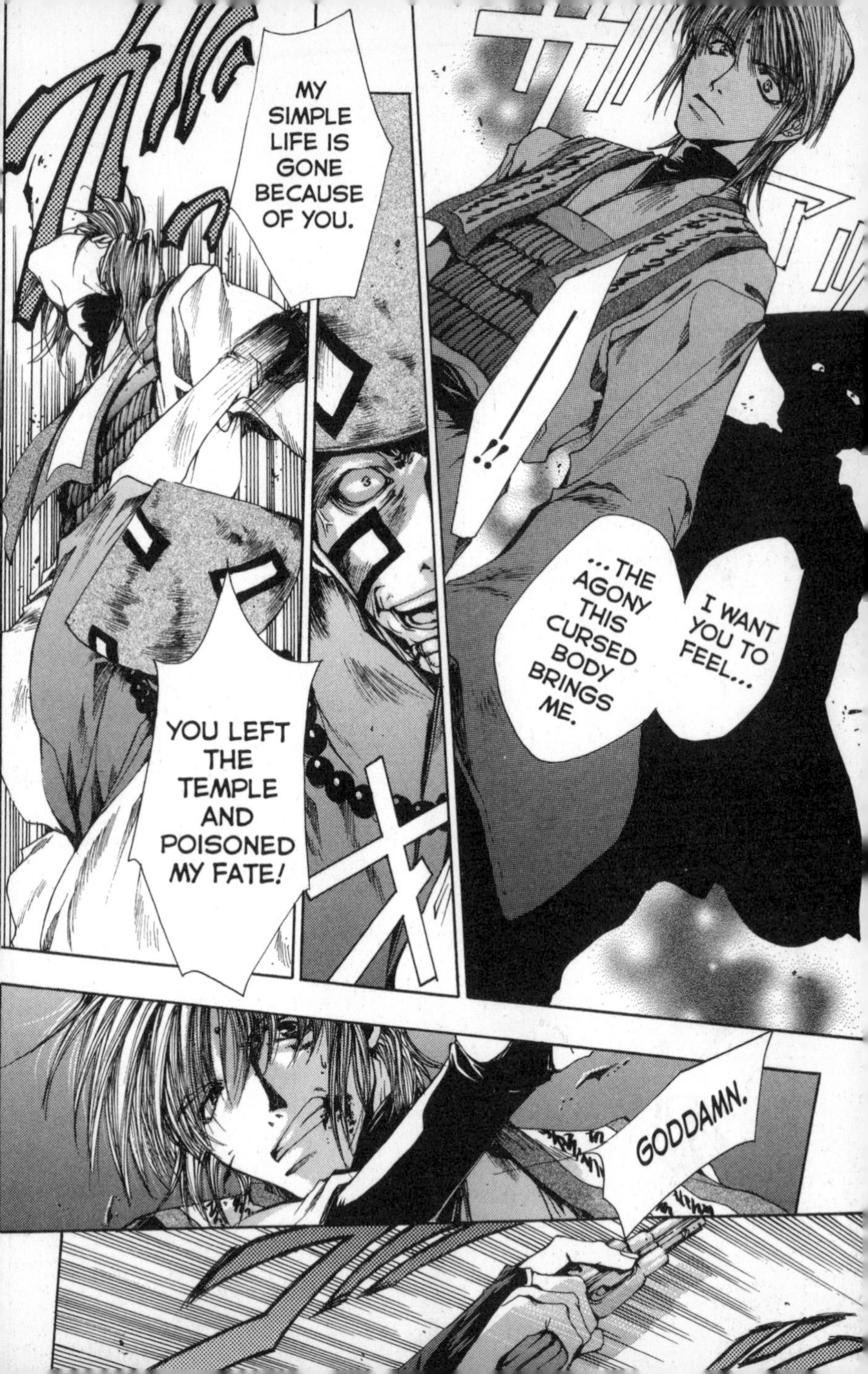
I WANT YOU TO FEEL...
...THE AGONY THIS CURSED BODY BRINGS ME.
!!
MY SIMPLE LIFE IS GONE BECAUSE OF YOU.
YOU LEFT THE TEMPLE AND POISONED MY FATE!
GODDAMN.

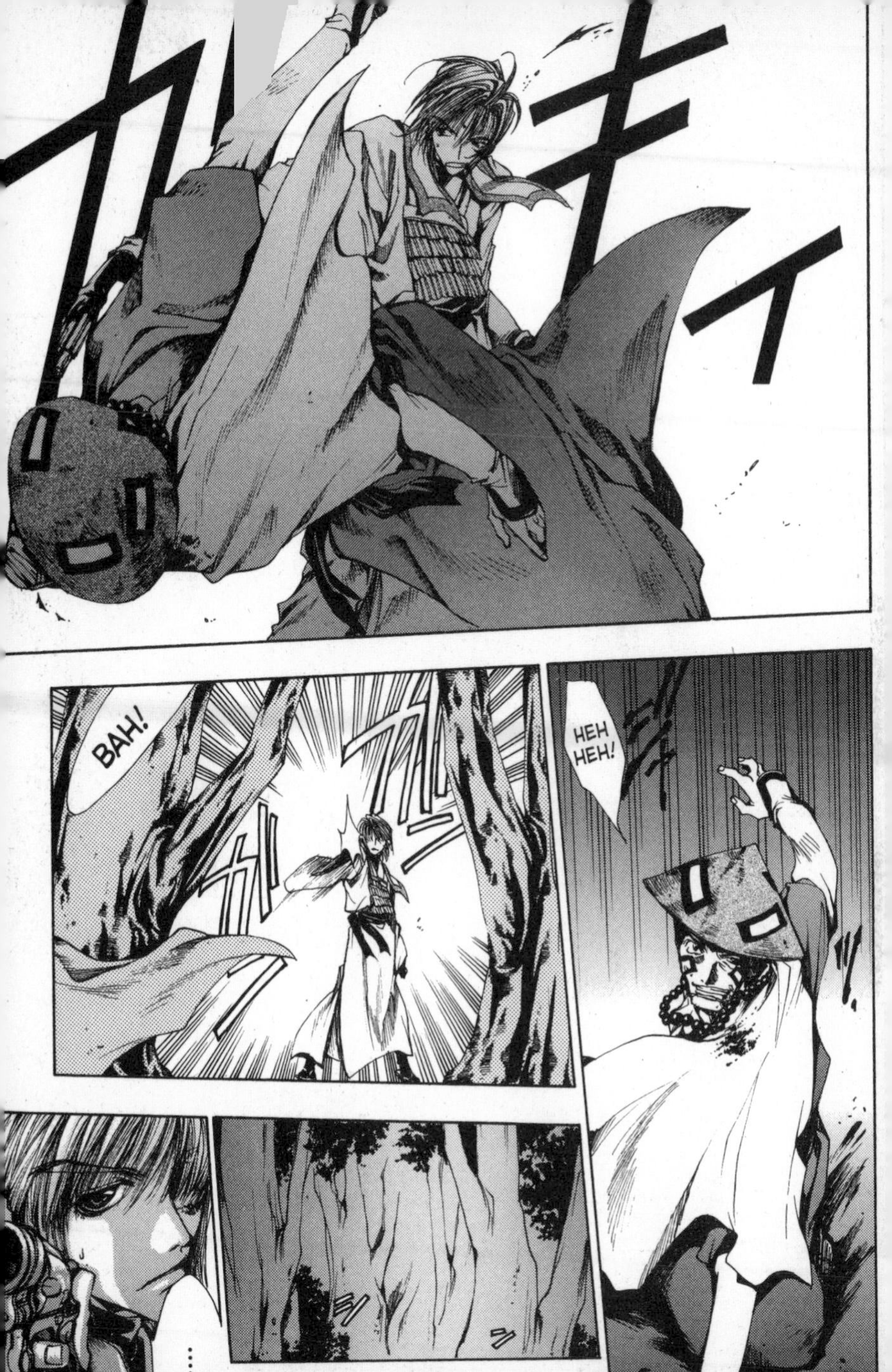
HEH HEH!
BAH!

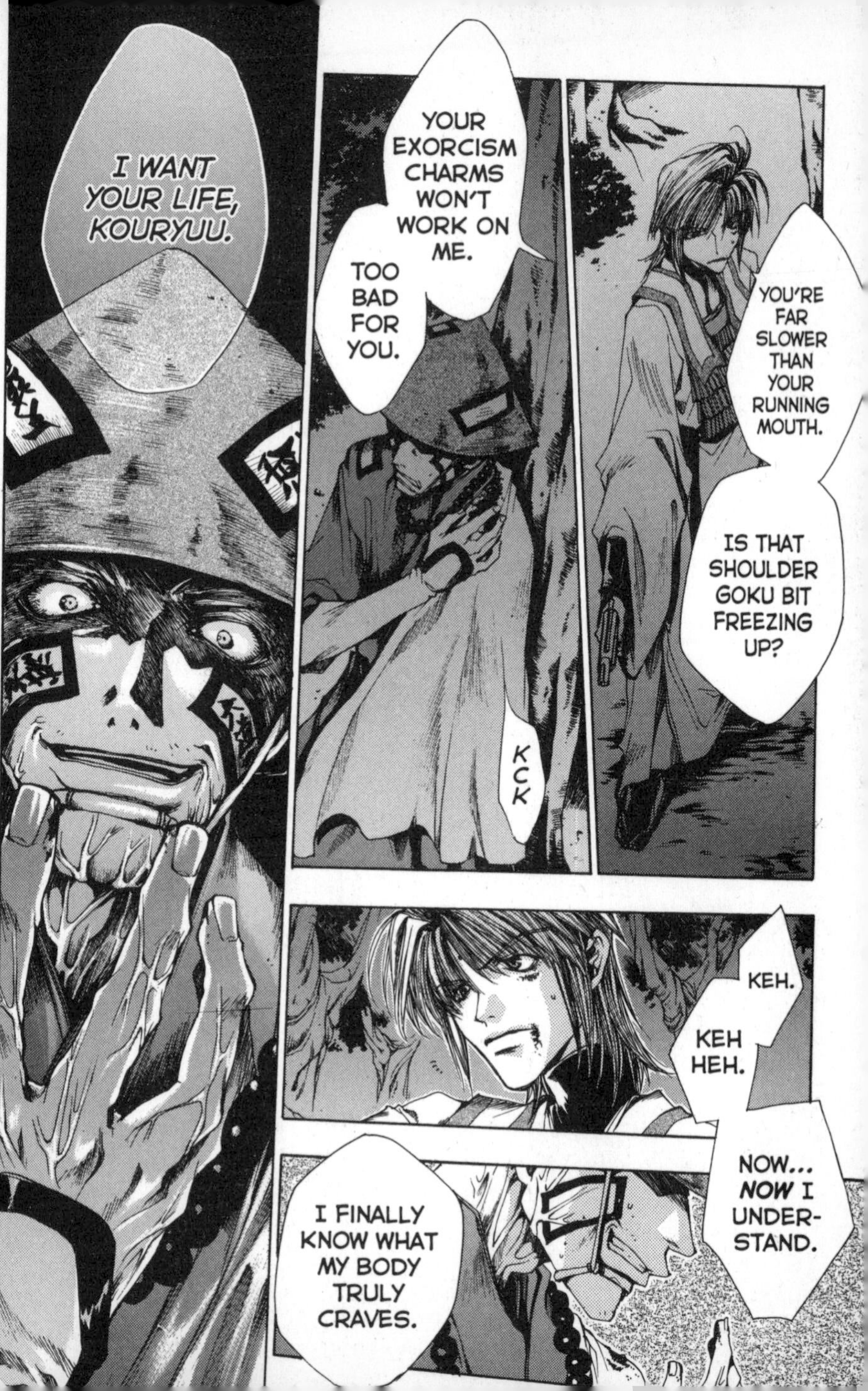
YOU'RE FAR SLOWER THAN YOUR RUNNING MOUTH.
IS THAT SHOULDER GOKU BIT FREEZING UP?
YOUR EXORCISM CHARMS WON'T WORK ON ME.
TOO BAD FOR YOU.
KCK
KEH.
KEH HEH.
NOW... *NOW* I UNDER-STAND.
I FINALLY KNOW WHAT MY BODY TRULY CRAVES.
I WANT YOUR LIFE, KOURYUU.

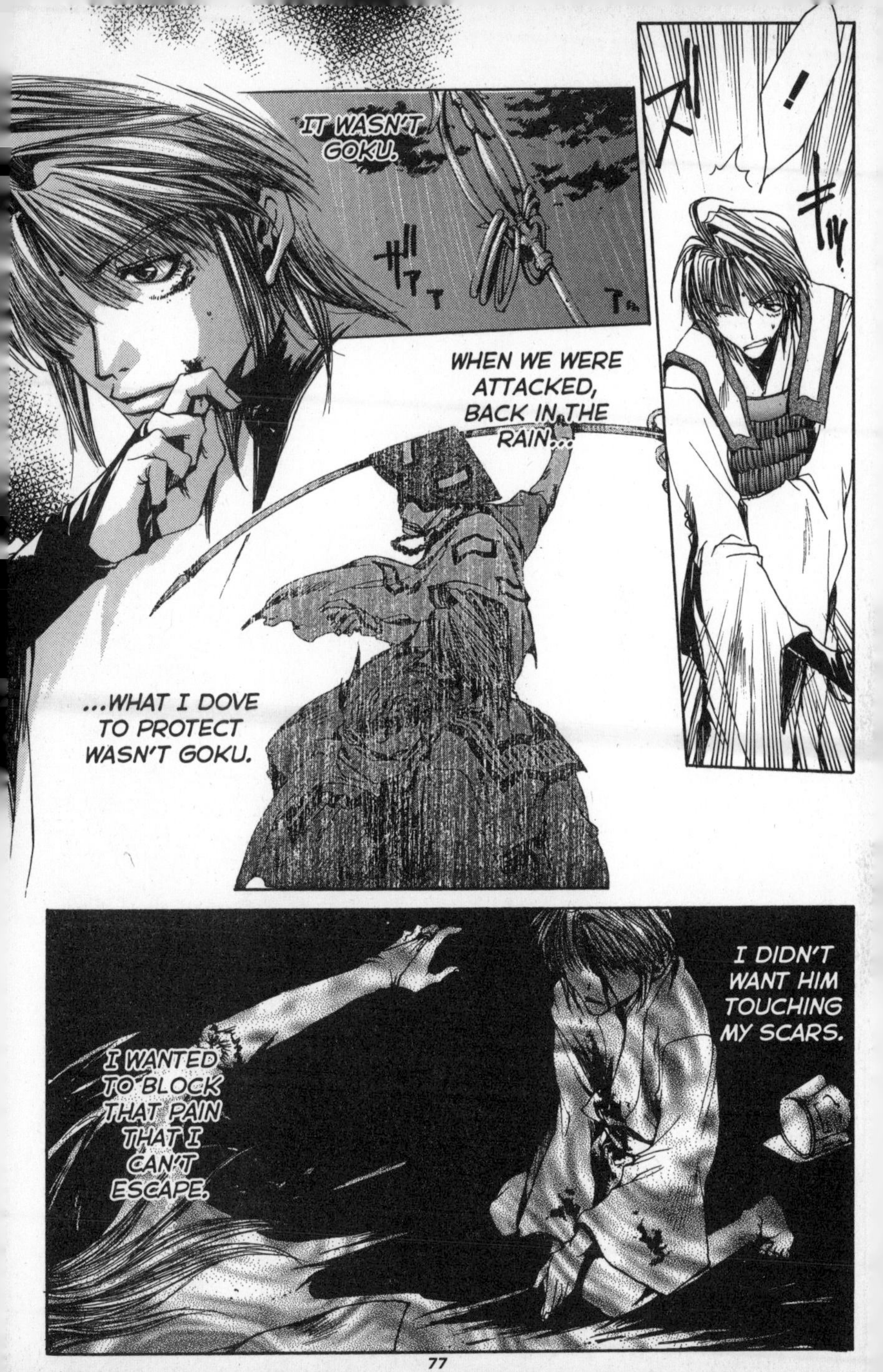
IT WASN'T GOKU.
WHEN WE WERE ATTACKED, BACK IN THE RAIN...
...WHAT I DOVE TO PROTECT WASN'T GOKU.
I DIDN'T WANT HIM TOUCHING MY SCARS.
I WANTED TO BLOCK THAT PAIN THAT I CAN'T ESCAPE.

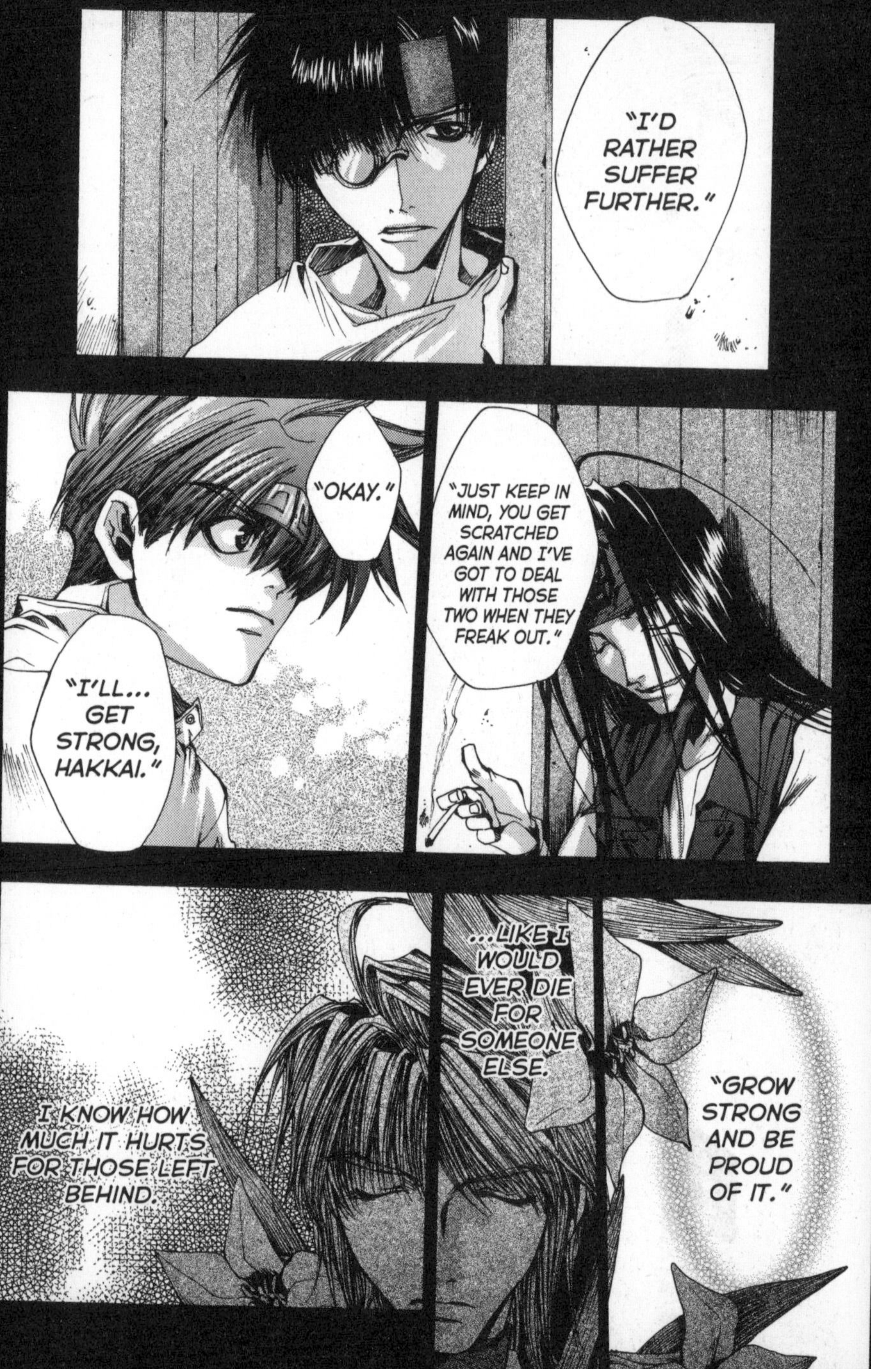
"I'D RATHER SUFFER FURTHER."
"JUST KEEP IN MIND, YOU GET SCRATCHED AGAIN AND I'VE GOT TO DEAL WITH THOSE TWO WHEN THEY FREAK OUT."
"OKAY."
"I'LL... GET STRONG, HAKKAI."
"GROW STRONG AND BE PROUD OF IT."
...LIKE I WOULD EVER DIE FOR SOMEONE ELSE.
I KNOW HOW MUCH IT HURTS FOR THOSE LEFT BEHIND.

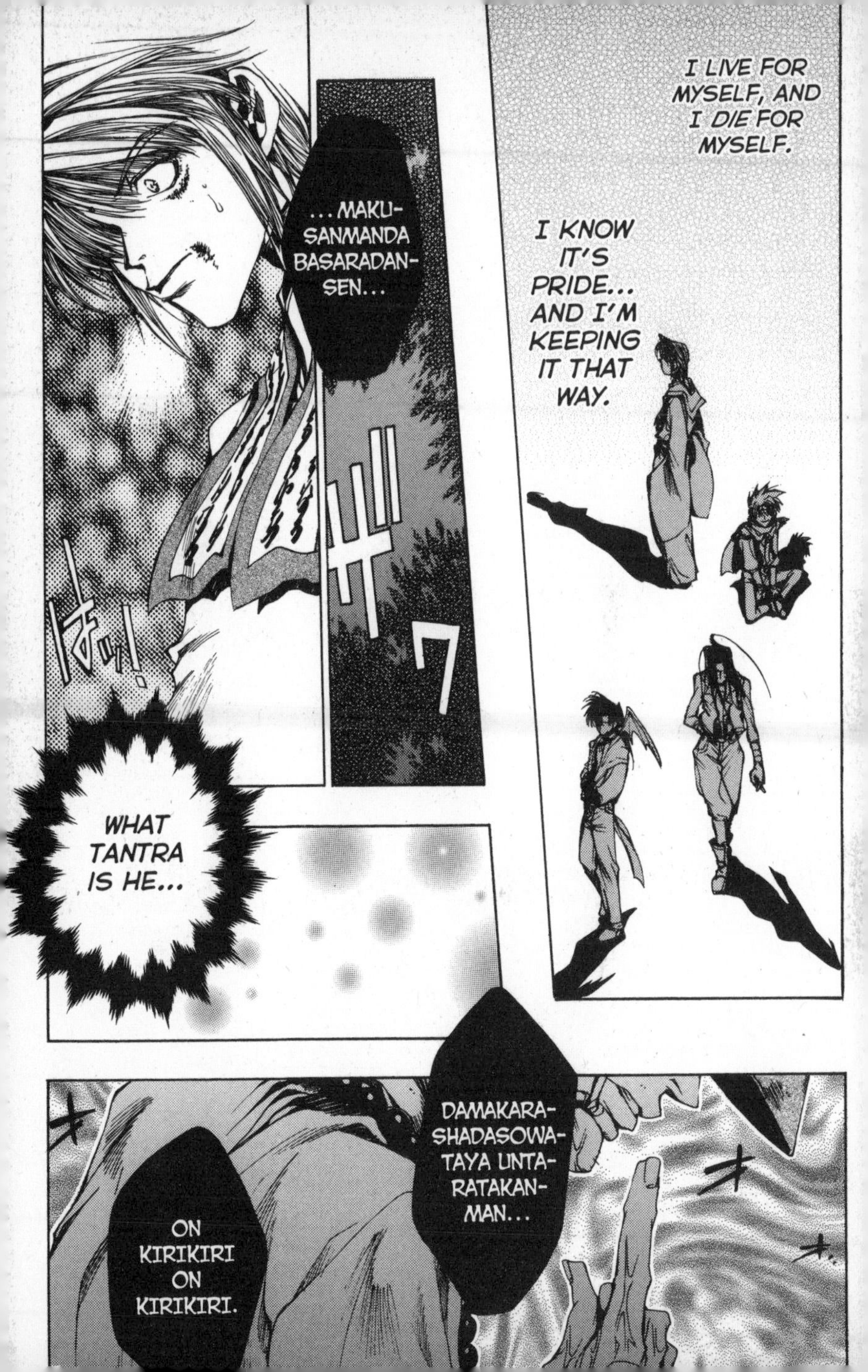
I LIVE FOR MYSELF, AND I DIE FOR MYSELF.
I KNOW IT'S PRIDE... AND I'M KEEPING IT THAT WAY.
...MAKU-SANMANDA BASARADAN-SEN...
はっ!
WHAT TANTRA IS HE...
DAMAKARA-SHADASOWA-TAYA UNTA-RATAKAN-MAN...
ON KIRIKIRI ON KIRIKIRI.

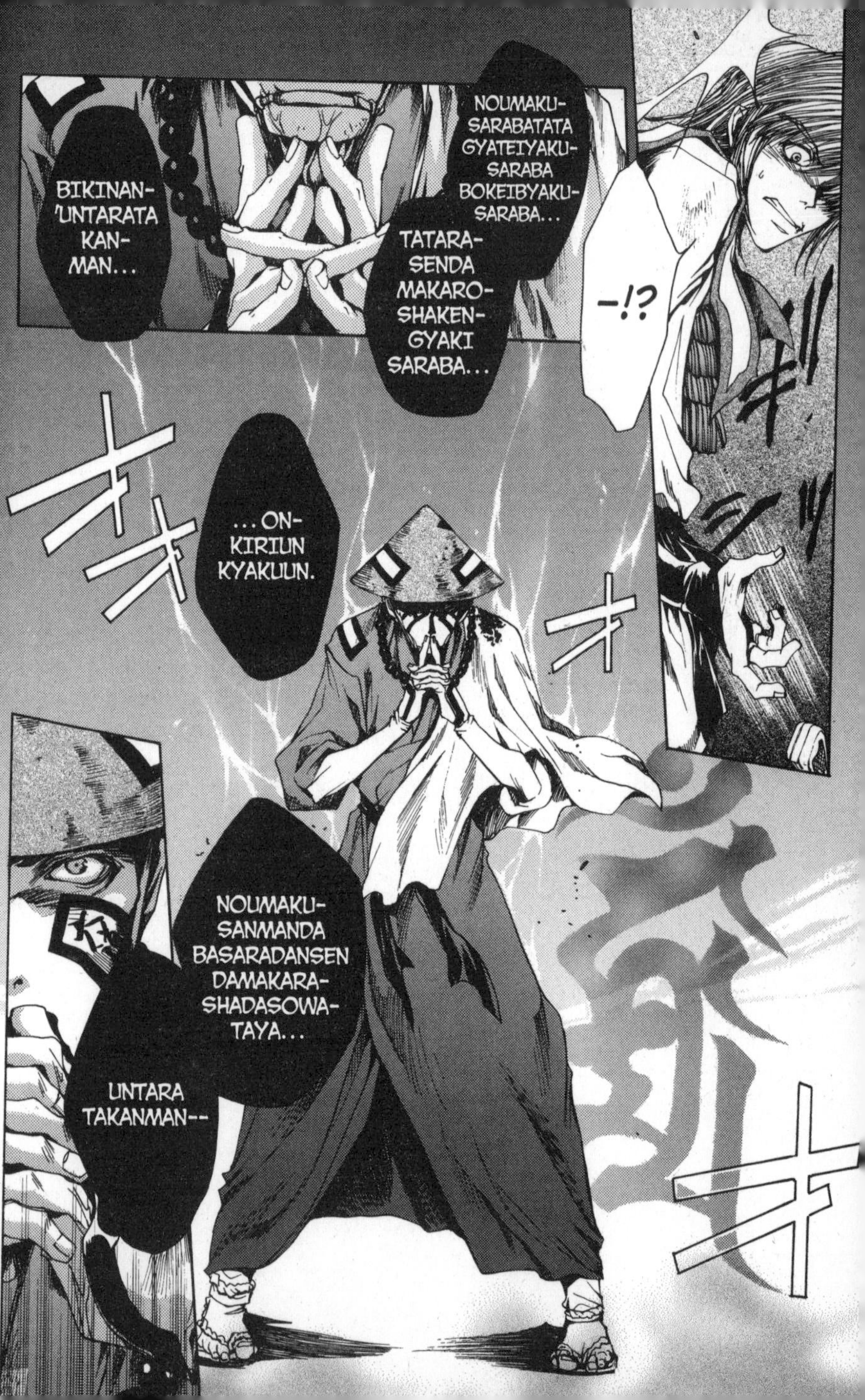
-!?
NOUMAKU-SARABATATA GYATEIYAKU-SARABA BOKEIBYAKU-SARABA...
TATARA-SENDA MAKARO-SHAKEN-GYAKI SARABA...
BIKINAN-'UNTARATA KAN-MAN...
...ON-KIRIUN KYAKUUN.
NOUMAKU-SANMANDA BASARADANSEN DAMAKARA-SHADASOWA-TAYA...
UNTARA TAKANMAN--

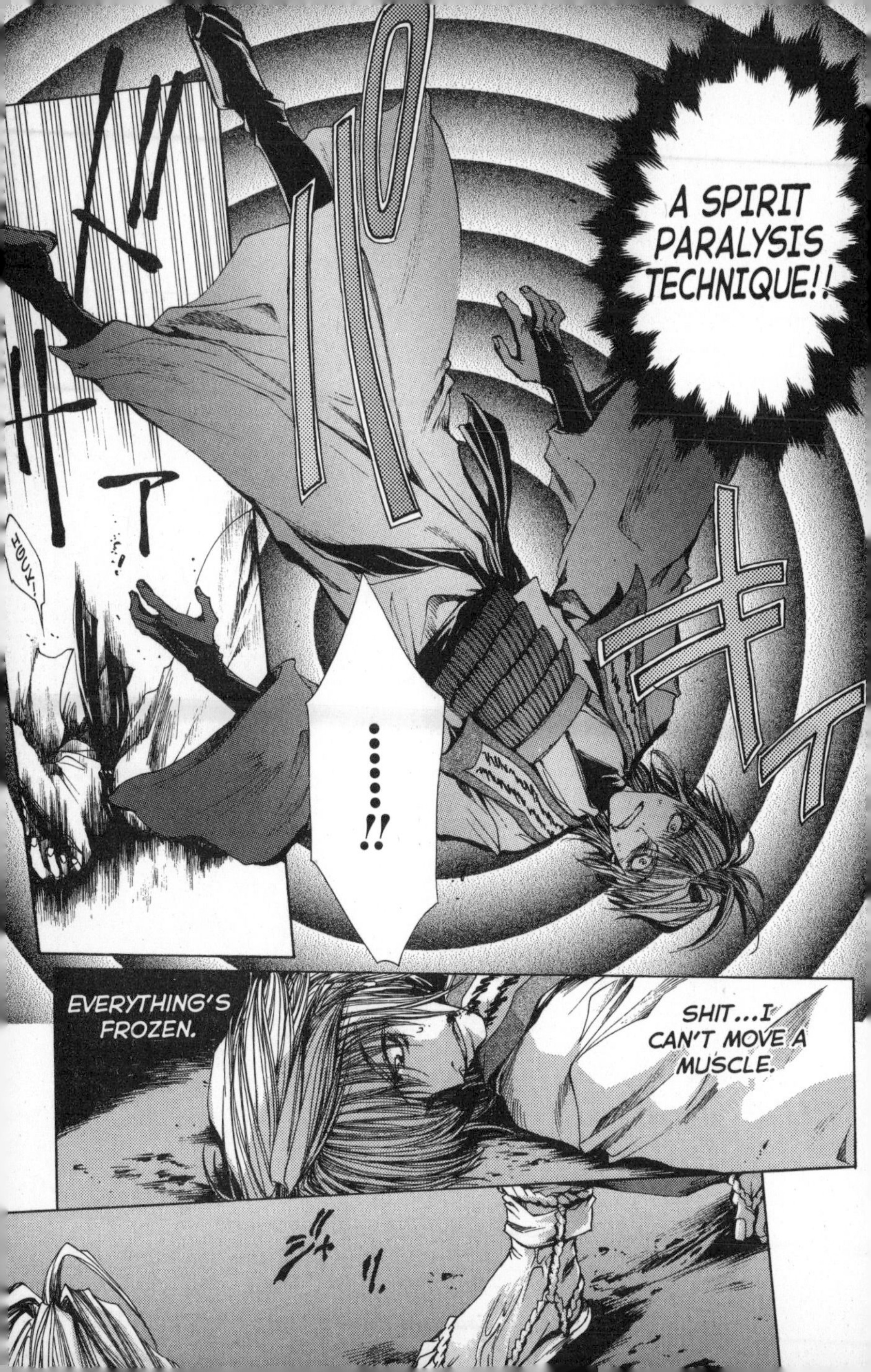
A SPIRIT PARALYSIS TECHNIQUE!!
......!!
HOUK!
SHIT...I CAN'T MOVE A MUSCLE.
EVERYTHING'S FROZEN.

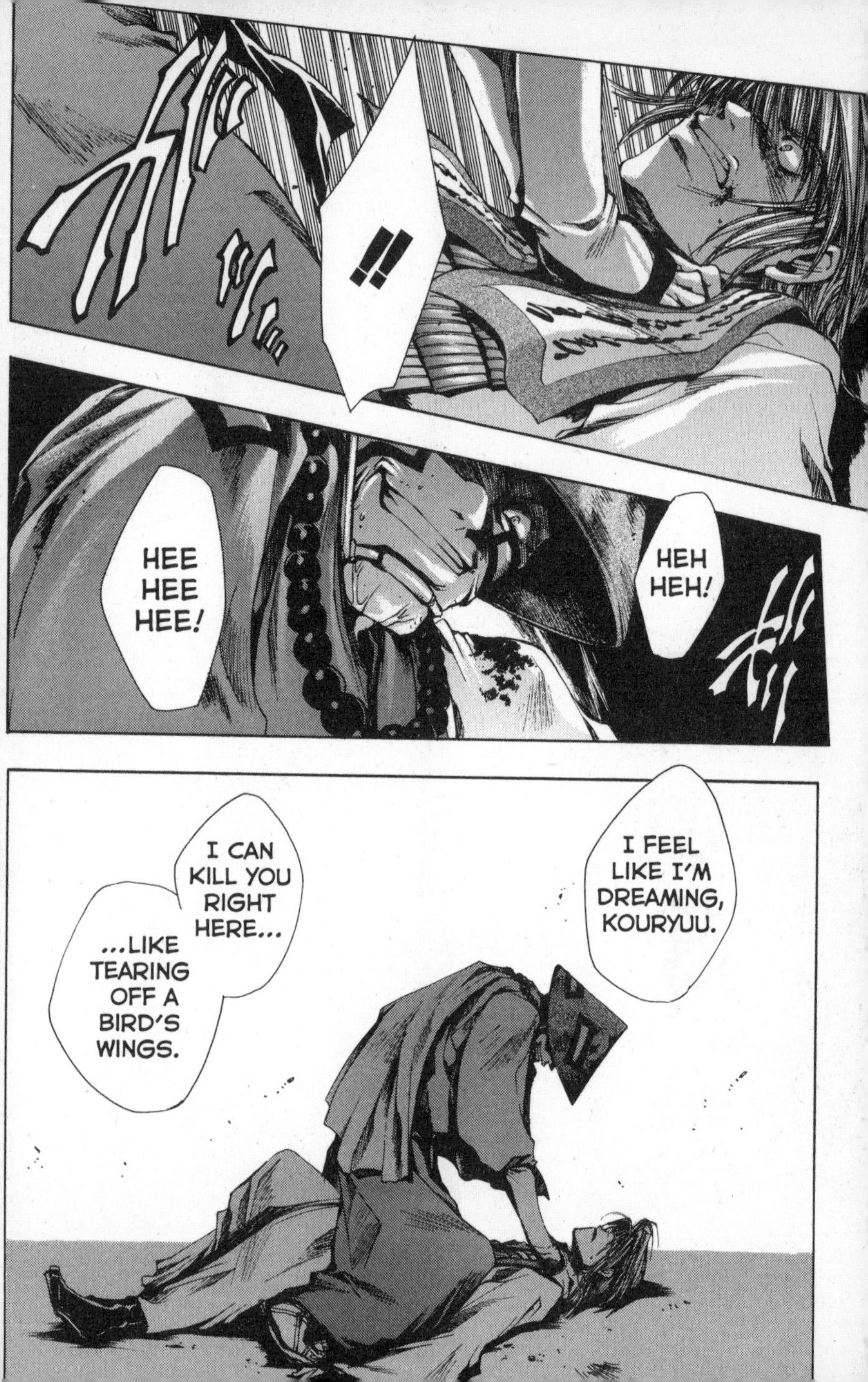
!!
HEH HEH!
HEE HEE HEE!
I FEEL LIKE I'M DREAMING, KOURYUU.
I CAN KILL YOU RIGHT HERE...
...LIKE TEARING OFF A BIRD'S WINGS.

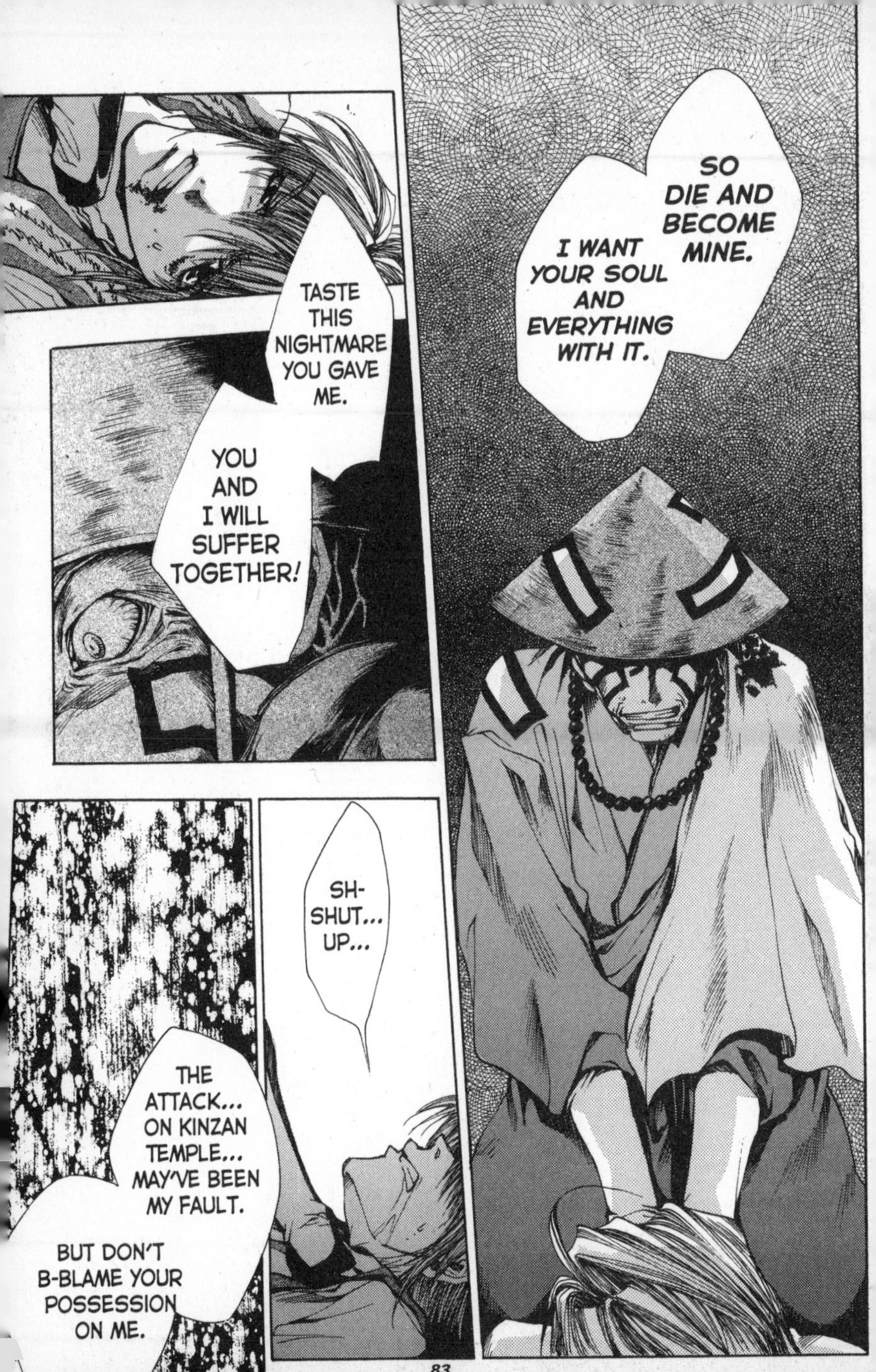
SO DIE AND BECOME MINE.
I WANT YOUR SOUL AND EVERYTHING WITH IT.
TASTE THIS NIGHTMARE YOU GAVE ME.
YOU AND I WILL SUFFER TOGETHER!
SH-SHUT... UP...
THE ATTACK... ON KINZAN TEMPLE... MAY'VE BEEN MY FAULT.
BUT DON'T B-BLAME YOUR POSSESSION ON ME.

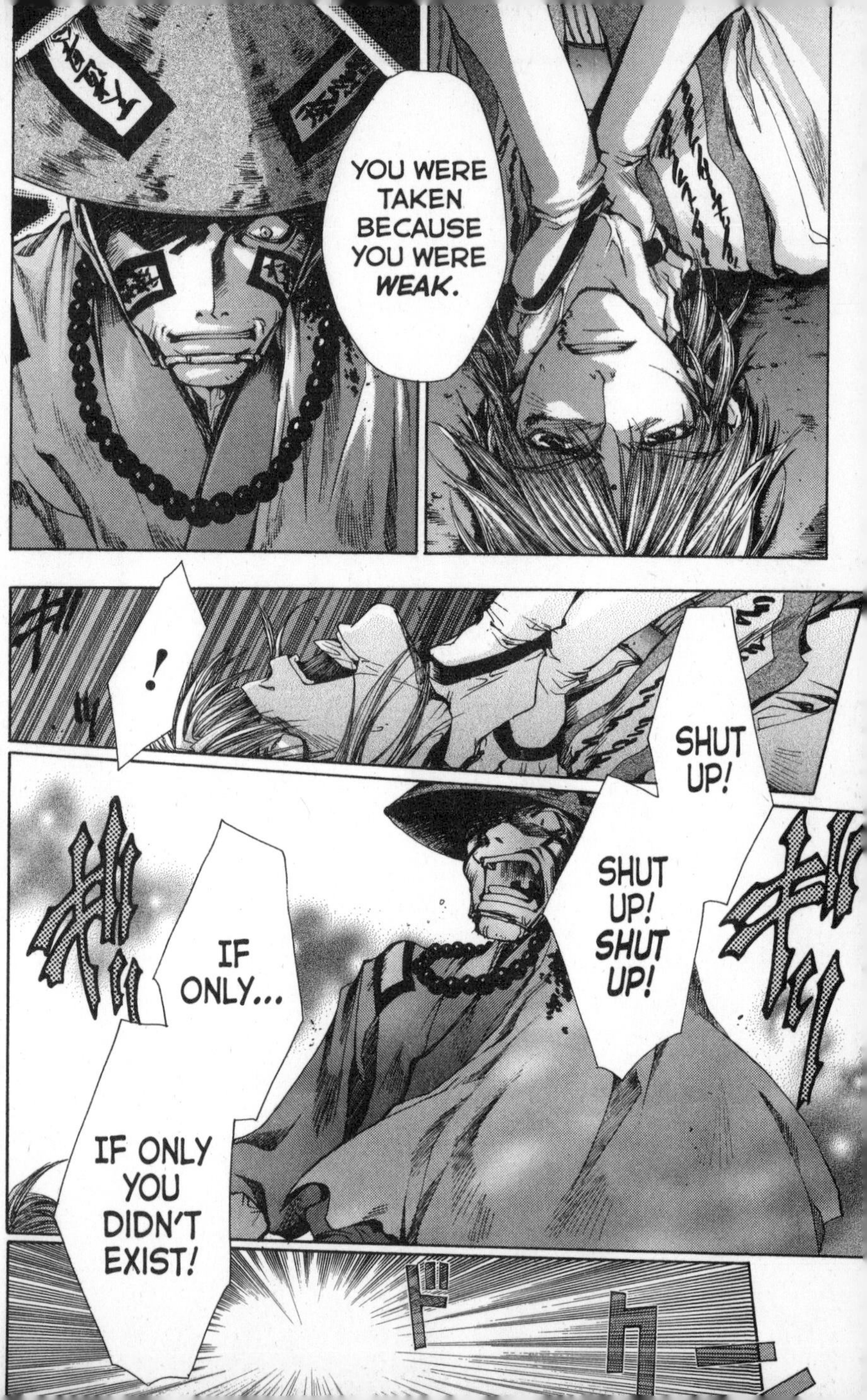
YOU WERE TAKEN BECAUSE YOU WERE *WEAK.*
!
SHUT UP!
SHUT UP! SHUT UP!
IF ONLY...
IF ONLY YOU DIDN'T EXIST!

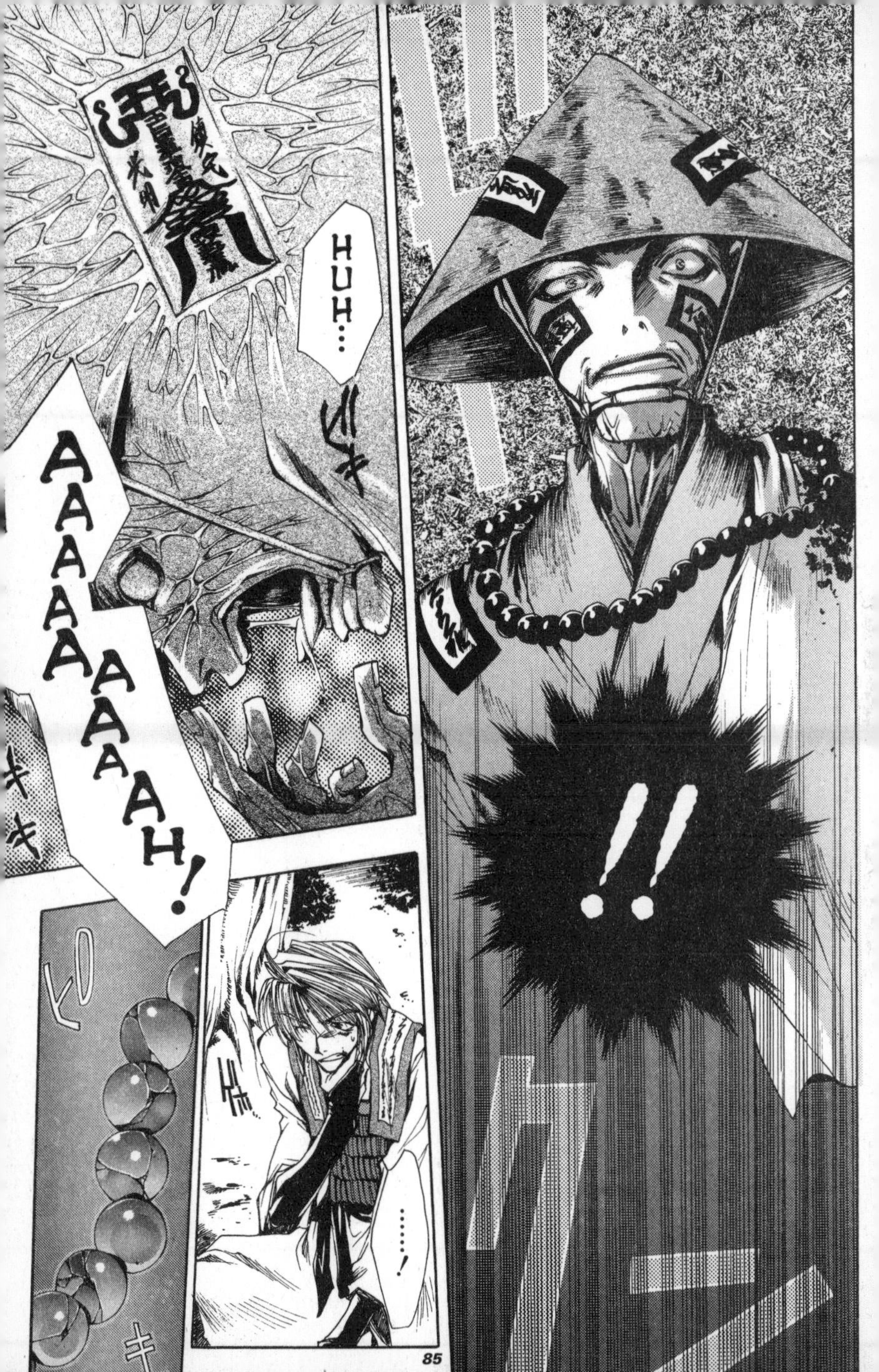
HUH...
AAAAAAAAAAH!
......!

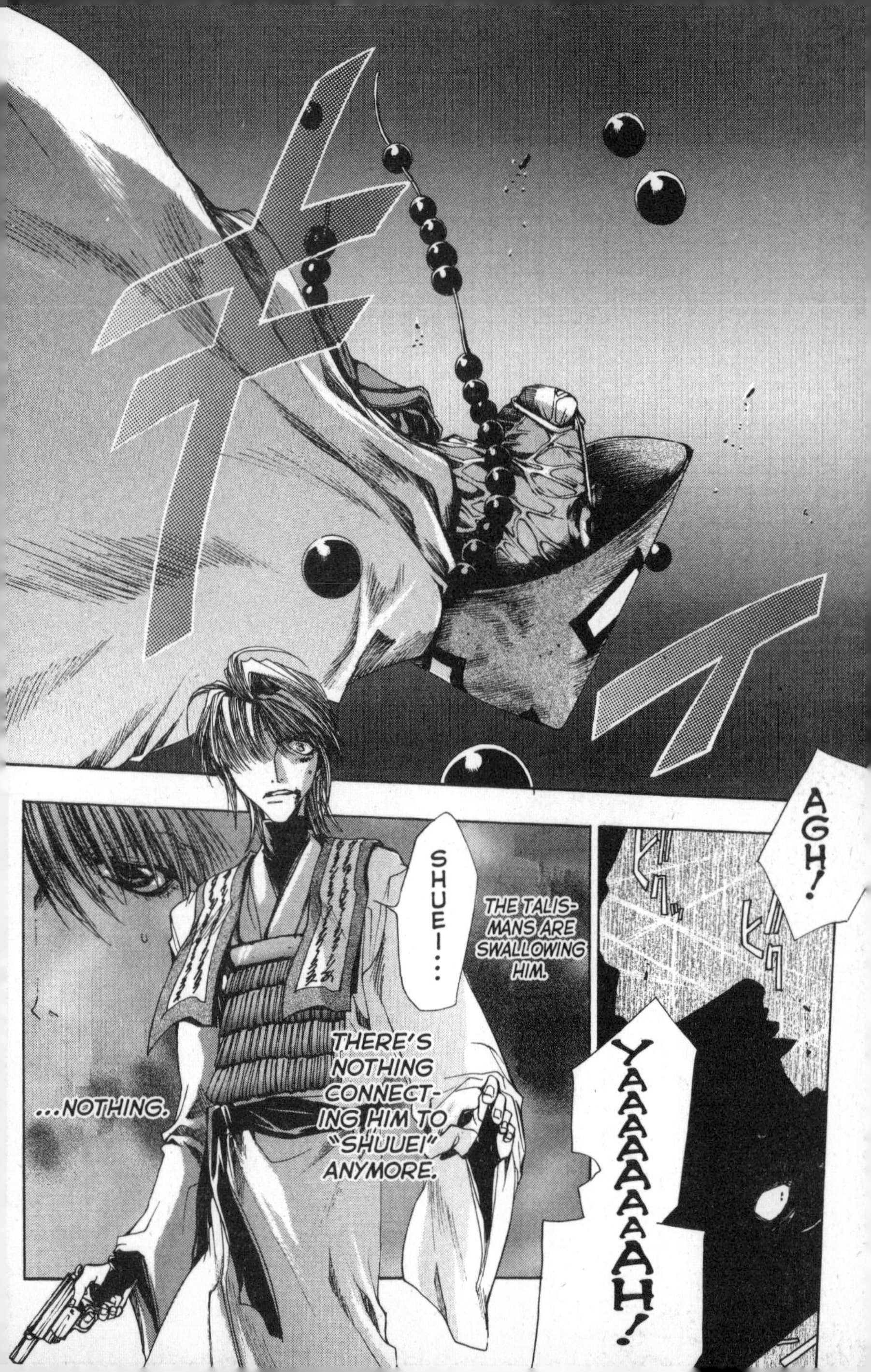
AGH!
YAAAAAAAAH!
SHUEI...
THE TALIS-MANS ARE SWALLOWING HIM.
THERE'S NOTHING CONNECT-ING HIM TO "SHUUEI" ANYMORE.
...NOTHING.

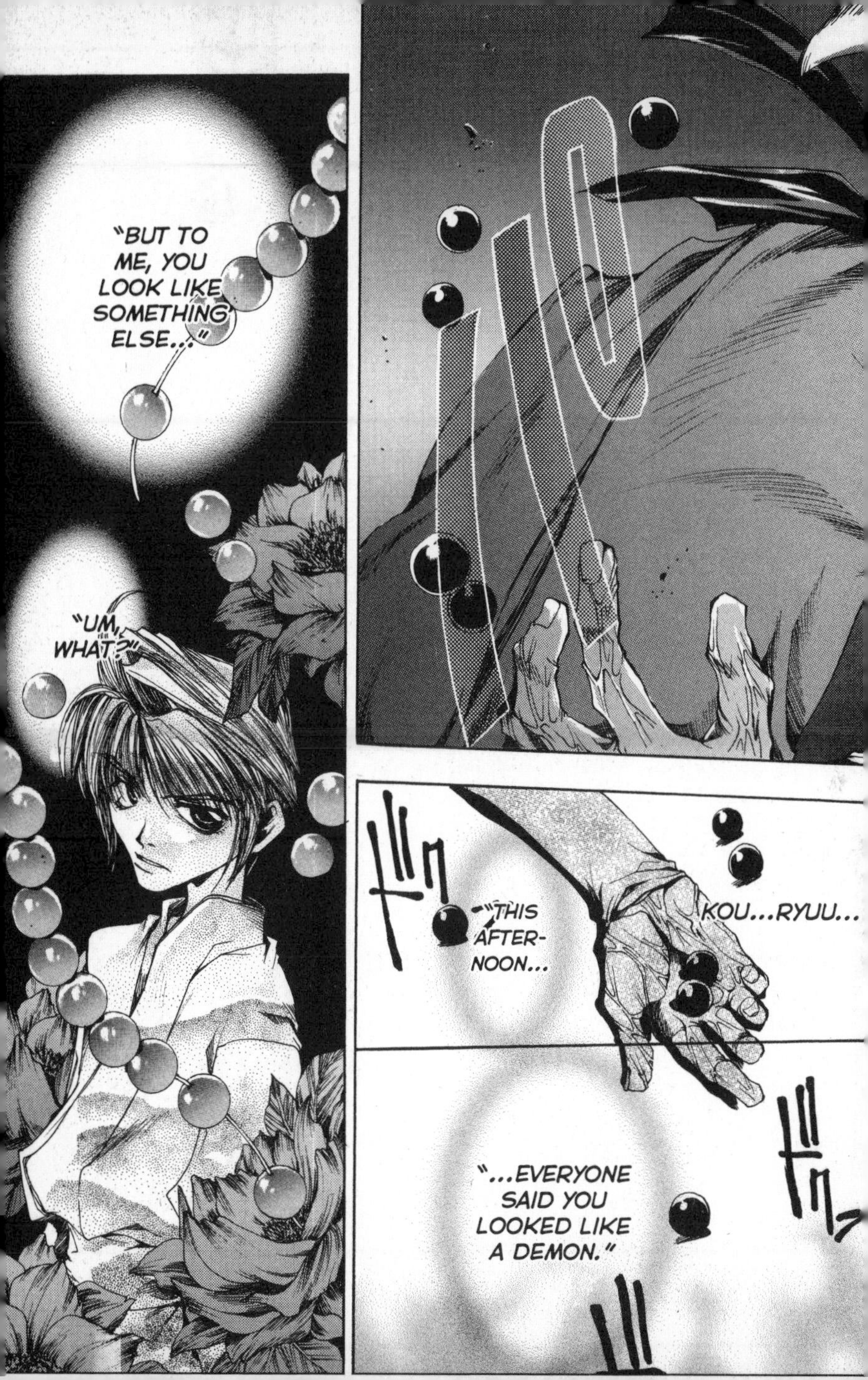
KOU...RYUU...
"THIS AFTERNOON...
"...EVERYONE SAID YOU LOOKED LIKE A DEMON."
"BUT TO ME, YOU LOOK LIKE SOMETHING ELSE..."
"UM, WHAT?"

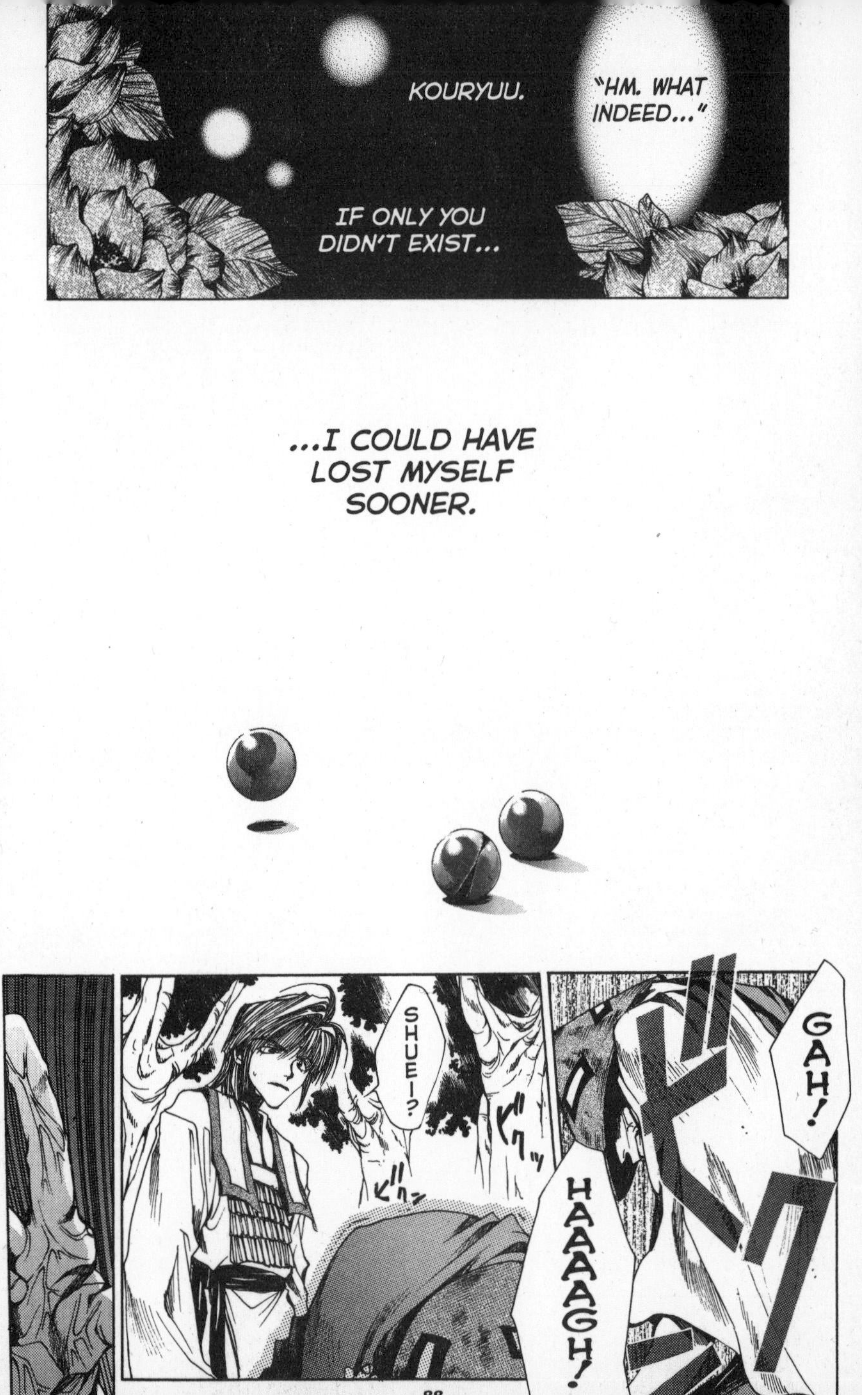
"HM. WHAT INDEED..."
KOURYUU.
IF ONLY YOU DIDN'T EXIST...
...I COULD HAVE LOST MYSELF SOONER.
GAH!
HAAAAGH!
SHUEI!?

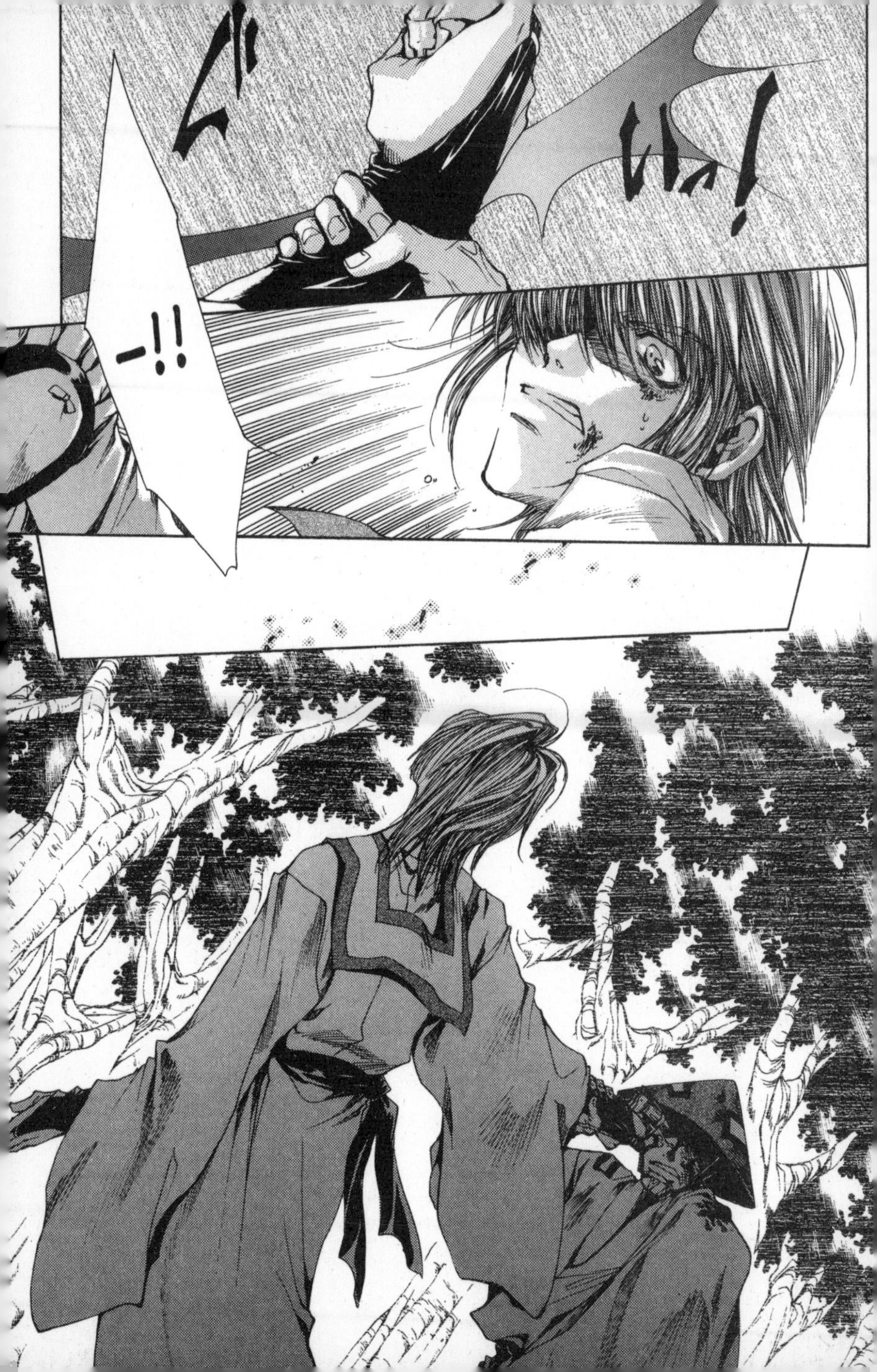
ぐいっ!
—!!

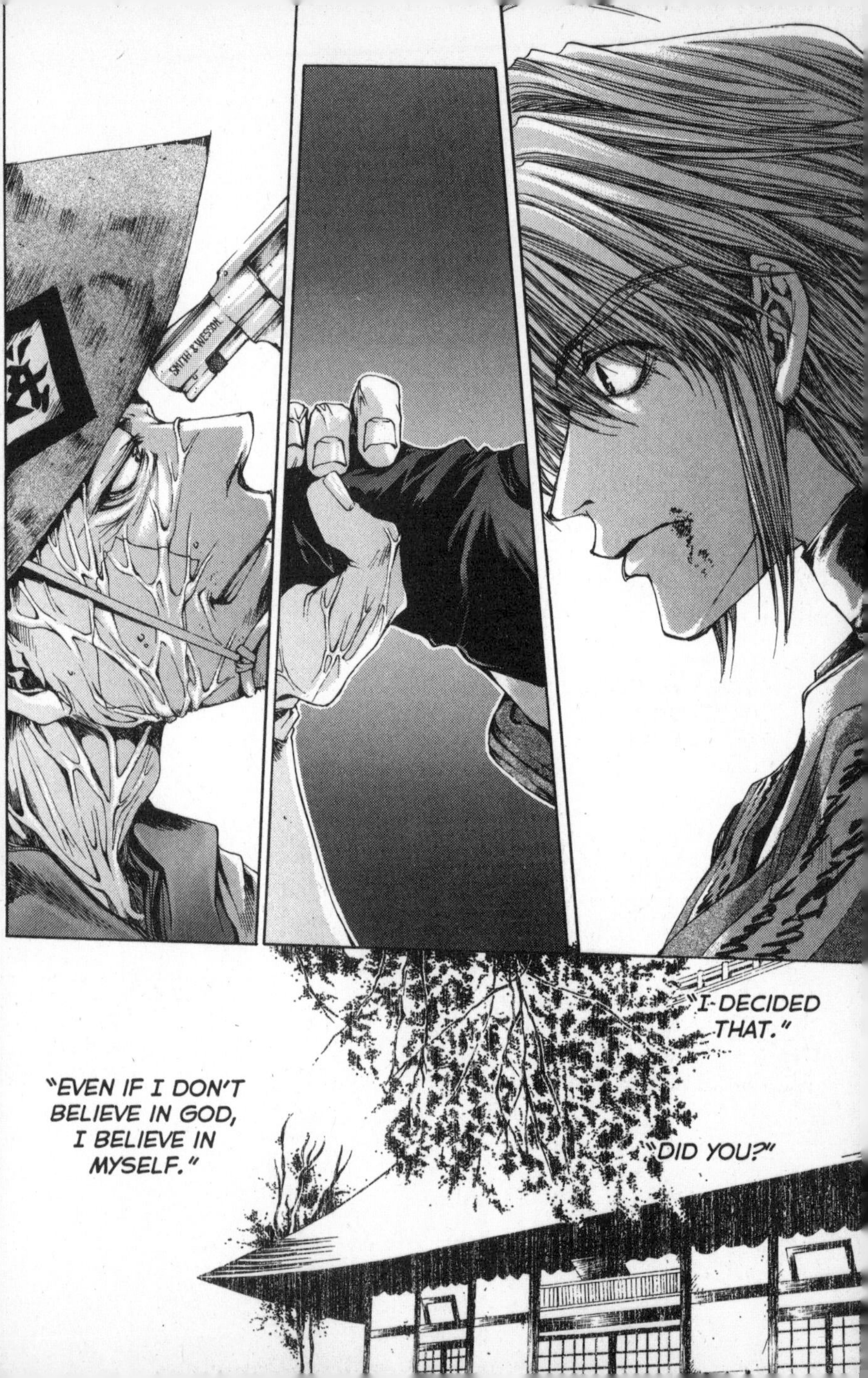
SMITH & WESSON
"EVEN IF I DON'T BELIEVE IN GOD, I BELIEVE IN MYSELF."
"I-DECIDED THAT."
"DID YOU?"

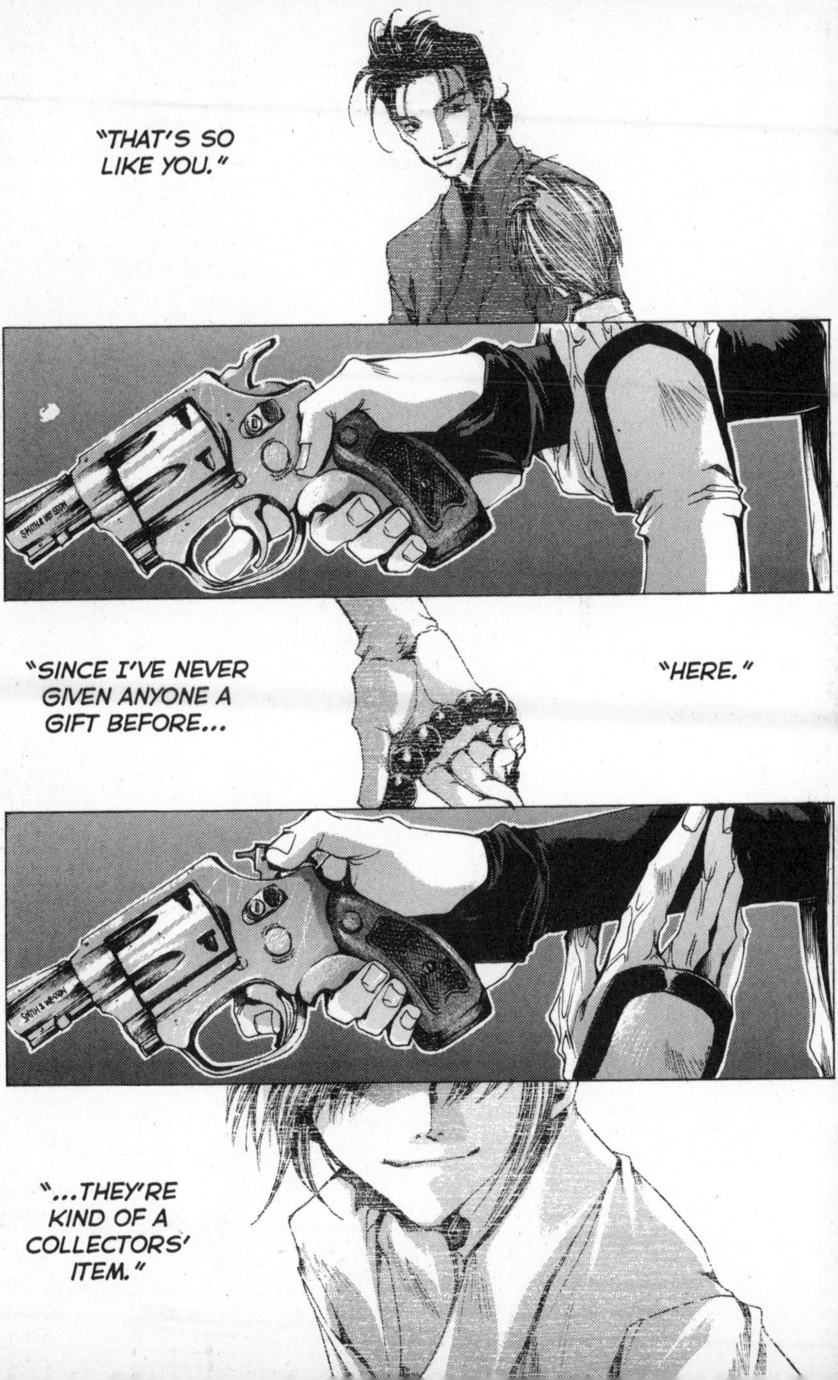
"THAT'S SO LIKE YOU."
"HERE."
"SINCE I'VE NEVER GIVEN ANYONE A GIFT BEFORE...
"...THEY'RE KIND OF A COLLECTORS' ITEM."

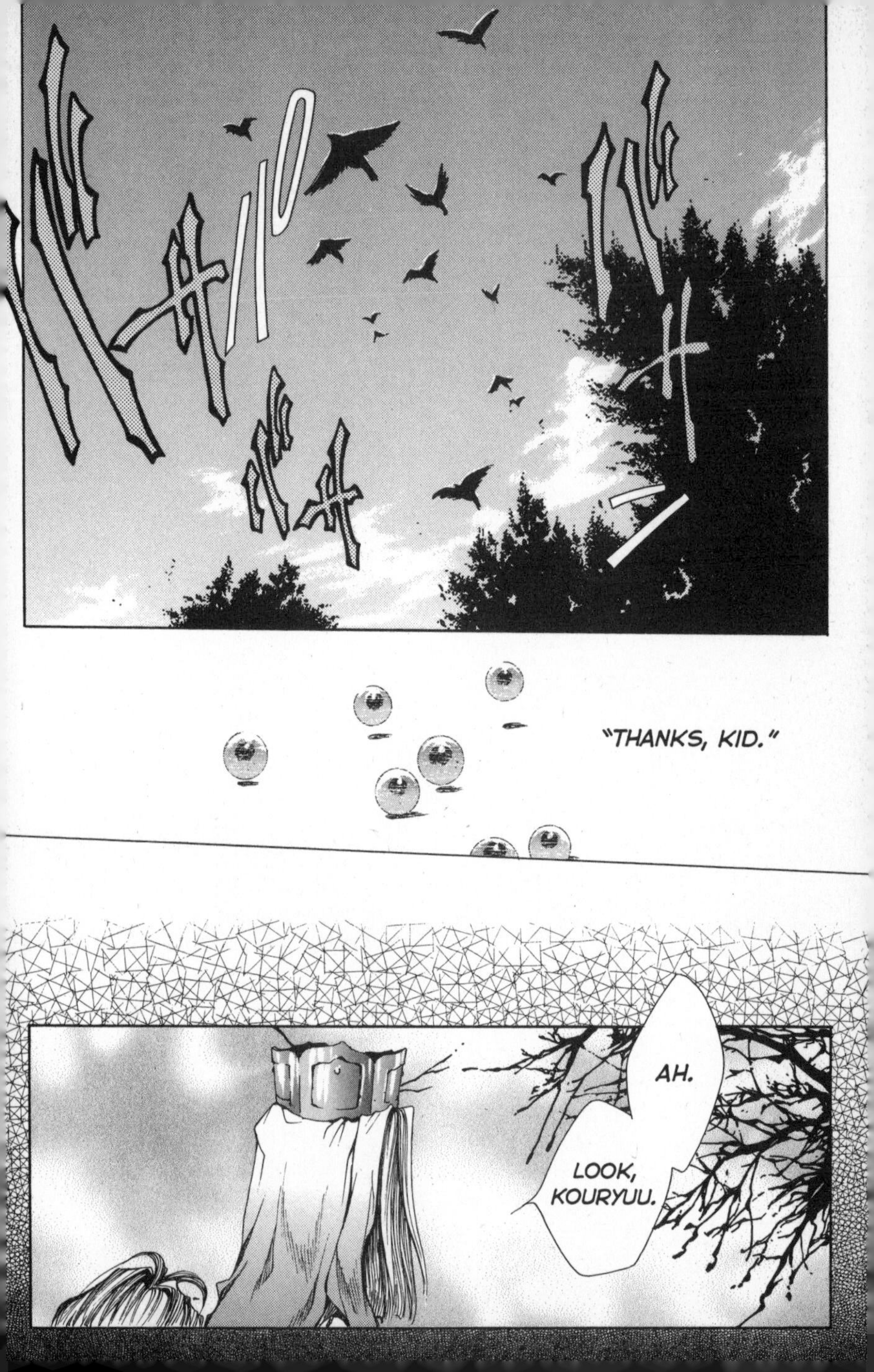
"THANKS, KID."
AH.
LOOK, KOURYUU.

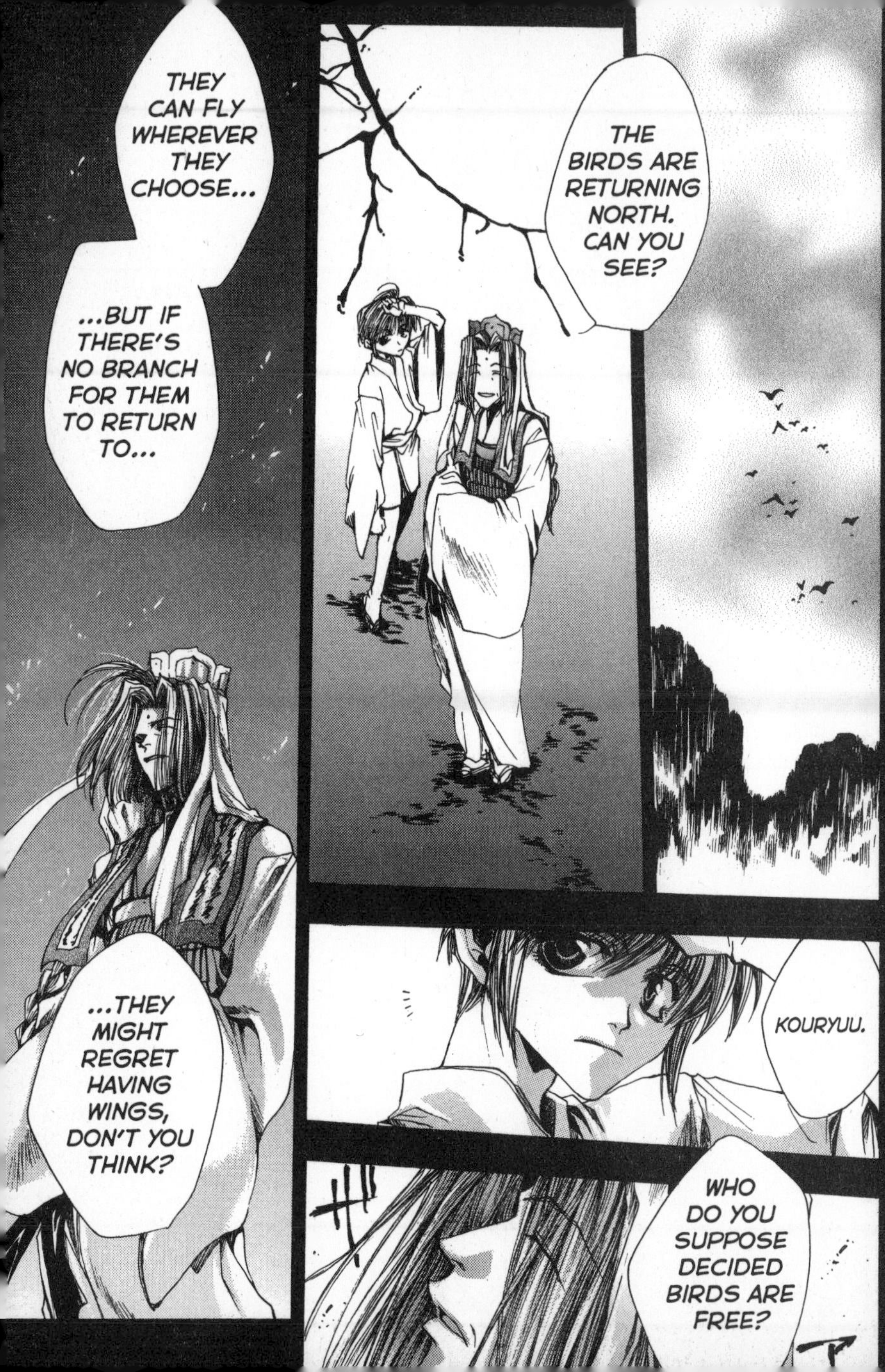
THE BIRDS ARE RETURNING NORTH. CAN YOU SEE?
KOURYUU.
WHO DO YOU SUPPOSE DECIDED BIRDS ARE FREE?
THEY CAN FLY WHEREVER THEY CHOOSE...
...BUT IF THERE'S NO BRANCH FOR THEM TO RETURN TO...
...THEY MIGHT REGRET HAVING WINGS, DON'T YOU THINK?

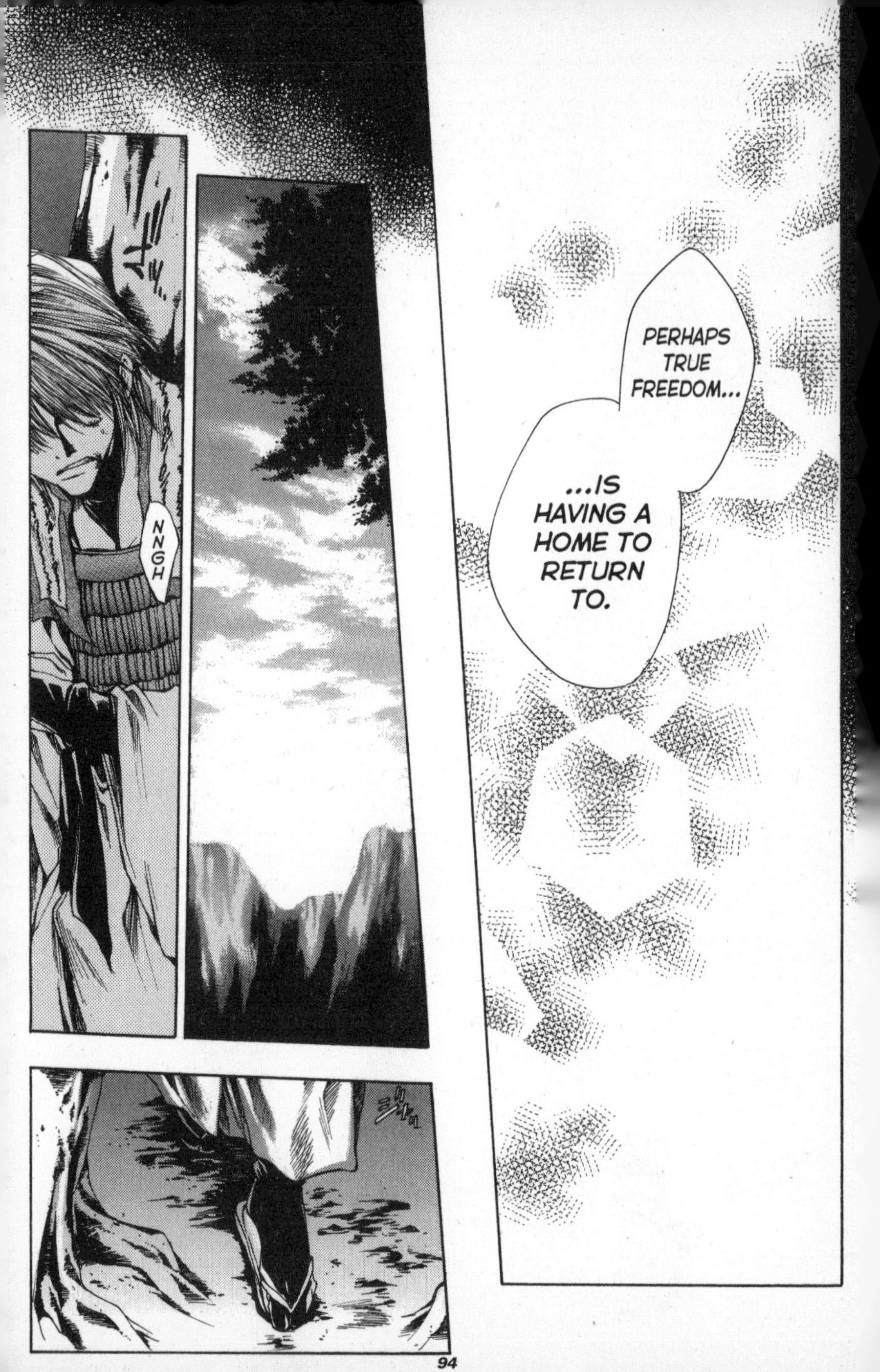
PERHAPS TRUE FREEDOM...
...IS HAVING A HOME TO RETURN TO.
NNGH

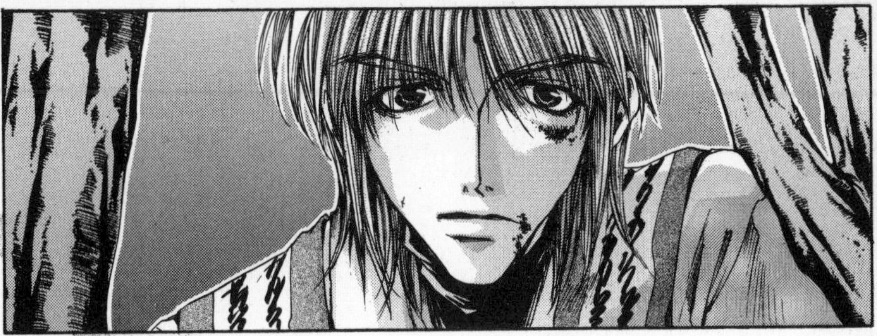
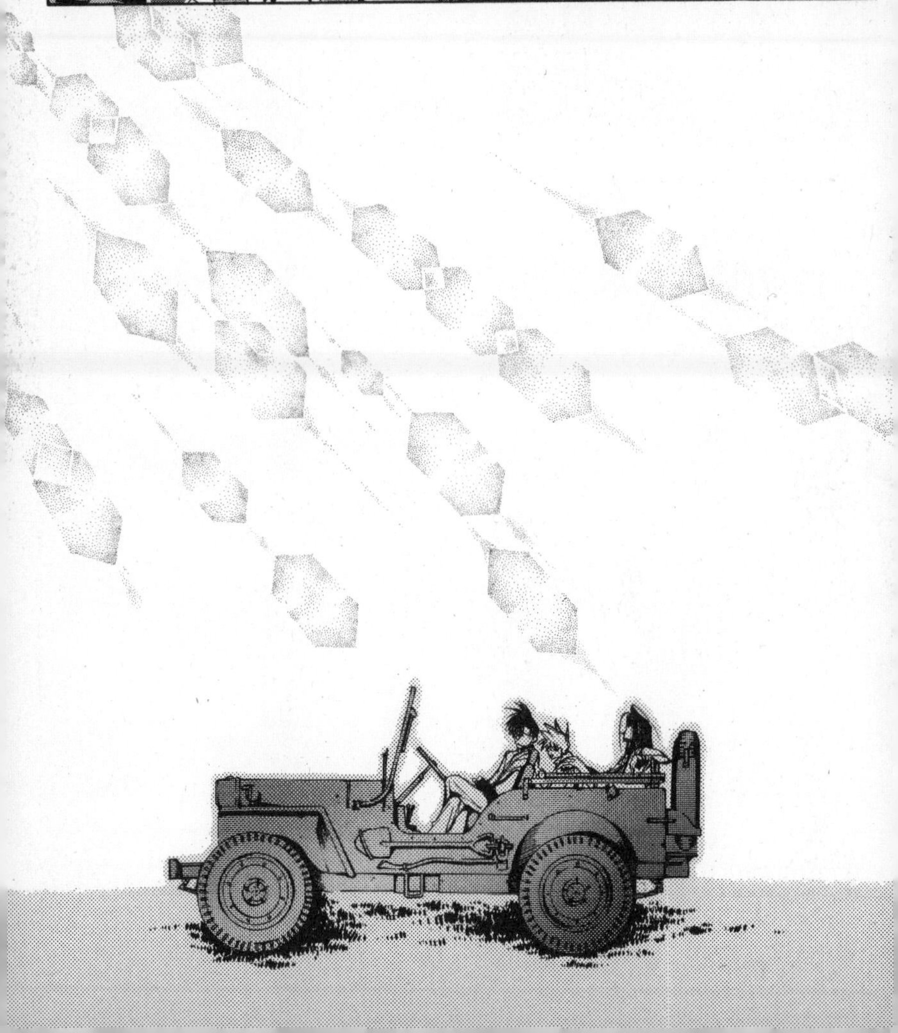

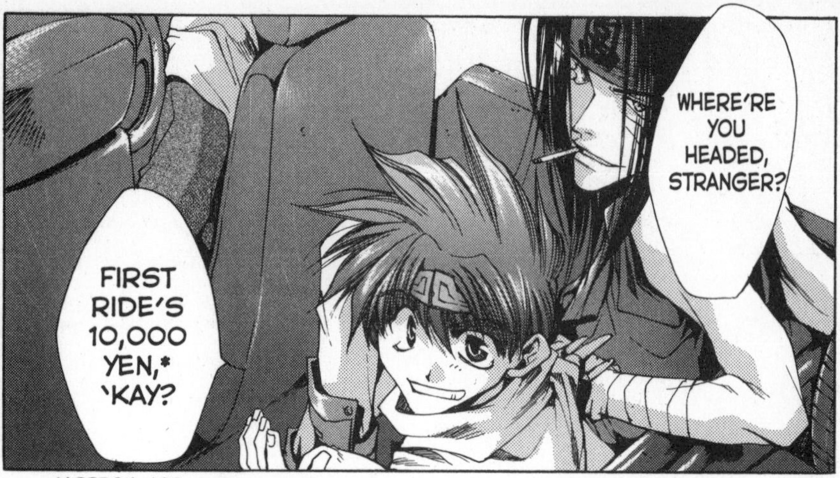
WHERE'RE YOU HEADED, STRANGER?
FIRST RIDE'S 10,000 YEN,* 'KAY?
*APPROX. $90

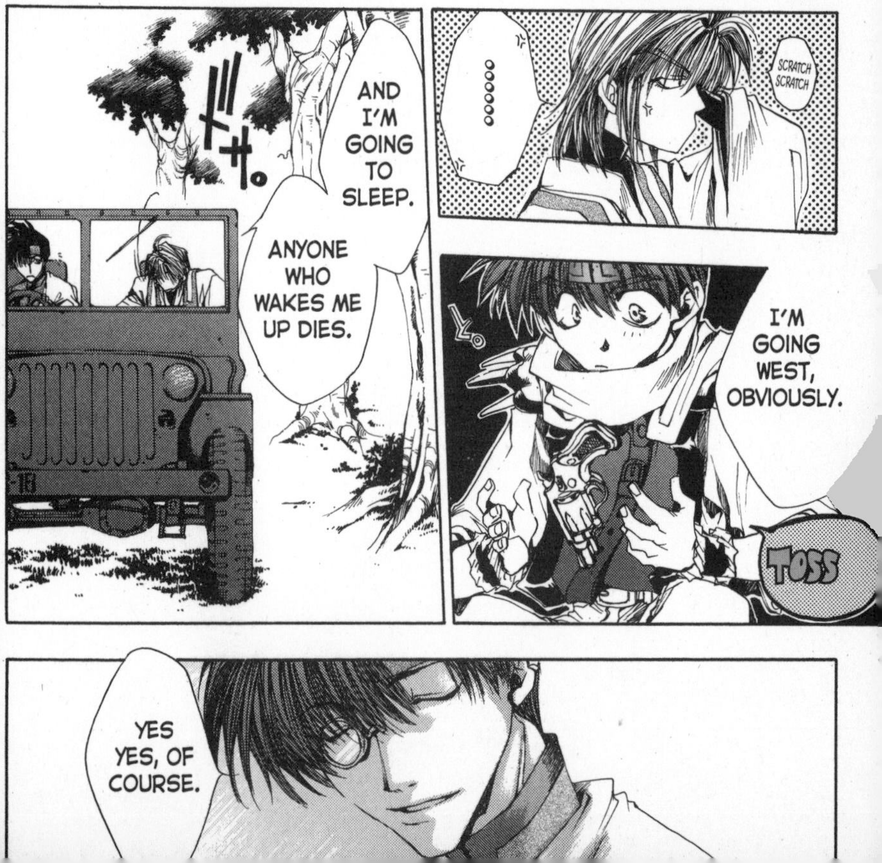
......
SCRATCH SCRATCH
I'M GOING WEST, OBVIOUSLY.
TOSS
AND I'M GOING TO SLEEP.
ANYONE WHO WAKES ME UP DIES.
YES YES, OF COURSE.

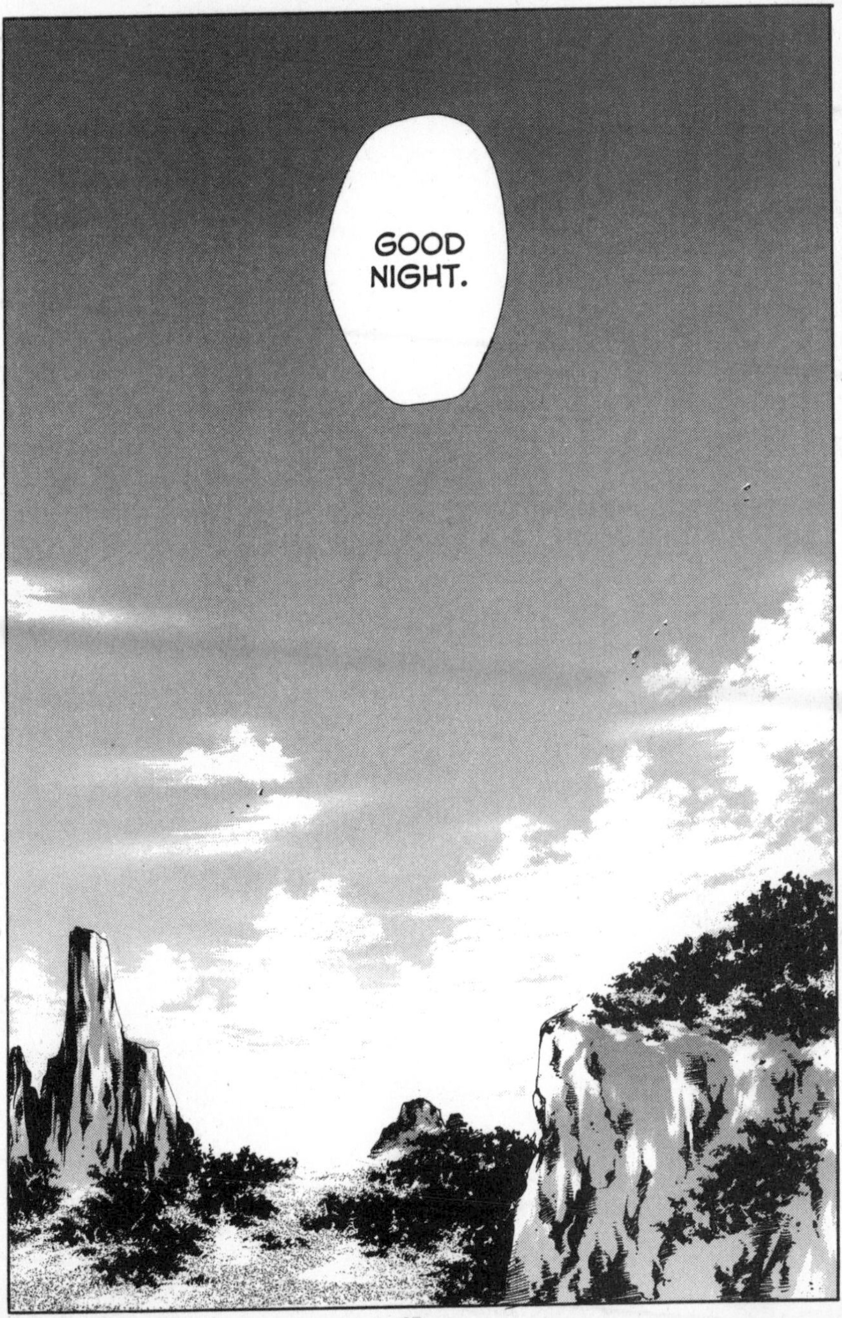
GOOD NIGHT.

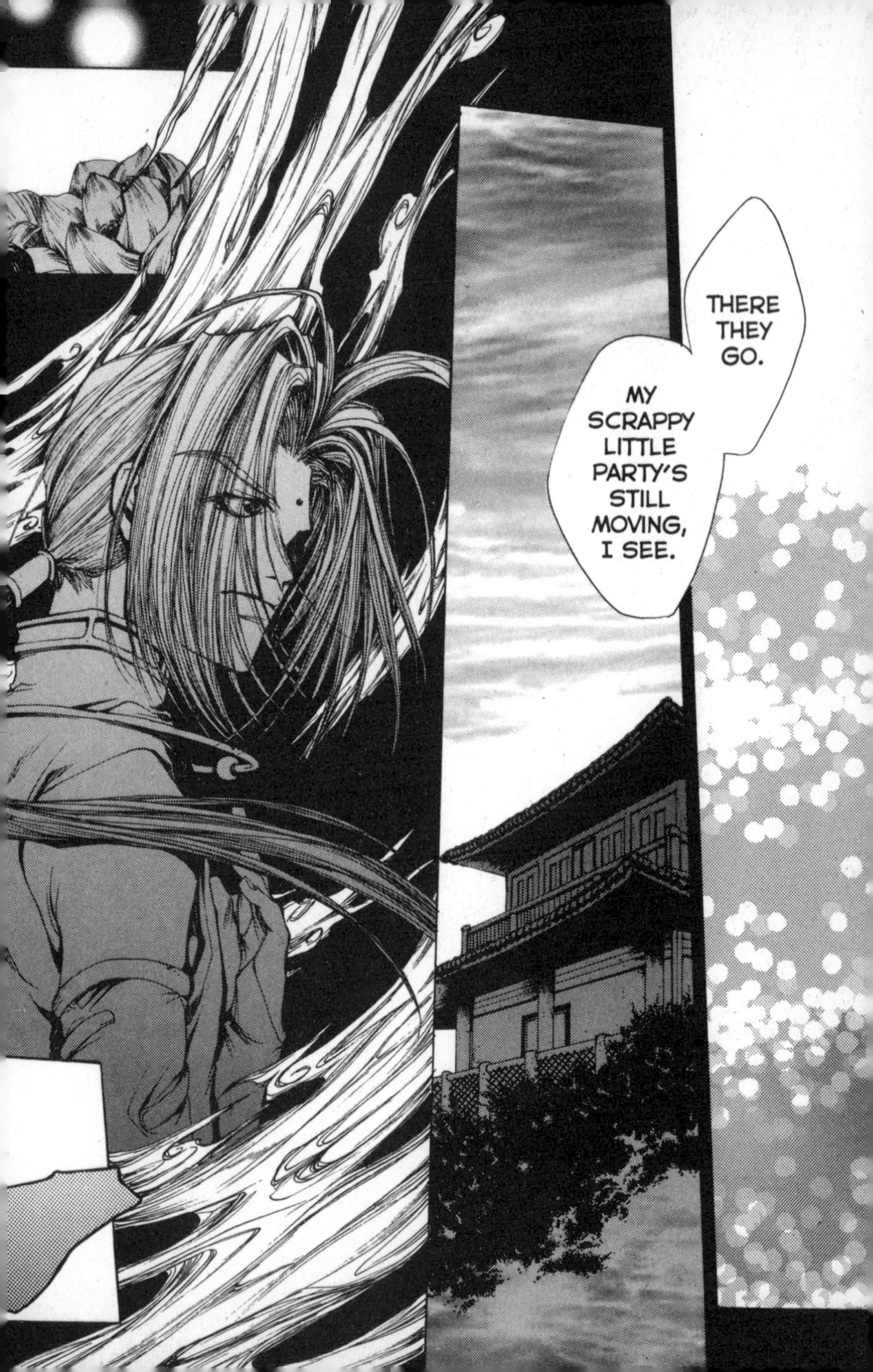
THERE THEY GO.
MY SCRAPPY LITTLE PARTY'S STILL MOVING, I SEE.

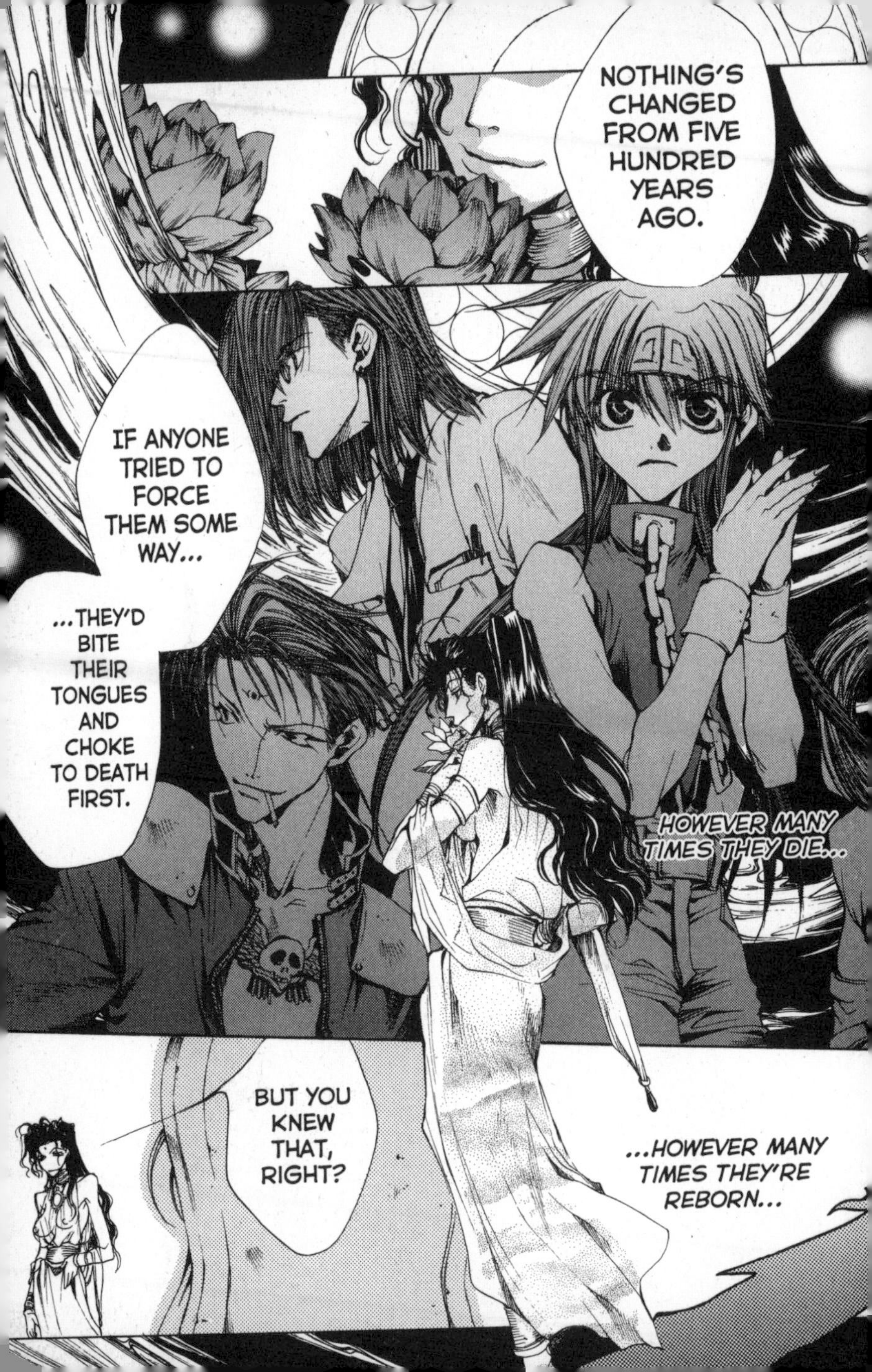
NOTHING'S CHANGED FROM FIVE HUNDRED YEARS AGO.
IF ANYONE TRIED TO FORCE THEM SOME WAY...
...THEY'D BITE THEIR TONGUES AND CHOKE TO DEATH FIRST.
HOWEVER MANY TIMES THEY DIE...
...HOWEVER MANY TIMES THEY'RE REBORN...
BUT YOU KNEW THAT, RIGHT?

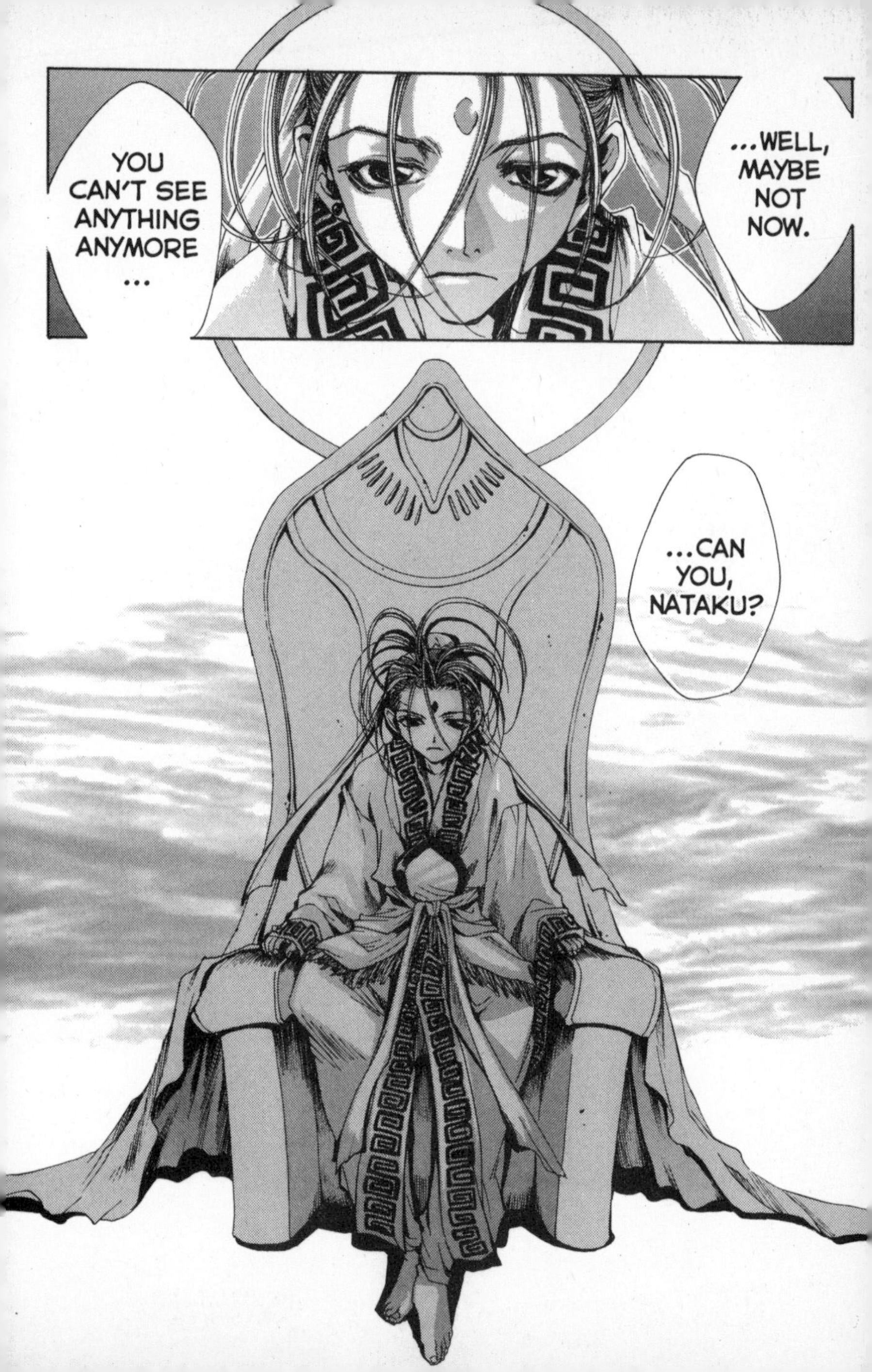
...WELL, MAYBE NOT NOW.
YOU CAN'T SEE ANYTHING ANYMORE ...
...CAN YOU, NATAKU?

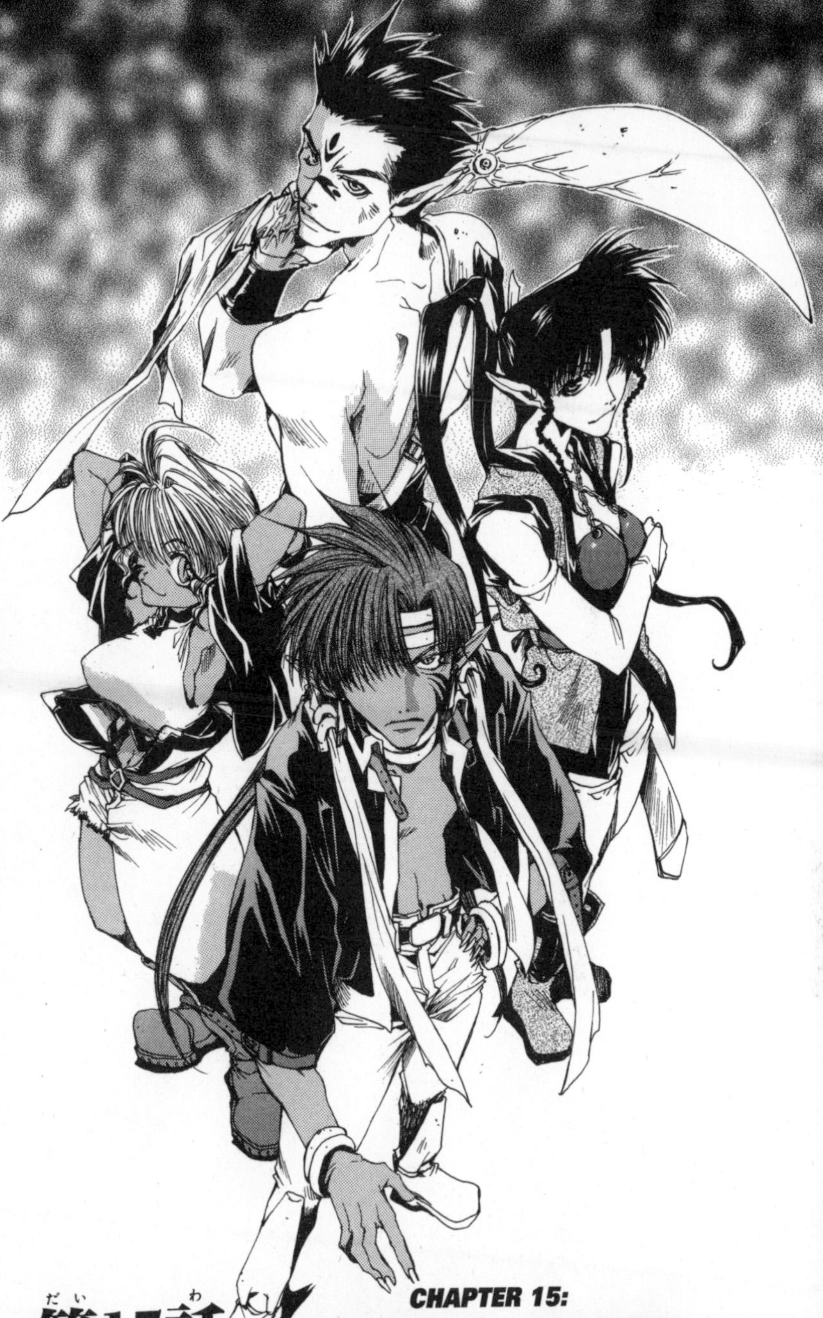

第15話 CHAPTER 15: DROP A BOMB

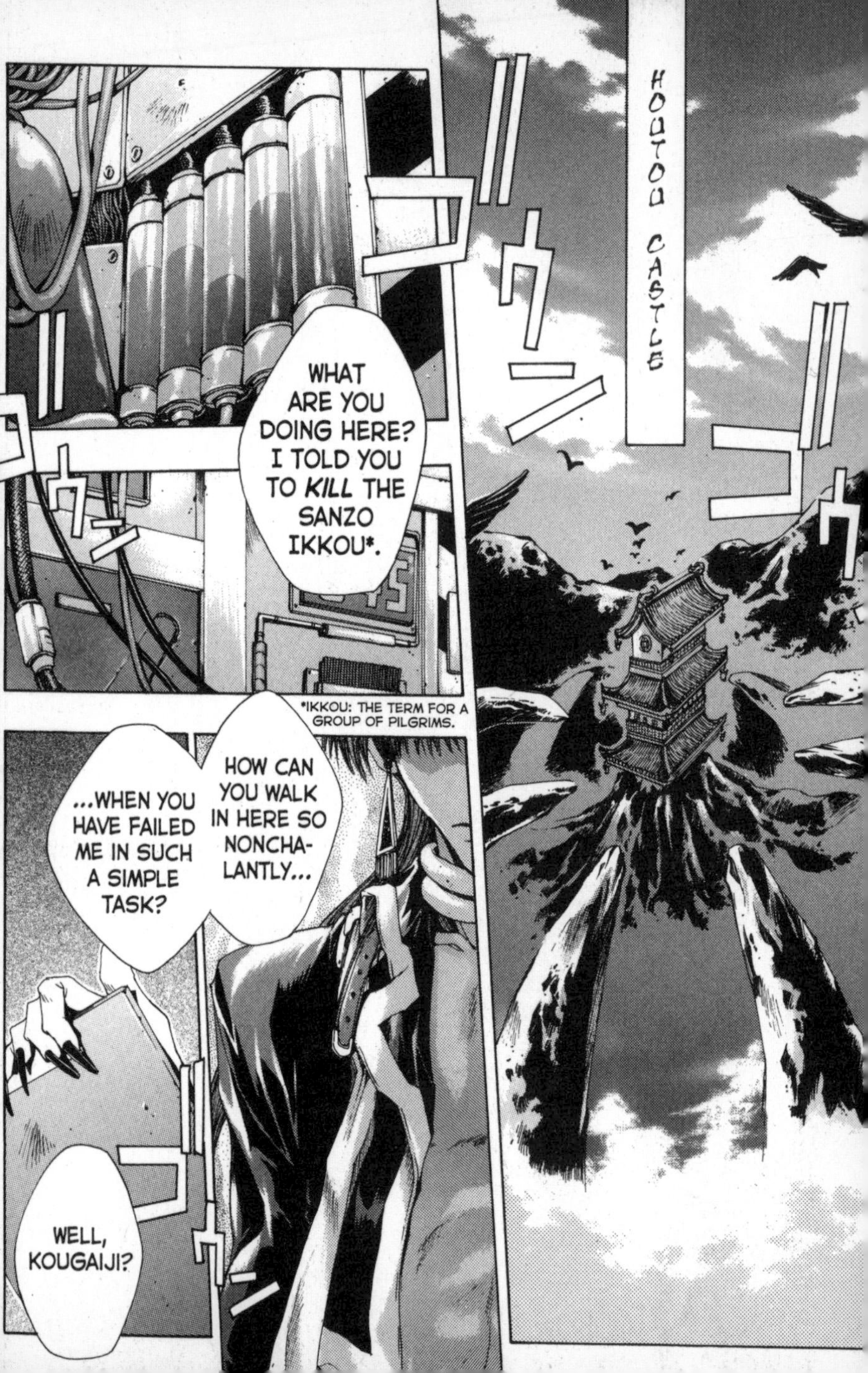
HOUTOU CASTLE
WHAT ARE YOU DOING HERE? I TOLD YOU TO *KILL* THE SANZO IKKOU*.
*IKKOU: THE TERM FOR A GROUP OF PILGRIMS.
HOW CAN YOU WALK IN HERE SO NONCHA-LANTLY...
...WHEN YOU HAVE FAILED ME IN SUCH A SIMPLE TASK?
WELL, KOUGAIJI?

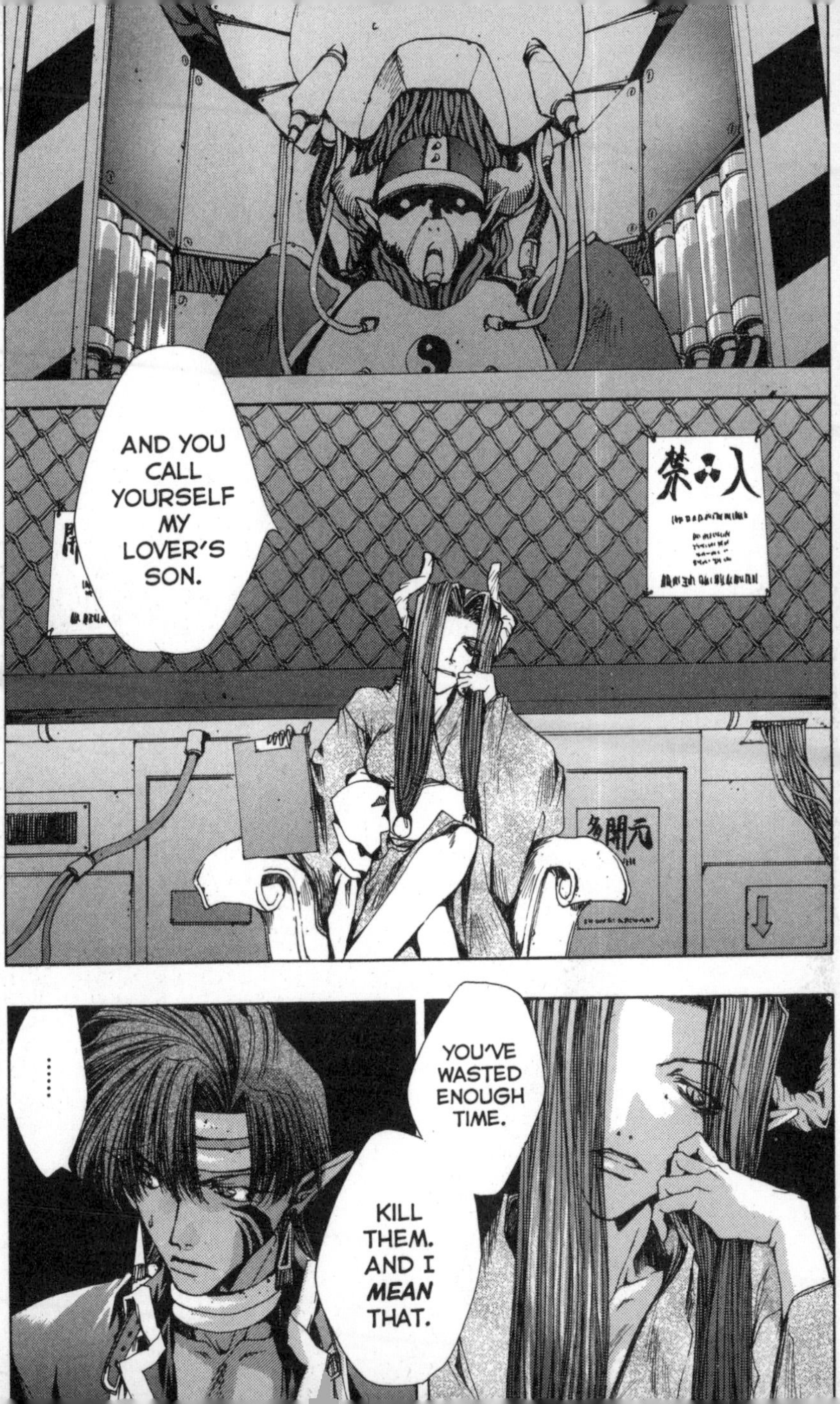
AND YOU CALL YOURSELF MY LOVER'S SON.
YOU'VE WASTED ENOUGH TIME.
KILL THEM. AND I *MEAN* THAT.
......

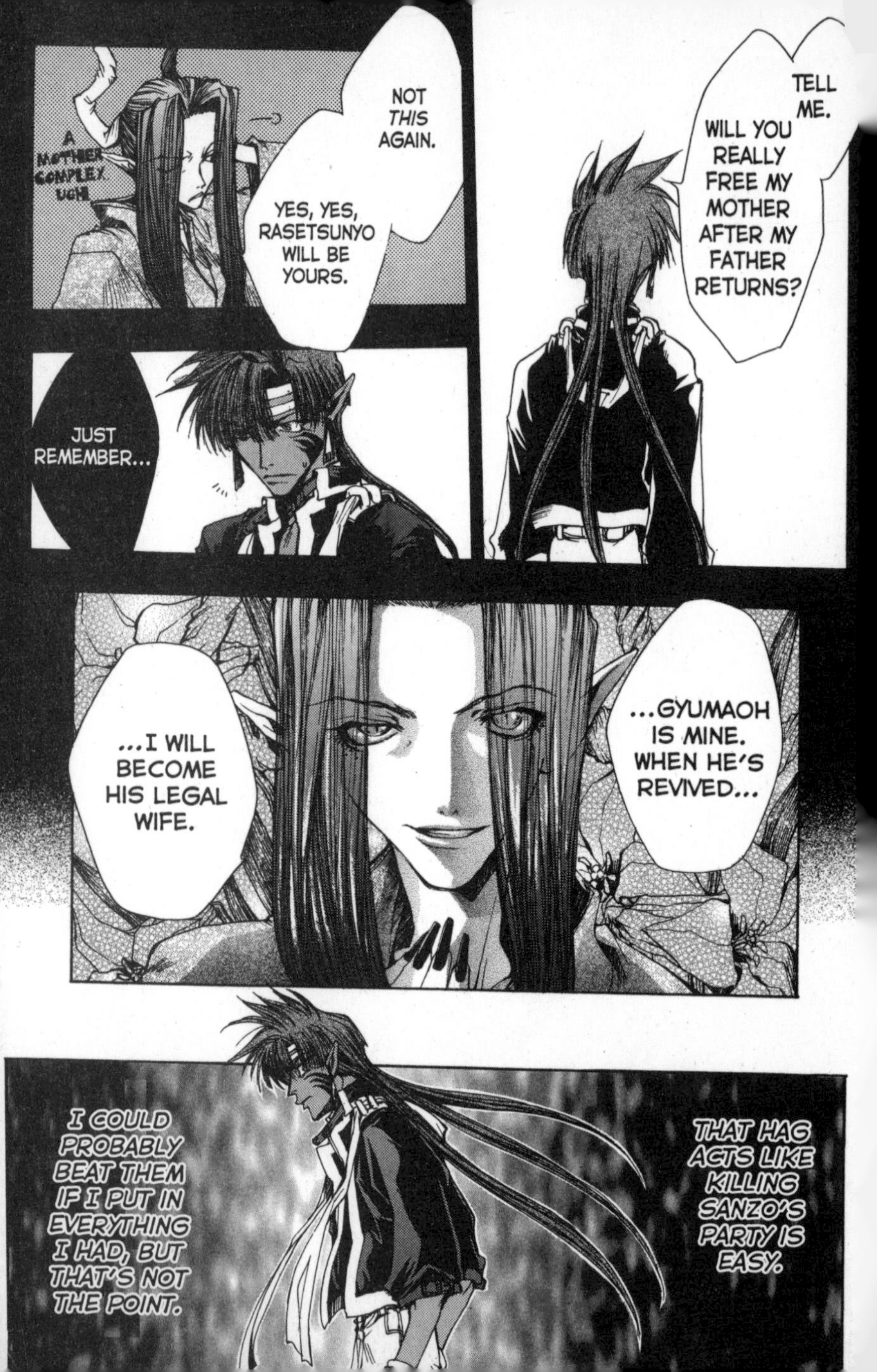
TELL ME. WILL YOU REALLY FREE MY MOTHER AFTER MY FATHER RETURNS?
NOT THIS AGAIN.
YES, YES, RASETSUNYO WILL BE YOURS.
A MOTHER COMPLEX. UGH.
JUST REMEMBER...
...GYUMAOH IS MINE. WHEN HE'S REVIVED...
...I WILL BECOME HIS LEGAL WIFE.
THAT HAG ACTS LIKE KILLING SANZO'S PARTY IS EASY.
I COULD PROBABLY BEAT THEM IF I PUT IN EVERYTHING I HAD, BUT THAT'S NOT THE POINT.

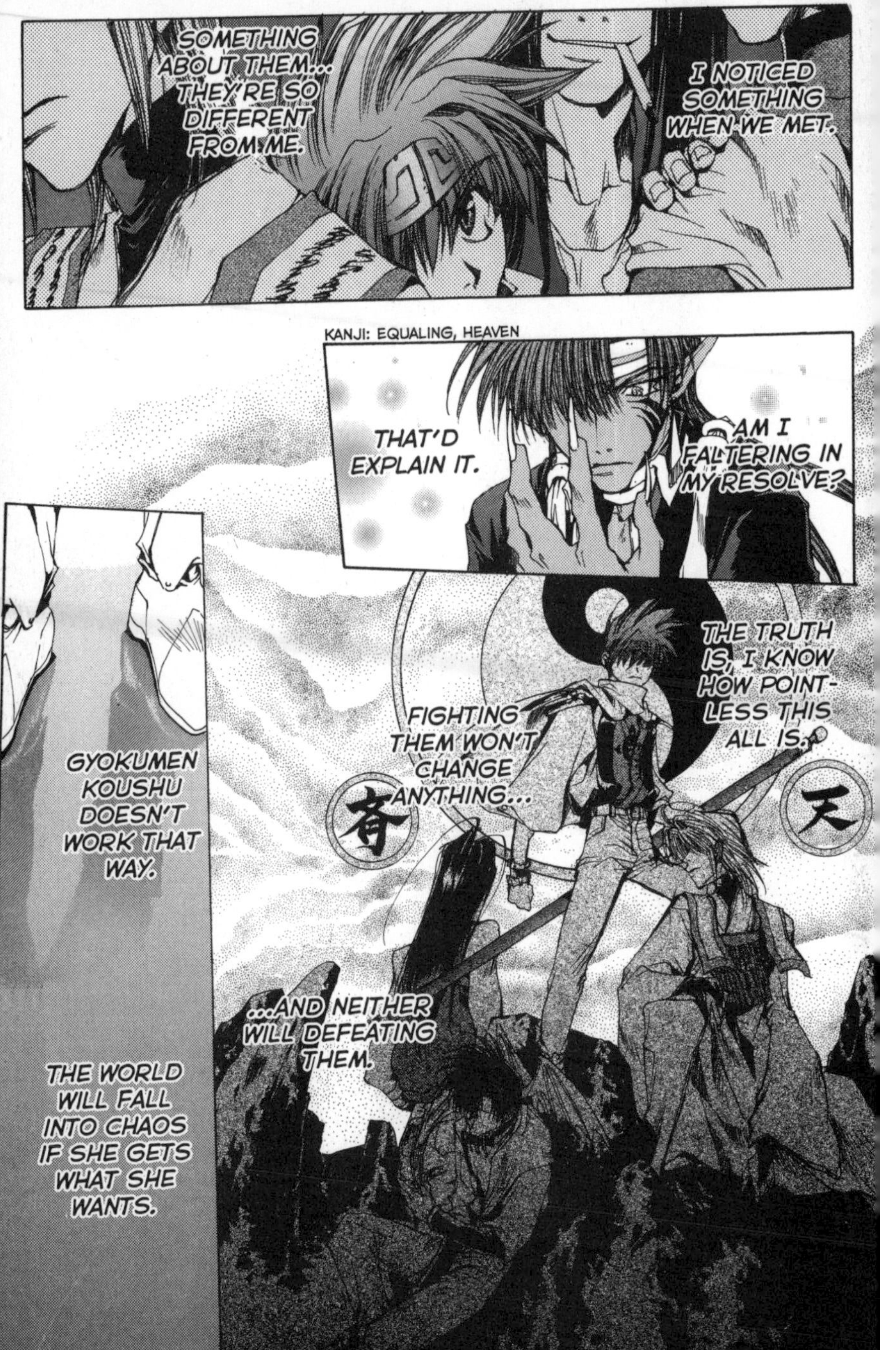
I NOTICED SOMETHING WHEN WE MET.
SOMETHING ABOUT THEM... THEY'RE SO DIFFERENT FROM ME.
KANJI: EQUALING, HEAVEN
AM I FALTERING IN MY RESOLVE?
THAT'D EXPLAIN IT.
THE TRUTH IS, I KNOW HOW POINTLESS THIS ALL IS.
天
FIGHTING THEM WON'T CHANGE ANYTHING...
斉
...AND NEITHER WILL DEFEATING THEM.
GYOKUMEN KOUSHU DOESN'T WORK THAT WAY.
THE WORLD WILL FALL INTO CHAOS IF SHE GETS WHAT SHE WANTS.

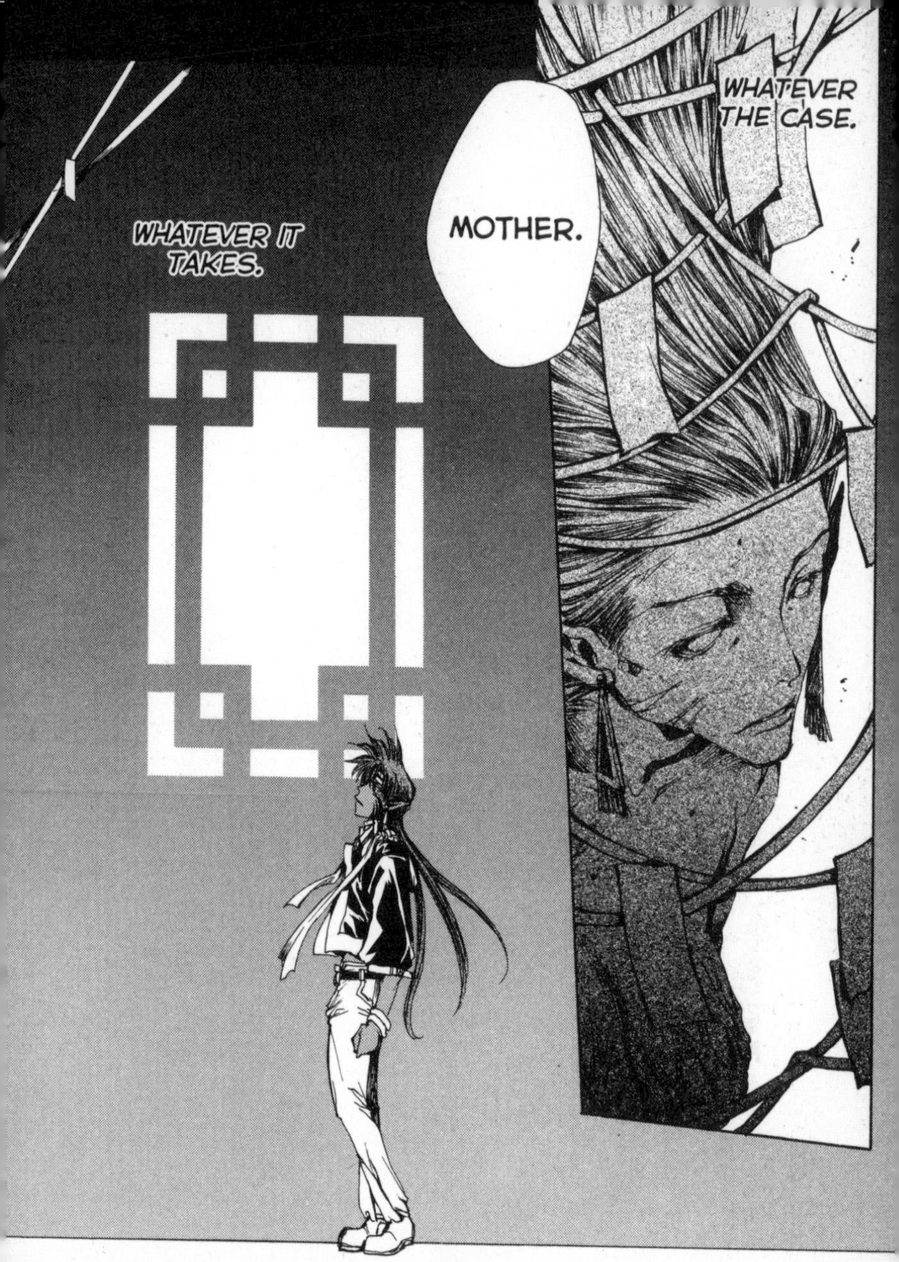
WHATEVER THE CASE.
MOTHER.
WHATEVER IT TAKES.

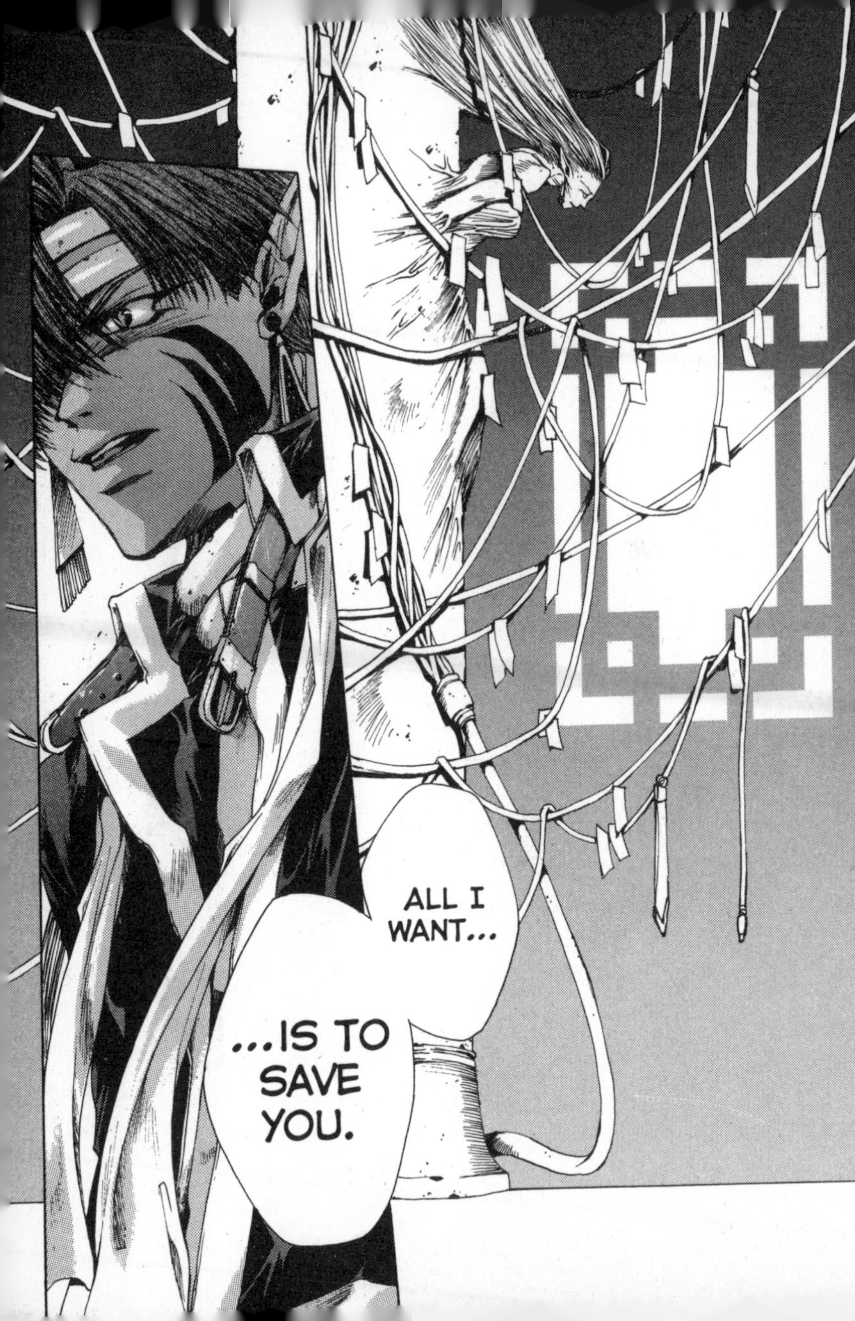
ALL I WANT...
...IS TO SAVE YOU.

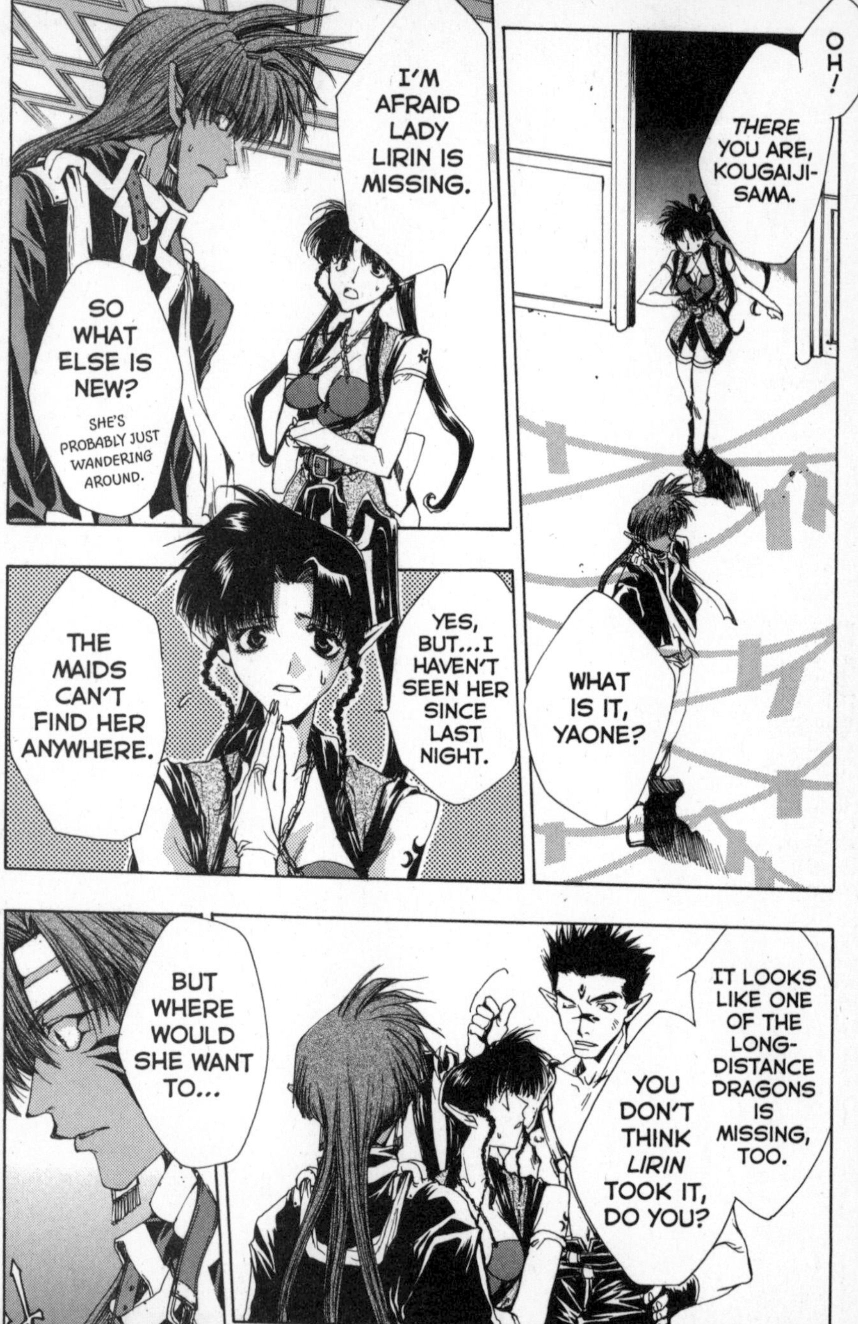
OH!
THERE YOU ARE, KOUGAIJI-SAMA.
WHAT IS IT, YAONE?
I'M AFRAID LADY LIRIN IS MISSING.
SO WHAT ELSE IS NEW?
SHE'S PROBABLY JUST WANDERING AROUND.
YES, BUT...I HAVEN'T SEEN HER SINCE LAST NIGHT.
THE MAIDS CAN'T FIND HER ANYWHERE.
IT LOOKS LIKE ONE OF THE LONG-DISTANCE DRAGONS IS MISSING, TOO.
YOU DON'T THINK *LIRIN* TOOK IT, DO YOU?
BUT WHERE WOULD SHE WANT TO...

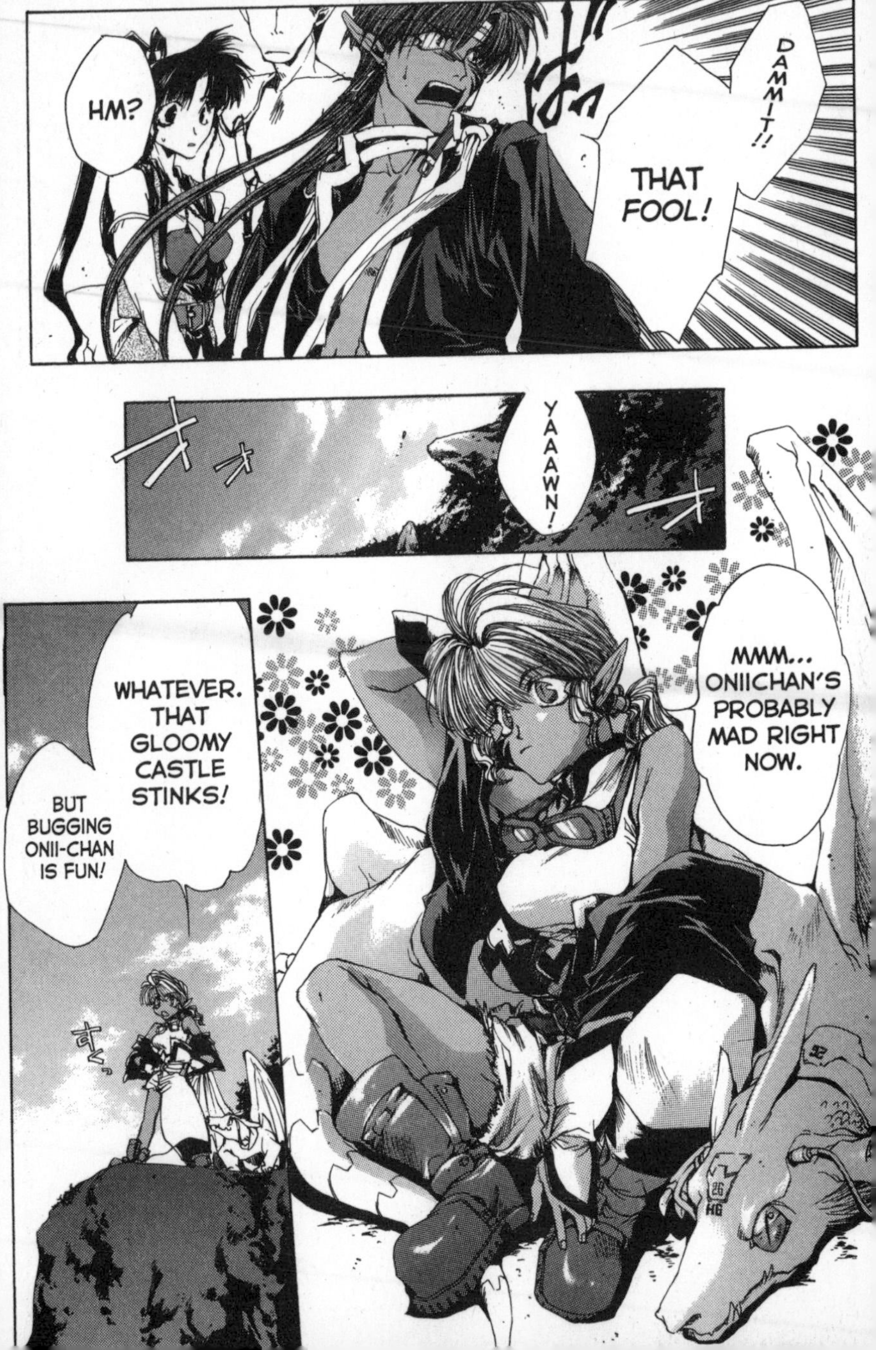
DAMMIT!!
THAT FOOL!
HM?
YAAAWN!
MMM... ONIICHAN'S PROBABLY MAD RIGHT NOW.
WHATEVER. THAT GLOOMY CASTLE STINKS!
BUT BUGGING ONII-CHAN IS FUN!

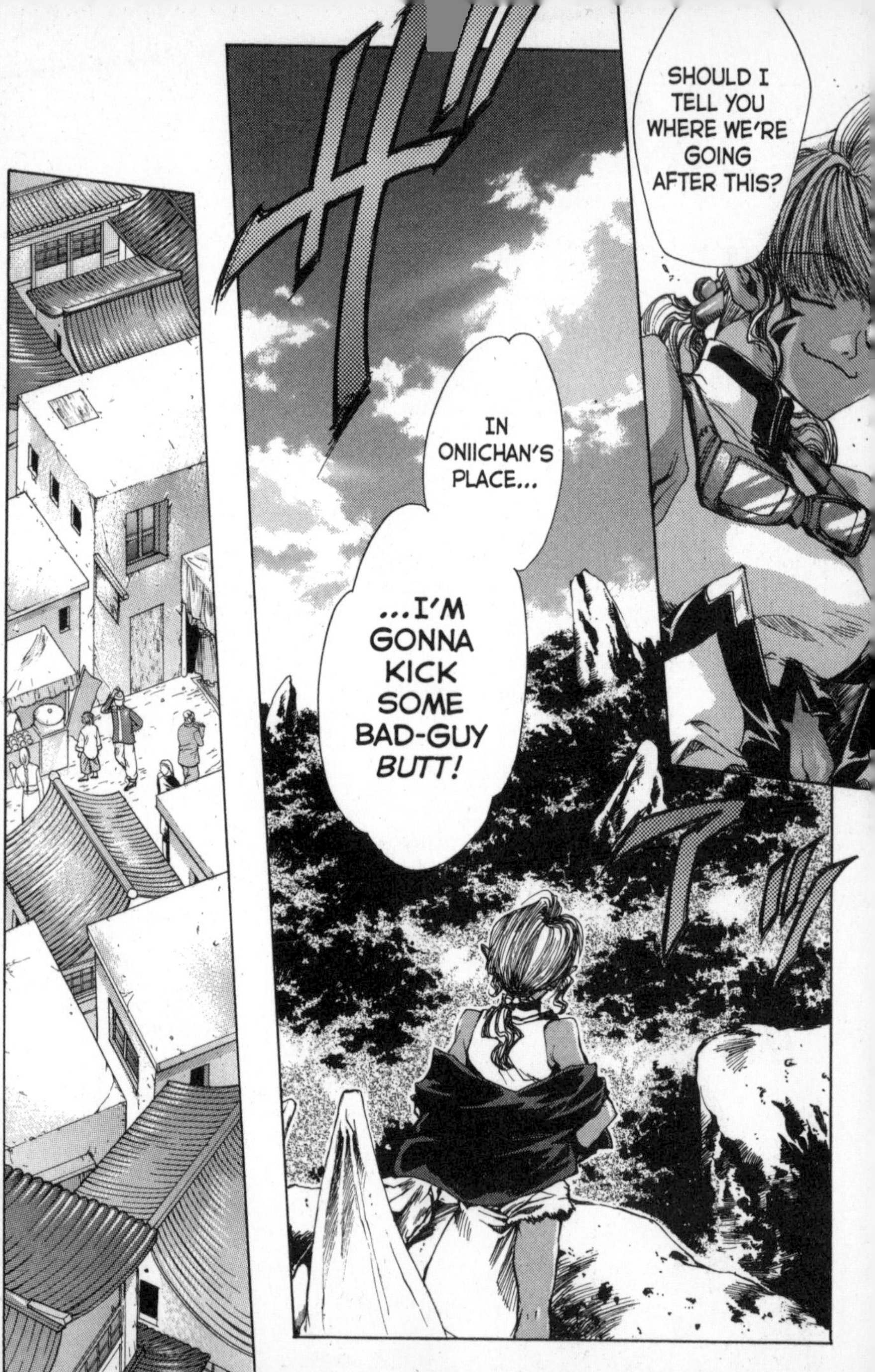
SHOULD I TELL YOU WHERE WE'RE GOING AFTER THIS?
IN ONIICHAN'S PLACE...
...I'M GONNA KICK SOME BAD-GUY *BUTT!*

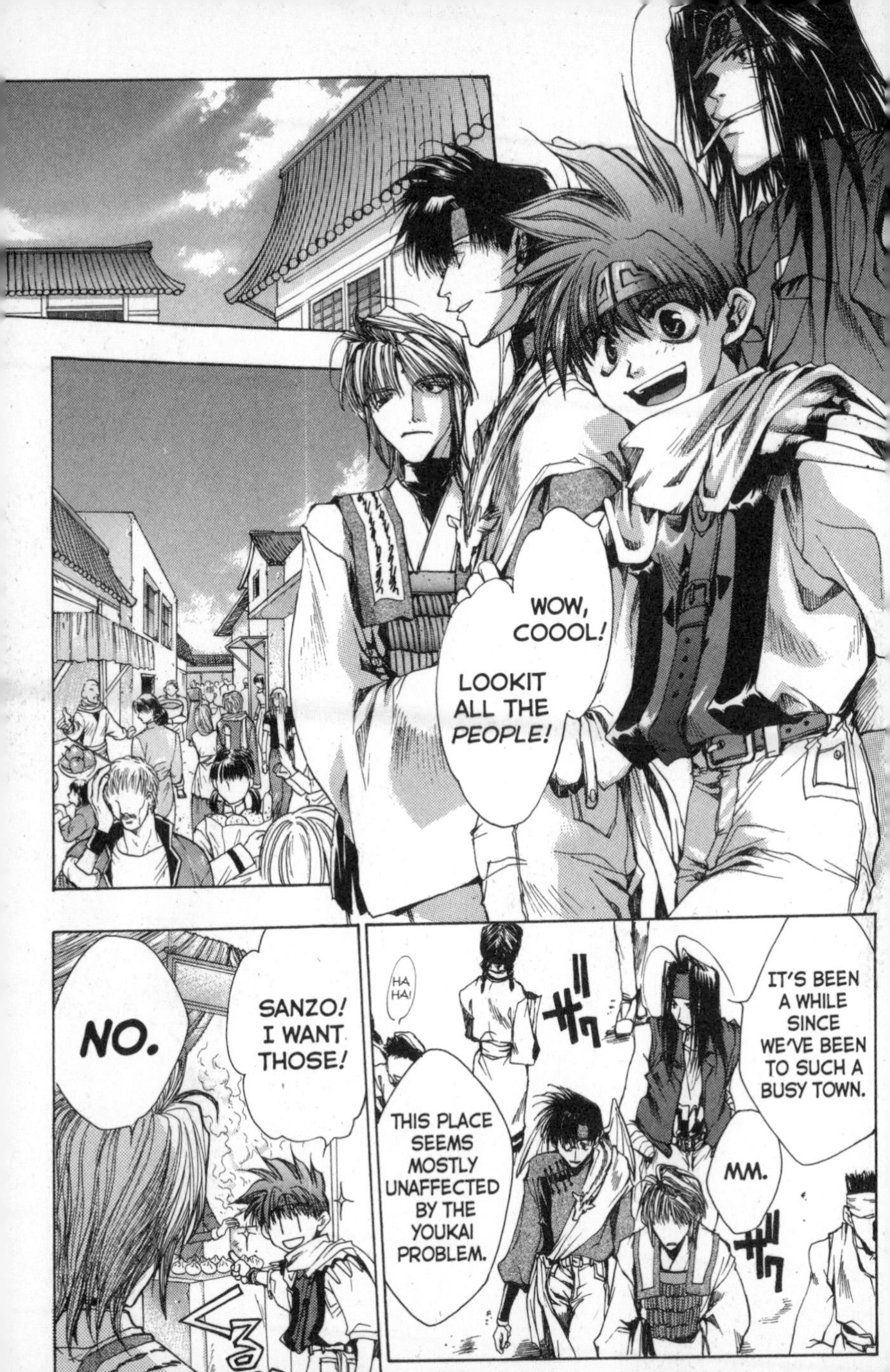
WOW, COOOL!
LOOKIT ALL THE *PEOPLE!*
IT'S BEEN A WHILE SINCE WE'VE BEEN TO SUCH A BUSY TOWN.
MM.
THIS PLACE SEEMS MOSTLY UNAFFECTED BY THE YOUKAI PROBLEM.
HA HA!
SANZO! I WANT THOSE!
NO.

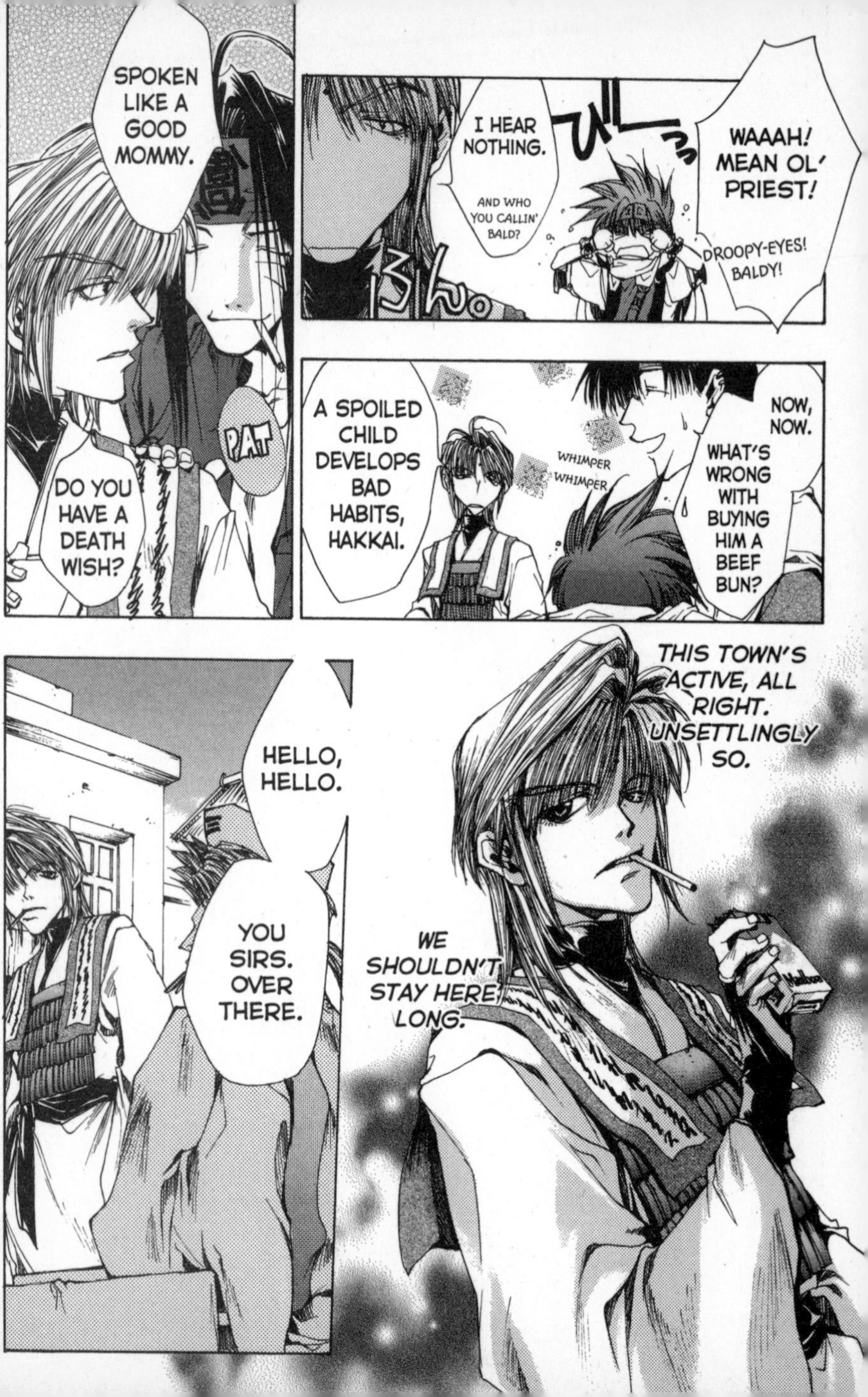
WAAAH! MEAN OL' PRIEST!
DROOPY-EYES! BALDY!
びーっ
I HEAR NOTHING.
AND WHO YOU CALLIN' BALD?
ふん。
NOW, NOW. WHAT'S WRONG WITH BUYING HIM A BEEF BUN?
WHIMPER WHIMPER
A SPOILED CHILD DEVELOPS BAD HABITS, HAKKAI.
SPOKEN LIKE A GOOD MOMMY.
PAT
DO YOU HAVE A DEATH WISH?
THIS TOWN'S ACTIVE, ALL RIGHT. UNSETTLINGLY SO.
WE SHOULDN'T STAY HERE LONG.
HELLO, HELLO.
YOU SIRS. OVER THERE.

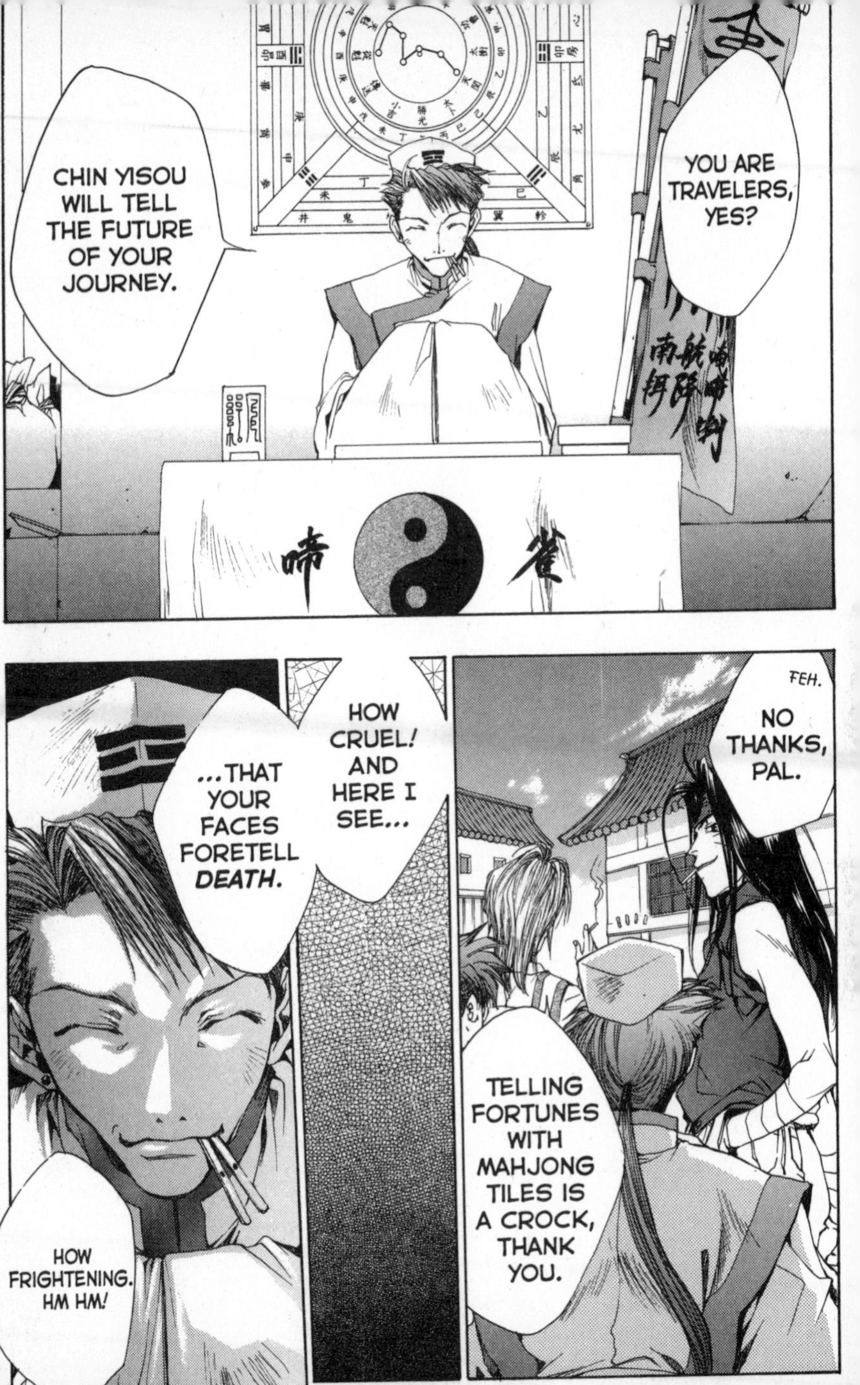
YOU ARE TRAVELERS, YES?
CHIN YISOU WILL TELL THE FUTURE OF YOUR JOURNEY.
FEH.
NO THANKS, PAL.
TELLING FORTUNES WITH MAHJONG TILES IS A CROCK, THANK YOU.
HOW CRUEL! AND HERE I SEE...
...THAT YOUR FACES FORETELL DEATH.
HOW FRIGHTENING. HM HM!

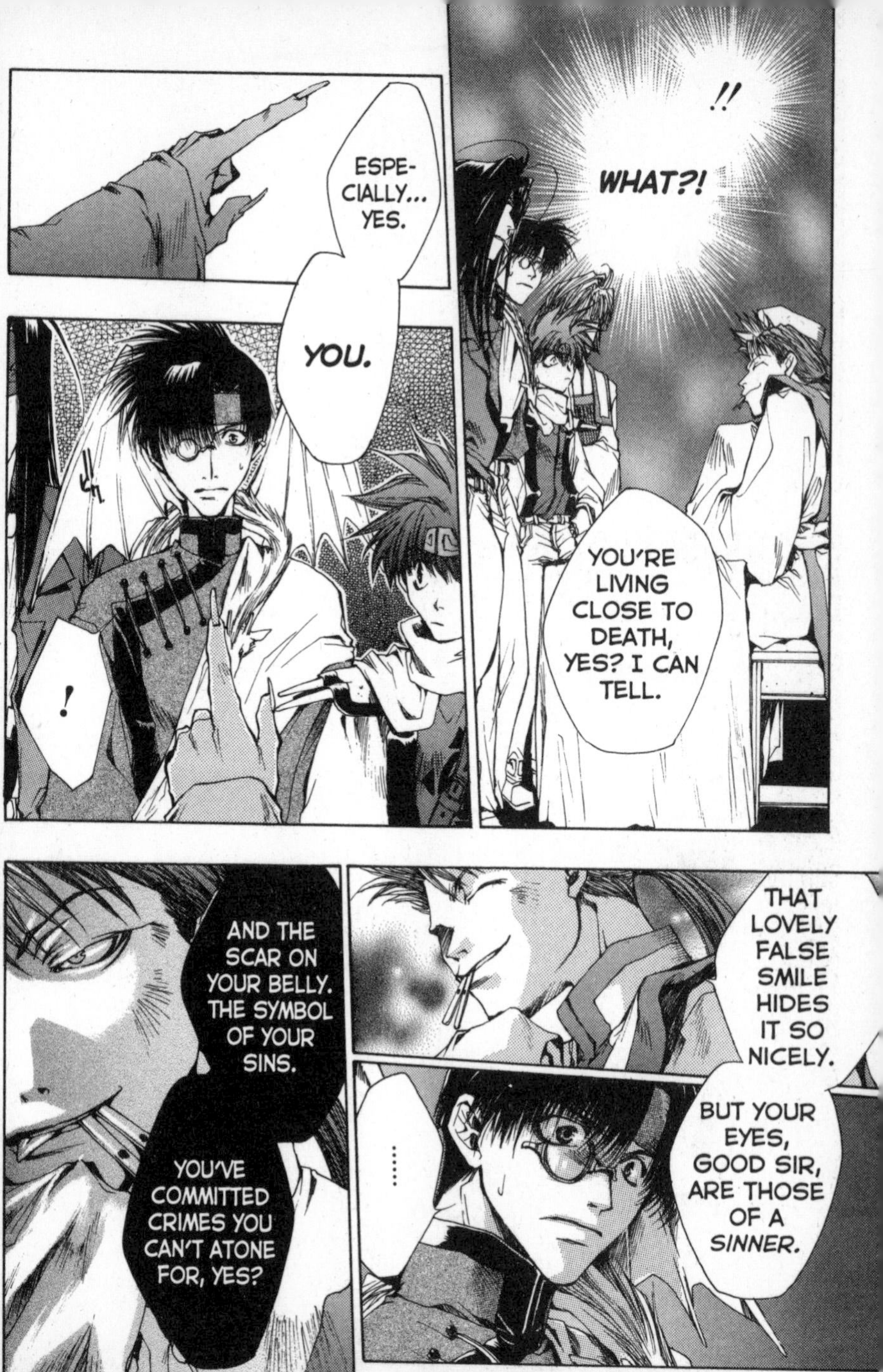
!!
WHAT?!
YOU'RE LIVING CLOSE TO DEATH, YES? I CAN TELL.
ESPECIALLY... YES.
YOU.
!
THAT LOVELY FALSE SMILE HIDES IT SO NICELY.
BUT YOUR EYES, GOOD SIR, ARE THOSE OF A SINNER.
......
AND THE SCAR ON YOUR BELLY. THE SYMBOL OF YOUR SINS.
YOU'VE COMMITTED CRIMES YOU CAN'T ATONE FOR, YES?

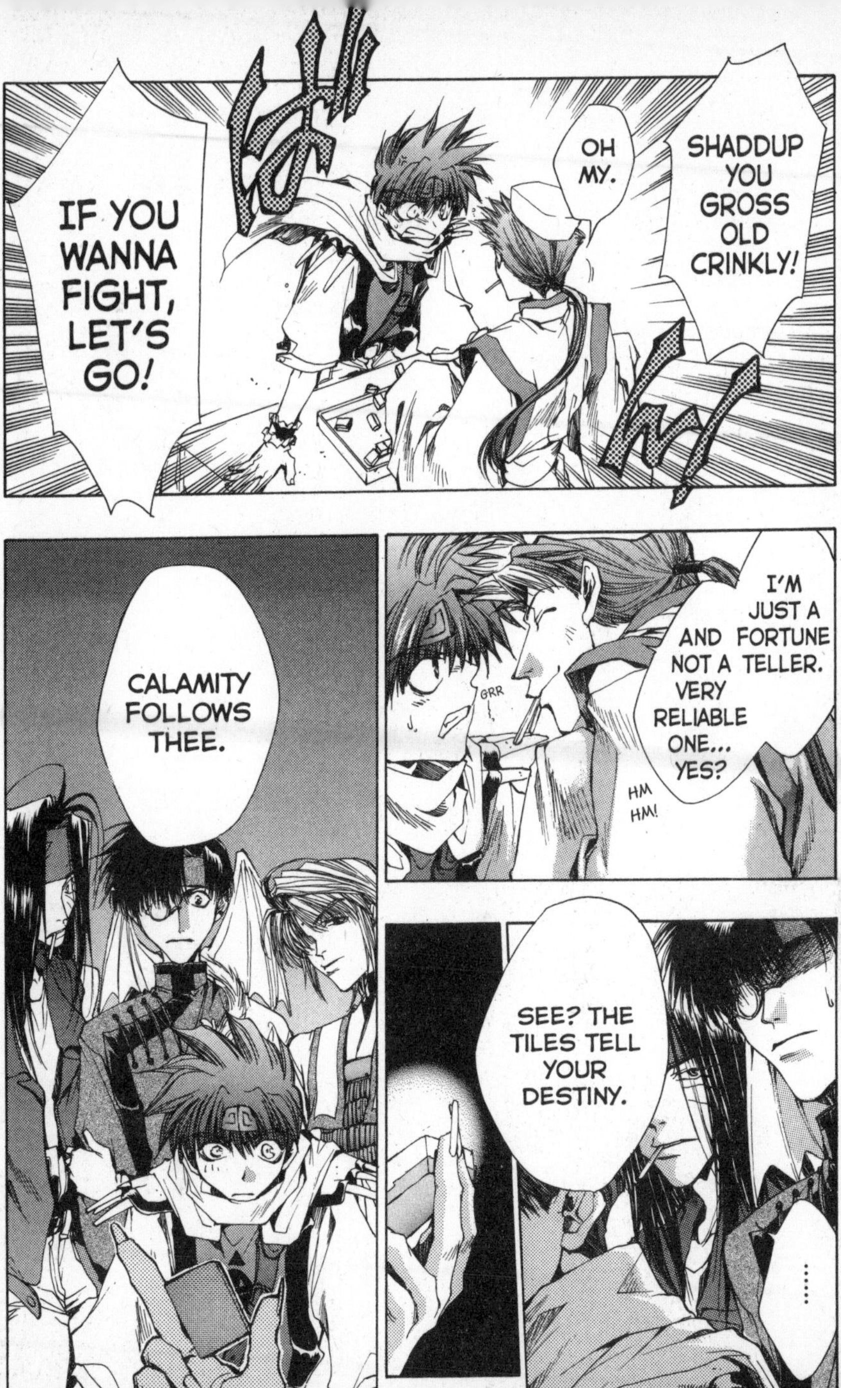
SHADDUP YOU GROSS OLD CRINKLY!
OH MY.
IF YOU WANNA FIGHT, LET'S GO!
I'M JUST A FORTUNE TELLER. AND NOT A VERY RELIABLE ONE... YES?
GRR
HM HM!
SEE? THE TILES TELL YOUR DESTINY.
......
CALAMITY FOLLOWS THEE.

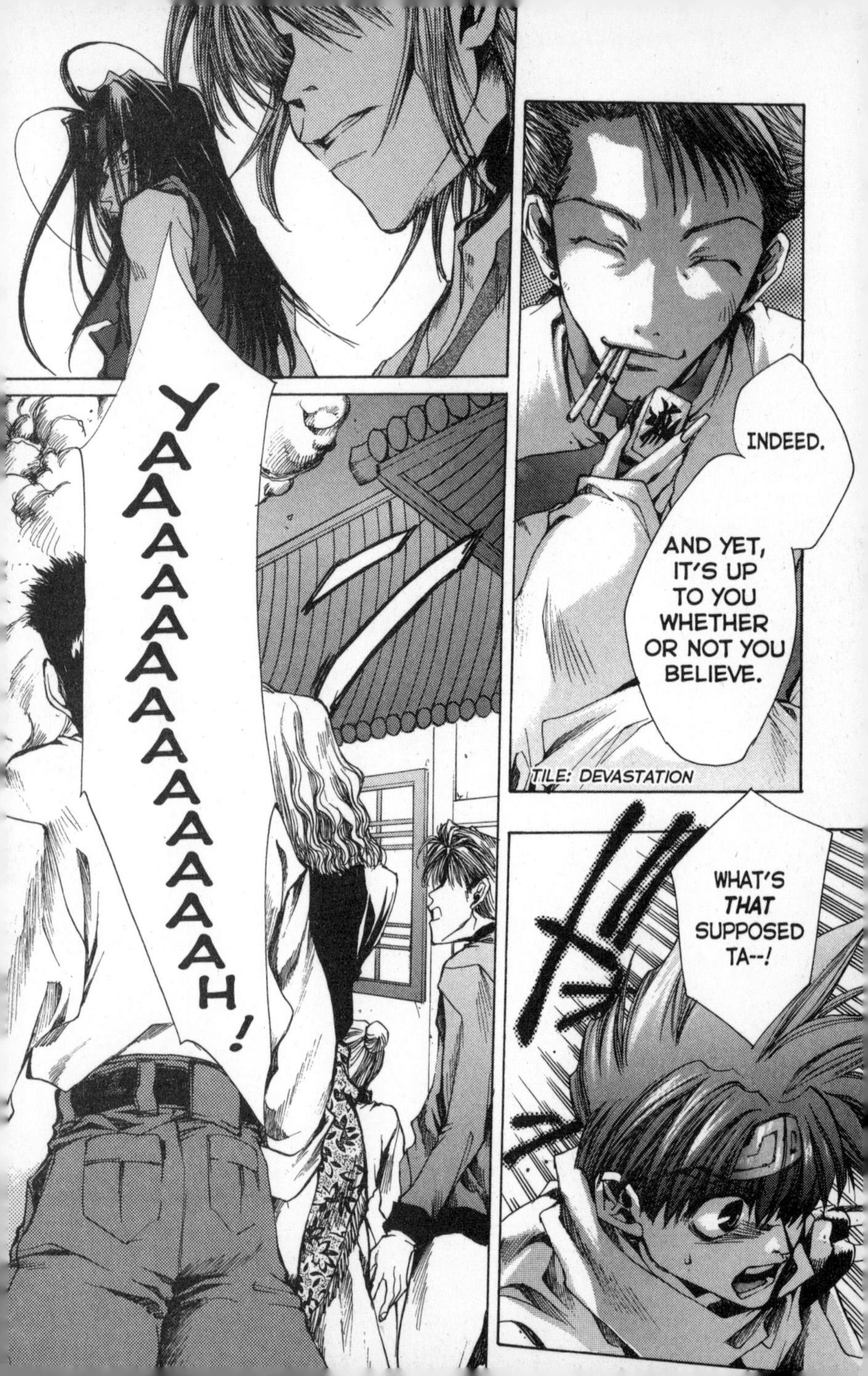
INDEED.
AND YET, IT'S UP TO YOU WHETHER OR NOT YOU BELIEVE.
TILE: DEVASTATION
YAAAAAAAAAAAAAH!
WHAT'S *THAT* SUPPOSED TA--!

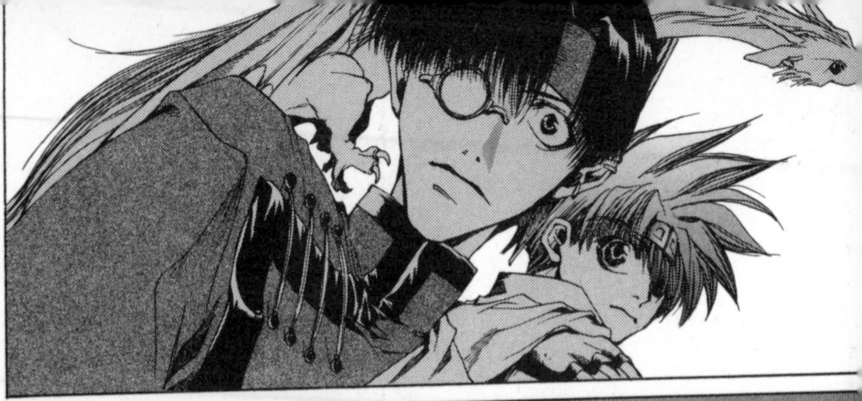
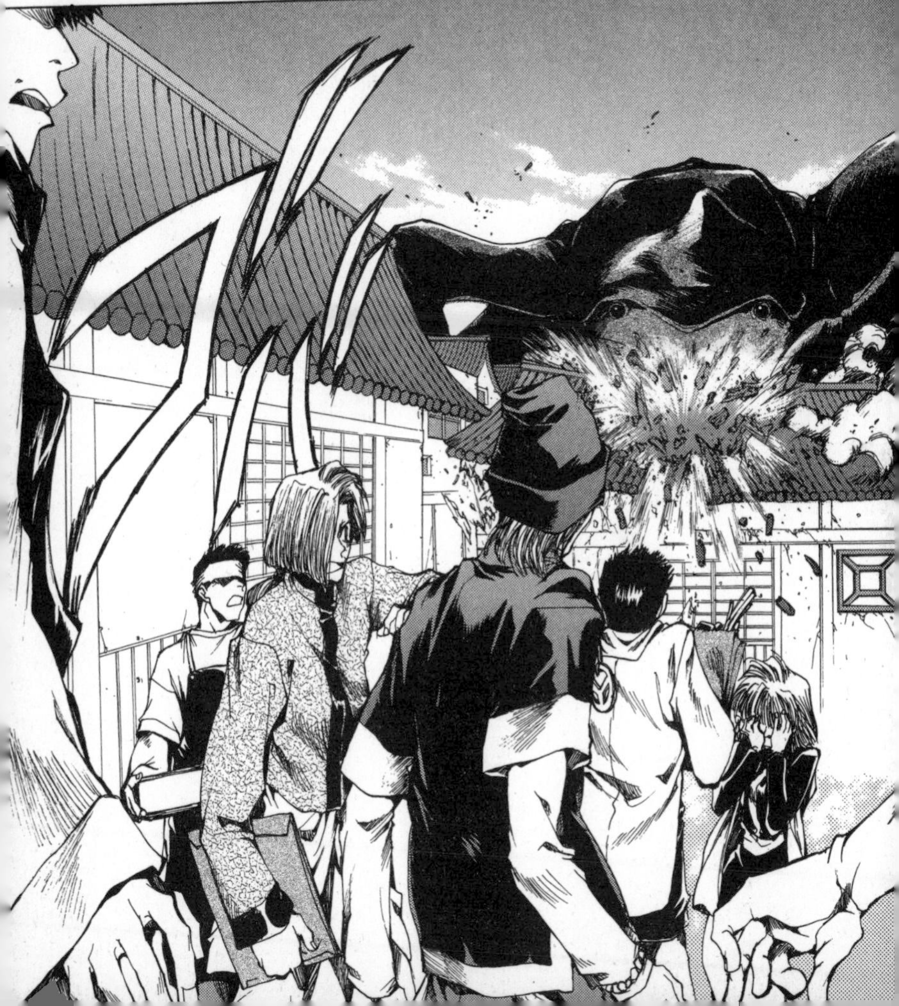

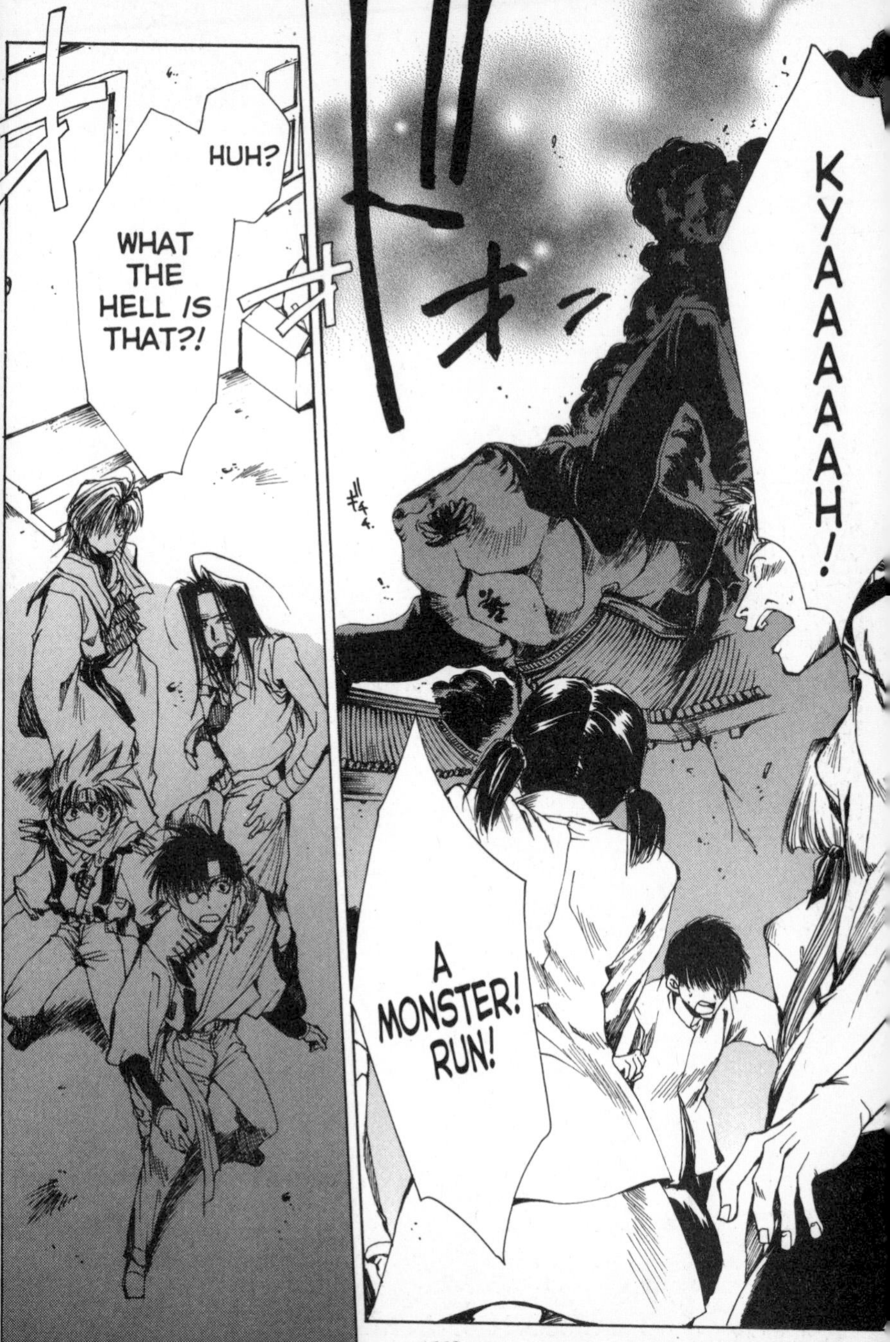
KYAAAAAAH!
A MONSTER! RUN!
HUH?
WHAT THE HELL IS THAT?!

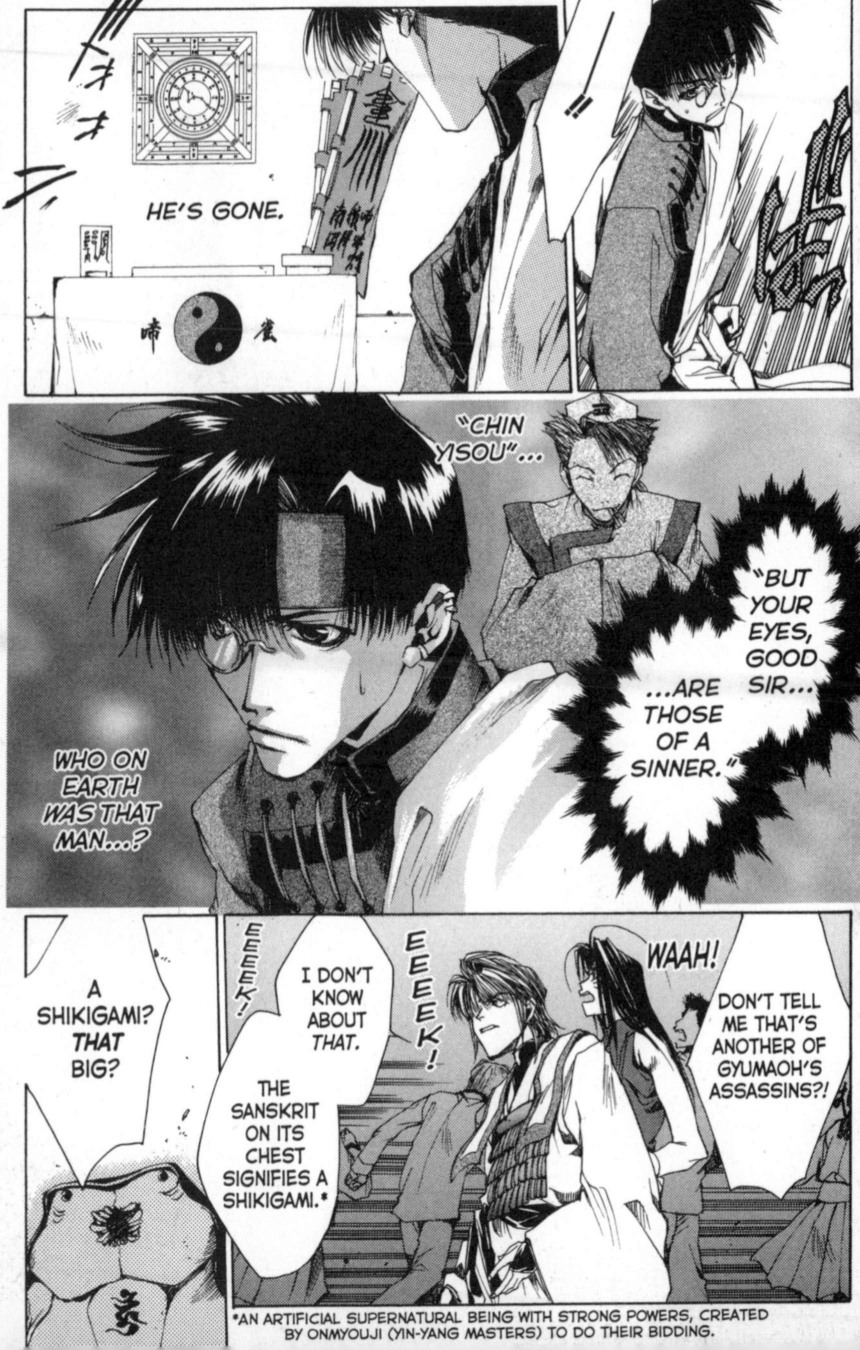
HE'S GONE.
"CHIN YISOU"...
"BUT YOUR EYES, GOOD SIR...
...ARE THOSE OF A SINNER."
WHO ON EARTH WAS THAT MAN...?
WAAH!
DON'T TELL ME THAT'S ANOTHER OF GYUMAOH'S ASSASSINS?!
EEEEK!
EEEEK!
I DON'T KNOW ABOUT THAT.
THE SANSKRIT ON ITS CHEST SIGNIFIES A SHIKIGAMI.*
A SHIKIGAMI? THAT BIG?

*AN ARTIFICIAL SUPERNATURAL BEING WITH STRONG POWERS, CREATED BY ONMYOUJI (YIN-YANG MASTERS) TO DO THEIR BIDDING.

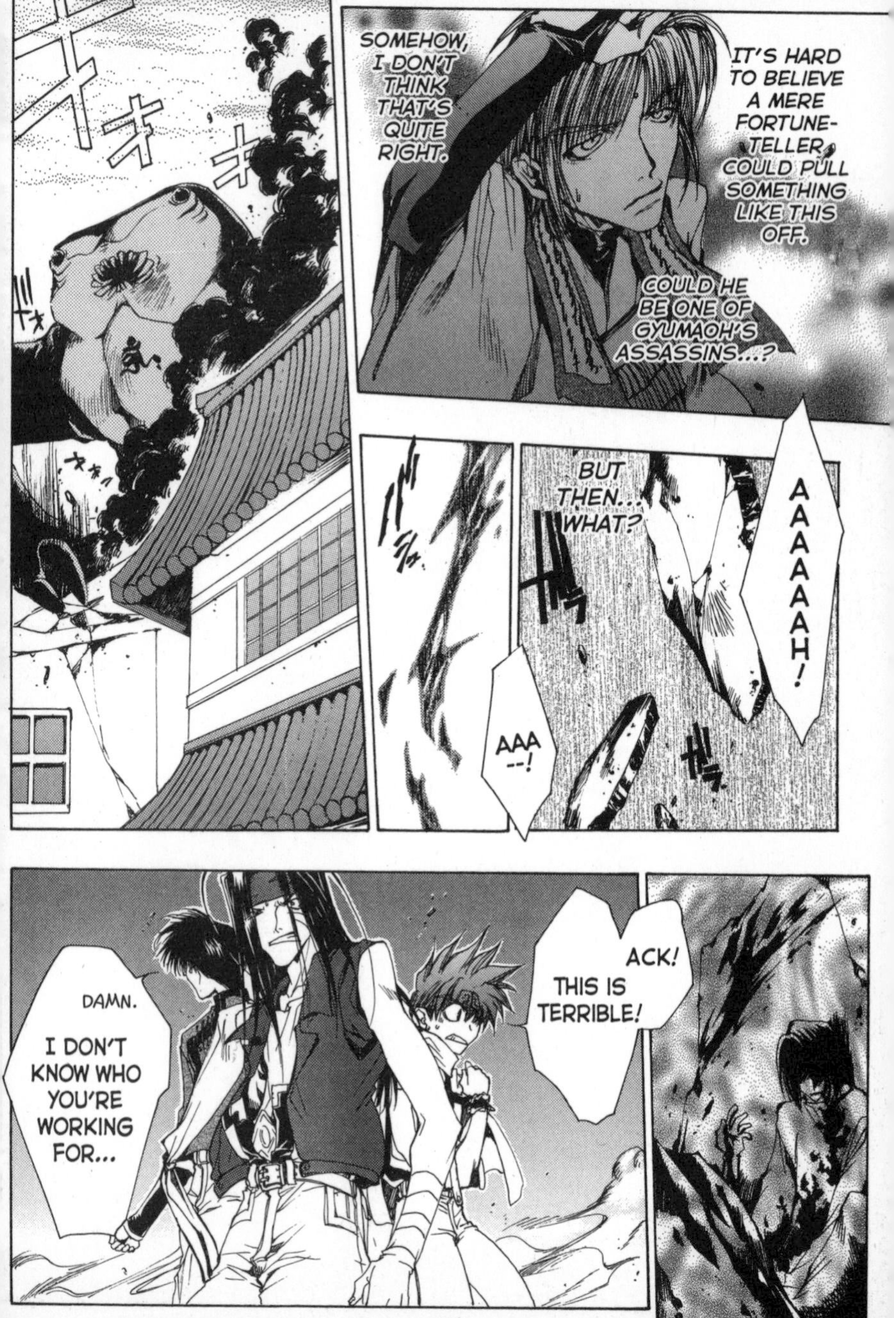
IT'S HARD TO BELIEVE A MERE FORTUNE-TELLER COULD PULL SOMETHING LIKE THIS OFF.
SOMEHOW, I DON'T THINK THAT'S QUITE RIGHT.
COULD HE BE ONE OF GYUMAOH'S ASSASSINS...?
AAAAAAAH!
BUT THEN... WHAT?
AAA--!
ACK! THIS IS TERRIBLE!
DAMN.
I DON'T KNOW WHO YOU'RE WORKING FOR...

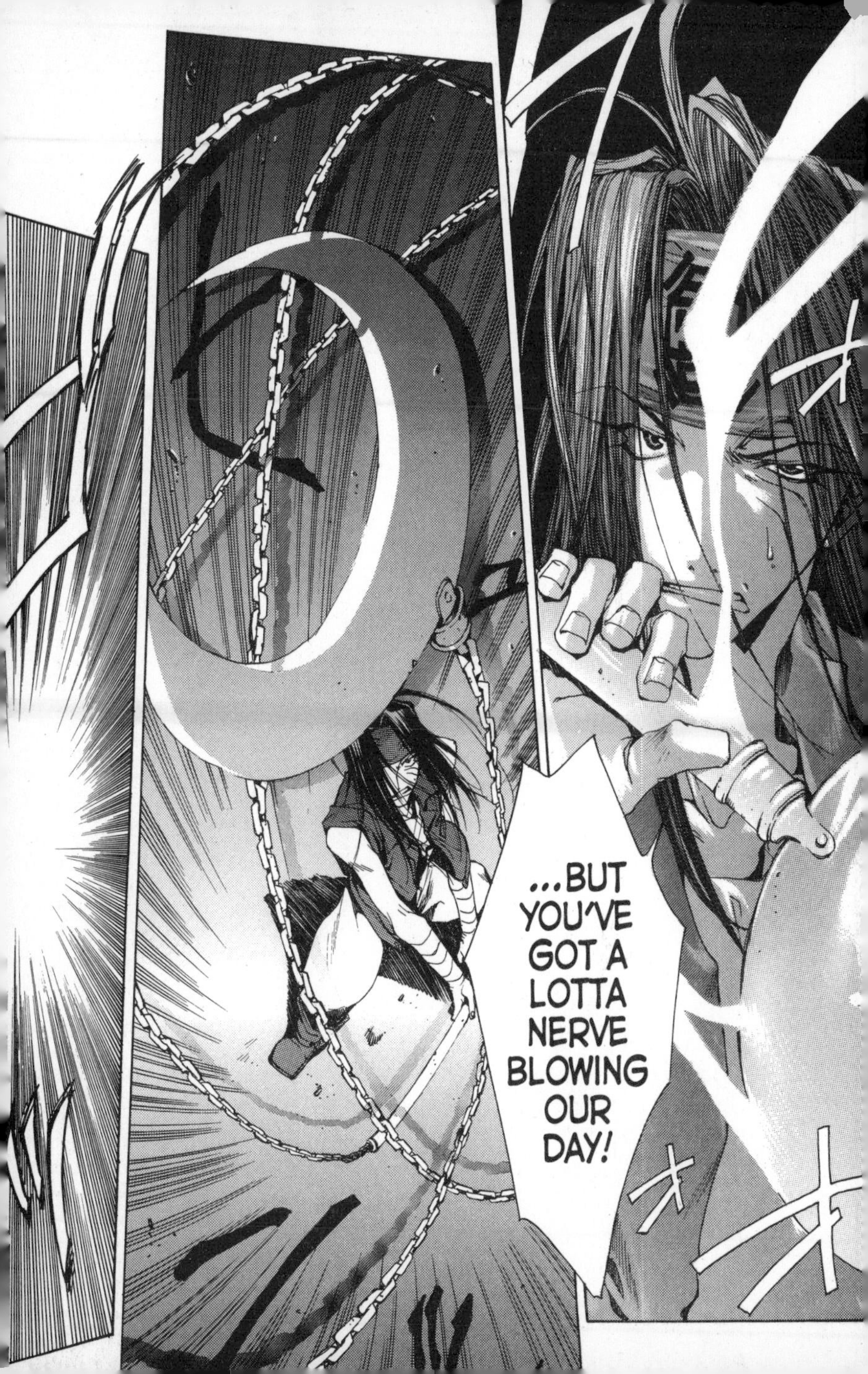
...BUT YOU'VE GOT A LOTTA NERVE BLOWING OUR DAY!

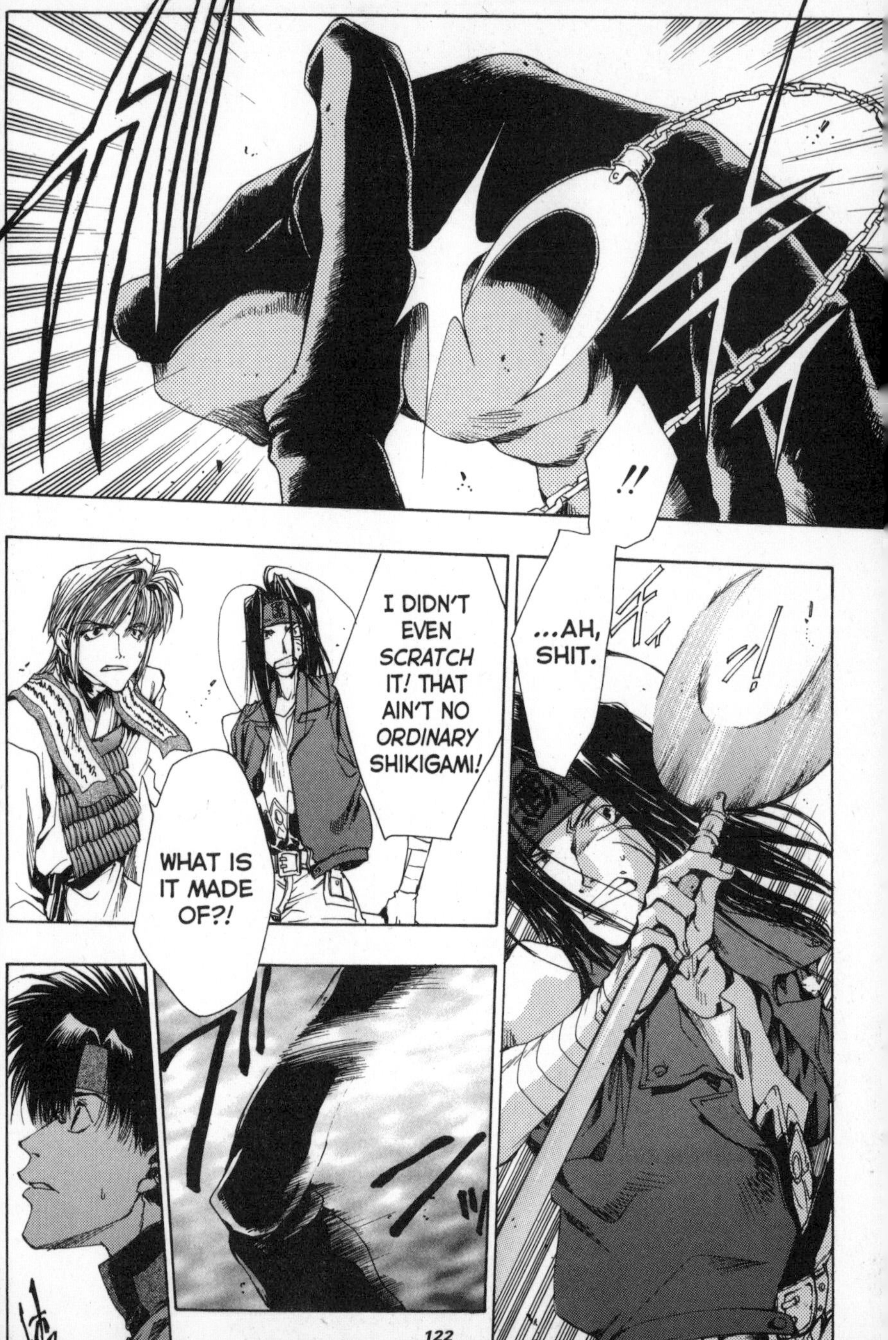
!!
...AH, SHIT.
I DIDN'T EVEN *SCRATCH* IT! THAT AIN'T NO *ORDINARY* SHIKIGAMI!
WHAT IS IT MADE OF?!

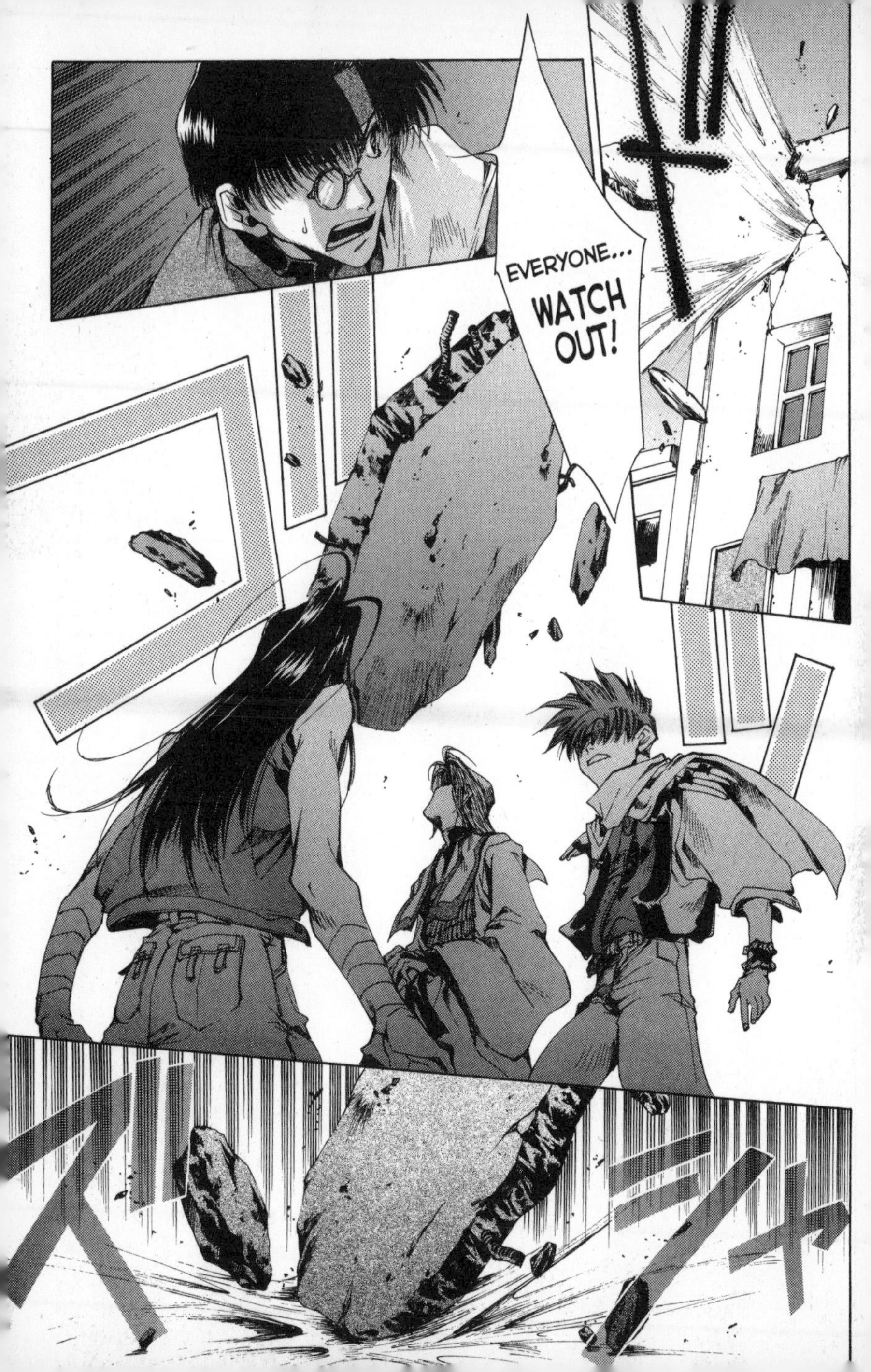
EVERYONE...
WATCH OUT!

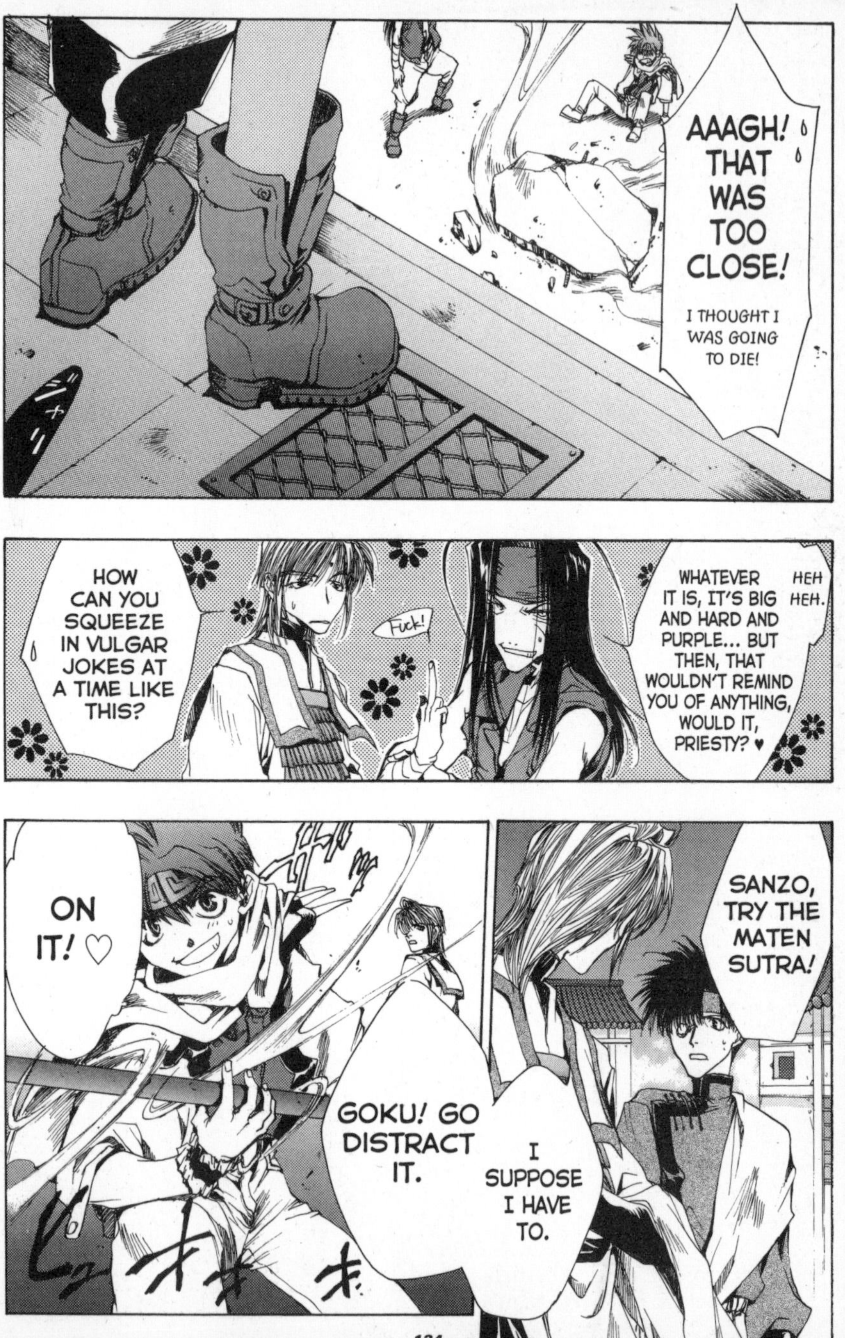
AAAGH! THAT WAS TOO CLOSE!
I THOUGHT I WAS GOING TO DIE!
HEH HEH.
WHATEVER IT IS, IT'S BIG AND HARD AND PURPLE... BUT THEN, THAT WOULDN'T REMIND YOU OF ANYTHING, WOULD IT, PRIESTY? ♥
Fuck!
HOW CAN YOU SQUEEZE IN VULGAR JOKES AT A TIME LIKE THIS?
SANZO, TRY THE MATEN SUTRA!
I SUPPOSE I HAVE TO.
GOKU! GO DISTRACT IT.
ON IT! ♡

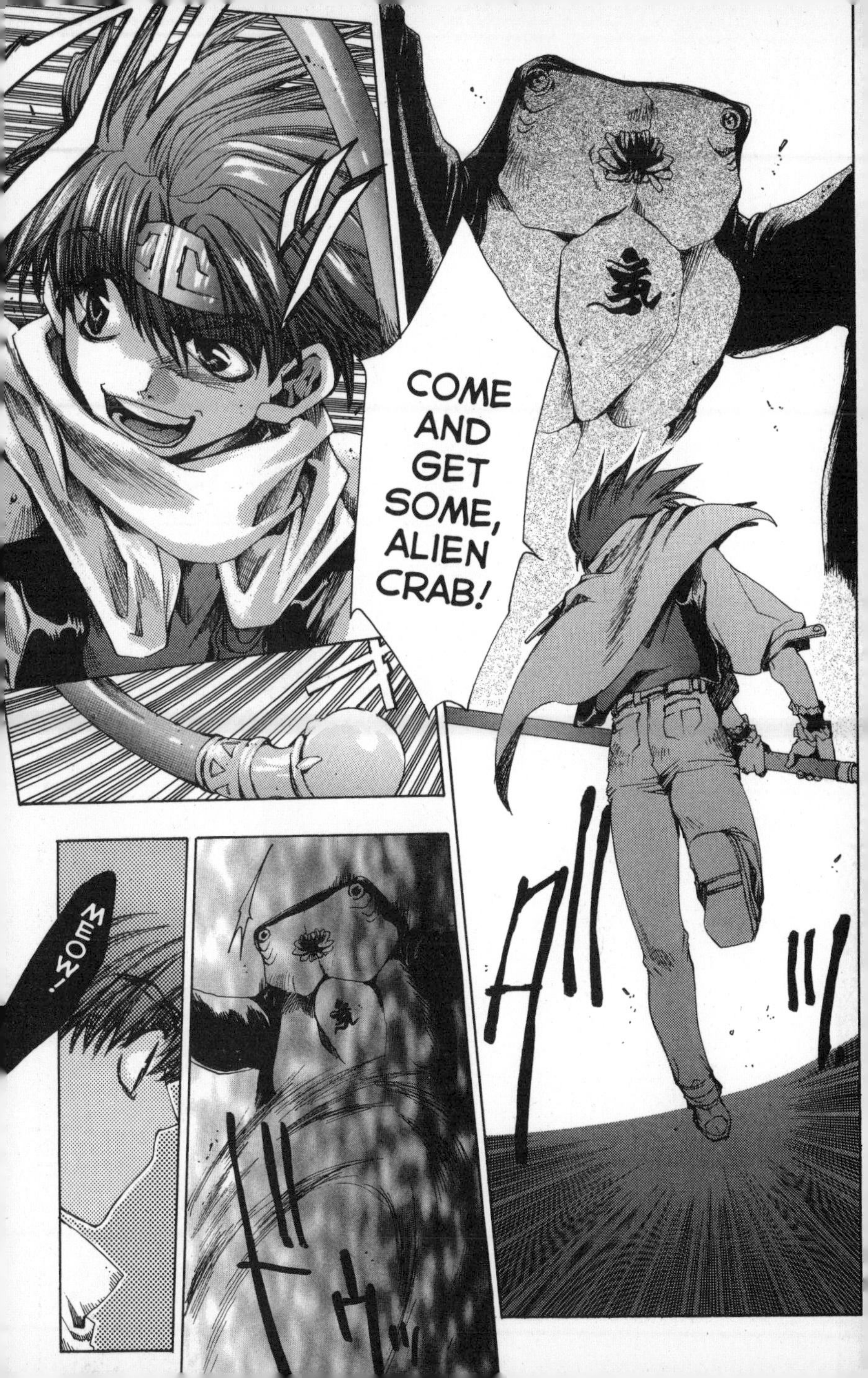
COME AND GET SOME, ALIEN CRAB!
MEOW!-

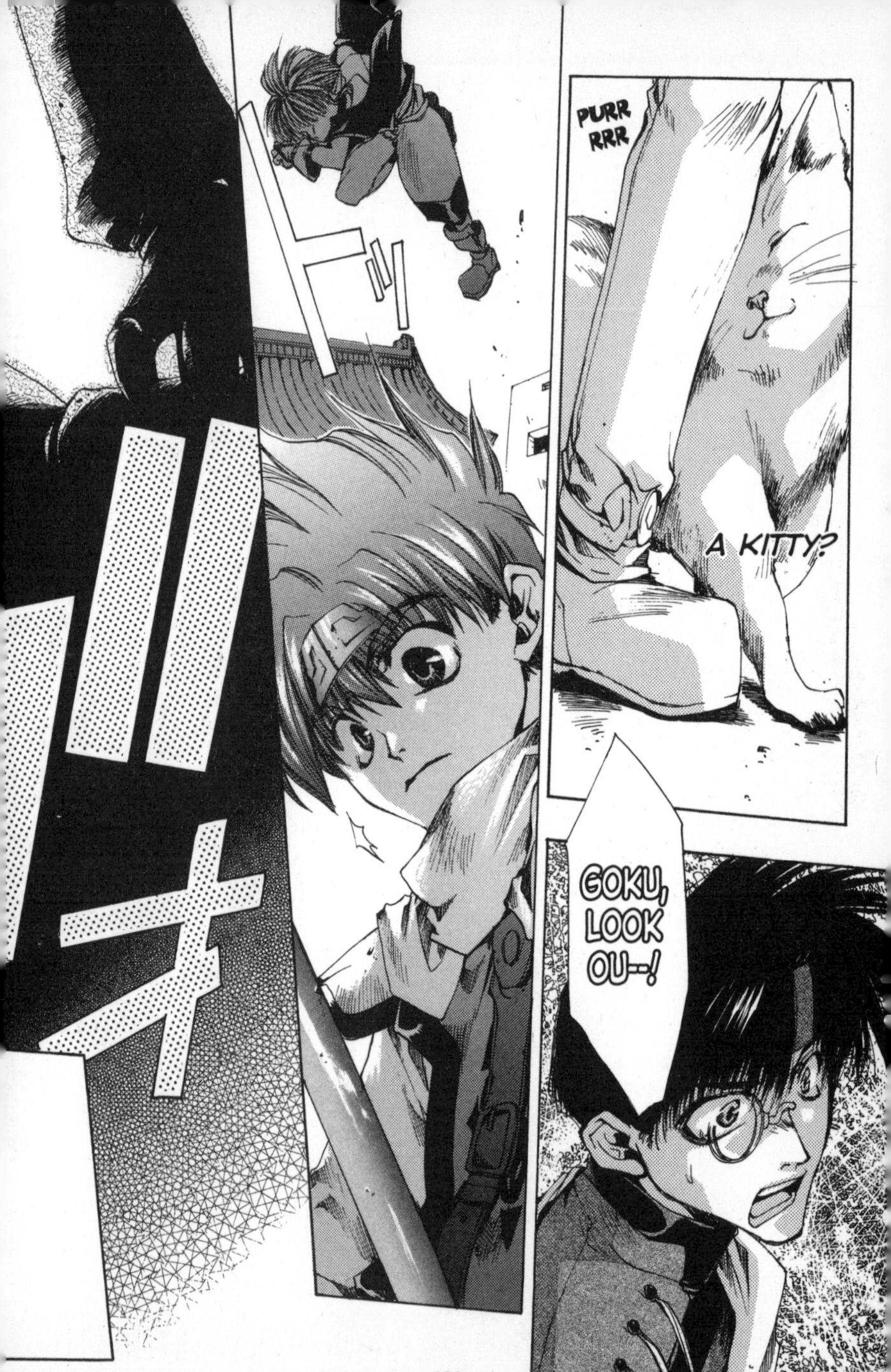
PURR RRR
A KITTY?
GOKU, LOOK OU--!

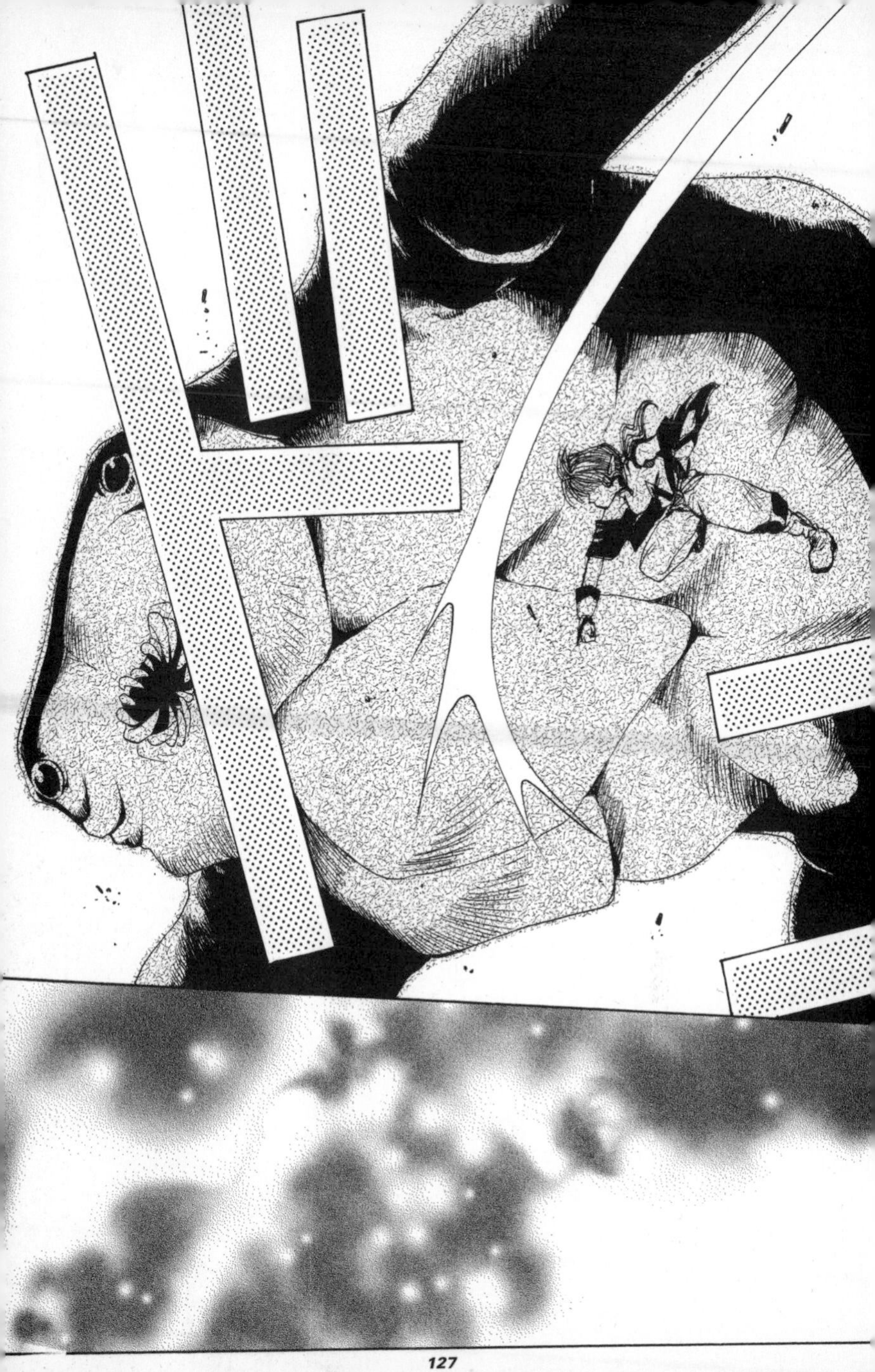

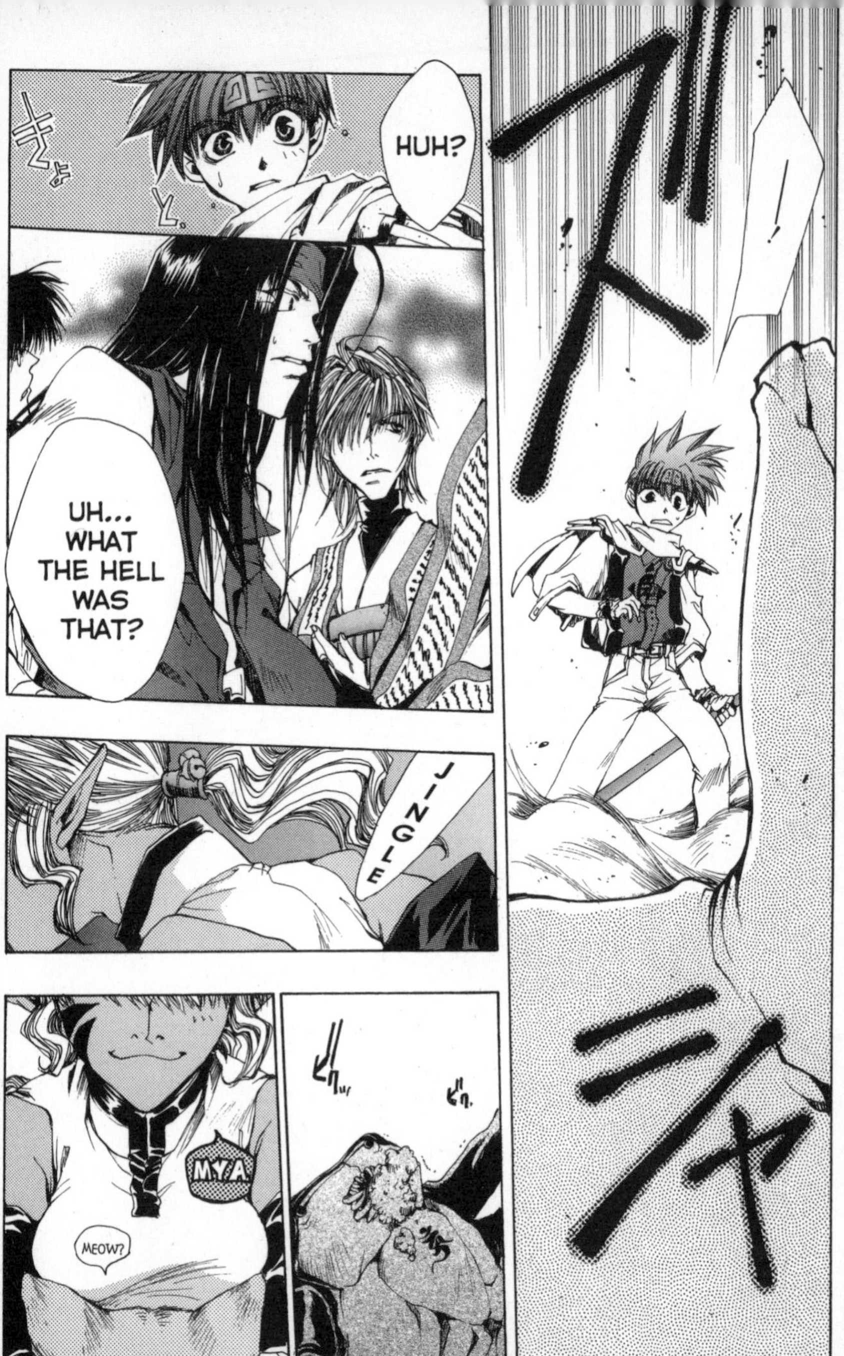
!
HUH?
UH... WHAT THE HELL WAS THAT?
JINGLE
M.Y.A.
MEOW?

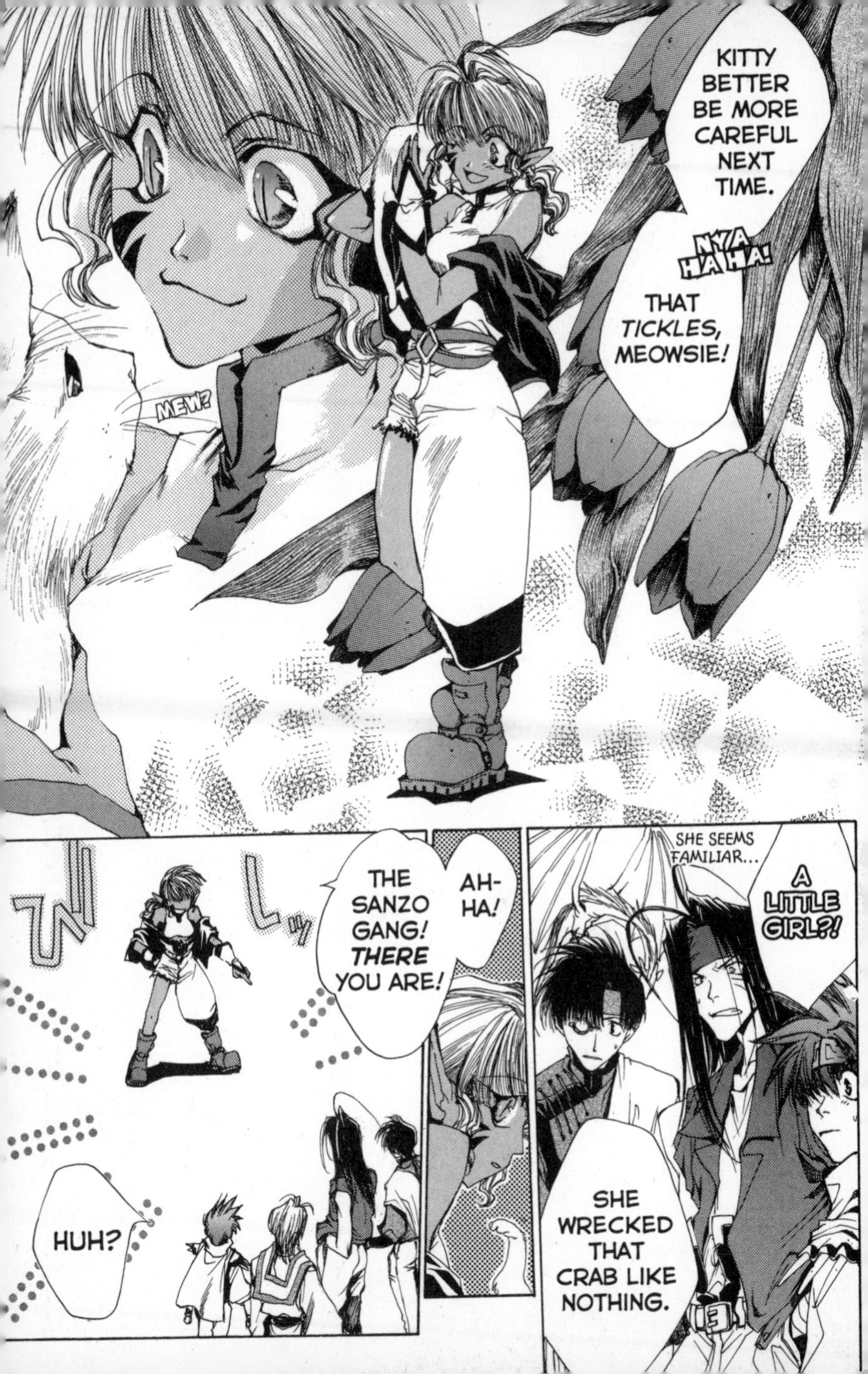
KITTY BETTER BE MORE CAREFUL NEXT TIME.
NYA HA HA!
THAT *TICKLES,* MEOWSIE!
MEW?
SHE SEEMS FAMILIAR...
A LITTLE GIRL?!
SHE WRECKED THAT CRAB LIKE NOTHING.
AH-HA!
THE SANZO GANG! *THERE* YOU ARE!
HUH?

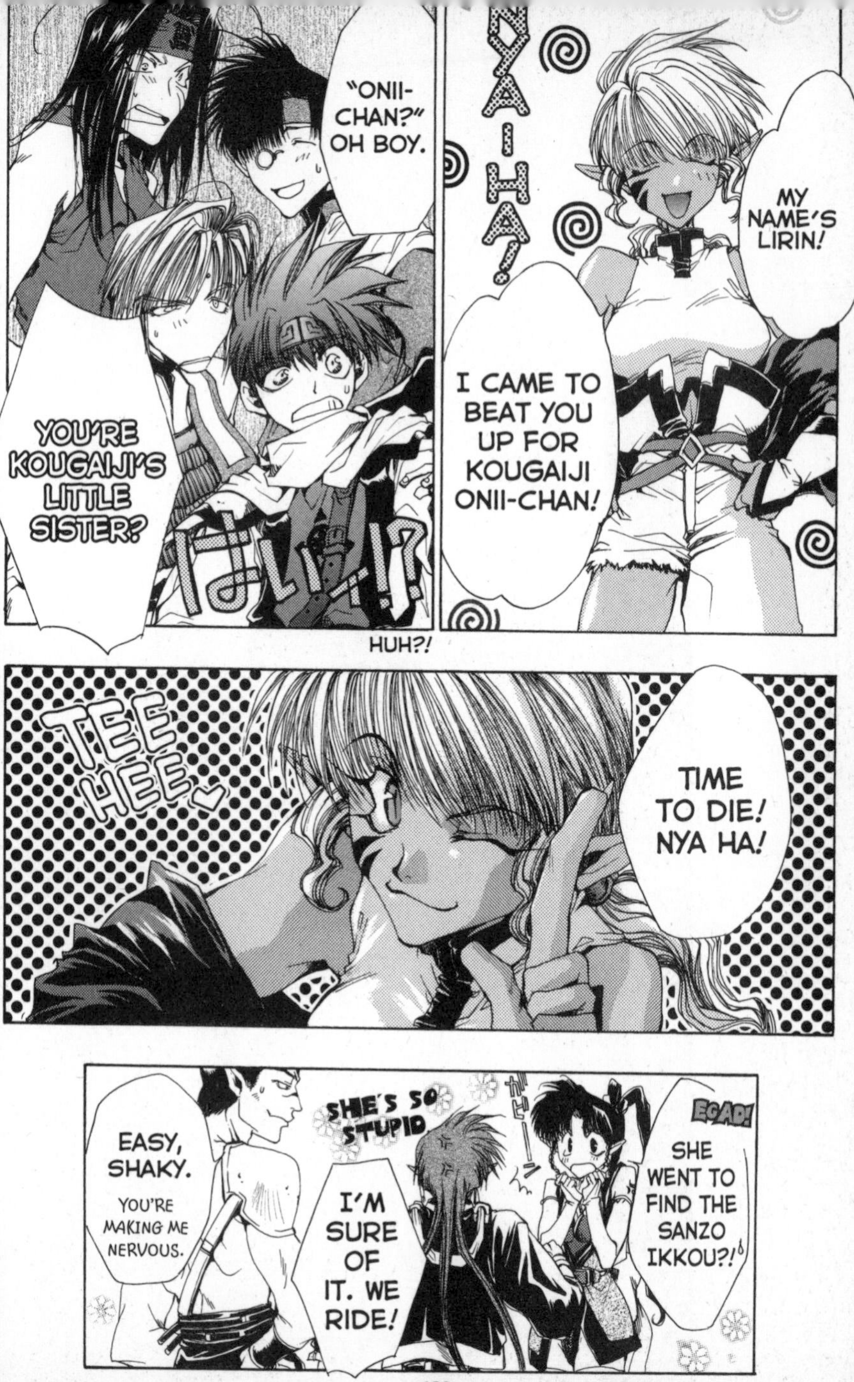
NYA-HA?!
MY NAME'S LIRIN!
I CAME TO BEAT YOU UP FOR KOUGAIJI ONII-CHAN!
"ONII-CHAN?" OH BOY.
YOU'RE KOUGAIJI'S LITTLE SISTER?
HUH?!
TEE HEE
TIME TO DIE! NYA HA!
EGAD!
SHE WENT TO FIND THE SANZO IKKOU?!
SHE'S SO STUPID
I'M SURE OF IT. WE RIDE!
EASY, SHAKY.
YOU'RE MAKING ME NERVOUS.

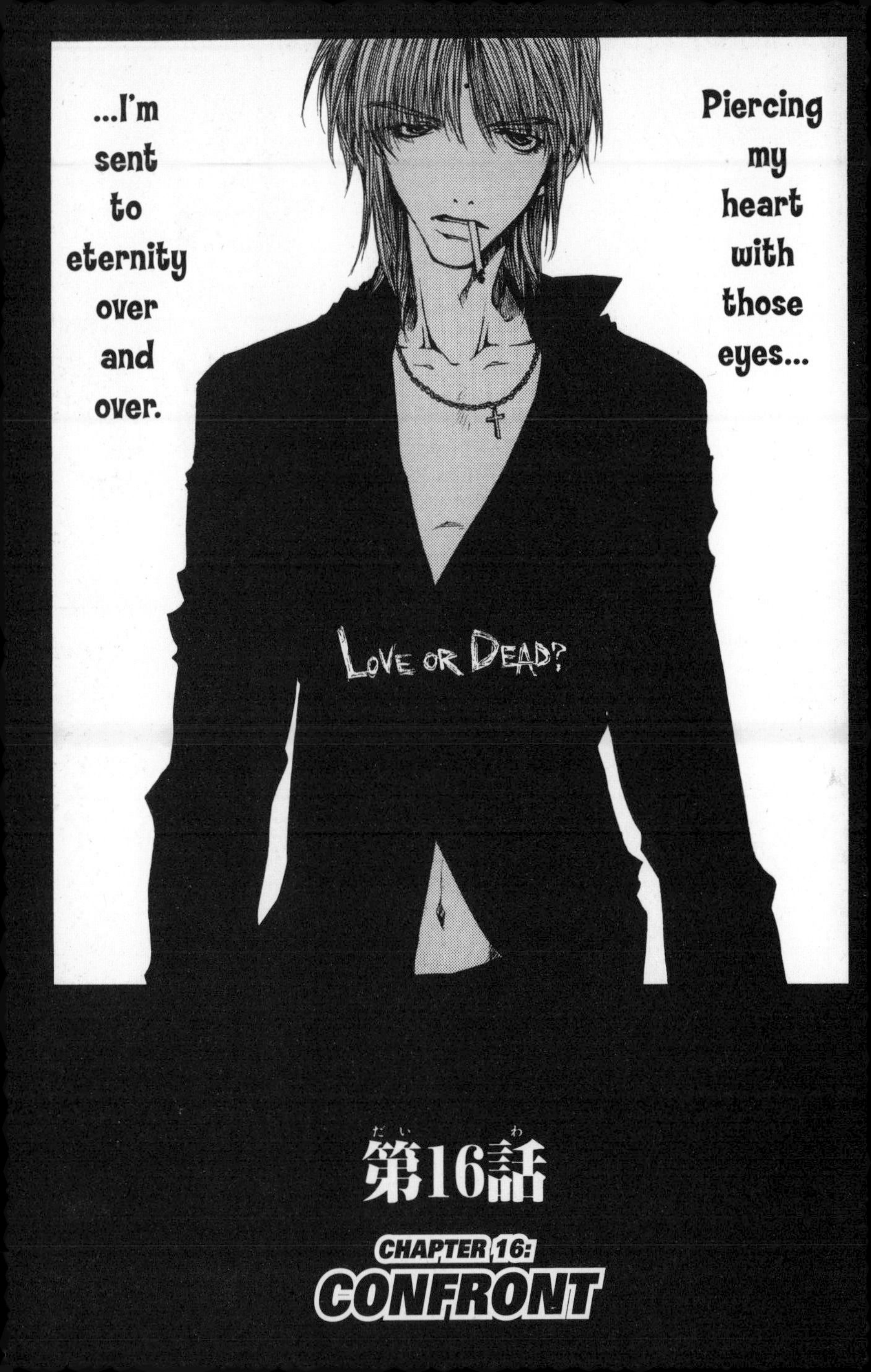
Piercing my heart with those eyes...
...I'm sent to eternity over and over.
LOVE OR DEAD?
第16話
CHAPTER 16:
CONFRONT

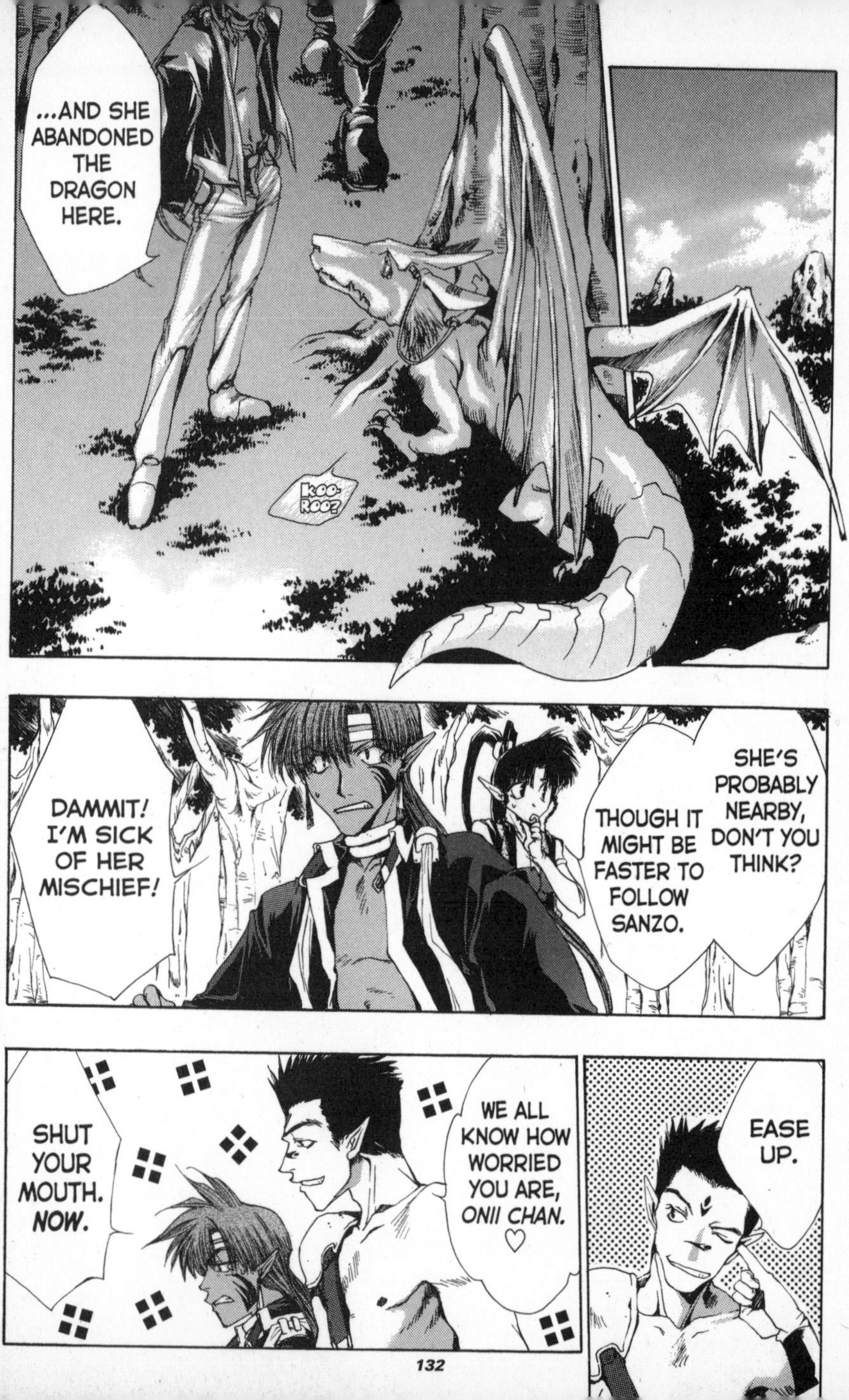
...AND SHE ABANDONED THE DRAGON HERE.
KOO-ROO?
SHE'S PROBABLY NEARBY, DON'T YOU THINK?
THOUGH IT MIGHT BE FASTER TO FOLLOW SANZO.
DAMMIT! I'M SICK OF HER MISCHIEF!
EASE UP.
WE ALL KNOW HOW WORRIED YOU ARE, ONII CHAN. ♡
SHUT YOUR MOUTH. *NOW.*

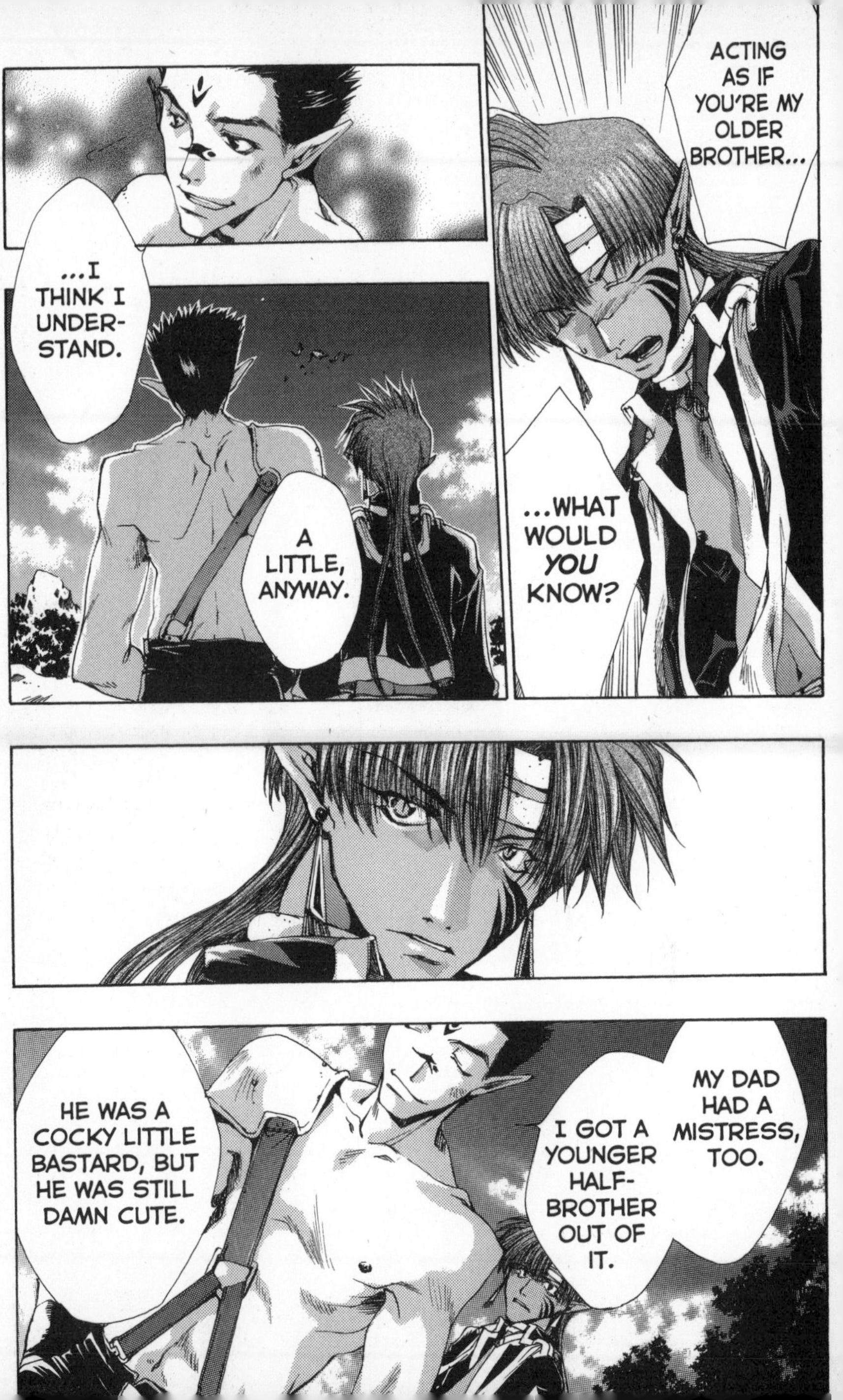
ACTING AS IF YOU'RE MY OLDER BROTHER...
...WHAT WOULD *YOU* KNOW?
...I THINK I UNDER-STAND.
A LITTLE, ANYWAY.
MY DAD HAD A MISTRESS, TOO.
I GOT A YOUNGER HALF-BROTHER OUT OF IT.
HE WAS A COCKY LITTLE BASTARD, BUT HE WAS STILL DAMN CUTE.

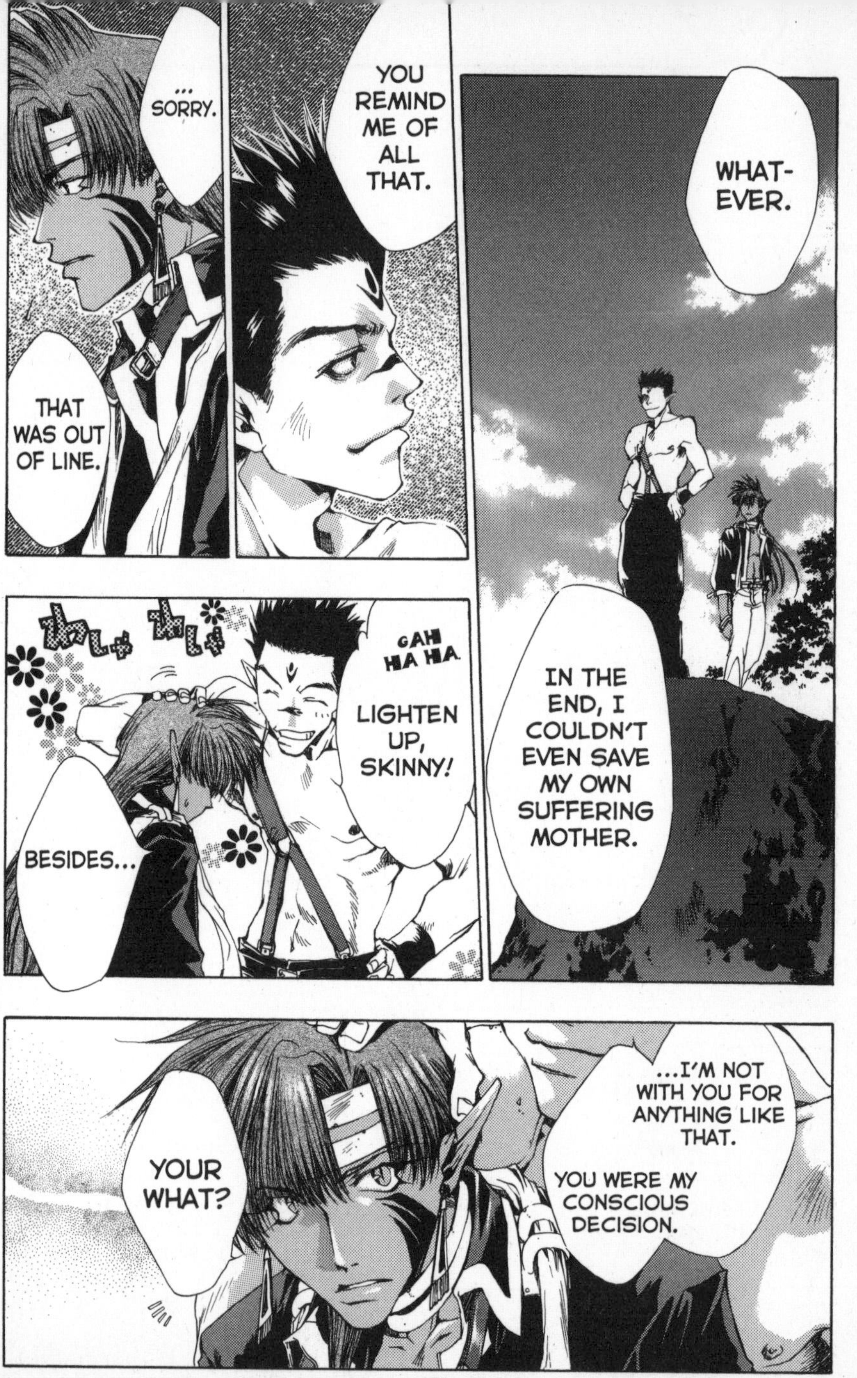
YOU REMIND ME OF ALL THAT.
... SORRY.
THAT WAS OUT OF LINE.
WHAT-EVER.
IN THE END, I COULDN'T EVEN SAVE MY OWN SUFFERING MOTHER.
GAH HA HA.
LIGHTEN UP, SKINNY!
BESIDES...
...I'M NOT WITH YOU FOR ANYTHING LIKE THAT.
YOU WERE MY CONSCIOUS DECISION.
YOUR WHAT?

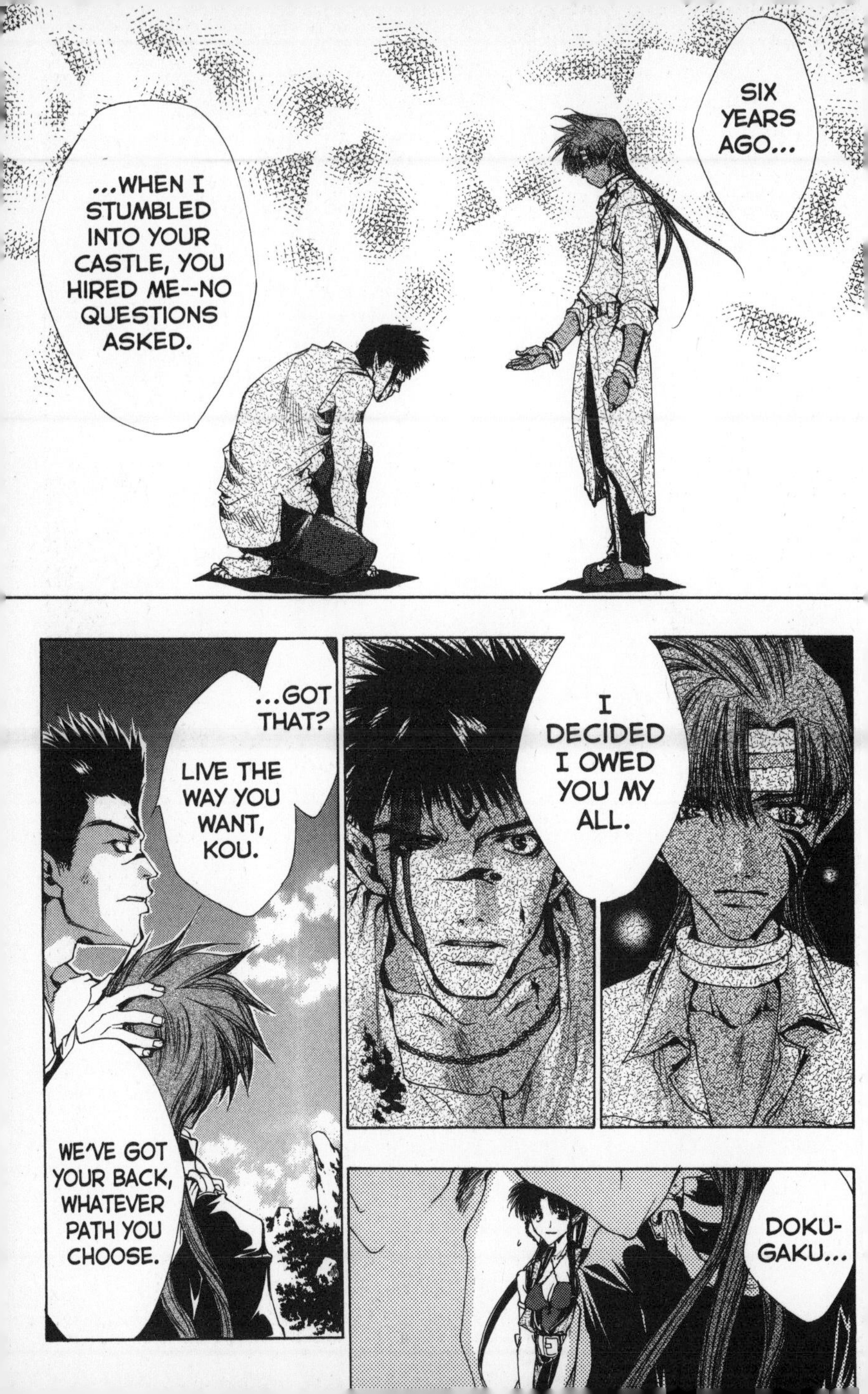
SIX YEARS AGO...
...WHEN I STUMBLED INTO YOUR CASTLE, YOU HIRED ME--NO QUESTIONS ASKED.
I DECIDED I OWED YOU MY ALL.
DOKU-GAKU...
...GOT THAT?
LIVE THE WAY YOU WANT, KOU.
WE'VE GOT YOUR BACK, WHATEVER PATH YOU CHOOSE.

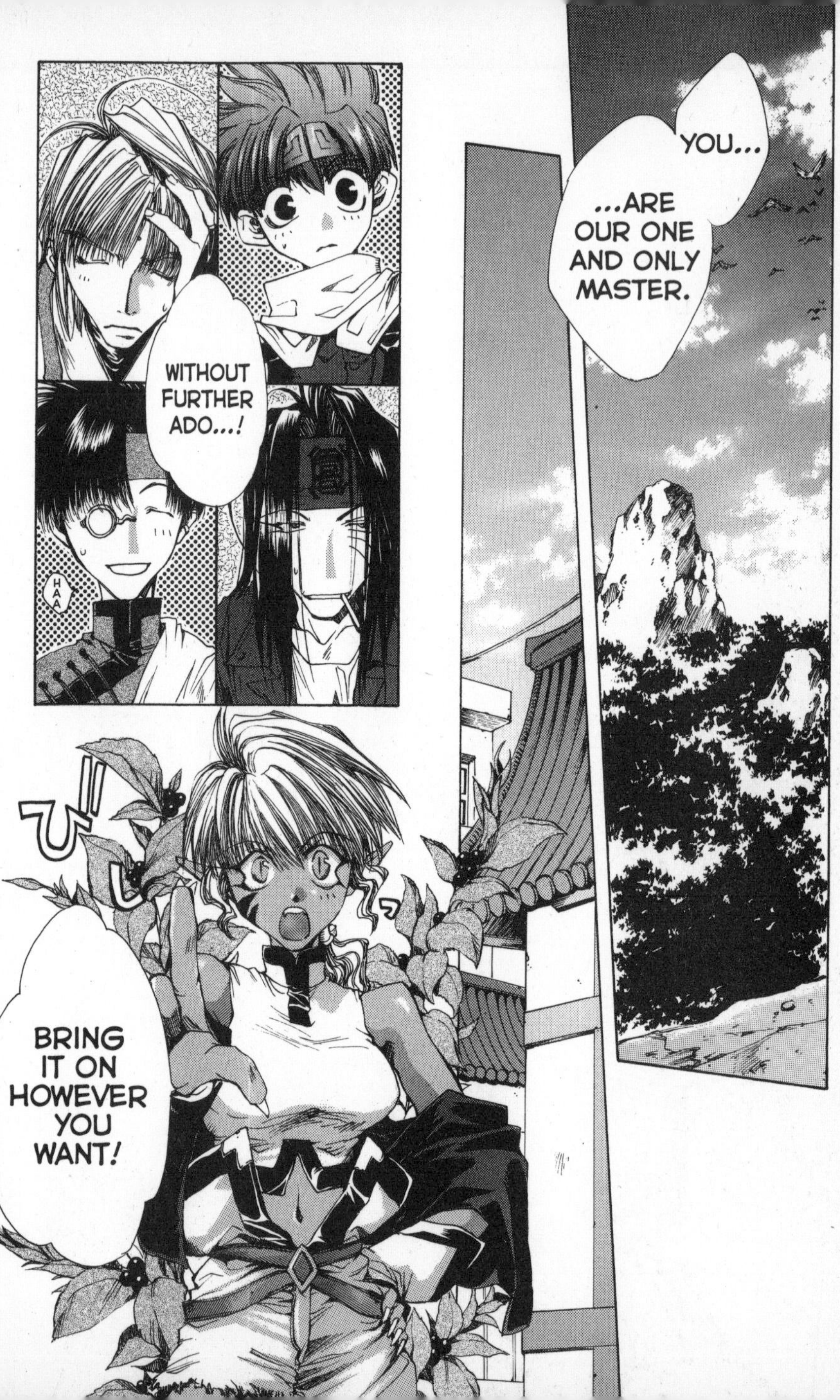
YOU...
...ARE OUR ONE AND ONLY MASTER.
WITHOUT FURTHER ADO...!
HAA
BRING IT ON HOWEVER YOU WANT!

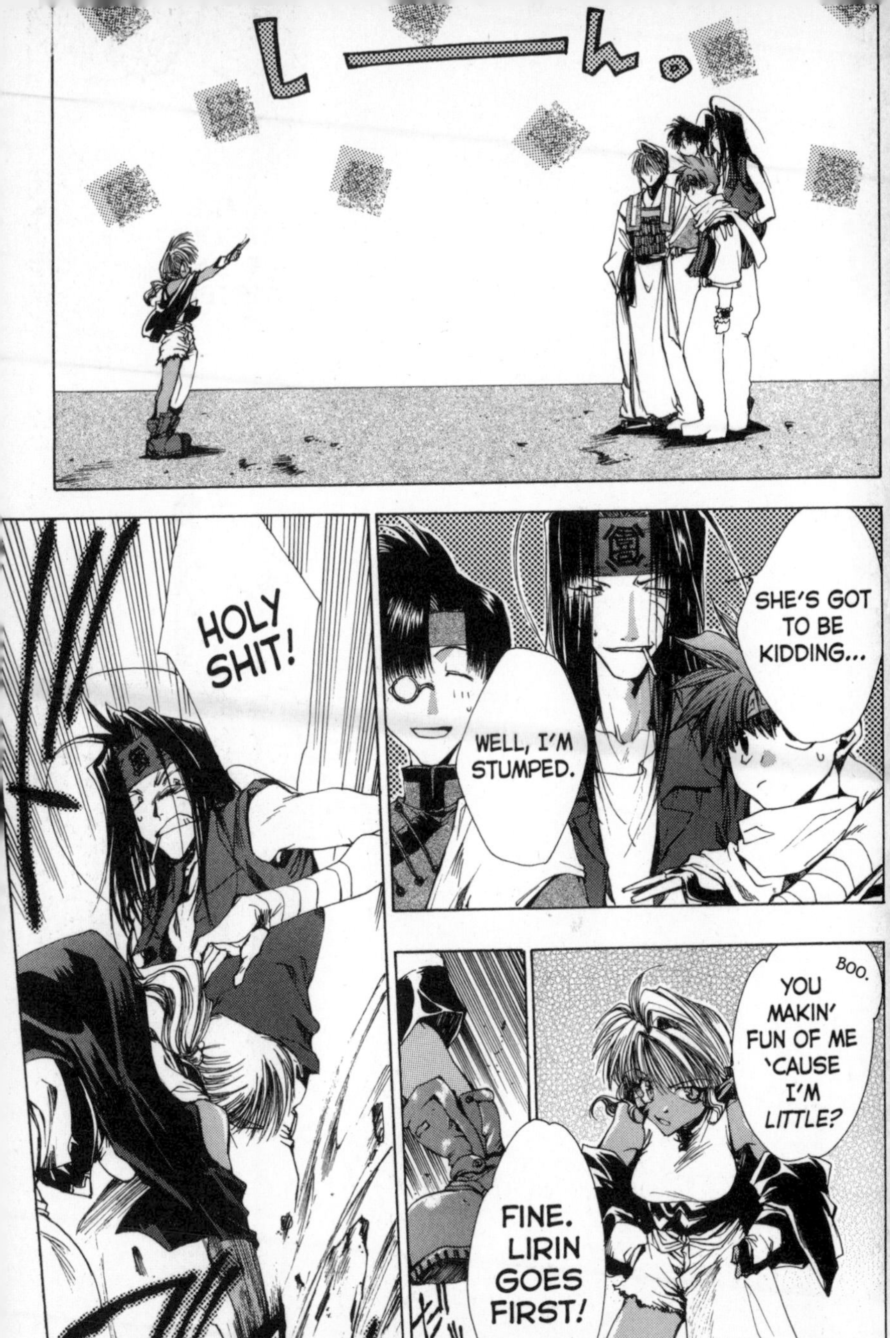
し———ん。
SHE'S GOT TO BE KIDDING...
WELL, I'M STUMPED.
BOO.
YOU MAKIN' FUN OF ME 'CAUSE I'M LITTLE?
FINE. LIRIN GOES FIRST!
HOLY SHIT!

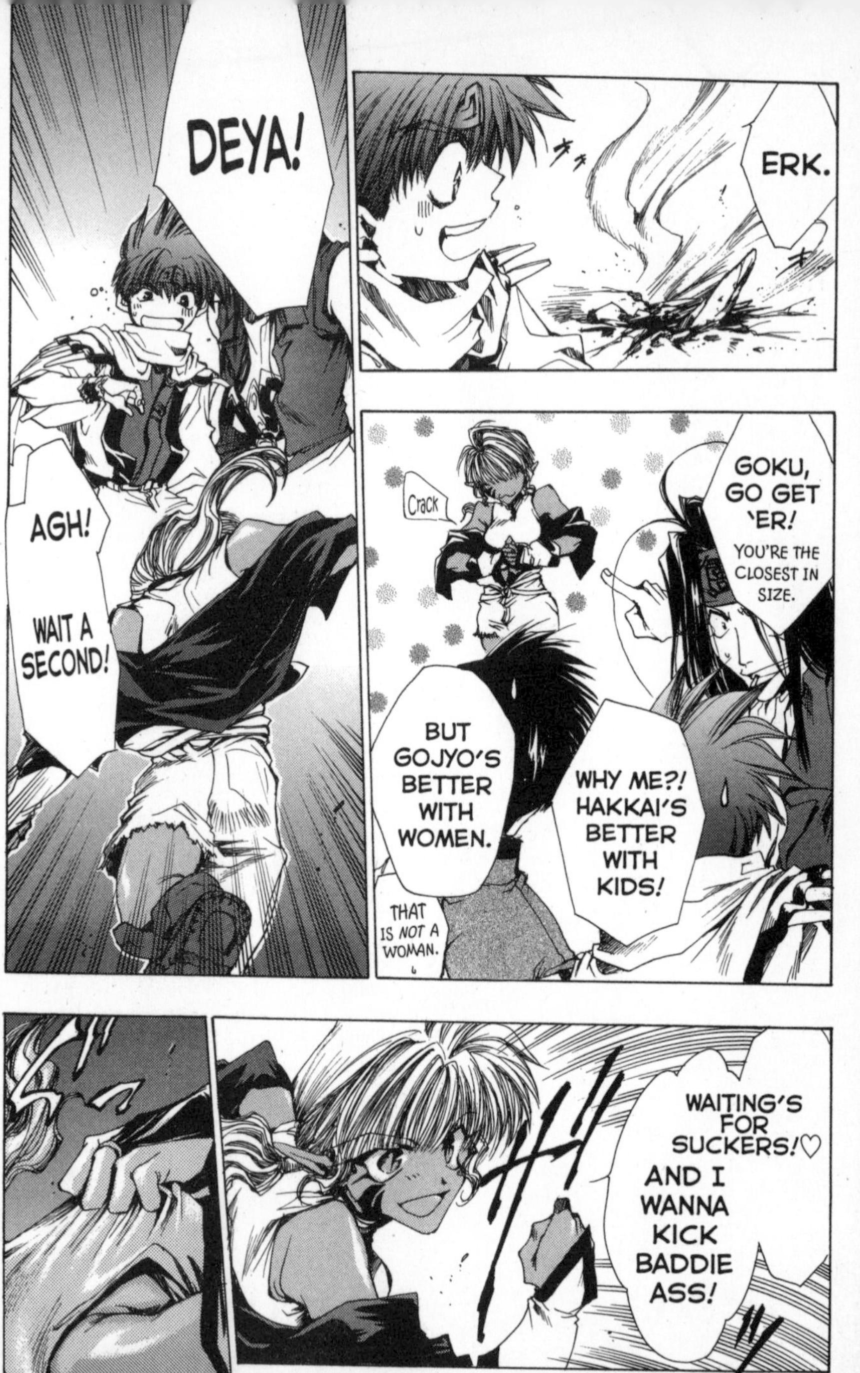
ERK.
Crack
GOKU, GO GET 'ER!
YOU'RE THE CLOSEST IN SIZE.
WHY ME?! HAKKAI'S BETTER WITH KIDS!
BUT GOJYO'S BETTER WITH WOMEN.
THAT IS *NOT* A WOMAN.
DEYA!
AGH!
WAIT A SECOND!
WAITING'S FOR SUCKERS!♡
AND I WANNA KICK BADDIE ASS!

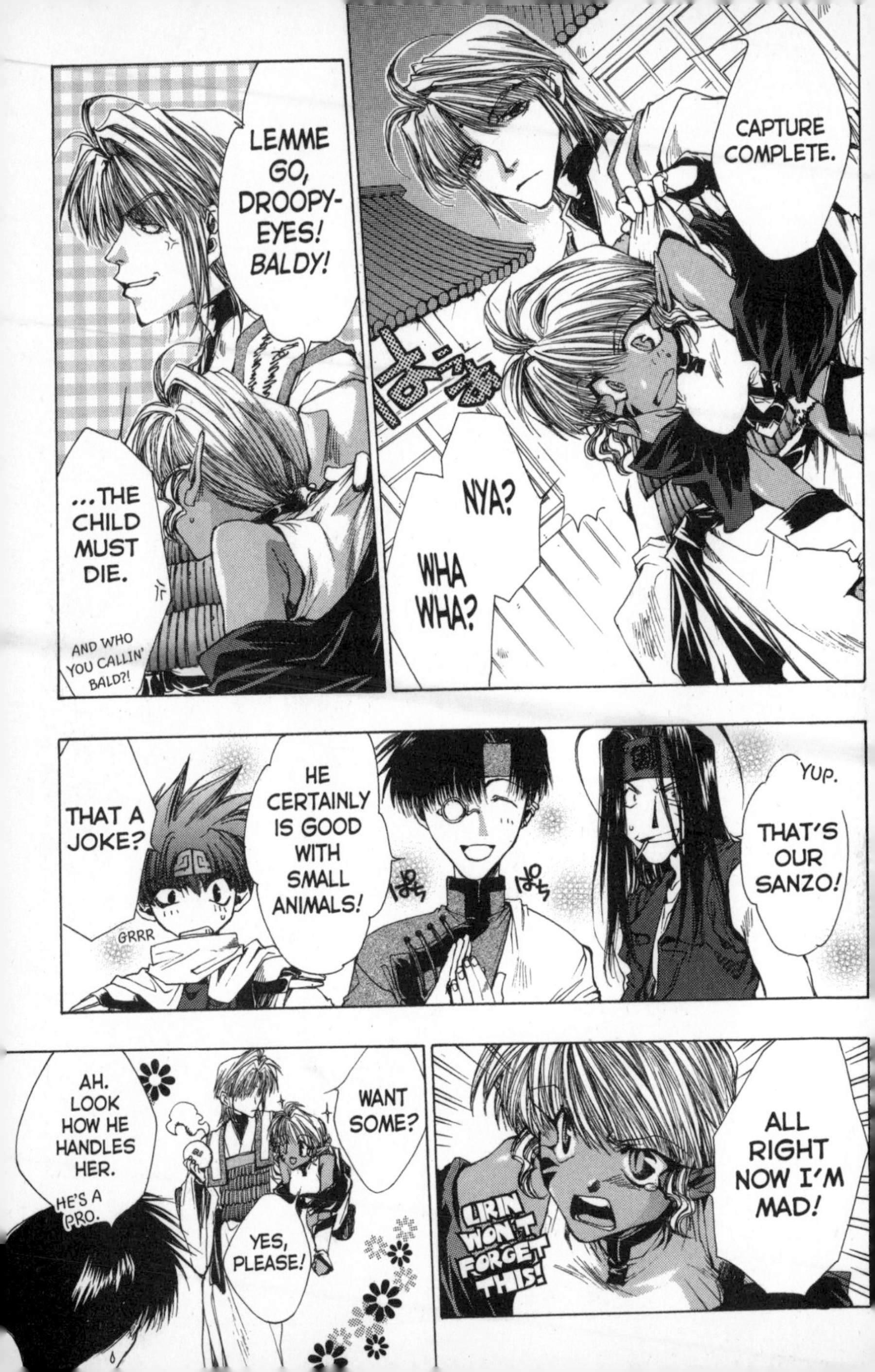
CAPTURE COMPLETE.
NYA?
WHA WHA?
LEMME GO, DROOPY-EYES! BALDY!
...THE CHILD MUST DIE.
AND WHO YOU CALLIN' BALD?!
YUP.
THAT'S OUR SANZO!
HE CERTAINLY IS GOOD WITH SMALL ANIMALS!
THAT A JOKE?
GRRR
ALL RIGHT NOW I'M MAD!
LIRIN WON'T FORGET THIS!
WANT SOME?
YES, PLEASE!
AH. LOOK HOW HE HANDLES HER.
HE'S A PRO.

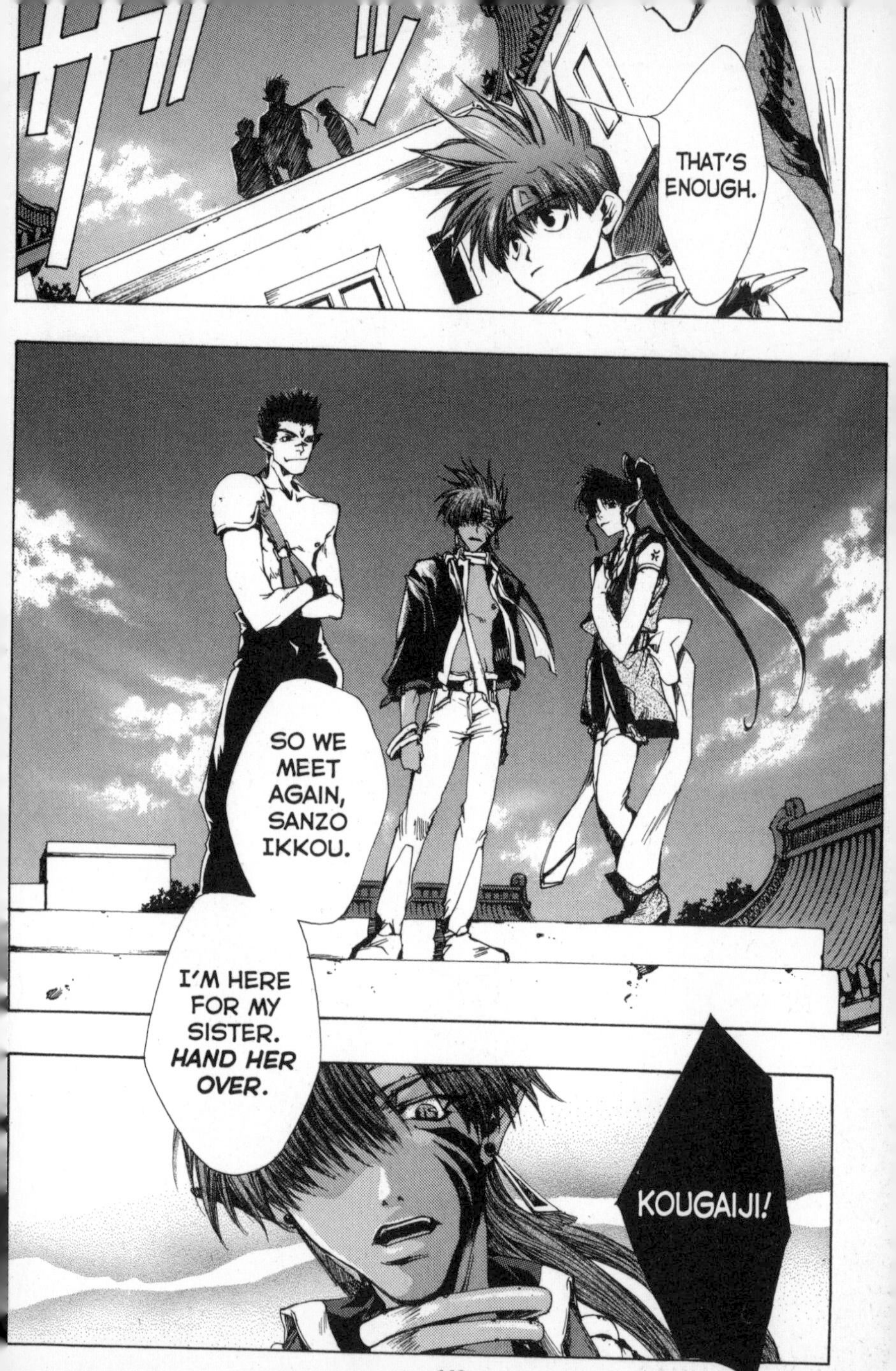
THAT'S ENOUGH.
SO WE MEET AGAIN, SANZO IKKOU.
I'M HERE FOR MY SISTER. HAND HER OVER.
KOUGAIJI!

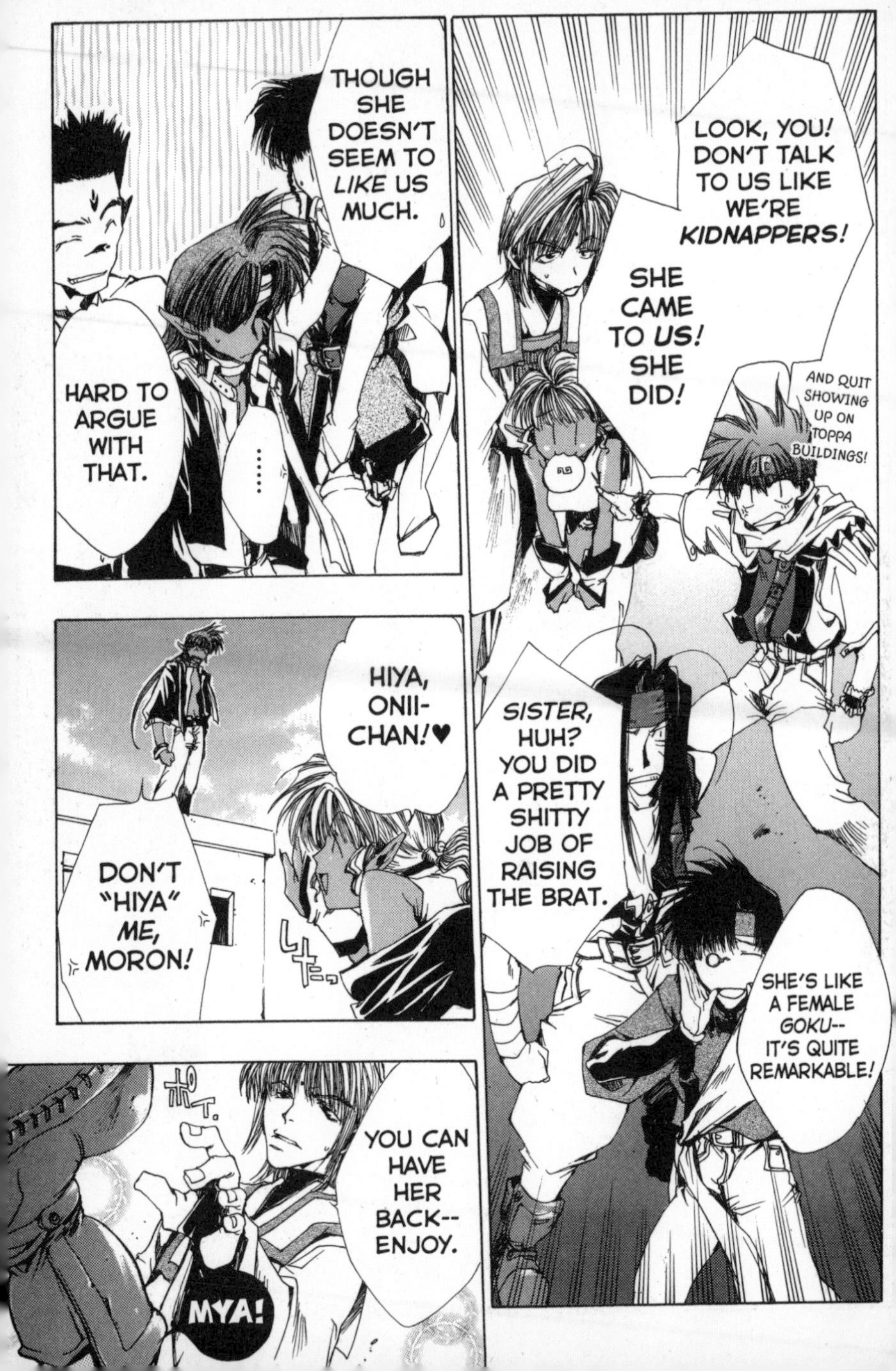
LOOK, YOU! DON'T TALK TO US LIKE WE'RE KIDNAPPERS!
SHE CAME TO US! SHE DID!
AND QUIT SHOWING UP ON TOPPA BUILDINGS!
SISTER, HUH? YOU DID A PRETTY SHITTY JOB OF RAISING THE BRAT.
SHE'S LIKE A FEMALE GOKU-- IT'S QUITE REMARKABLE!
THOUGH SHE DOESN'T SEEM TO LIKE US MUCH.
HARD TO ARGUE WITH THAT.
......
HIYA, ONII-CHAN!♥
DON'T "HIYA" ME, MORON!
YOU CAN HAVE HER BACK-- ENJOY.
MYA!

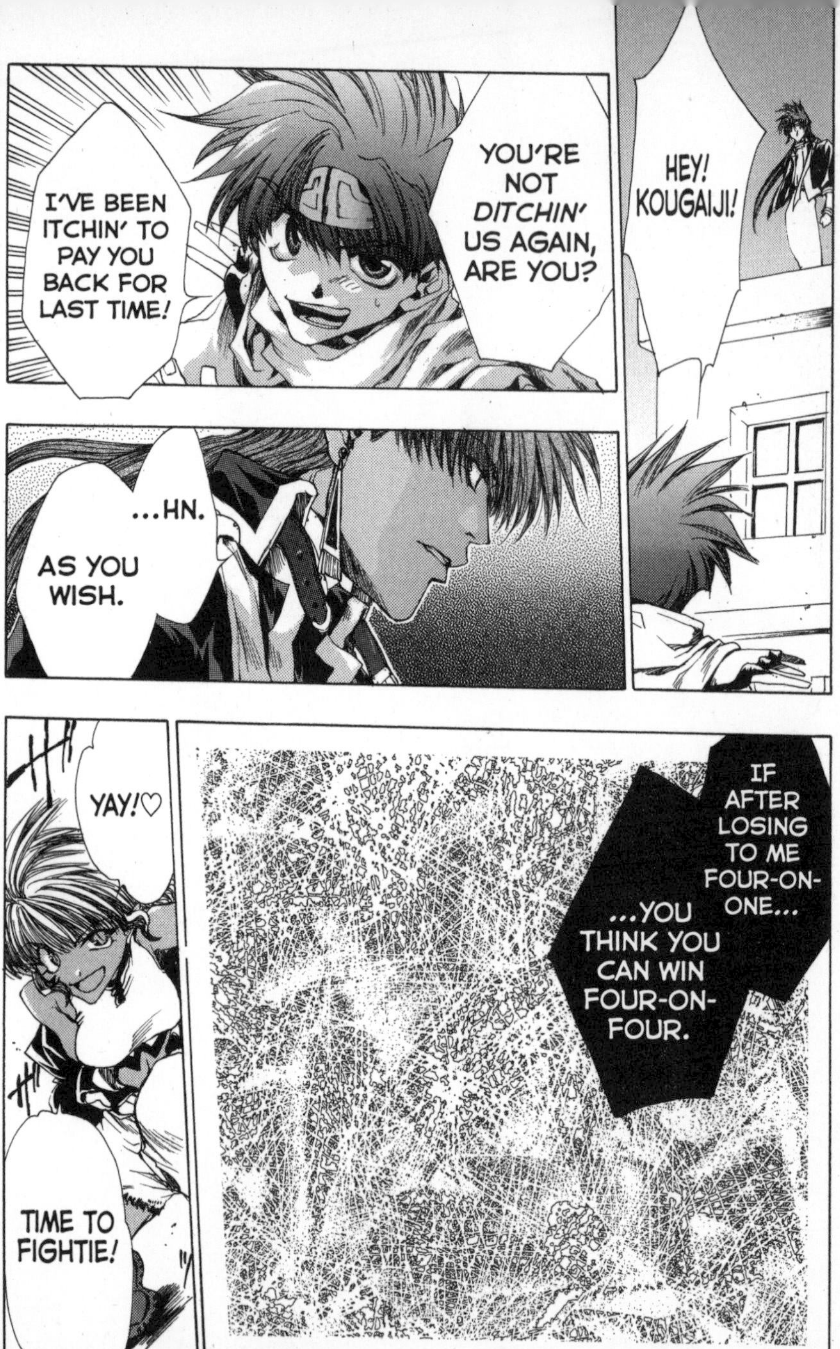
HEY! KOUGAIJI!
YOU'RE NOT *DITCHIN'* US AGAIN, ARE YOU?
I'VE BEEN ITCHIN' TO PAY YOU BACK FOR LAST TIME!
...HN.
AS YOU WISH.
IF AFTER LOSING TO ME FOUR-ON-ONE...
...YOU THINK YOU CAN WIN FOUR-ON-FOUR.
YAY!♡
TIME TO FIGHTIE!

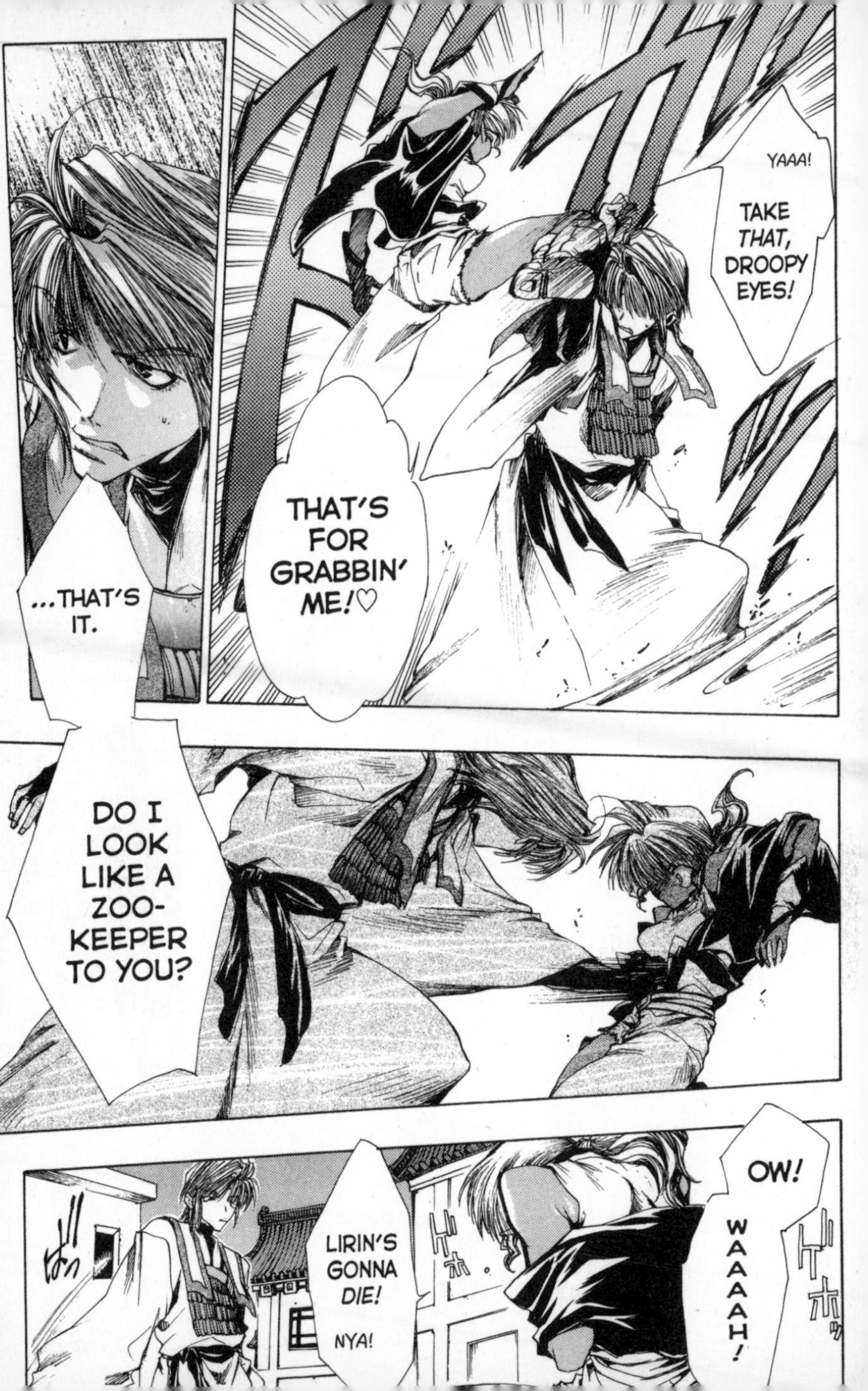
YAAA!
TAKE *THAT*, DROOPY EYES!
THAT'S FOR GRABBIN' ME!♡
...THAT'S IT.
DO I LOOK LIKE A ZOO-KEEPER TO YOU?
OW!
WAAAAH!
LIRIN'S GONNA *DIE!*
NYA!

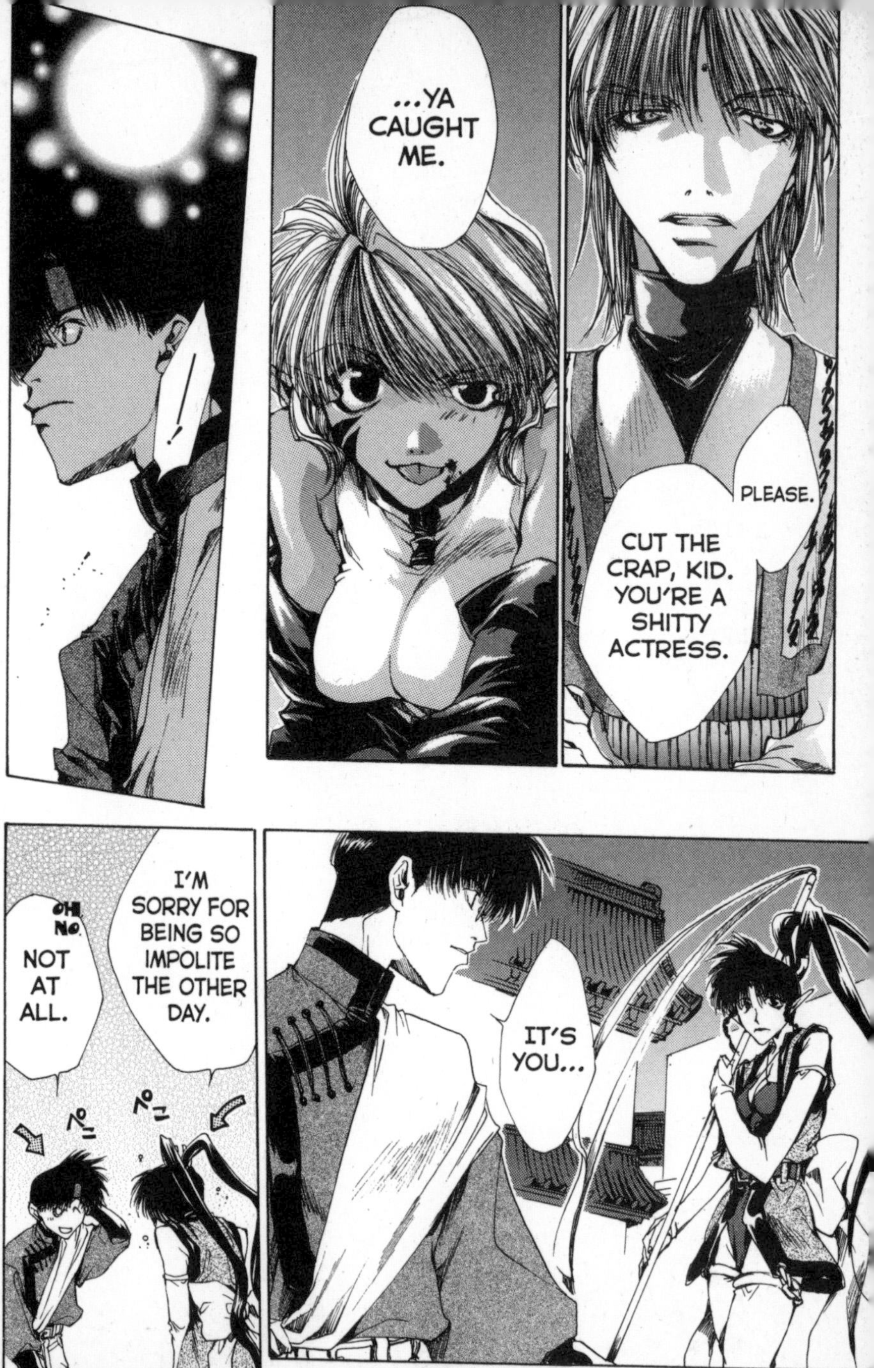
PLEASE.
CUT THE CRAP, KID. YOU'RE A SHITTY ACTRESS.
...YA CAUGHT ME.
!
IT'S YOU...
I'M SORRY FOR BEING SO IMPOLITE THE OTHER DAY.
OH, NO. NOT AT ALL.

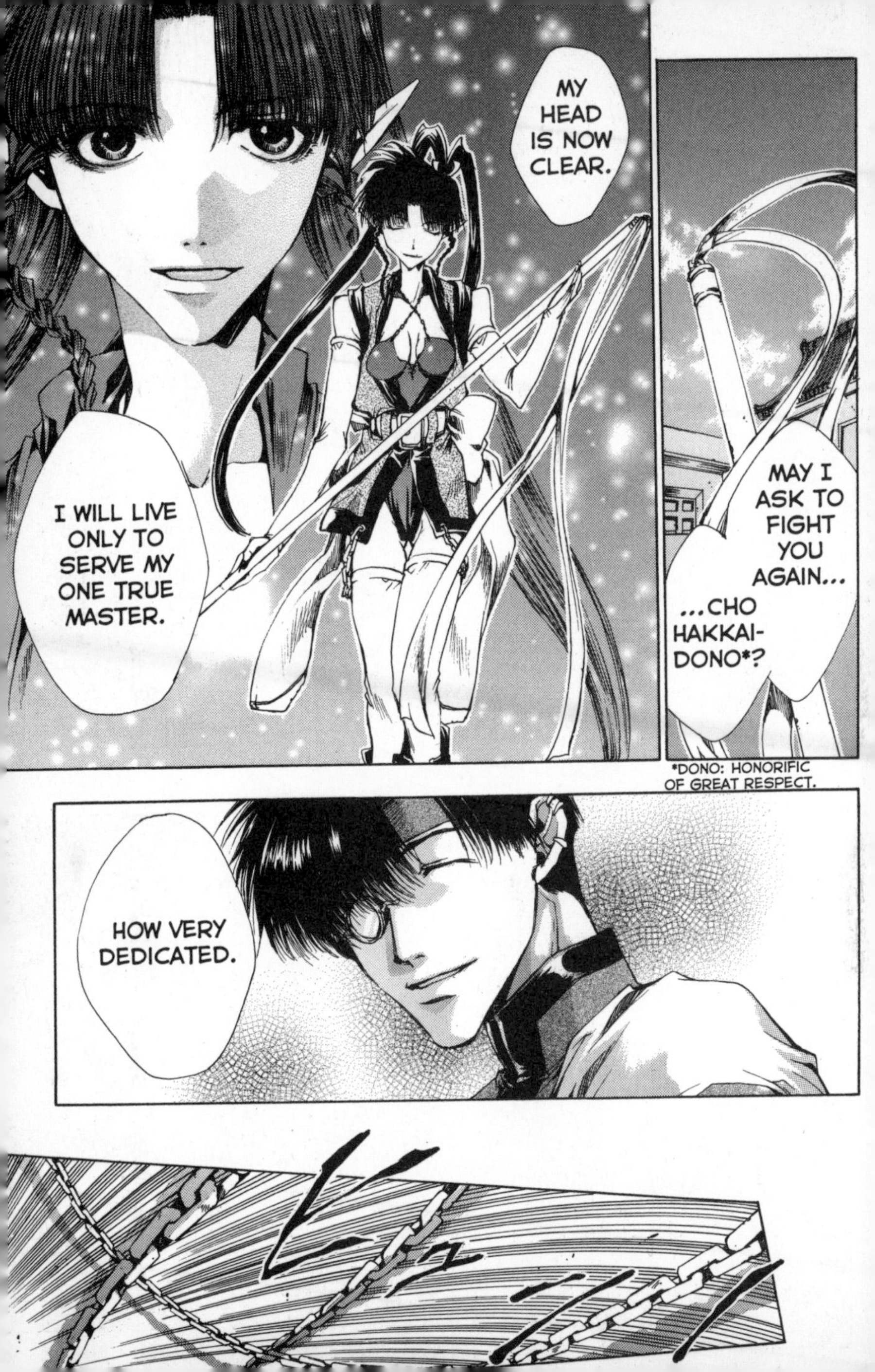
MAY I ASK TO FIGHT YOU AGAIN...
...CHO HAKKAI-DONO*?
MY HEAD IS NOW CLEAR.
I WILL LIVE ONLY TO SERVE MY ONE TRUE MASTER.
*DONO: HONORIFIC OF GREAT RESPECT.
HOW VERY DEDICATED.

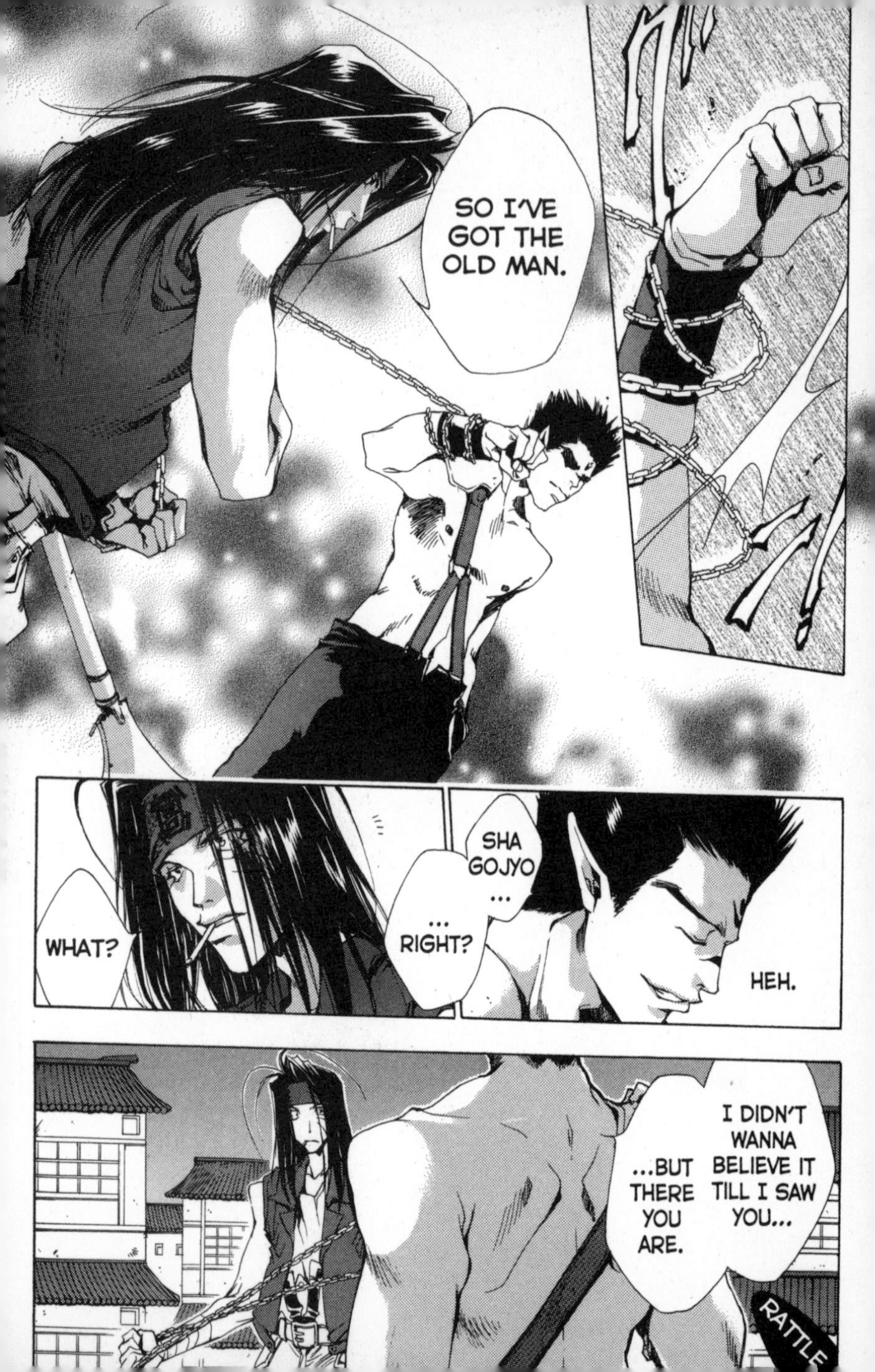
SO I'VE GOT THE OLD MAN.
SHA GOJYO ...
... RIGHT?
HEH.
WHAT?
I DIDN'T WANNA BELIEVE IT TILL I SAW YOU...
...BUT THERE YOU ARE.
RATTLE

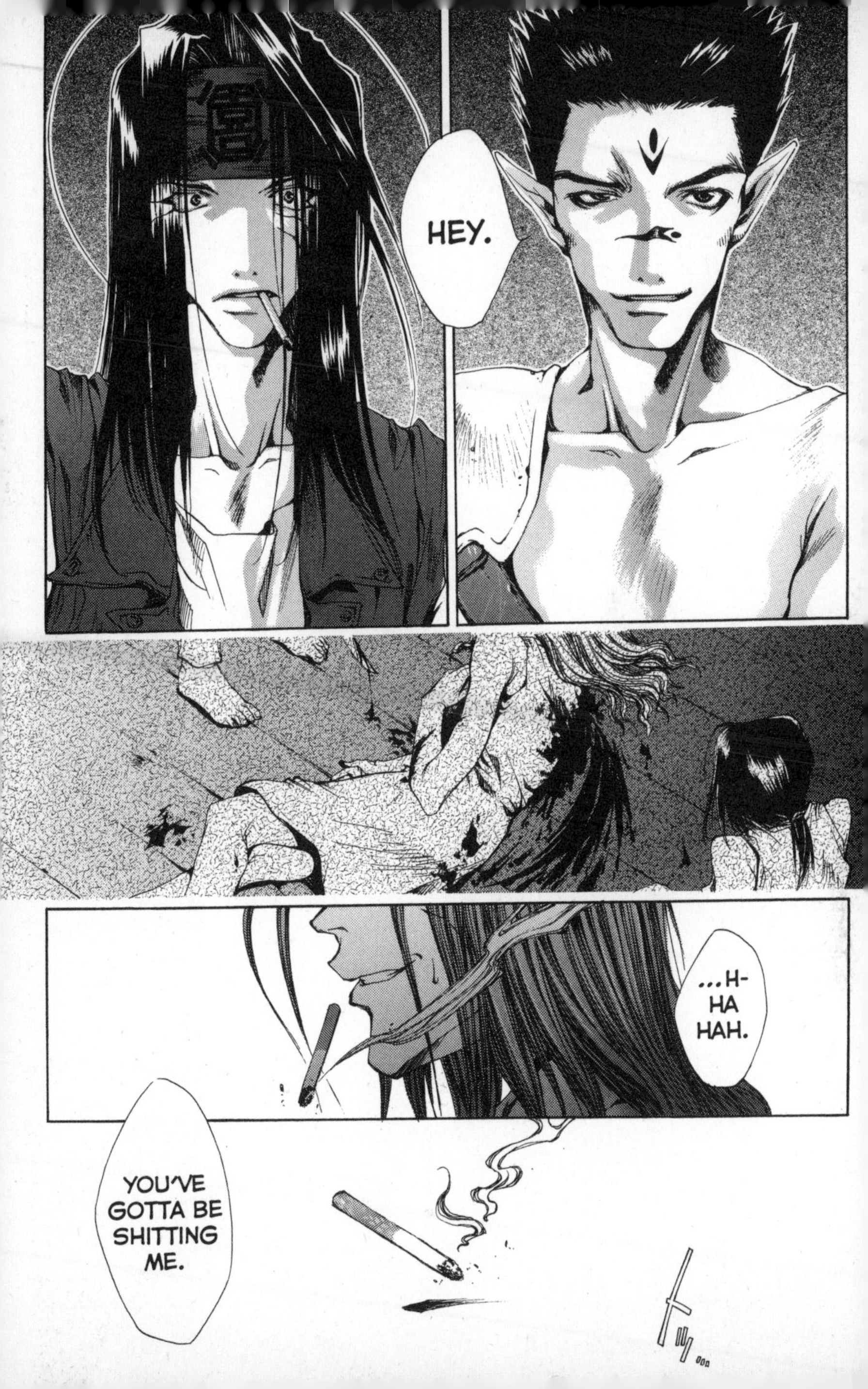
HEY.
...H-
HA
HAH.
YOU'VE
GOTTA BE
SHITTING
ME.

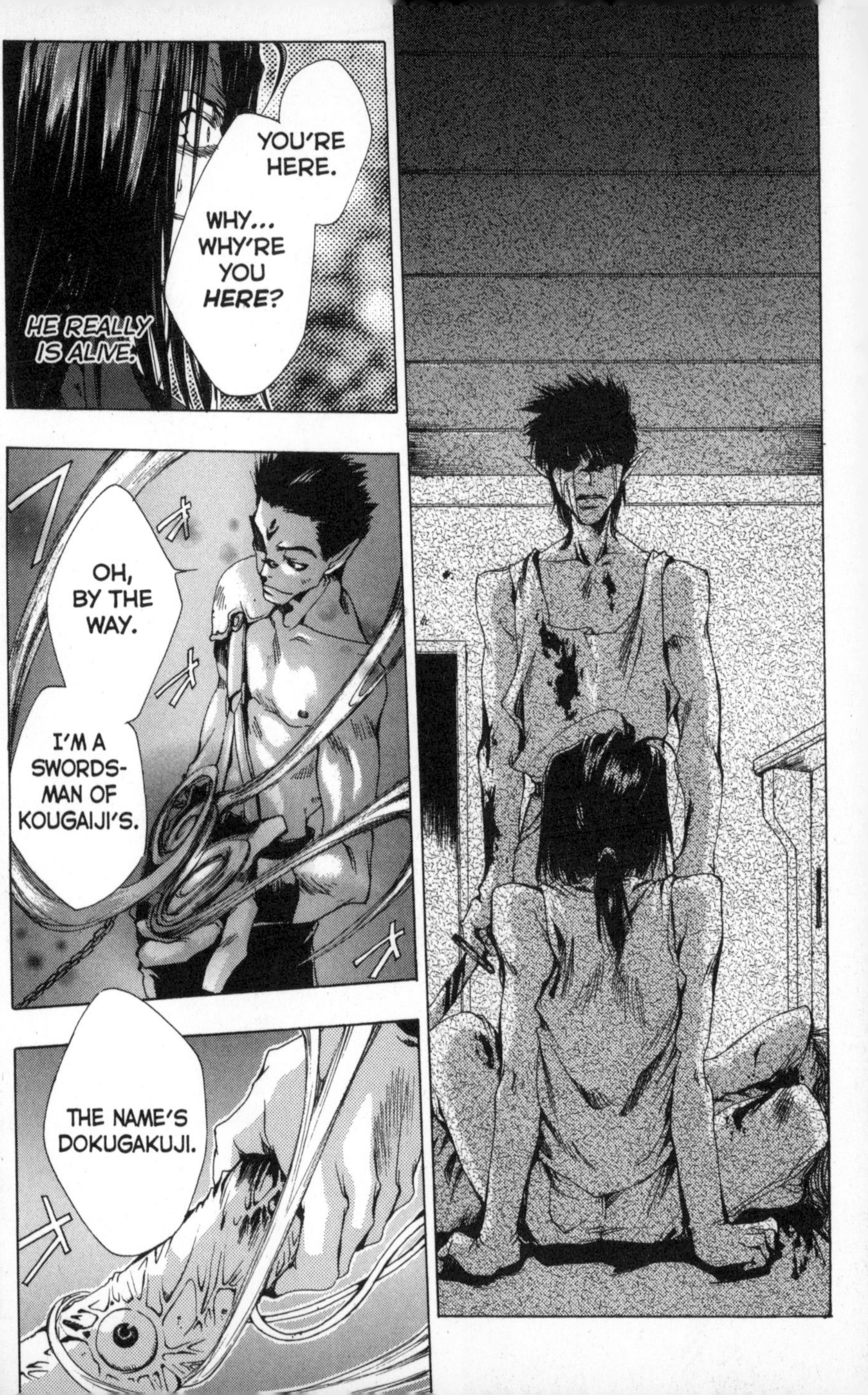
YOU'RE HERE.
WHY... WHY'RE YOU HERE?
HE REALLY IS ALIVE.
OH, BY THE WAY.
I'M A SWORDS-MAN OF KOUGAIJI'S.
THE NAME'S DOKUGAKUJI.

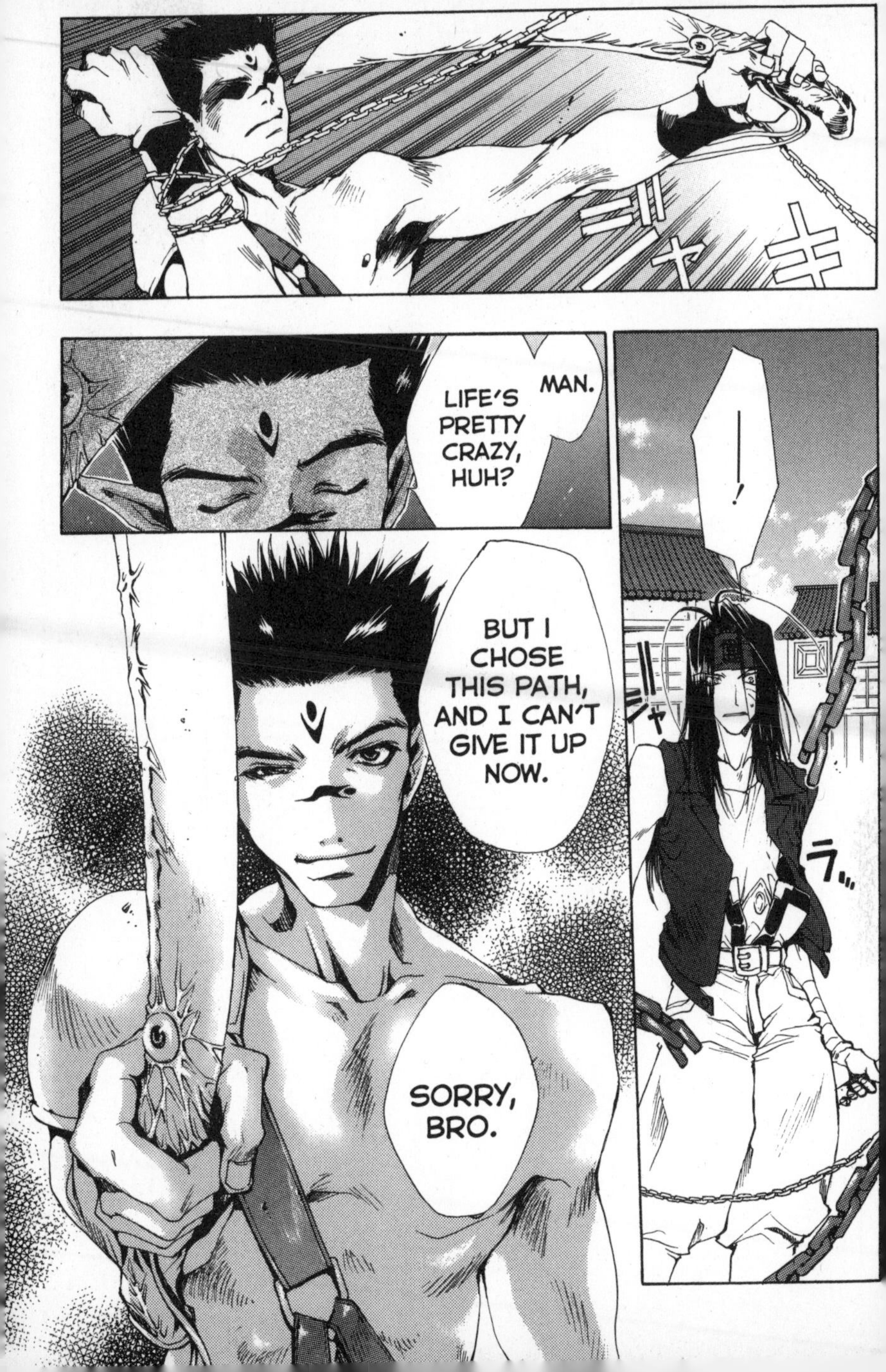

—!
MAN.
LIFE'S PRETTY CRAZY, HUH?
BUT I CHOSE THIS PATH, AND I CAN'T GIVE IT UP NOW.
SORRY, BRO.

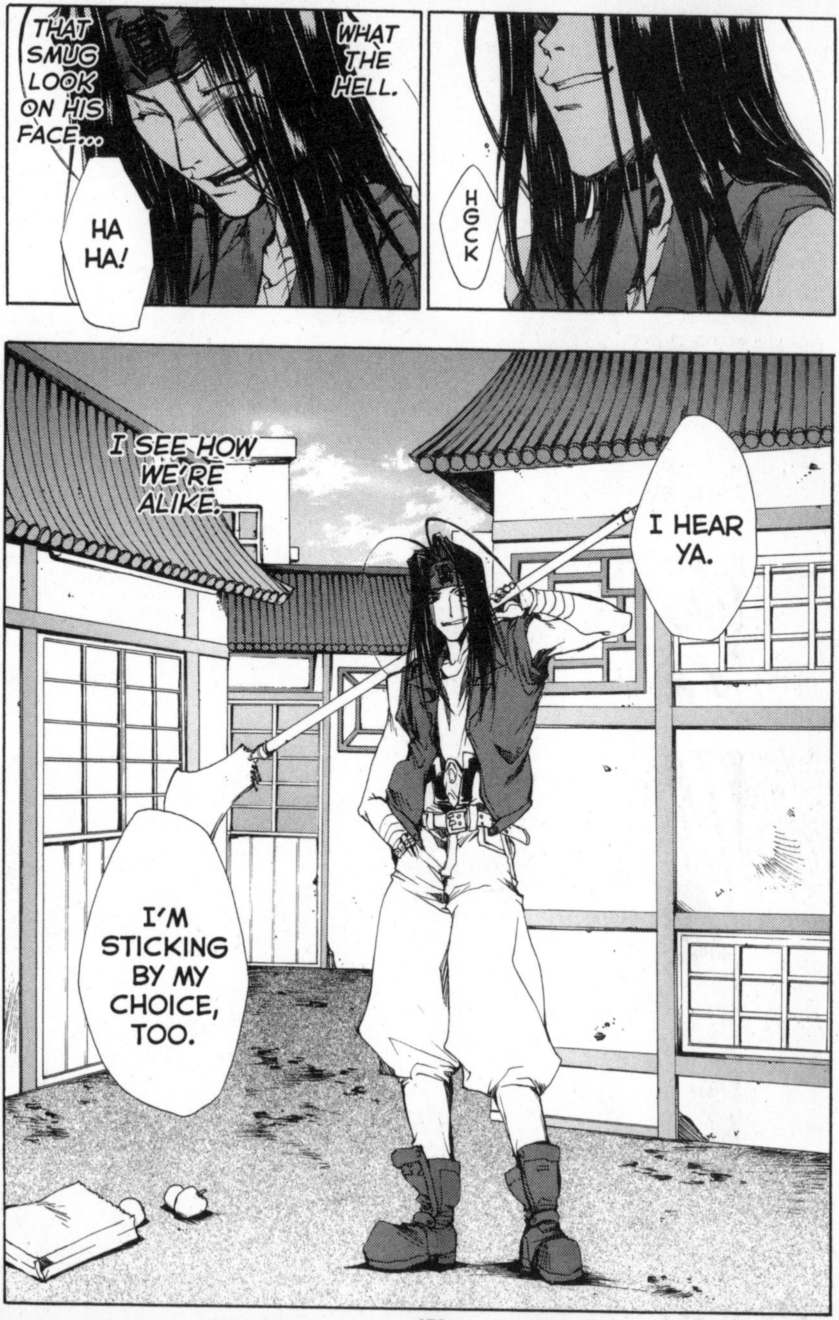
HGCK
WHAT THE HELL.
THAT SMUG LOOK ON HIS FACE...
HA HA!
I HEAR YA.
I SEE HOW WE'RE ALIKE.
I'M STICKING BY MY CHOICE, TOO.

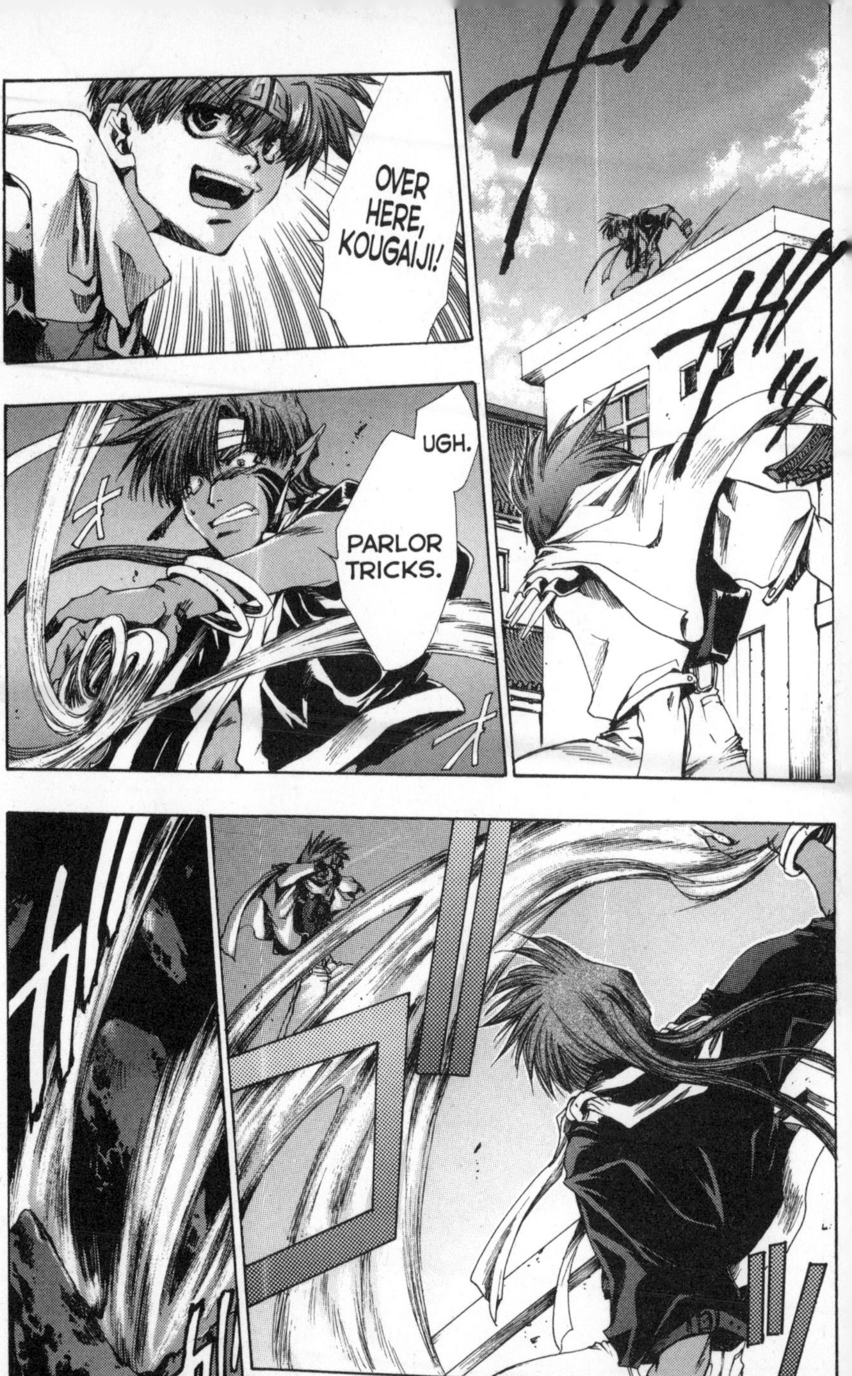
OVER HERE, KOUGAIJI!
UGH.
PARLOR TRICKS.

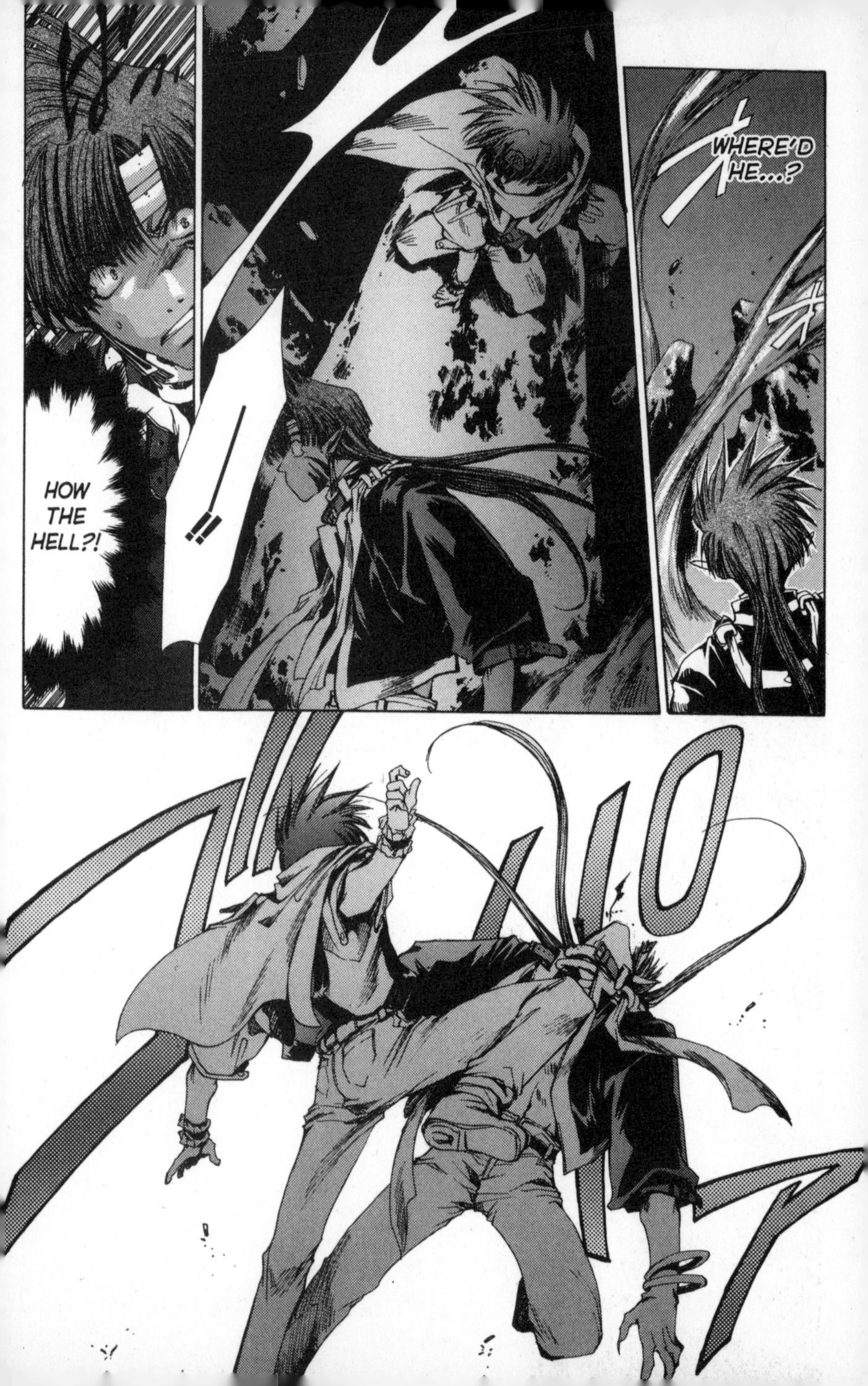
WHERE'D HE...?
HOW THE HELL?!

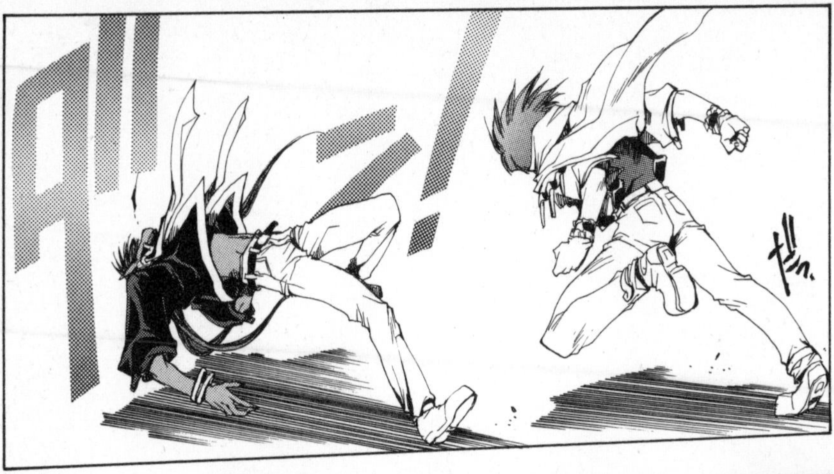

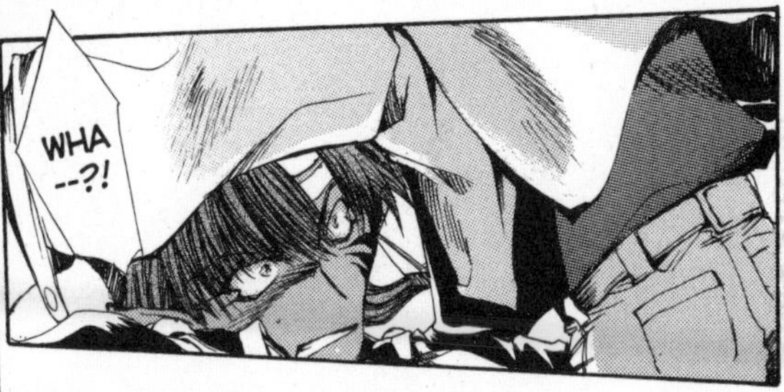
WHA
--?!

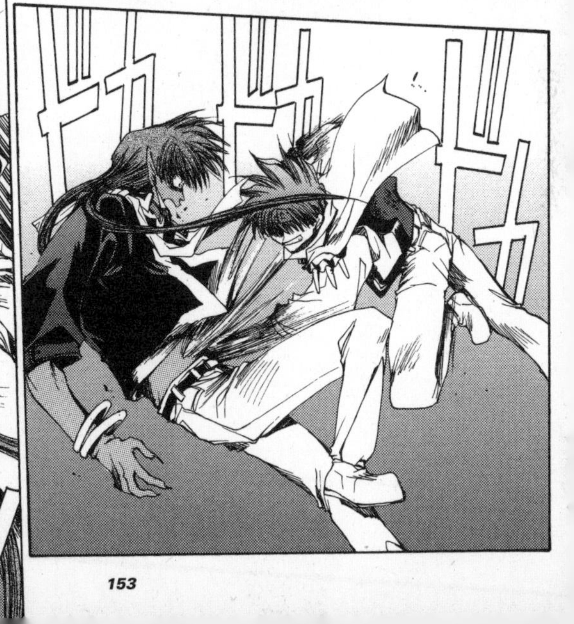

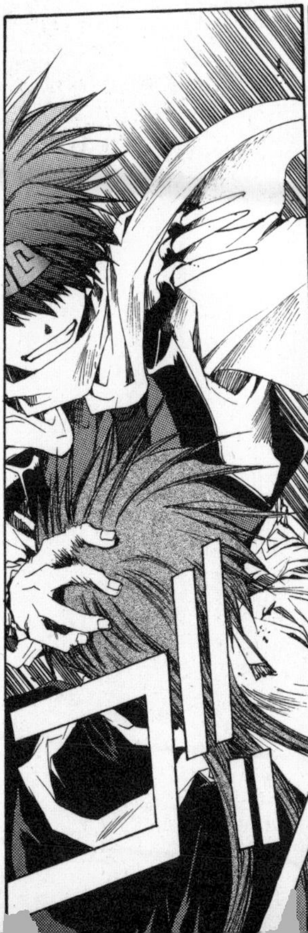

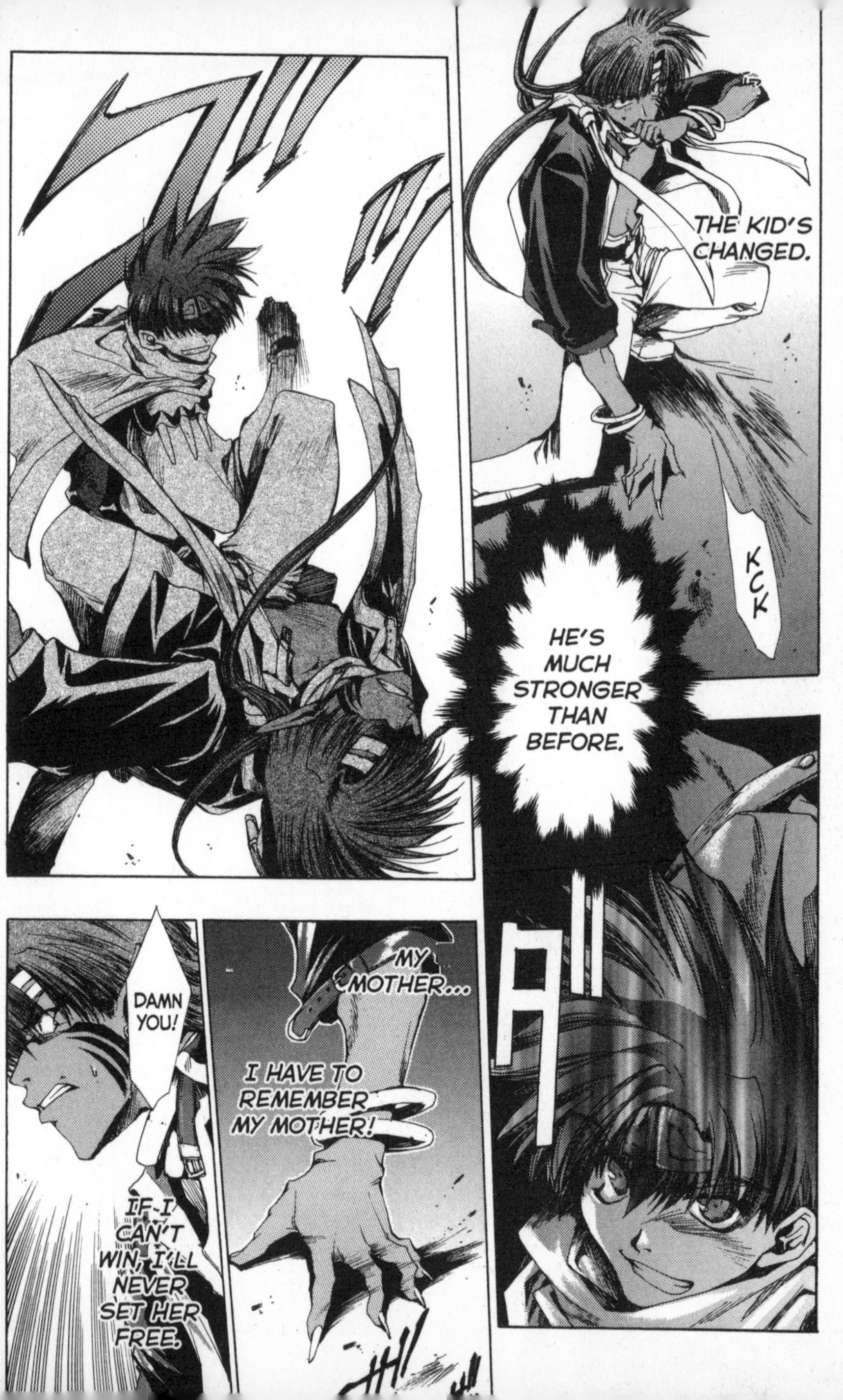
THE KID'S CHANGED.
KCK
HE'S MUCH STRONGER THAN BEFORE.
MY MOTHER...
I HAVE TO REMEMBER MY MOTHER!
DAMN YOU!
IF I CAN'T WIN, I'LL NEVER SET HER FREE.

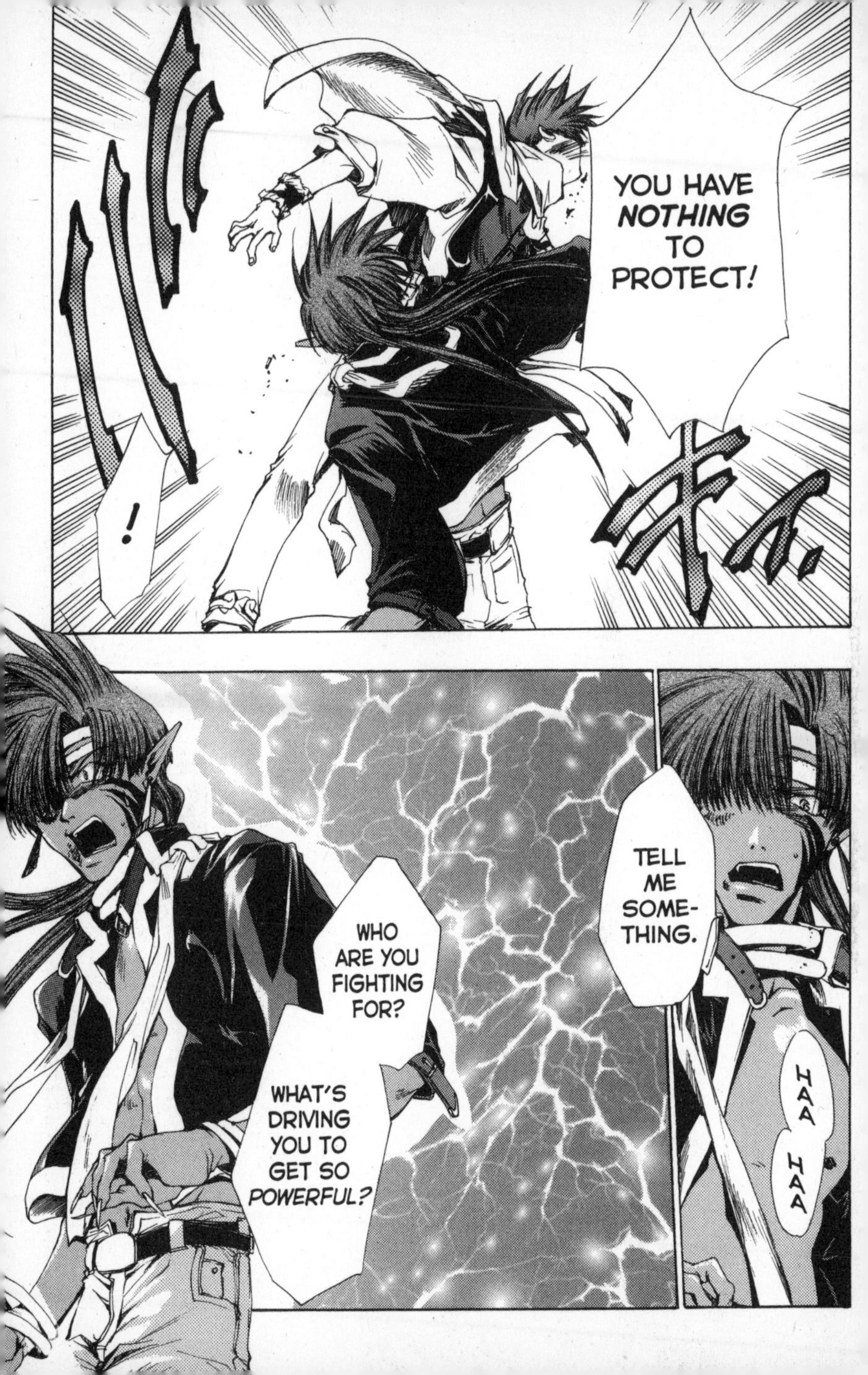
YOU HAVE NOTHING TO PROTECT!
!
TELL ME SOME-THING.
HAA HAA
WHO ARE YOU FIGHTING FOR?
WHAT'S DRIVING YOU TO GET SO POWERFUL?

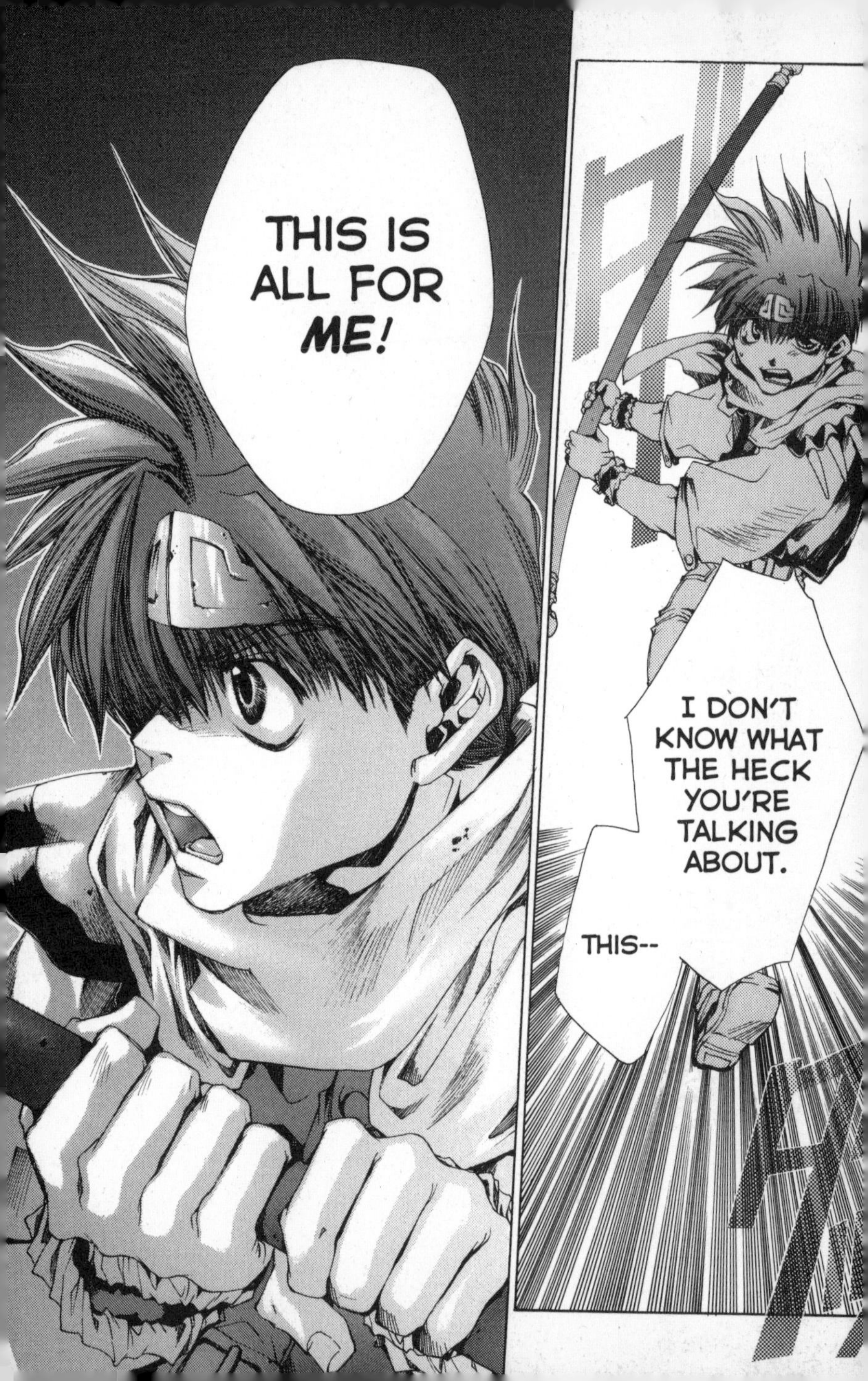
I DON'T KNOW WHAT THE HECK YOU'RE TALKING ABOUT.
THIS--
THIS IS ALL FOR *ME!*

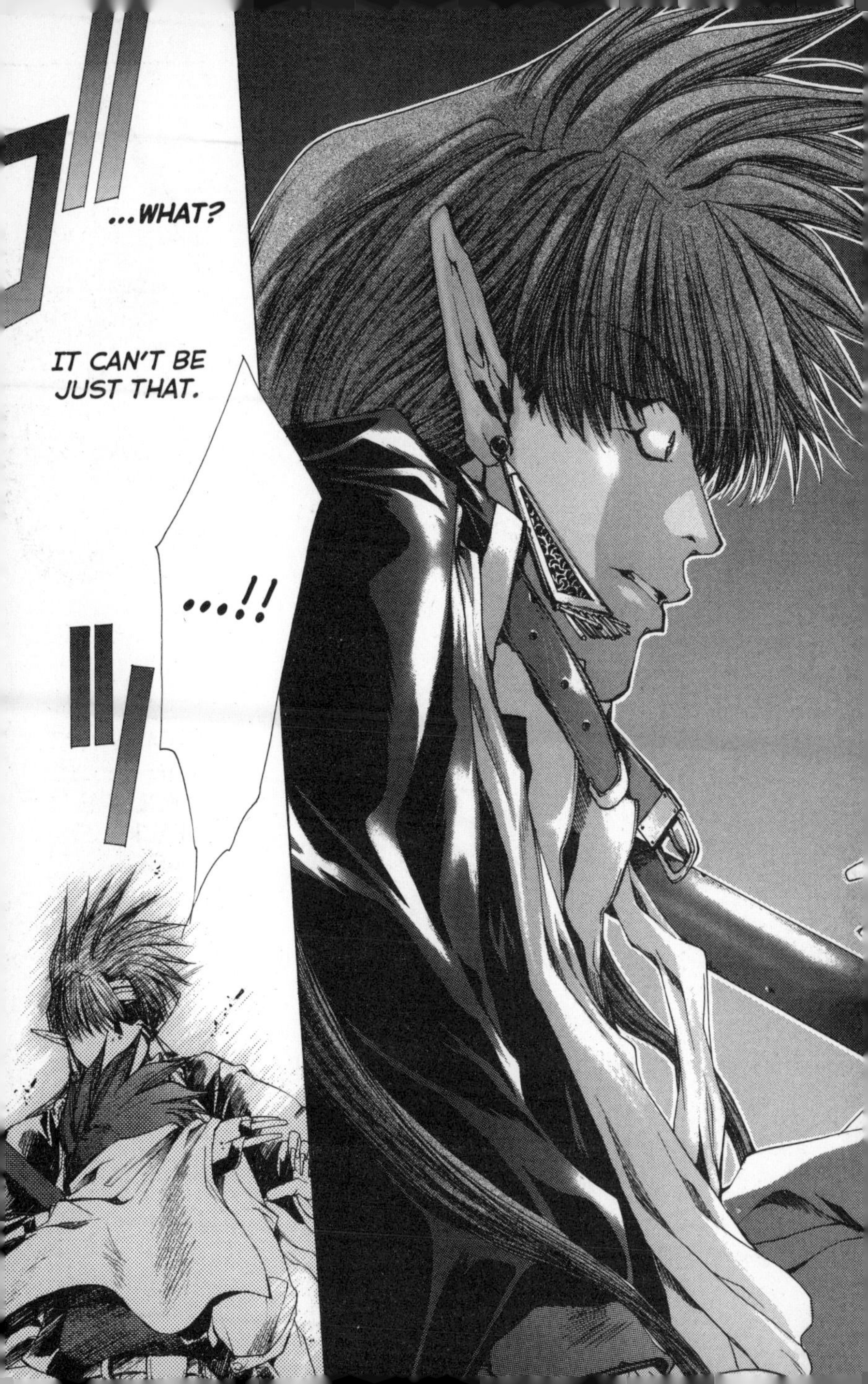
...WHAT?
IT CAN'T BE JUST THAT.
...!!

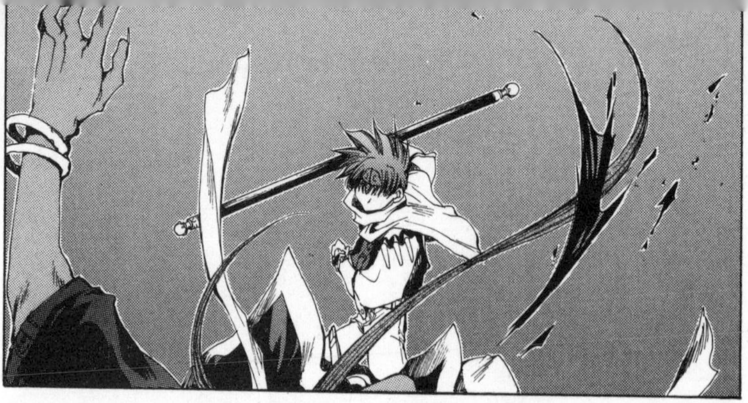

--OH...I THINK I UNDERSTAND...

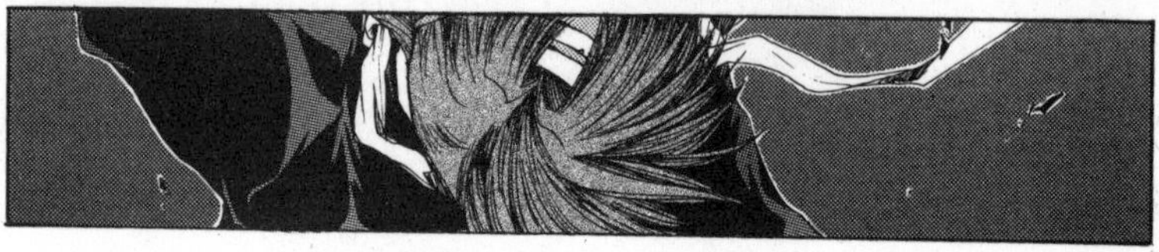

"IS THAT ALL?" YES...

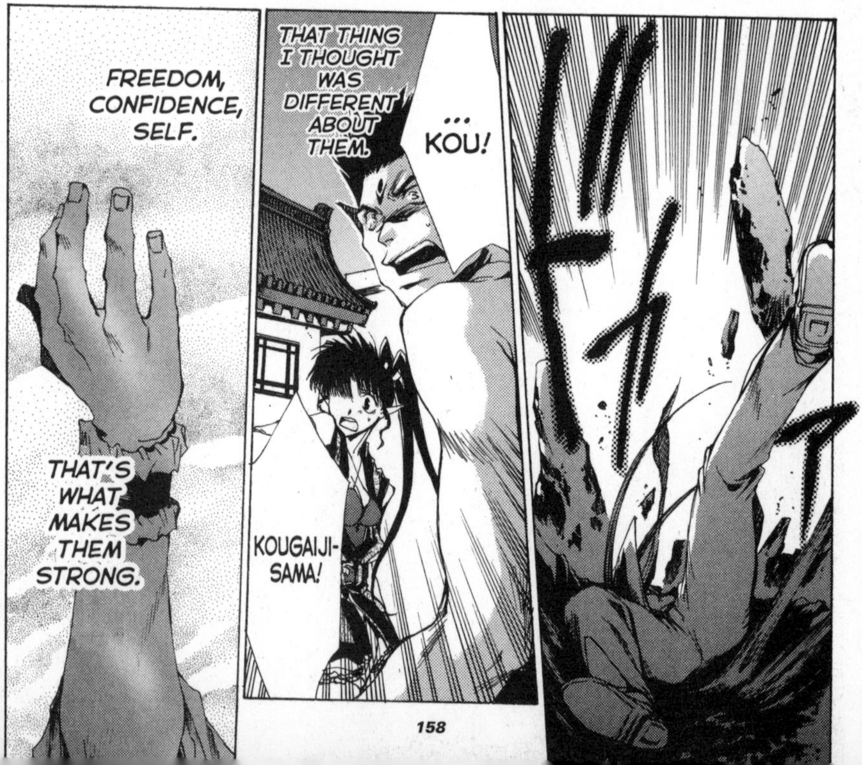
...KOU!
THAT THING I THOUGHT WAS DIFFERENT ABOUT THEM.
KOUGAIJI-SAMA!
FREEDOM, CONFIDENCE, SELF.
THAT'S WHAT MAKES THEM STRONG.

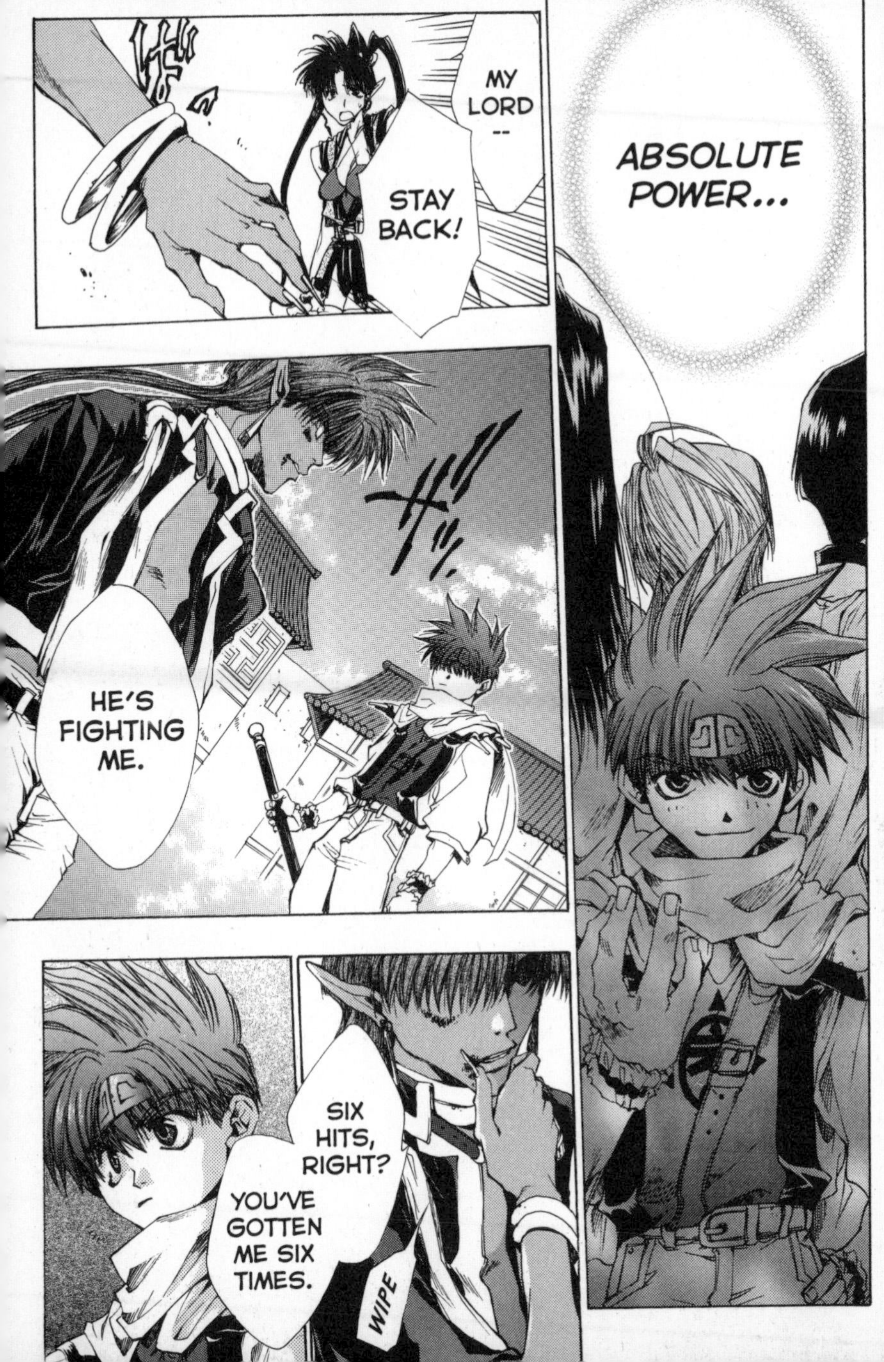
ABSOLUTE POWER...
MY LORD --
STAY BACK!
HE'S FIGHTING ME.
SIX HITS, RIGHT?
YOU'VE GOTTEN ME SIX TIMES.
WIPE

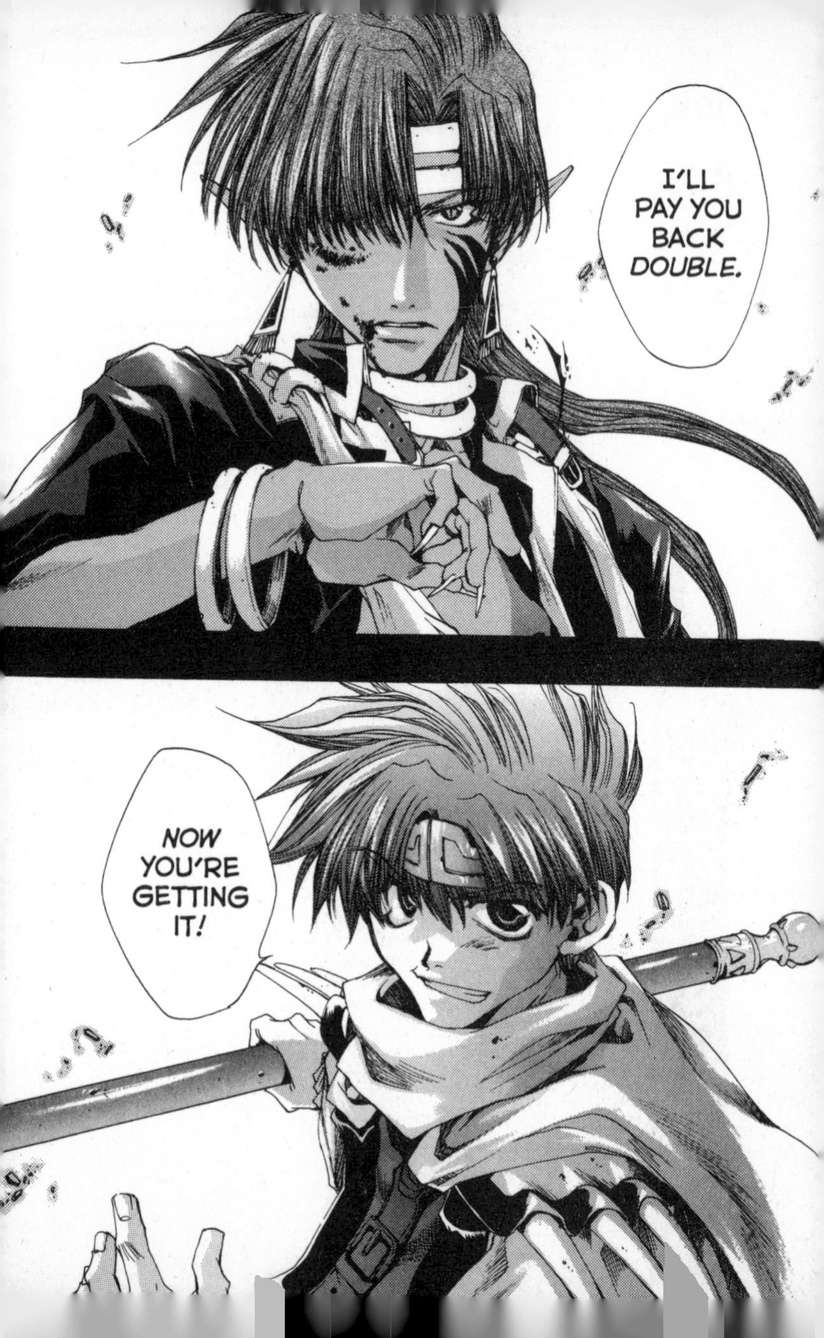
I'LL PAY YOU BACK DOUBLE.
NOW YOU'RE GETTING IT!

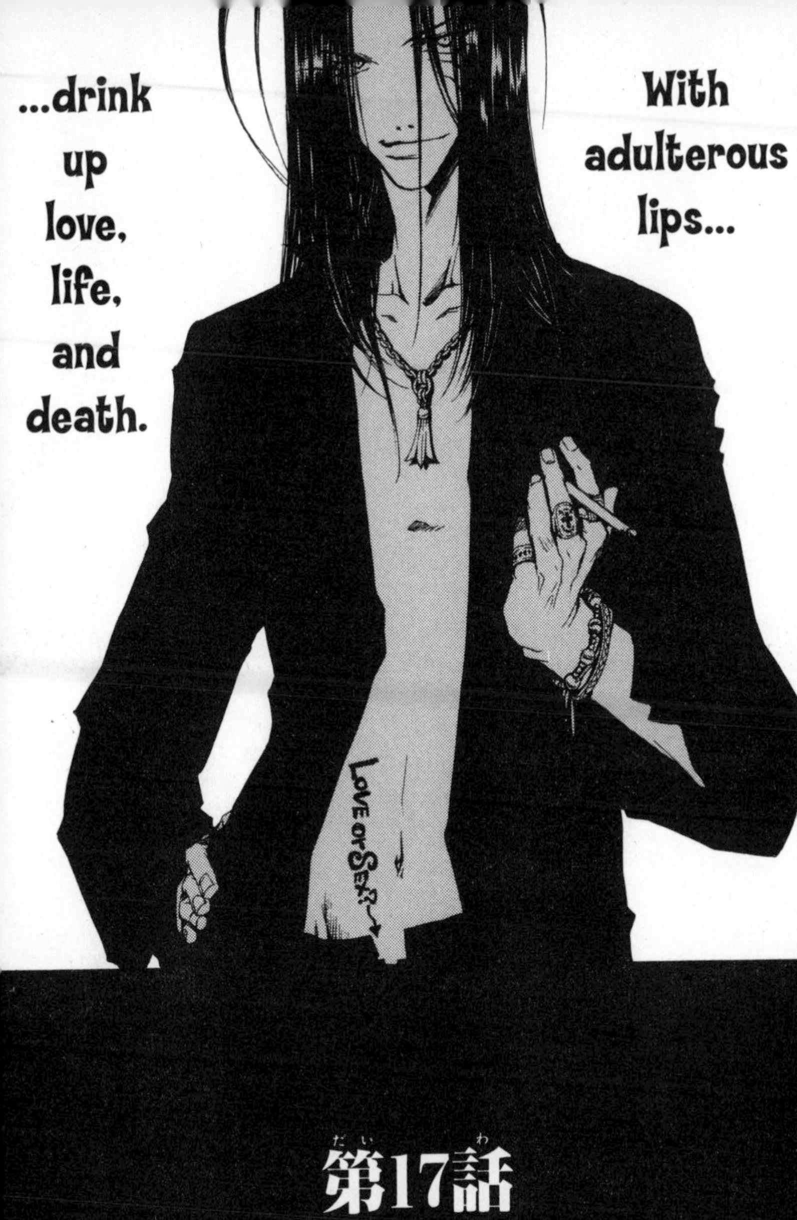

第17話

CHAPTER 17: OVERLAP EACH OTHER

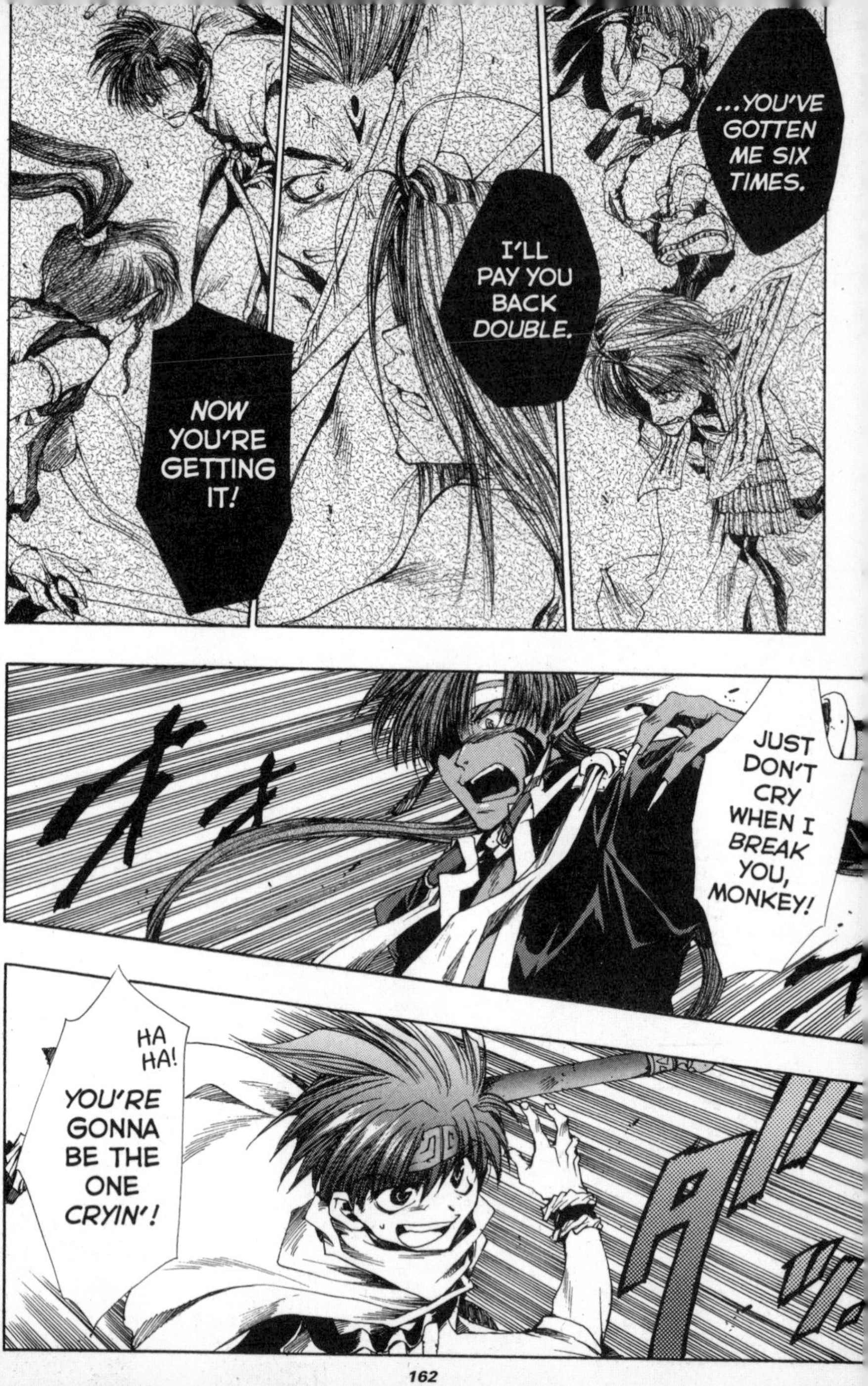
...YOU'VE GOTTEN ME SIX TIMES.
I'LL PAY YOU BACK DOUBLE.
NOW YOU'RE GETTING IT!
JUST DON'T CRY WHEN I BREAK YOU, MONKEY!
HA HA!
YOU'RE GONNA BE THE ONE CRYIN'!

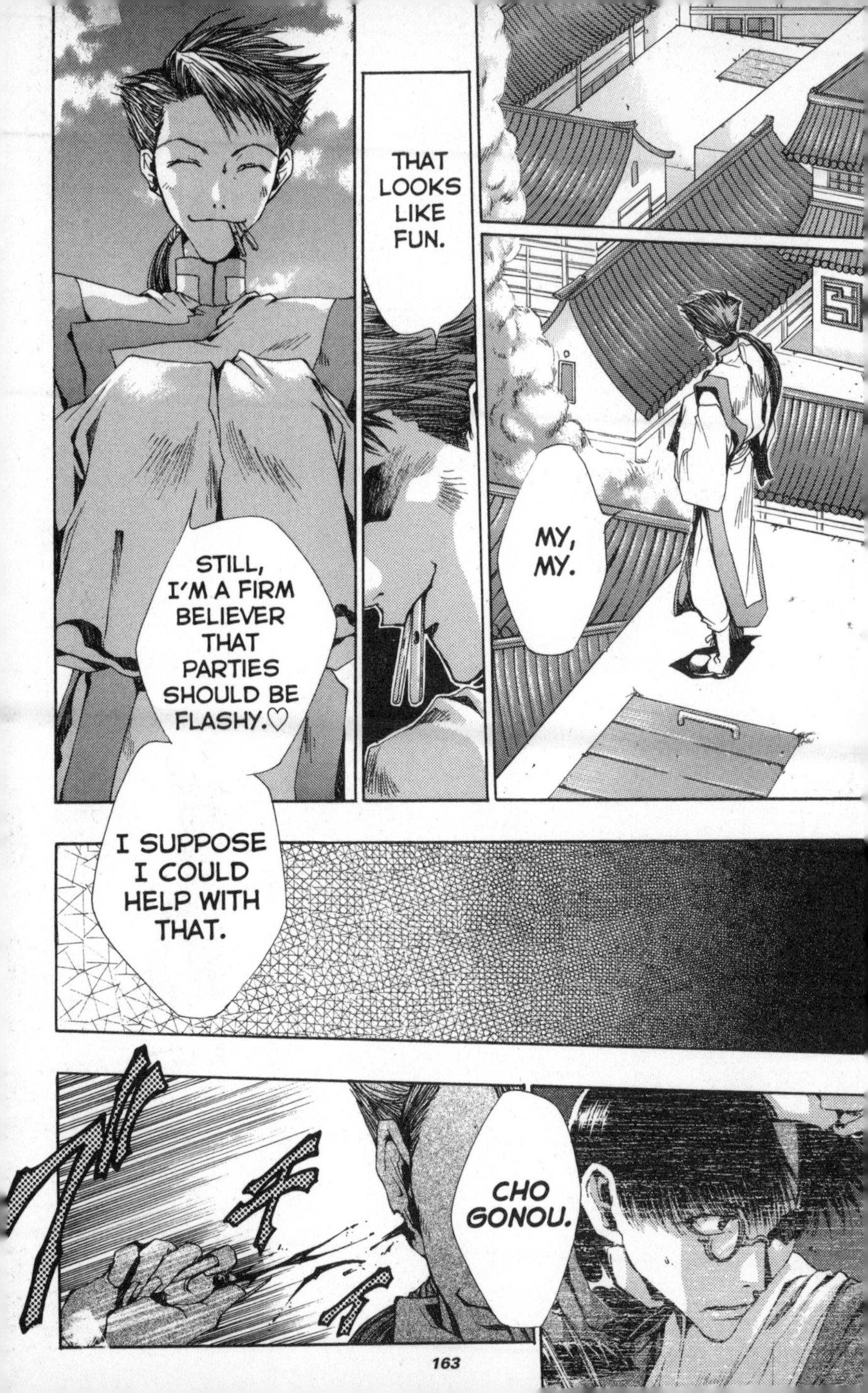
MY, MY.
THAT LOOKS LIKE FUN.
STILL, I'M A FIRM BELIEVER THAT PARTIES SHOULD BE FLASHY.♡
I SUPPOSE I COULD HELP WITH THAT.
CHO GONOU.

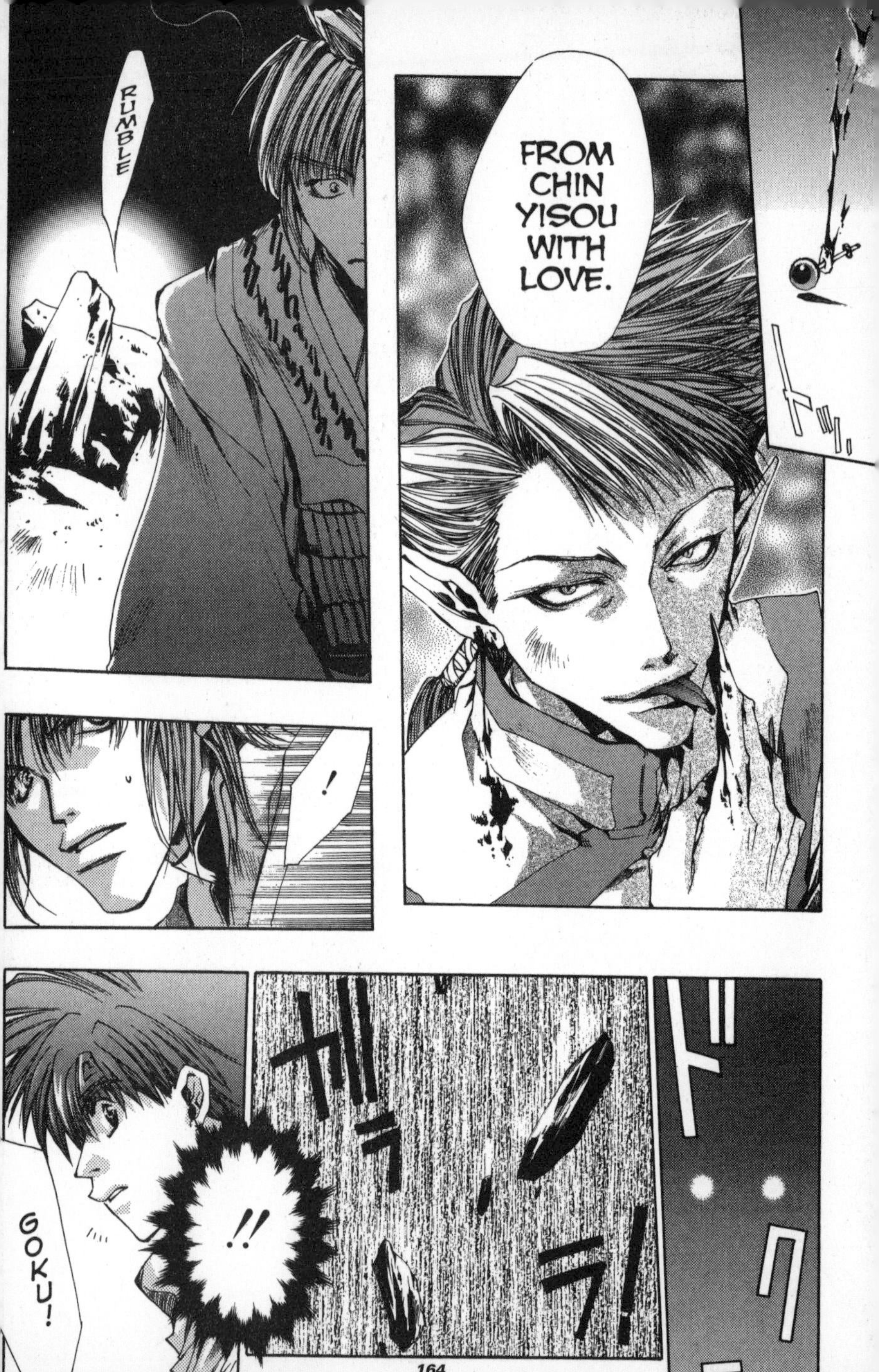
FROM CHIN YISOU WITH LOVE.
RUMBLE
!
!!
GOKU!

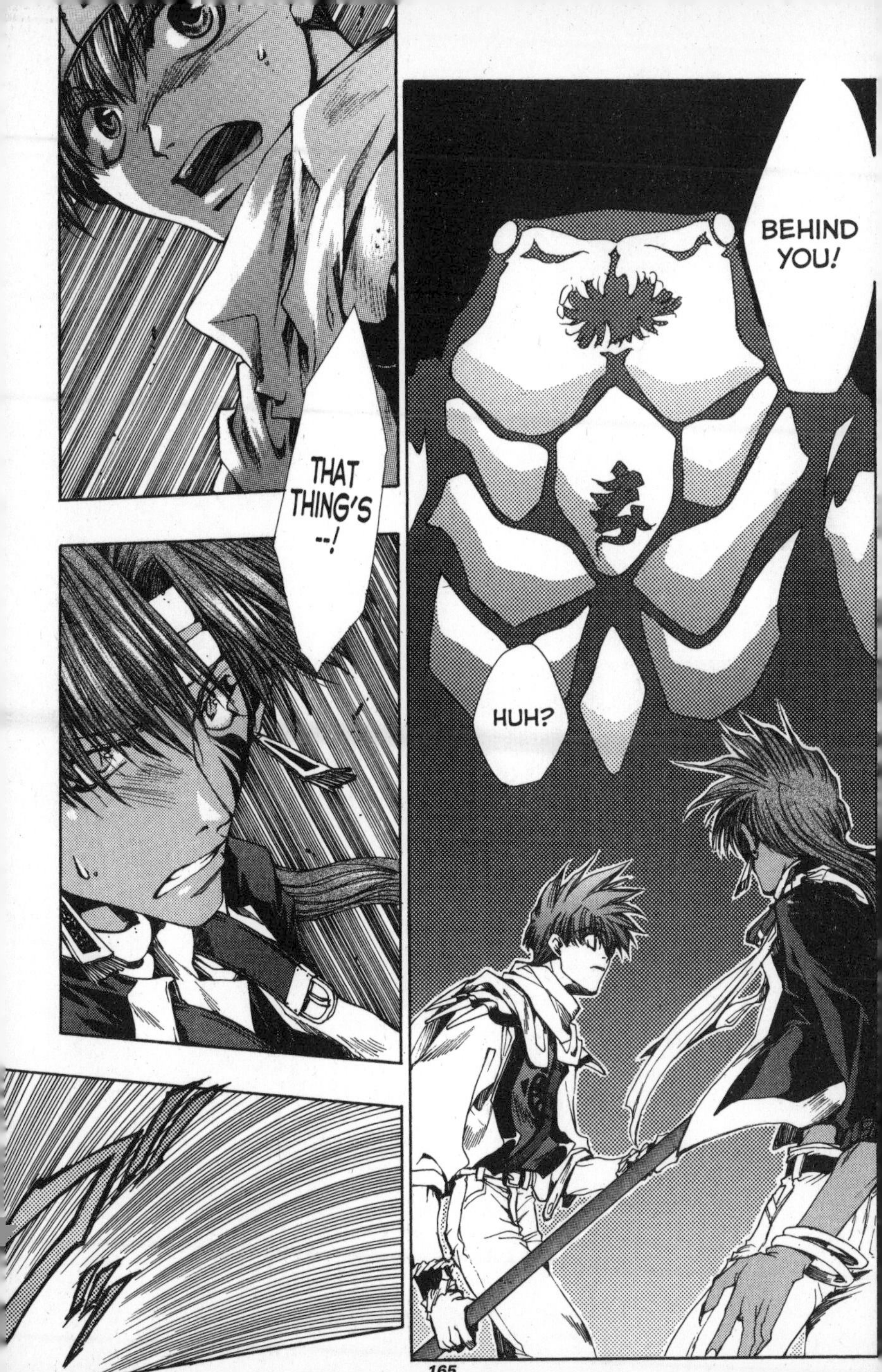
THAT THING'S --!
BEHIND YOU!
HUH?

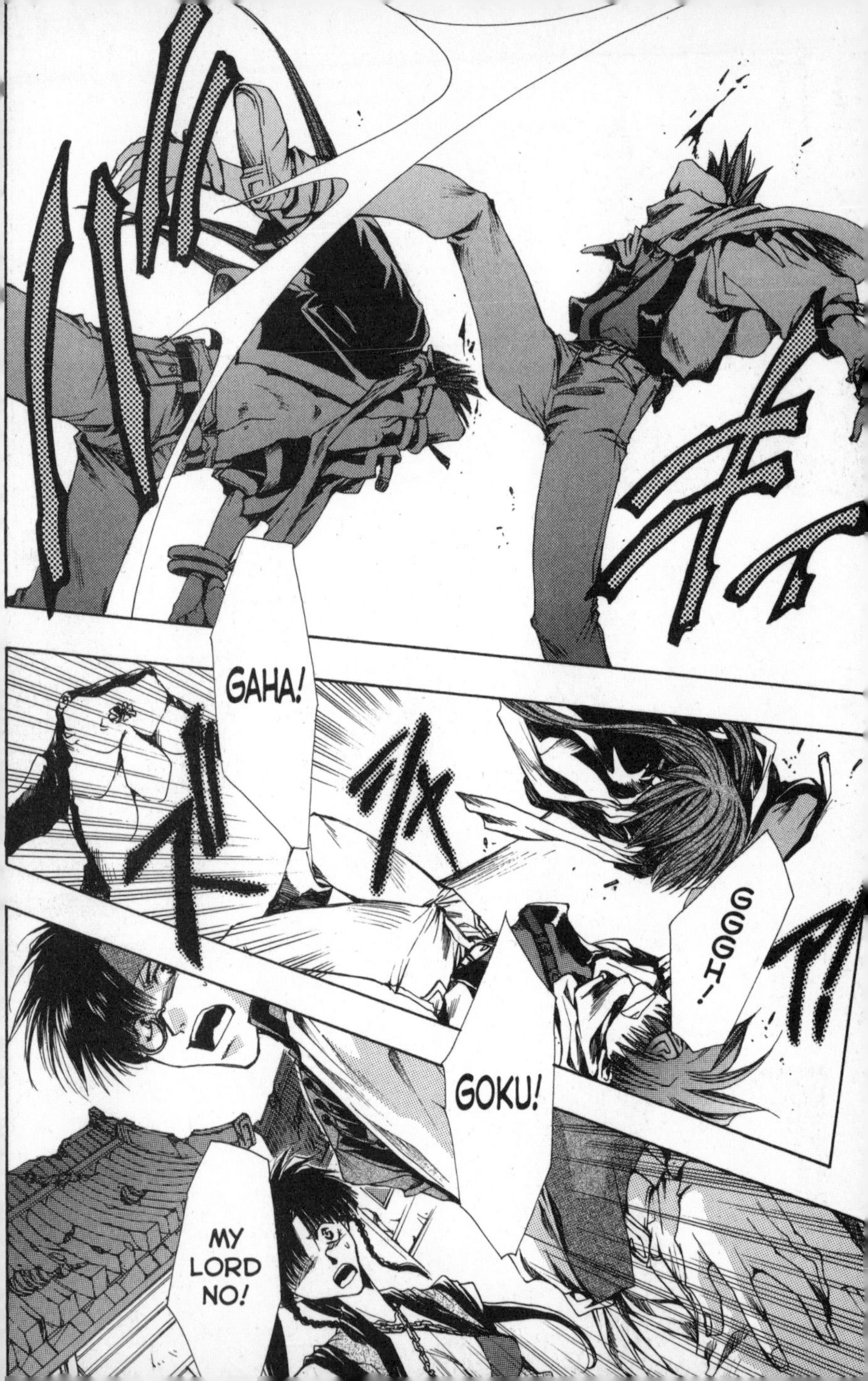
GGGH!
GAHA!
GOKU!
MY LORD NO!

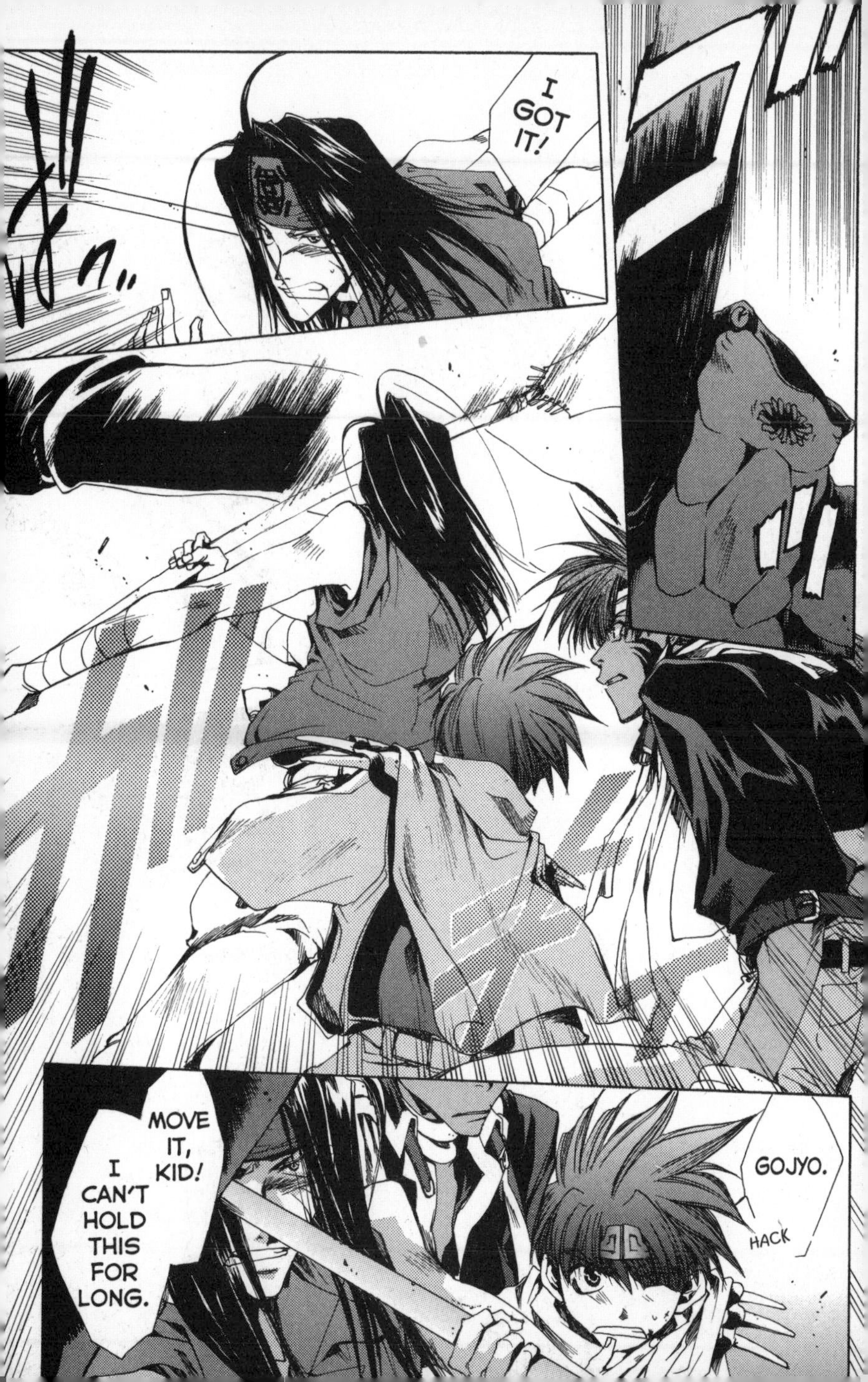
I GOT IT!
GOJYO.
HACK
MOVE IT, KID!
I CAN'T HOLD THIS FOR LONG.

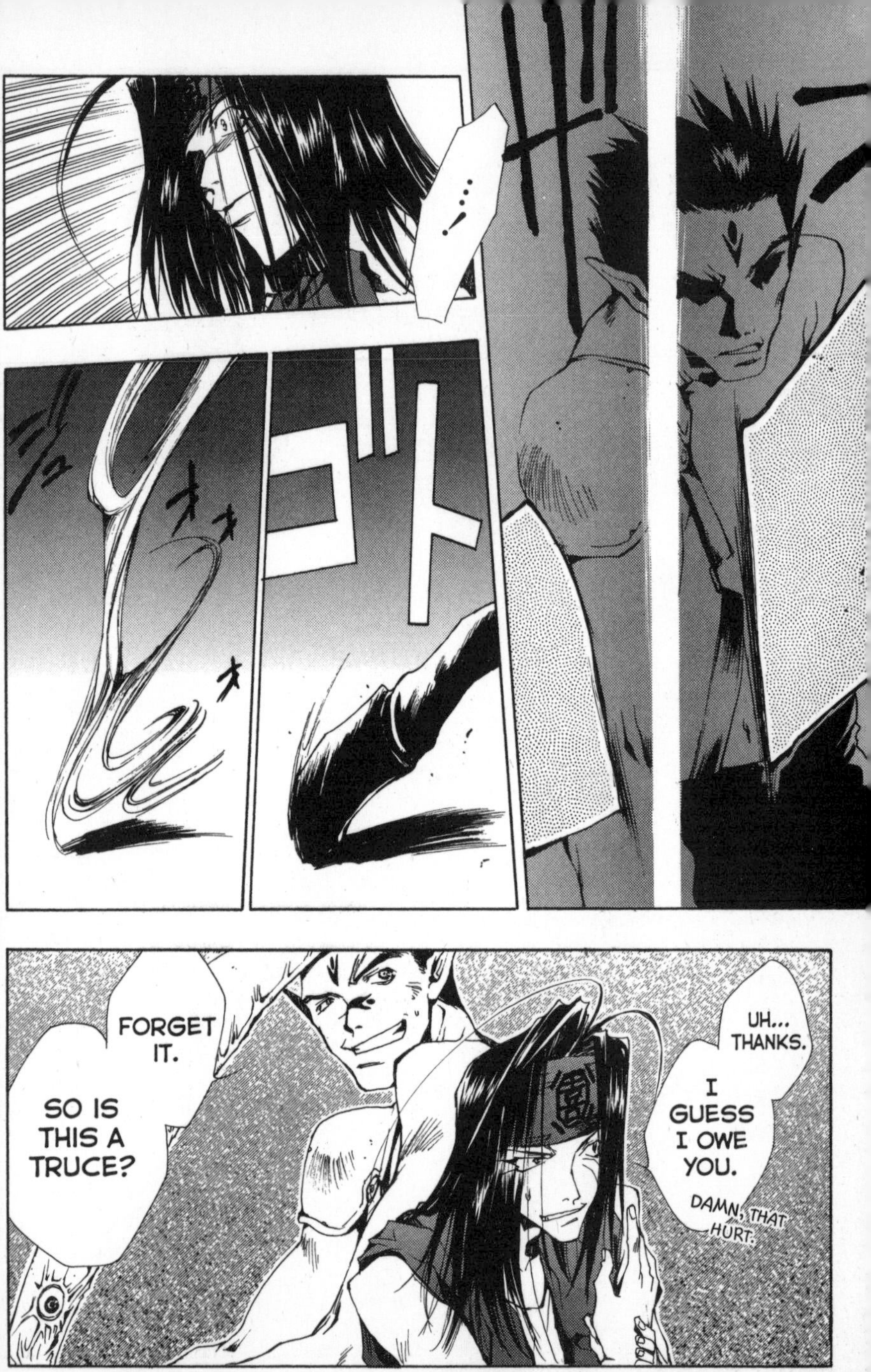
!...
UH... THANKS.
I GUESS I OWE YOU.
DAMN, THAT HURT.
FORGET IT.
SO IS THIS A TRUCE?

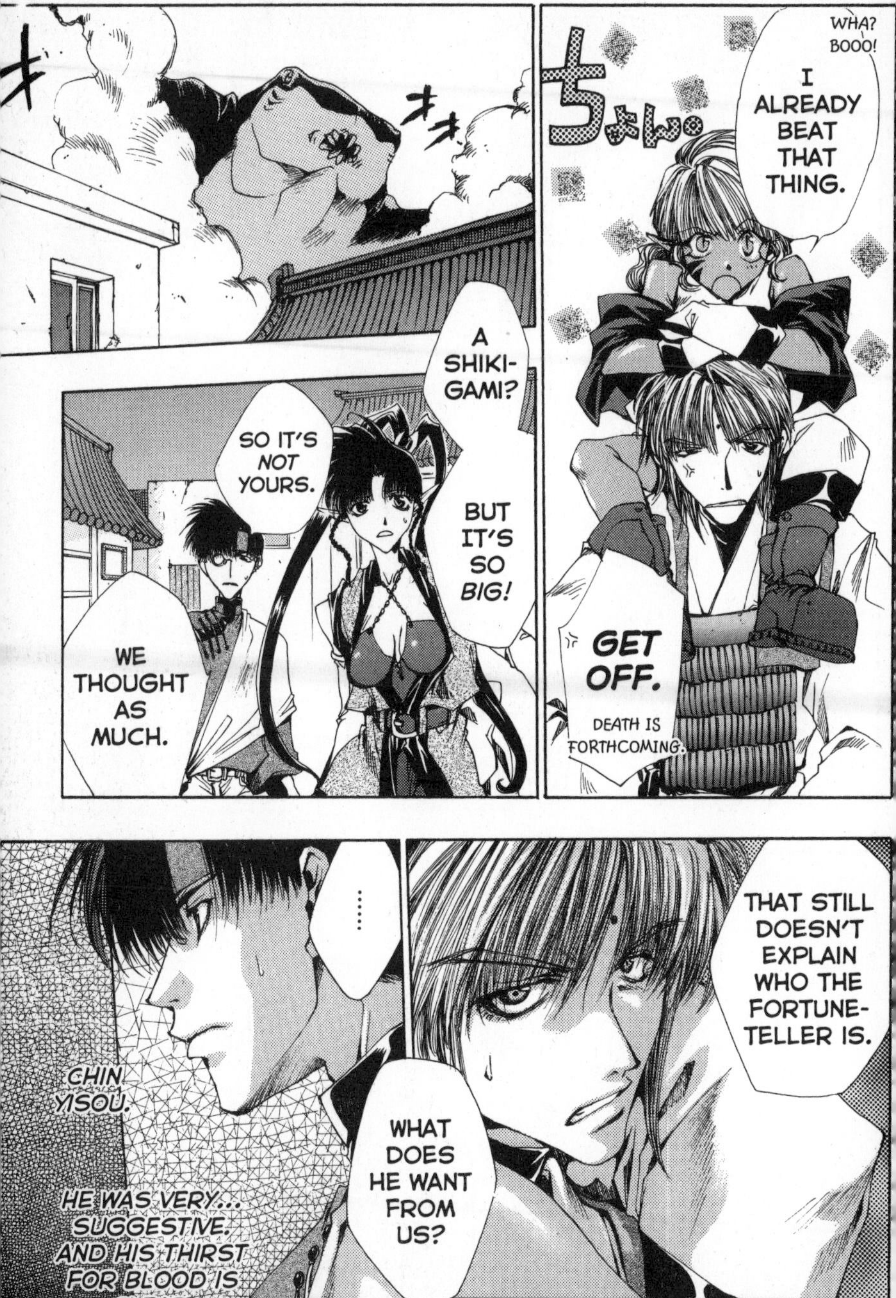

WHA? BOOO!
I ALREADY BEAT THAT THING.
ちょん。
GET OFF.
DEATH IS FORTHCOMING.
A SHIKI-GAMI?
BUT IT'S SO *BIG!*
SO IT'S *NOT* YOURS.
WE THOUGHT AS MUCH.
THAT STILL DOESN'T EXPLAIN WHO THE FORTUNE-TELLER IS.
......
WHAT DOES HE WANT FROM US?
CHIN YISOU.
HE WAS VERY... SUGGESTIVE. AND HIS THIRST FOR BLOOD IS CLEAR.

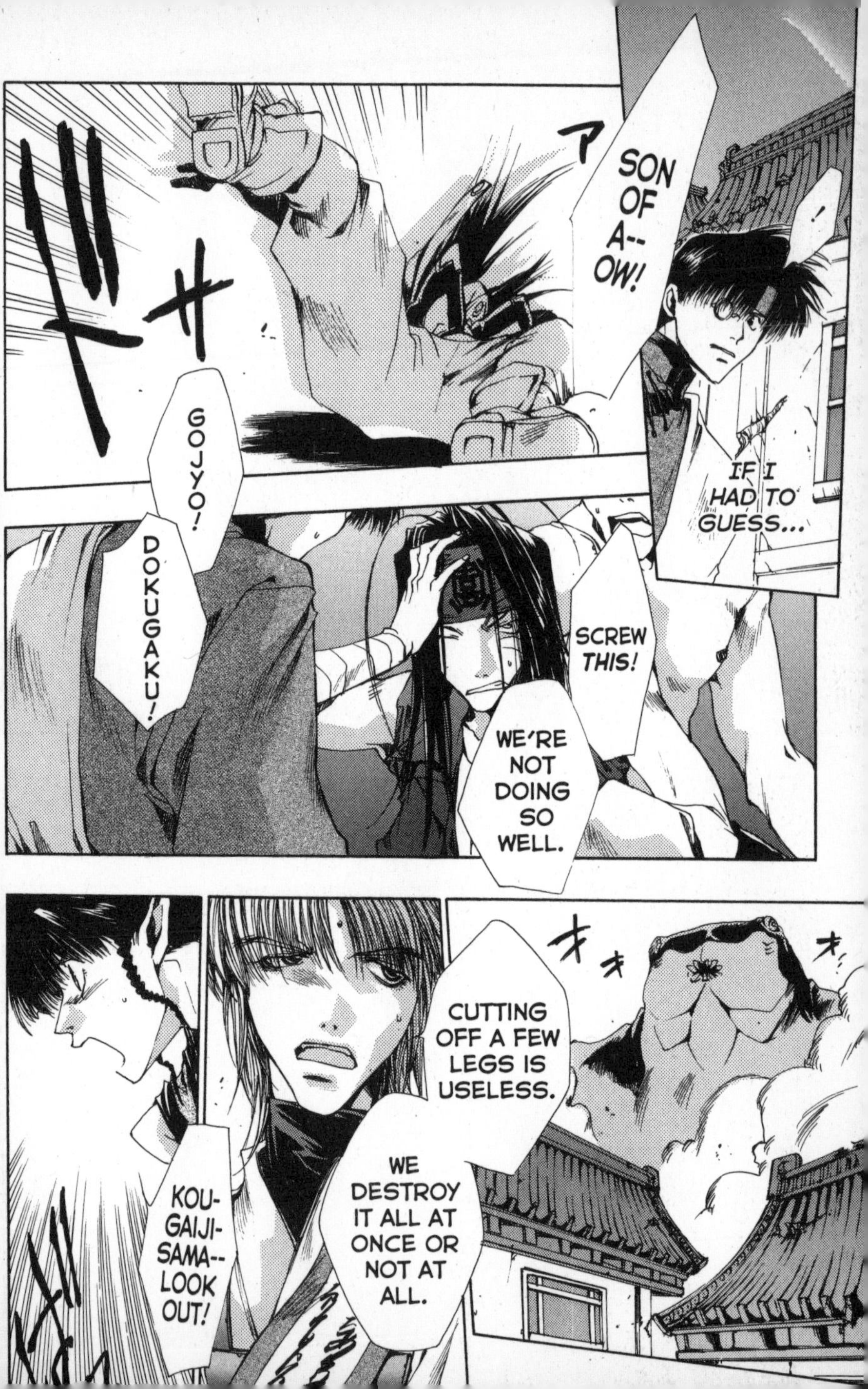

SON OF A-- OW!
GOJYO!
DOKUGAKU!
SCREW THIS!
WE'RE NOT DOING SO WELL.
!
IF I HAD TO GUESS...
CUTTING OFF A FEW LEGS IS USELESS.
WE DESTROY IT ALL AT ONCE OR NOT AT ALL.
KOU-GAIJI-SAMA-- LOOK OUT!

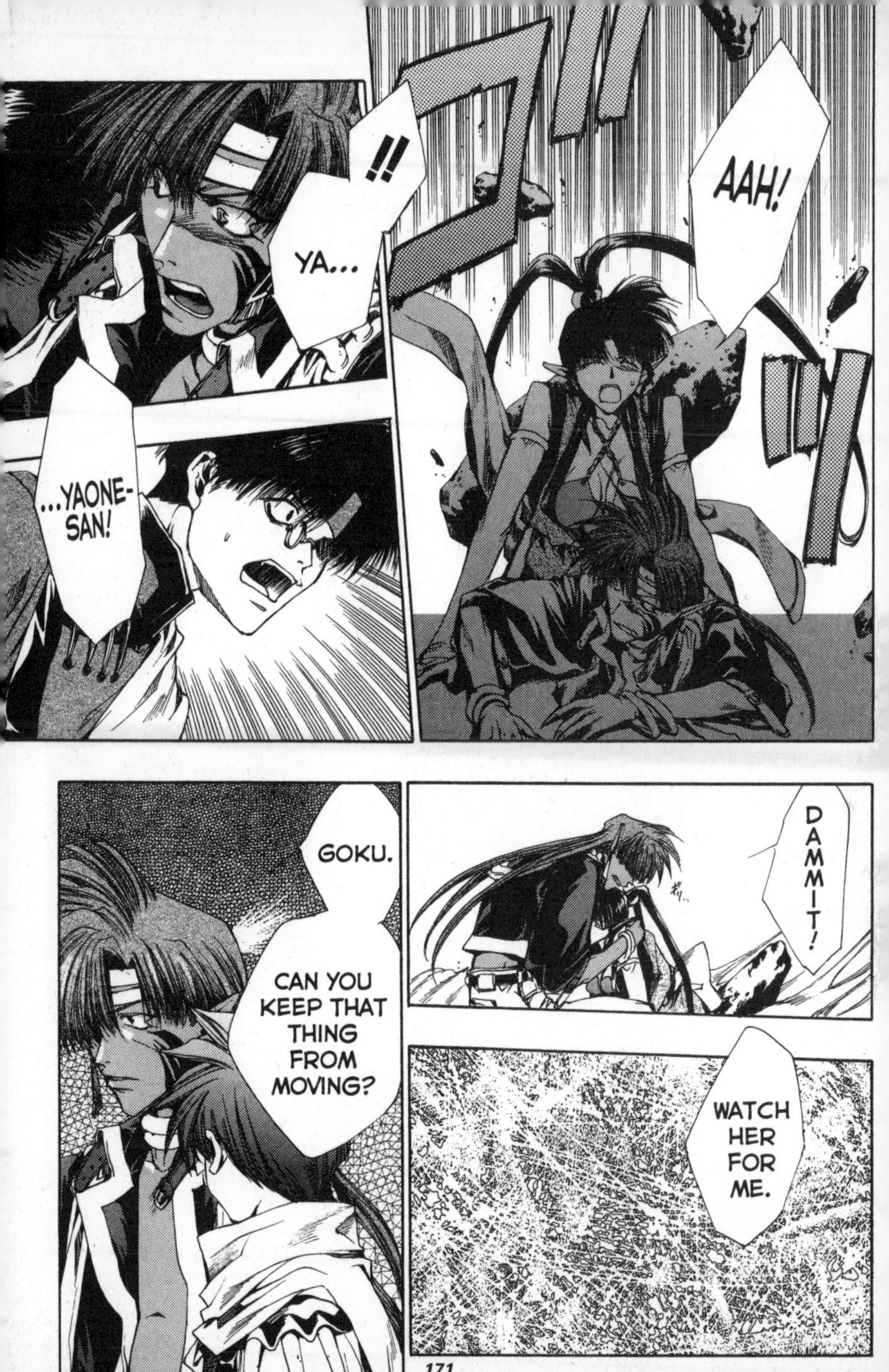
AAH!
!!
YA...
...YAONE-SAN!
DAMMIT!
WATCH HER FOR ME.
GOKU.
CAN YOU KEEP THAT THING FROM MOVING?

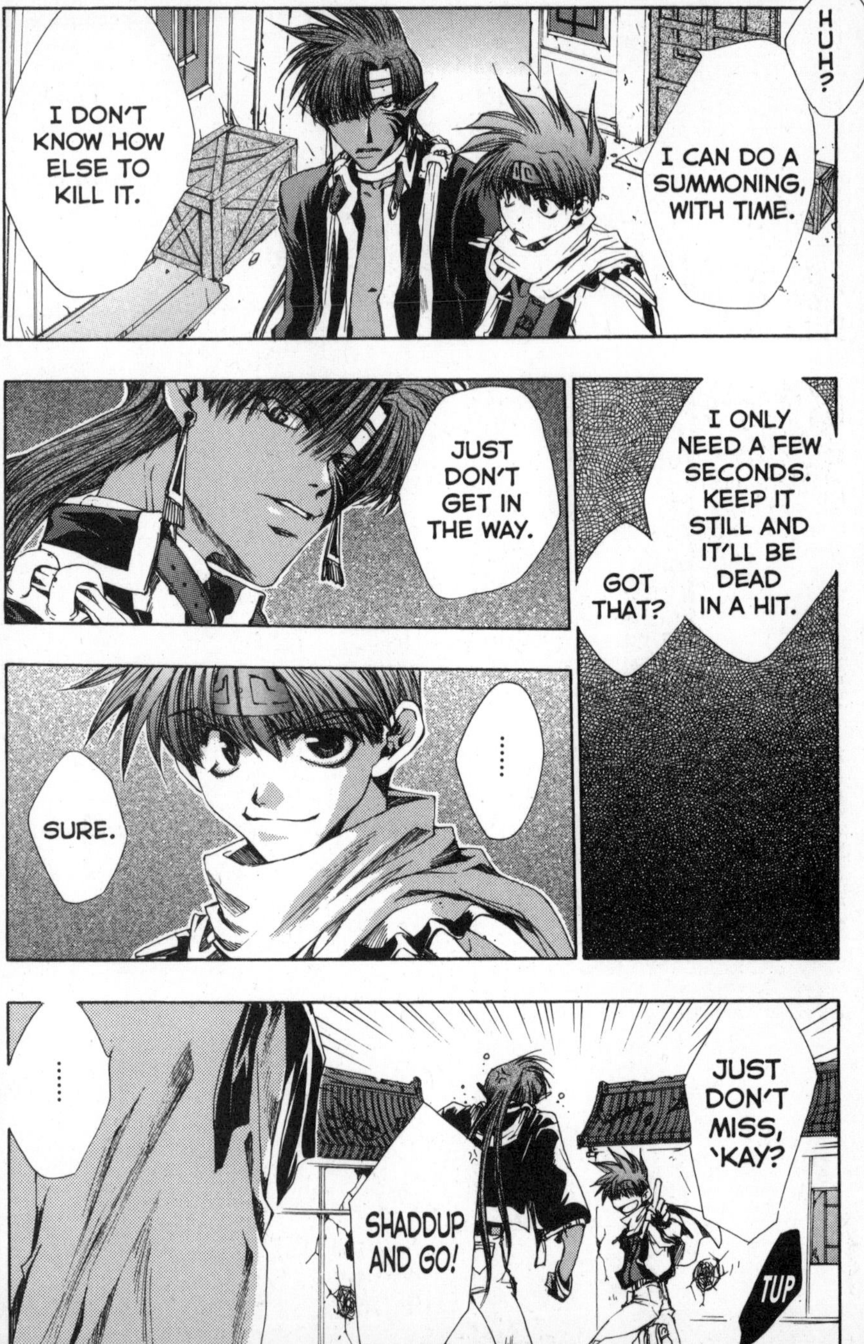
HUH?
I CAN DO A SUMMONING, WITH TIME.
I DON'T KNOW HOW ELSE TO KILL IT.
I ONLY NEED A FEW SECONDS. KEEP IT STILL AND IT'LL BE DEAD IN A HIT.
GOT THAT?
JUST DON'T GET IN THE WAY.
......
SURE.
JUST DON'T MISS, 'KAY?
SHADDUP AND GO!
TUP
......

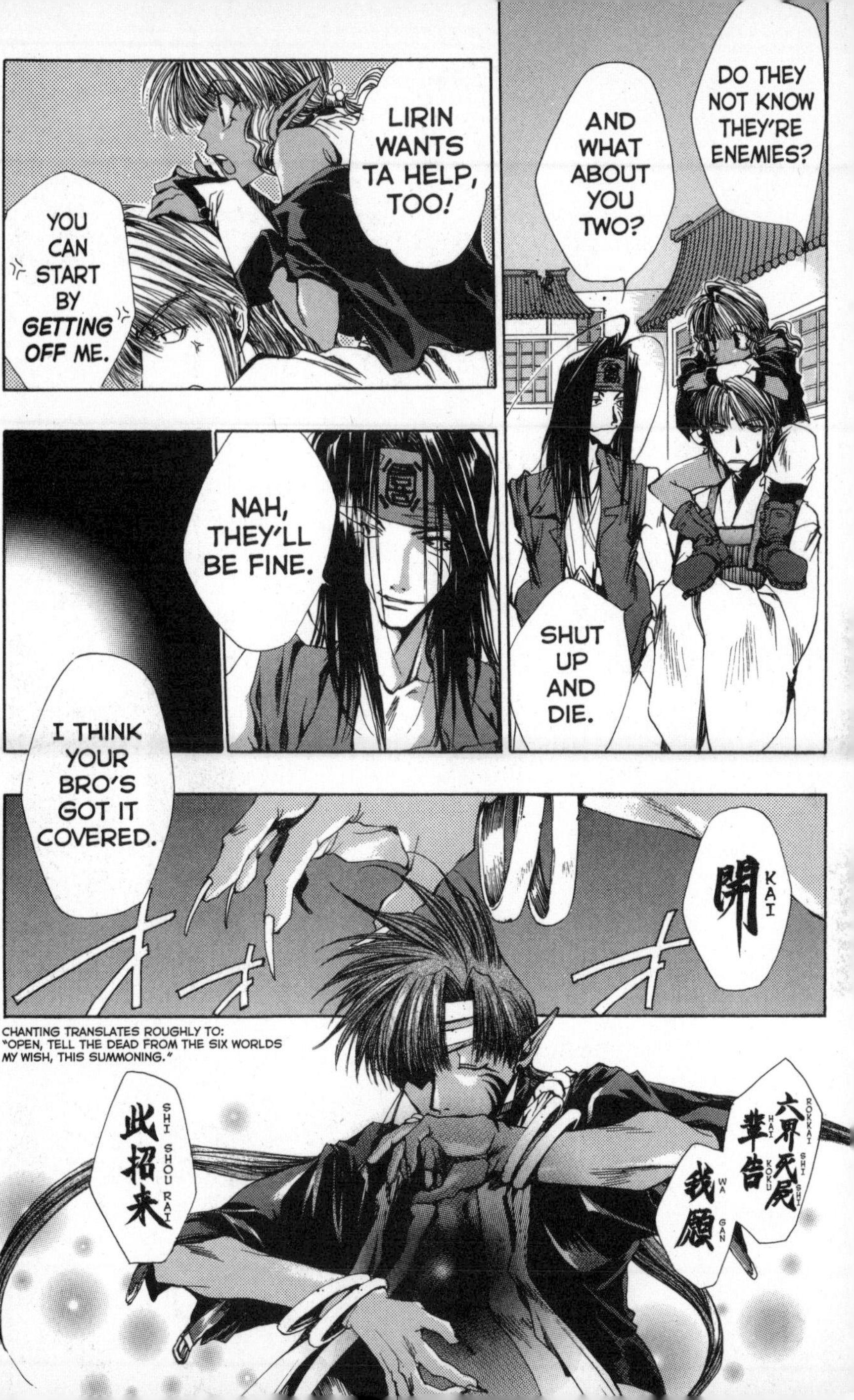
DO THEY NOT KNOW THEY'RE ENEMIES?
AND WHAT ABOUT YOU TWO?
LIRIN WANTS TA HELP, TOO!
YOU CAN START BY GETTING OFF ME.
NAH, THEY'LL BE FINE.
SHUT UP AND DIE.
I THINK YOUR BRO'S GOT IT COVERED.
開 KAI
六界死尸 ROKKAI SHI SHI
拝告 HAI KOKU
我願 WA GAN
此招来 SHI SHOU RAI
CHANTING TRANSLATES ROUGHLY TO: "OPEN, TELL THE DEAD FROM THE SIX WORLDS MY WISH, THIS SUMMONING."

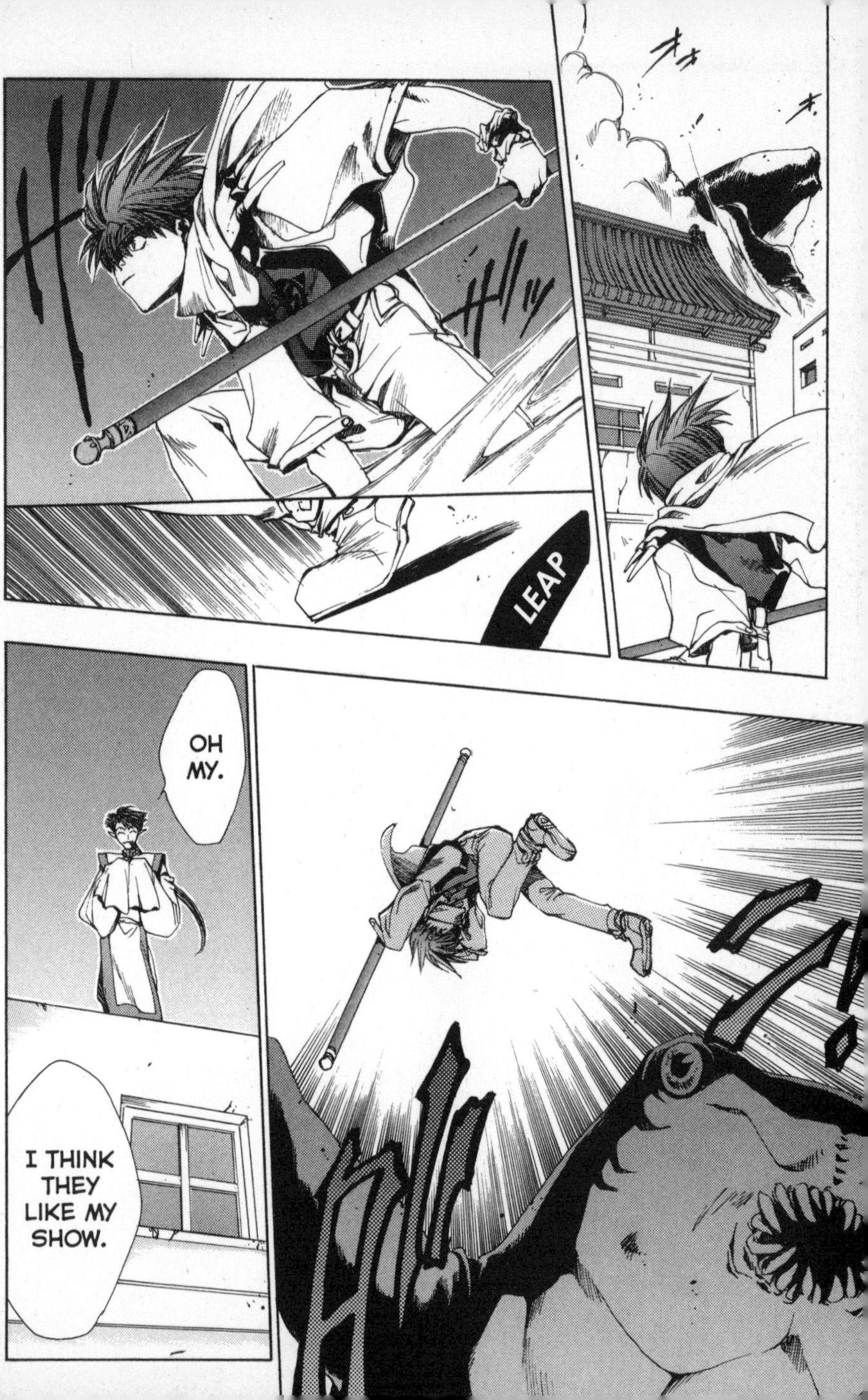
LEAP
OH MY.
I THINK THEY LIKE MY SHOW.

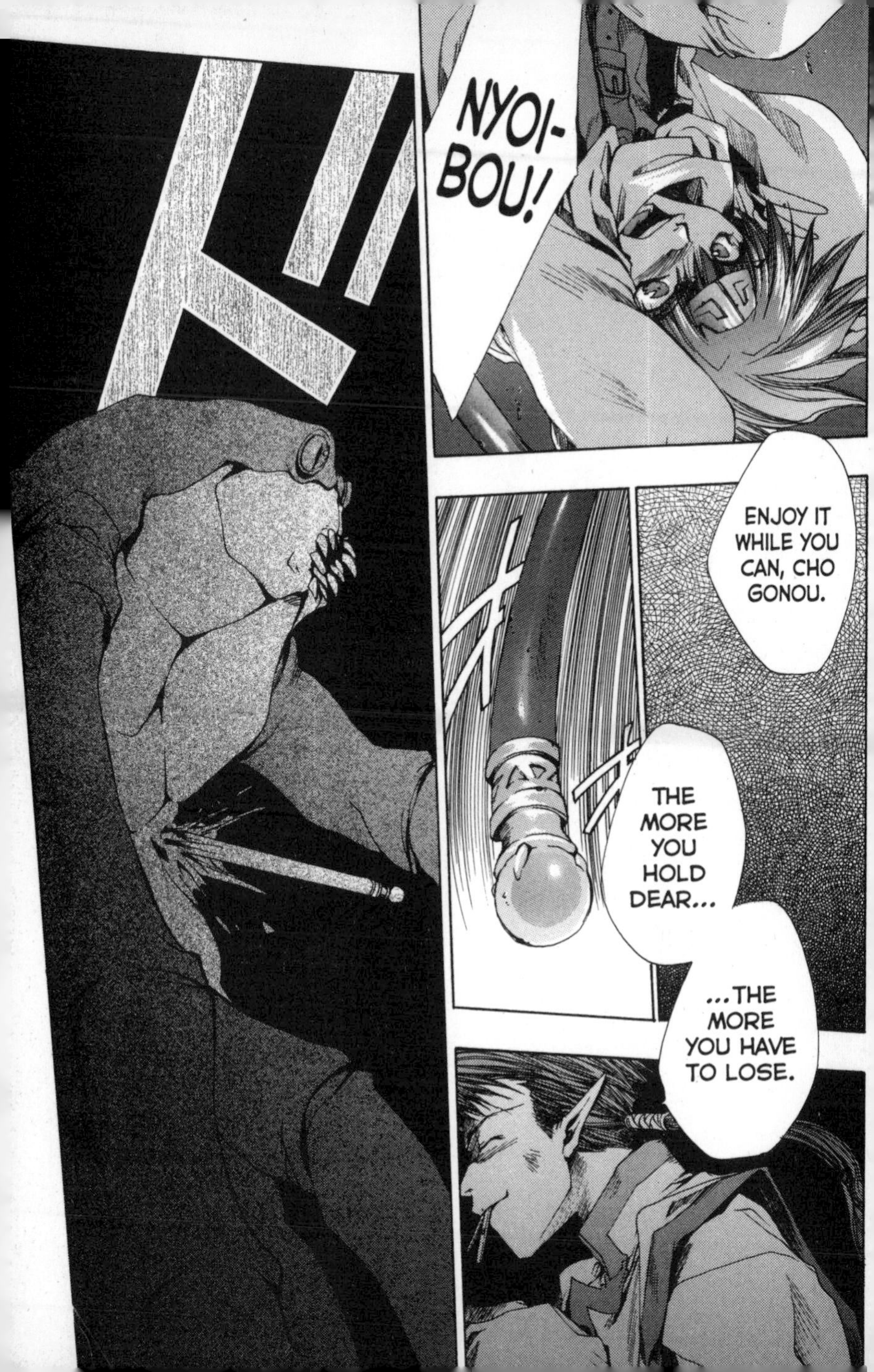

NYOI-BOU!
ENJOY IT WHILE YOU CAN, CHO GONOU.
THE MORE YOU HOLD DEAR...
...THE MORE YOU HAVE TO LOSE.

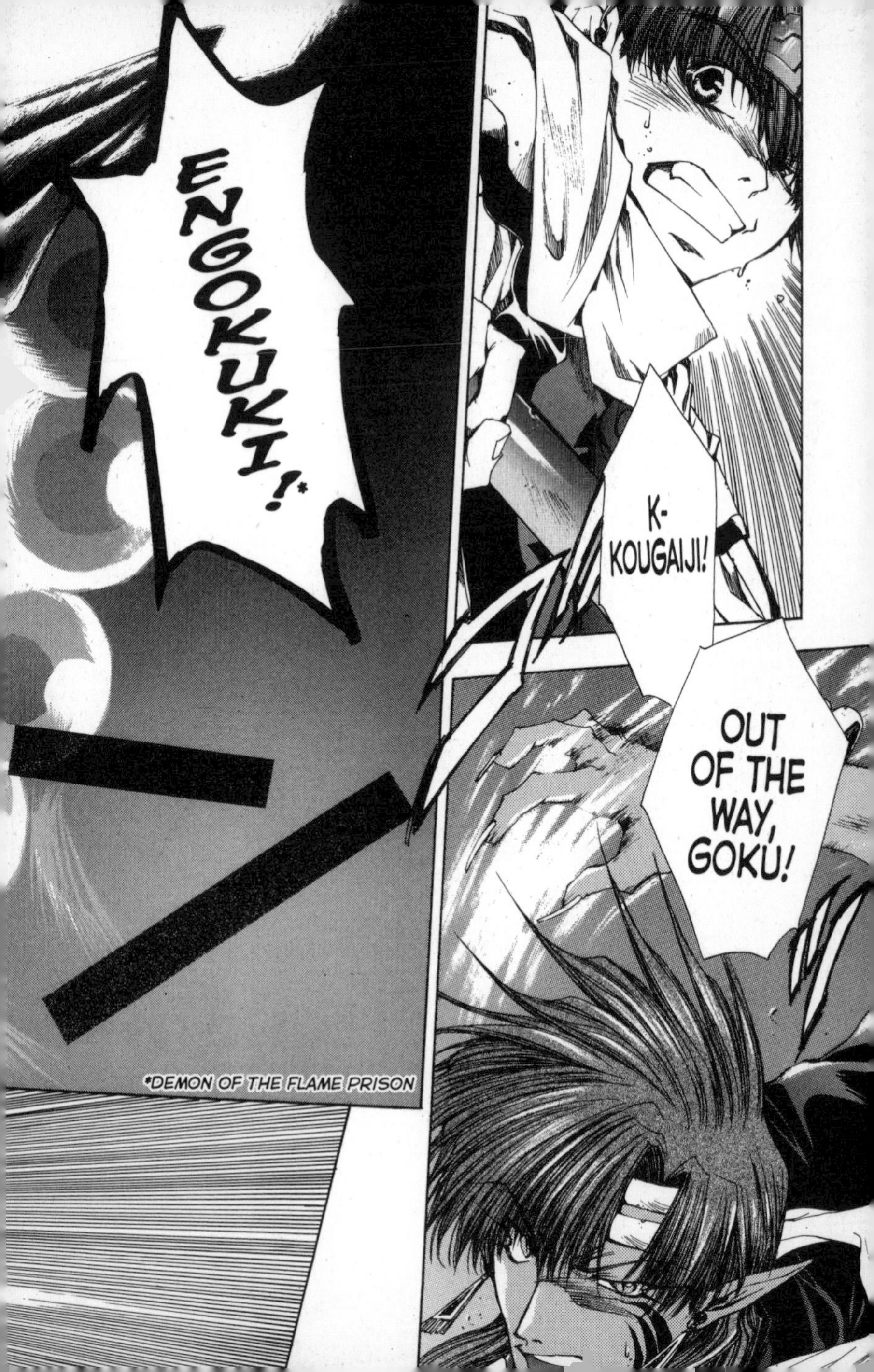
K-KOUGAIJI!
OUT OF THE WAY, GOKU!
ENGOKUKI!*
*DEMON OF THE FLAME PRISON

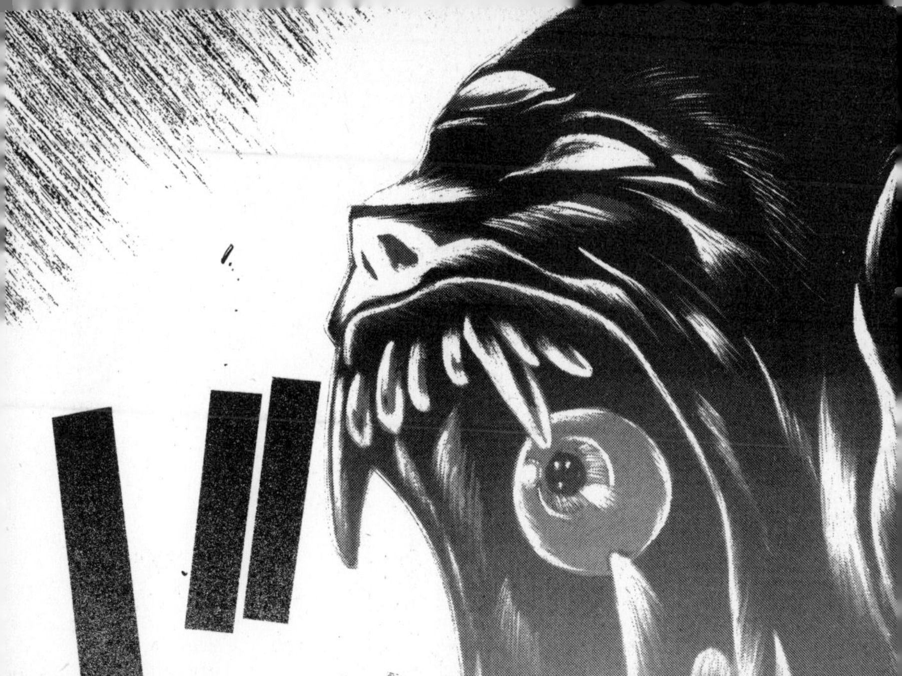
ド
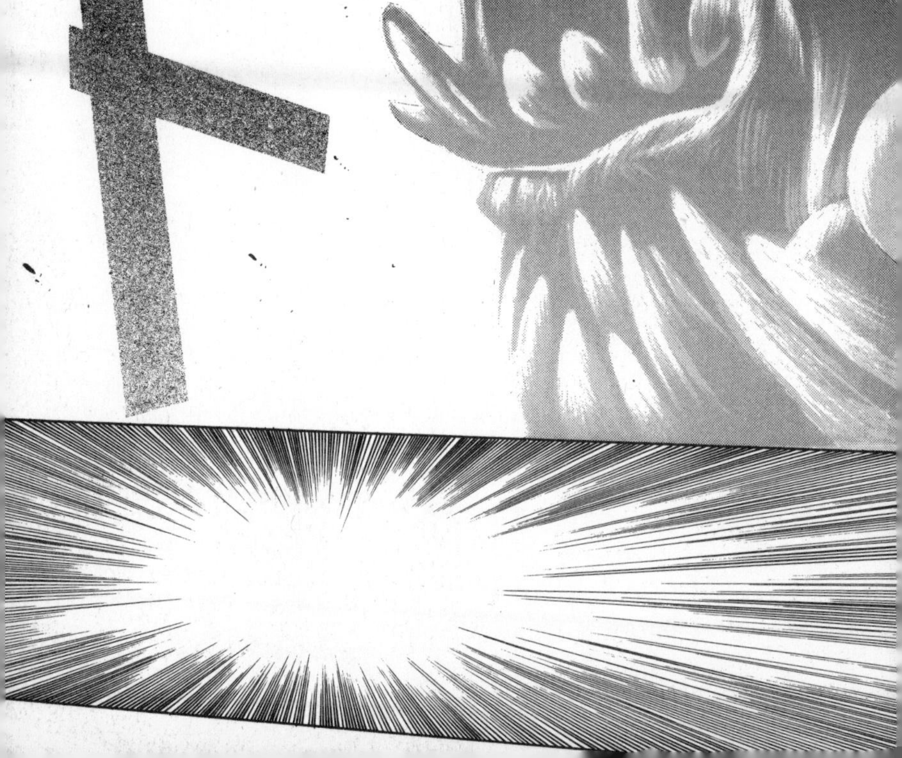

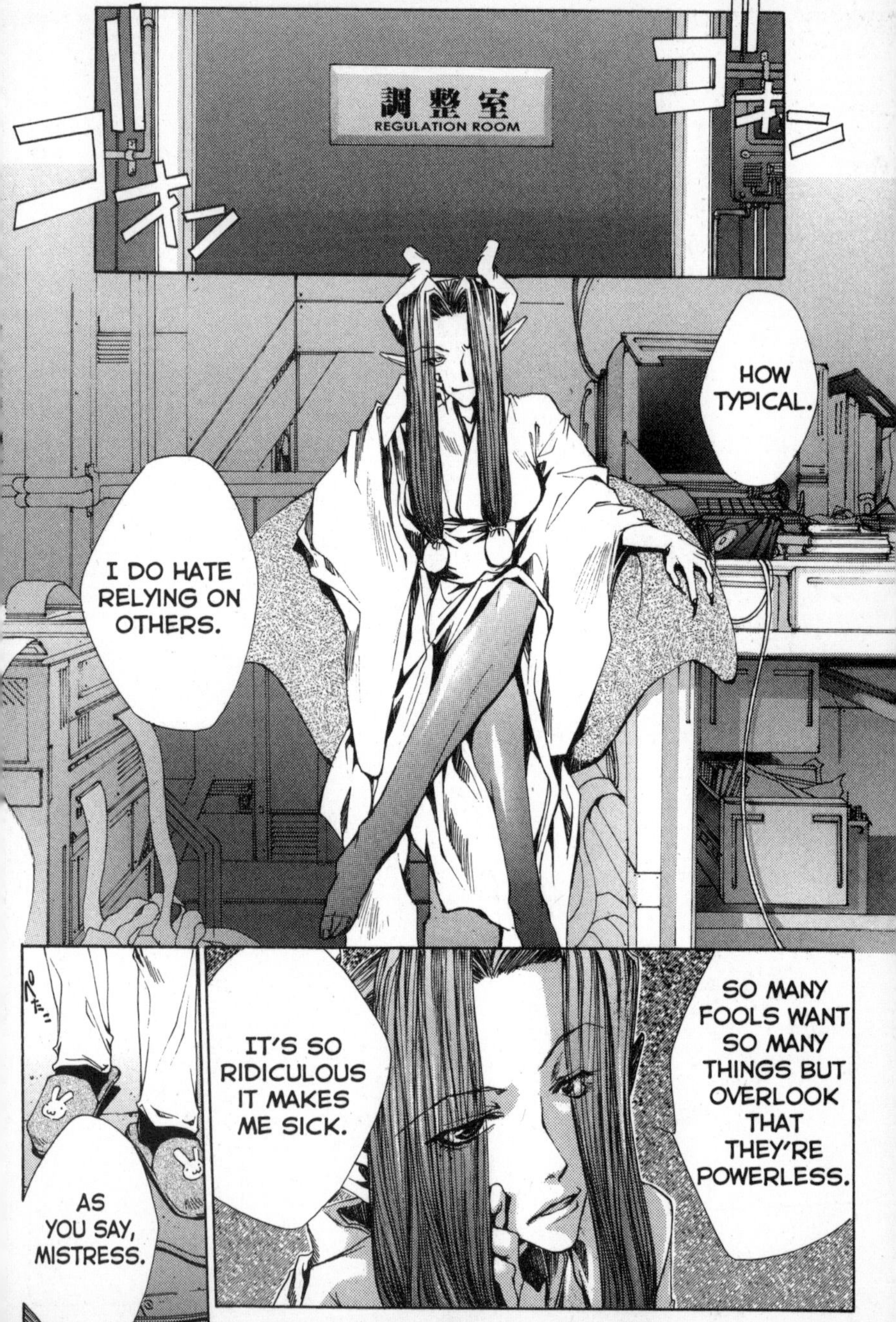
ゴォン
調整室
REGULATION ROOM
ゴォン
HOW TYPICAL.
I DO HATE RELYING ON OTHERS.
SO MANY FOOLS WANT SO MANY THINGS BUT OVERLOOK THAT THEY'RE POWERLESS.
IT'S SO RIDICULOUS IT MAKES ME SICK.
AS YOU SAY, MISTRESS.

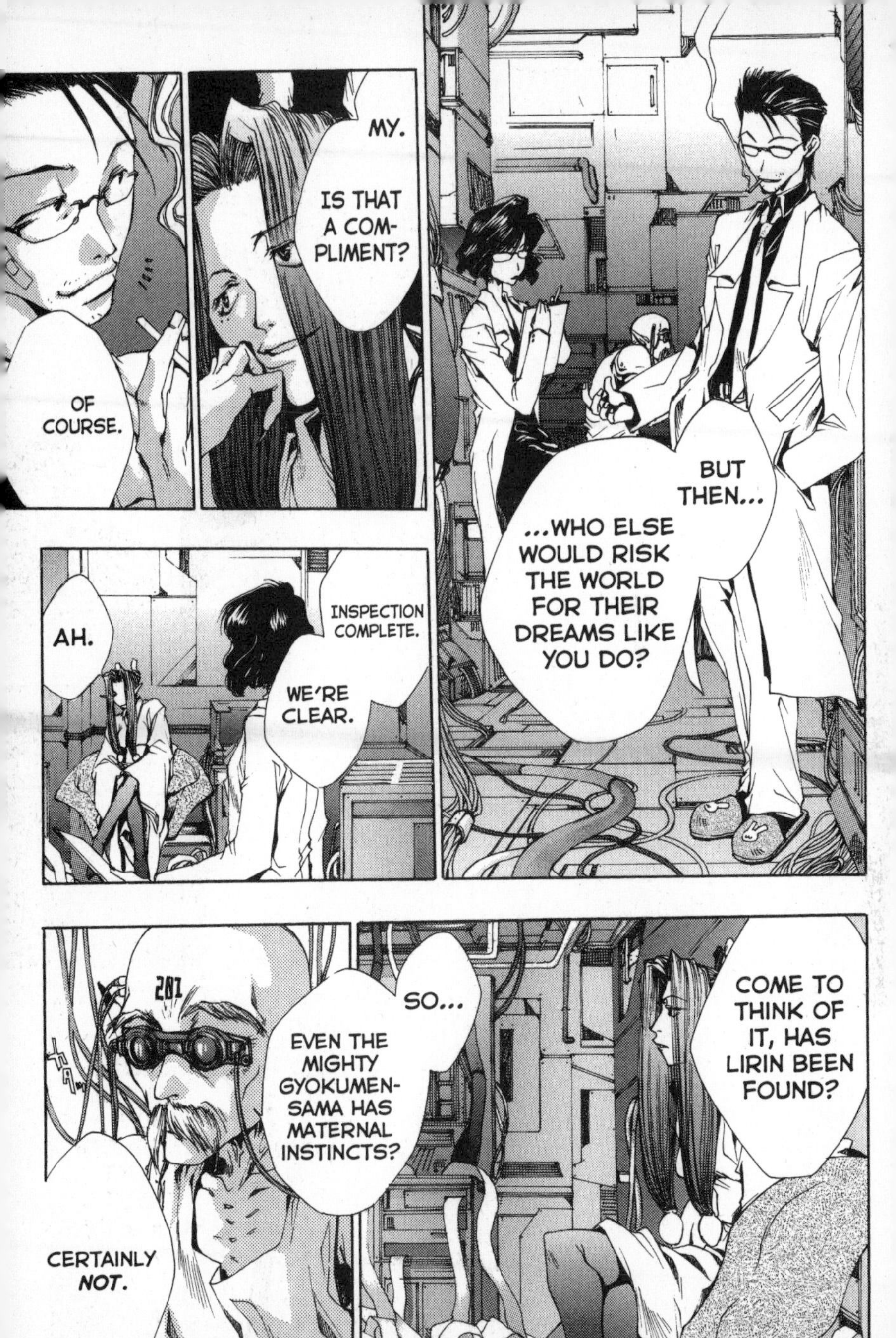
BUT THEN...
...WHO ELSE WOULD RISK THE WORLD FOR THEIR DREAMS LIKE YOU DO?
MY.
IS THAT A COMPLIMENT?
OF COURSE.
INSPECTION COMPLETE.
WE'RE CLEAR.
AH.
COME TO THINK OF IT, HAS LIRIN BEEN FOUND?
SO...
EVEN THE MIGHTY GYOKUMEN-SAMA HAS MATERNAL INSTINCTS?
CERTAINLY NOT.

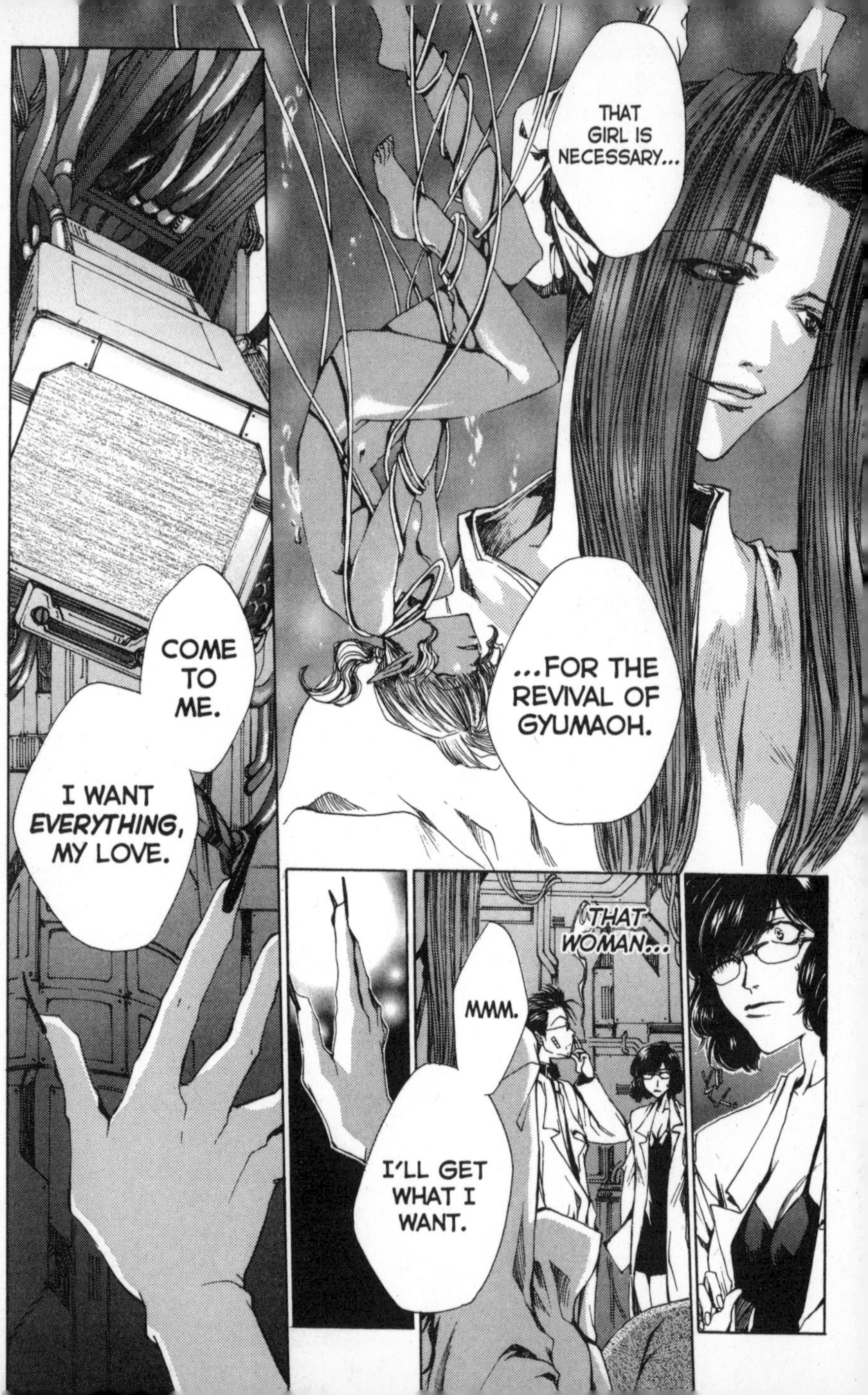
THAT GIRL IS NECESSARY...
...FOR THE REVIVAL OF GYUMAOH.
THAT WOMAN...
MMM.
I'LL GET WHAT I WANT.
COME TO ME.
I WANT *EVERYTHING*, MY LOVE.

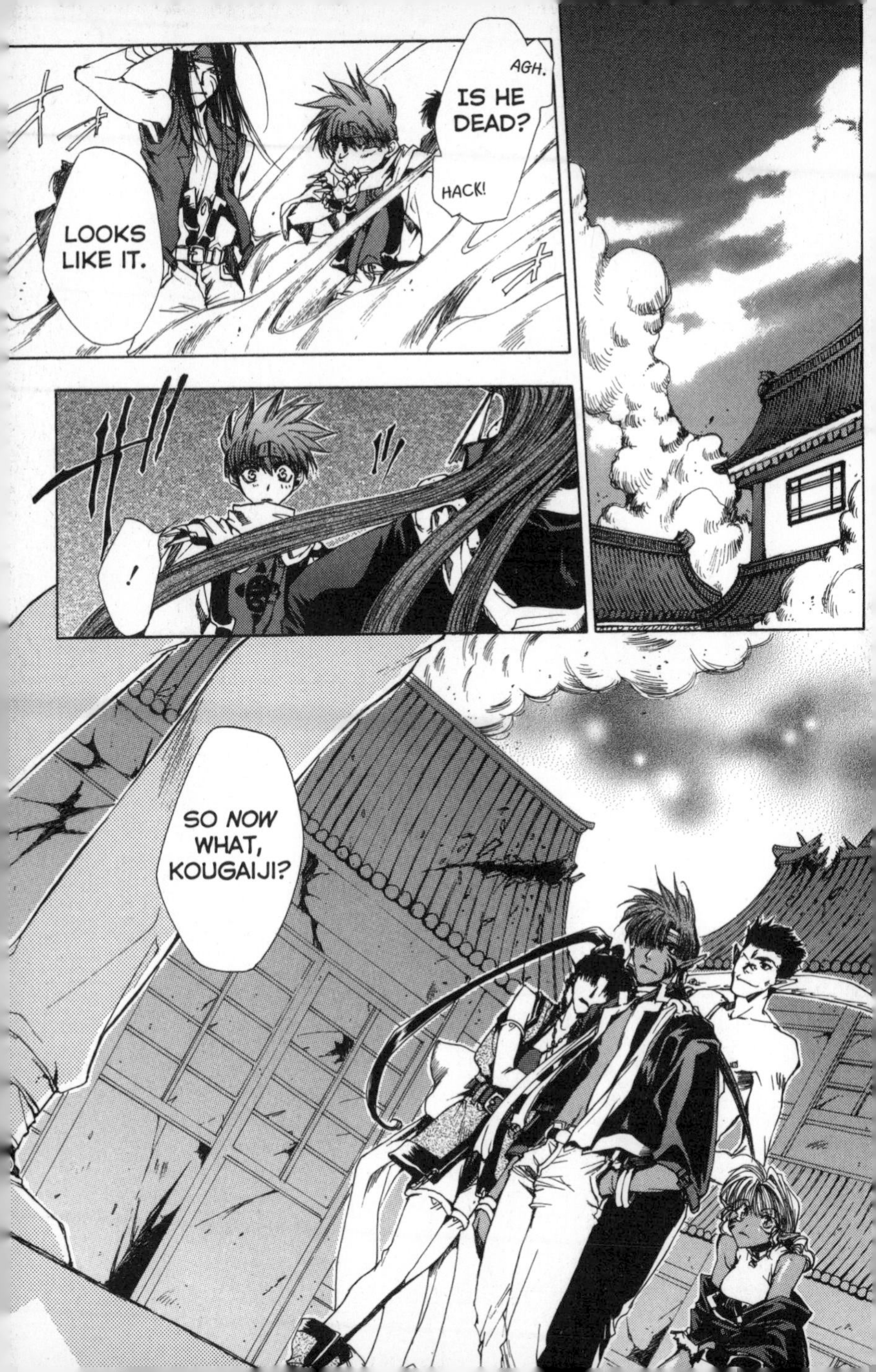
AGH. IS HE DEAD? HACK!
LOOKS LIKE IT.
!
SO NOW WHAT, KOUGAIJI?

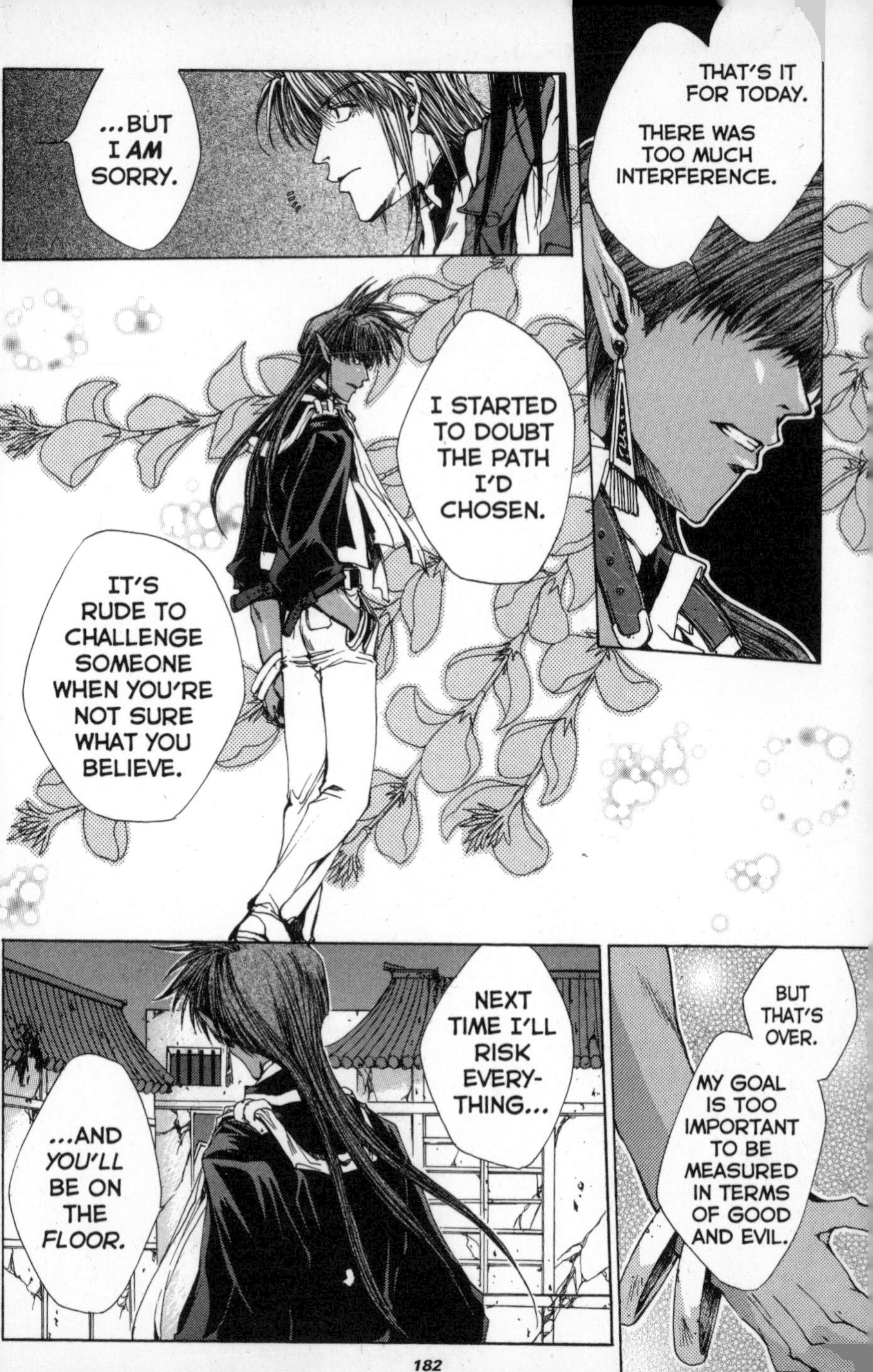
THAT'S IT FOR TODAY.
THERE WAS TOO MUCH INTERFERENCE.
...BUT I *AM* SORRY.
I STARTED TO DOUBT THE PATH I'D CHOSEN.
IT'S RUDE TO CHALLENGE SOMEONE WHEN YOU'RE NOT SURE WHAT YOU BELIEVE.
BUT THAT'S OVER.
MY GOAL IS TOO IMPORTANT TO BE MEASURED IN TERMS OF GOOD AND EVIL.
NEXT TIME I'LL RISK EVERY-THING...
...AND *YOU'LL* BE ON THE *FLOOR.*

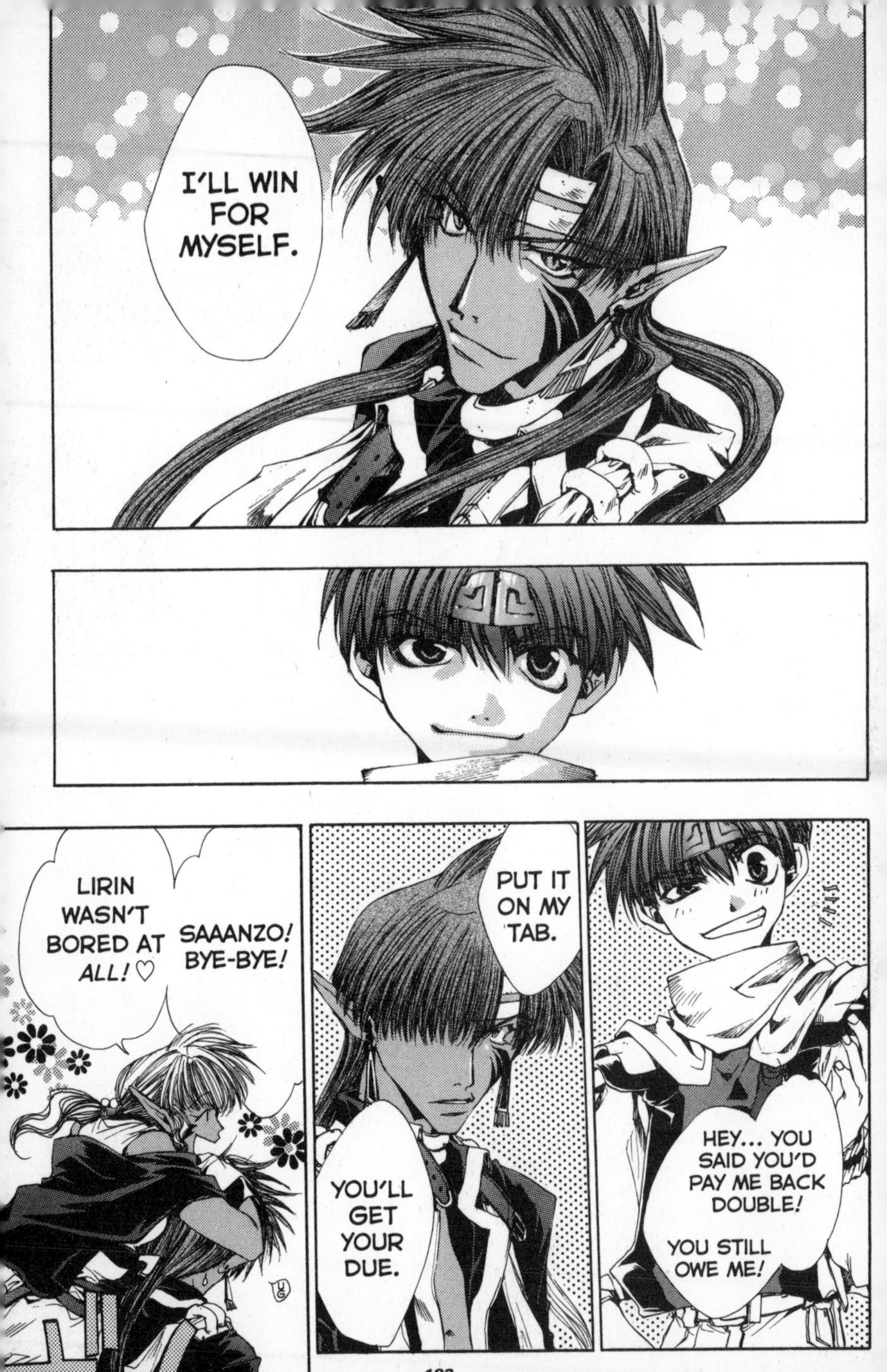
I'LL WIN FOR MYSELF.
HEY... YOU SAID YOU'D PAY ME BACK DOUBLE!
YOU STILL OWE ME!
PUT IT ON MY TAB.
YOU'LL GET YOUR DUE.
SAAANZO! BYE-BYE!
LIRIN WASN'T BORED AT ALL! ♡

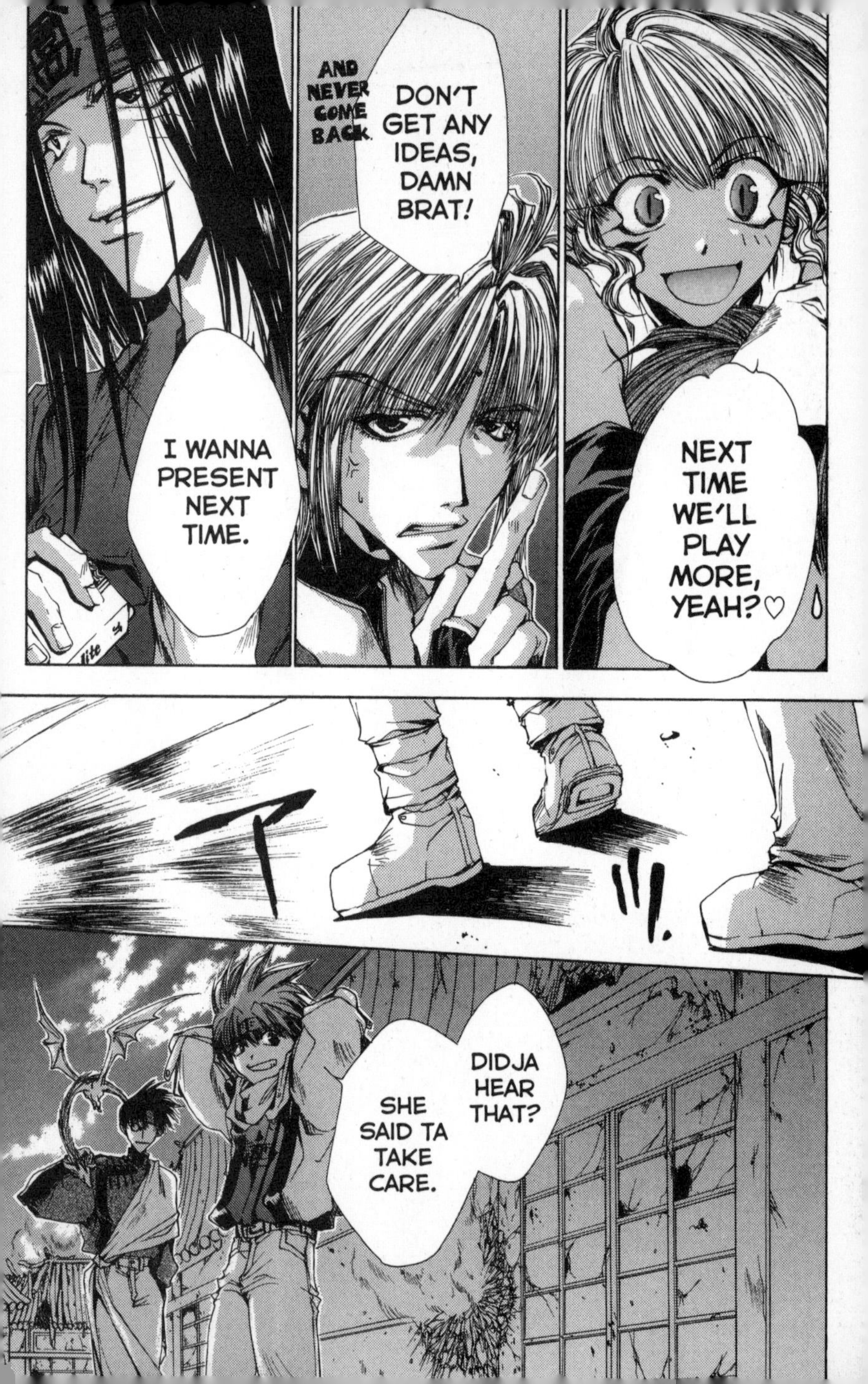
NEXT TIME WE'LL PLAY MORE, YEAH?♡
DON'T GET ANY IDEAS, DAMN BRAT!
AND NEVER COME BACK.
I WANNA PRESENT NEXT TIME.
DIDJA HEAR THAT?
SHE SAID TA TAKE CARE.

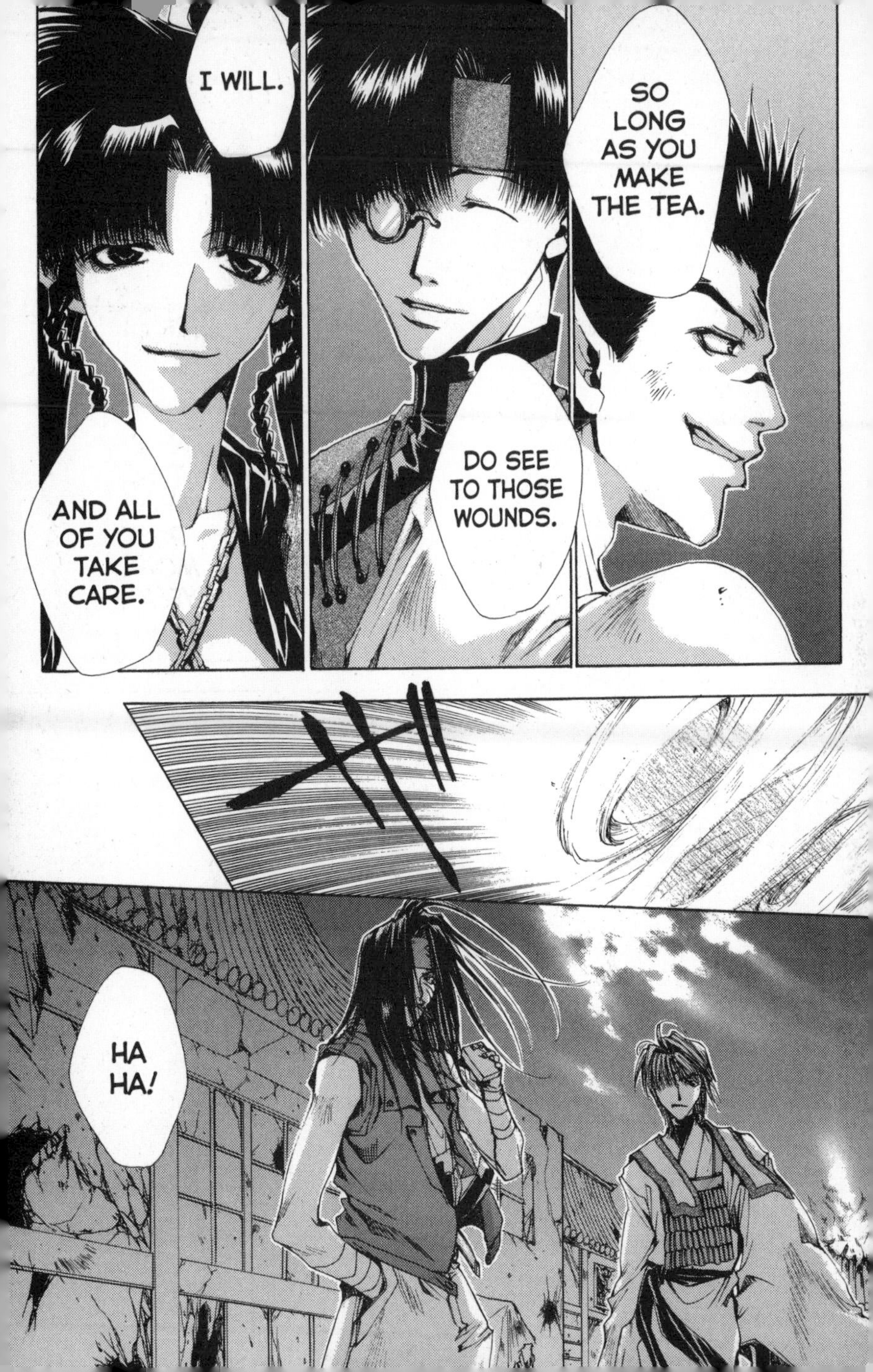
SO LONG AS YOU MAKE THE TEA.
DO SEE TO THOSE WOUNDS.
I WILL.
AND ALL OF YOU TAKE CARE.
HA HA!

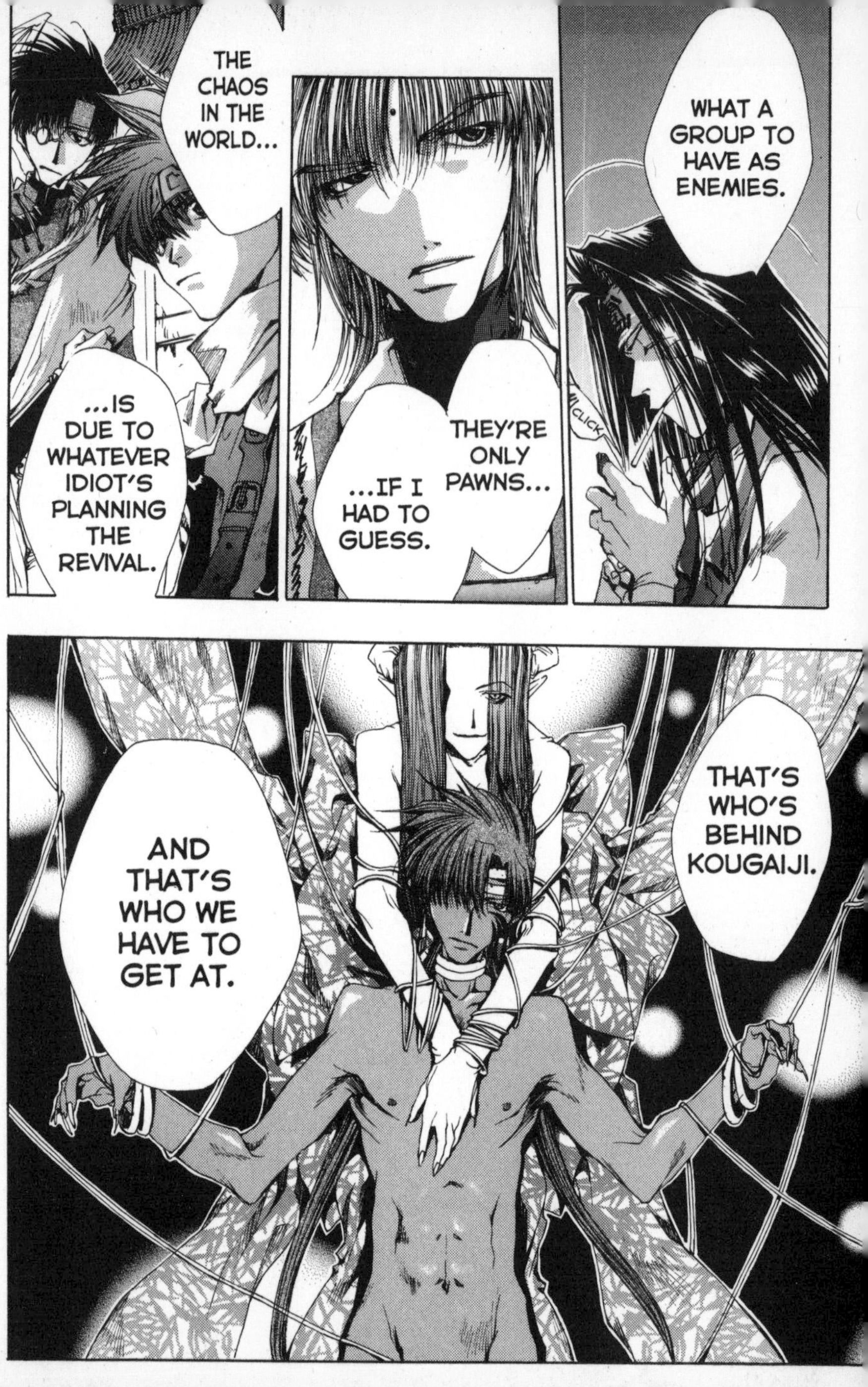
WHAT A GROUP TO HAVE AS ENEMIES.
CLICK
THEY'RE ONLY PAWNS...
...IF I HAD TO GUESS.
THE CHAOS IN THE WORLD...
...IS DUE TO WHATEVER IDIOT'S PLANNING THE REVIVAL.
THAT'S WHO'S BEHIND KOUGAIJI.
AND THAT'S WHO WE HAVE TO GET AT.

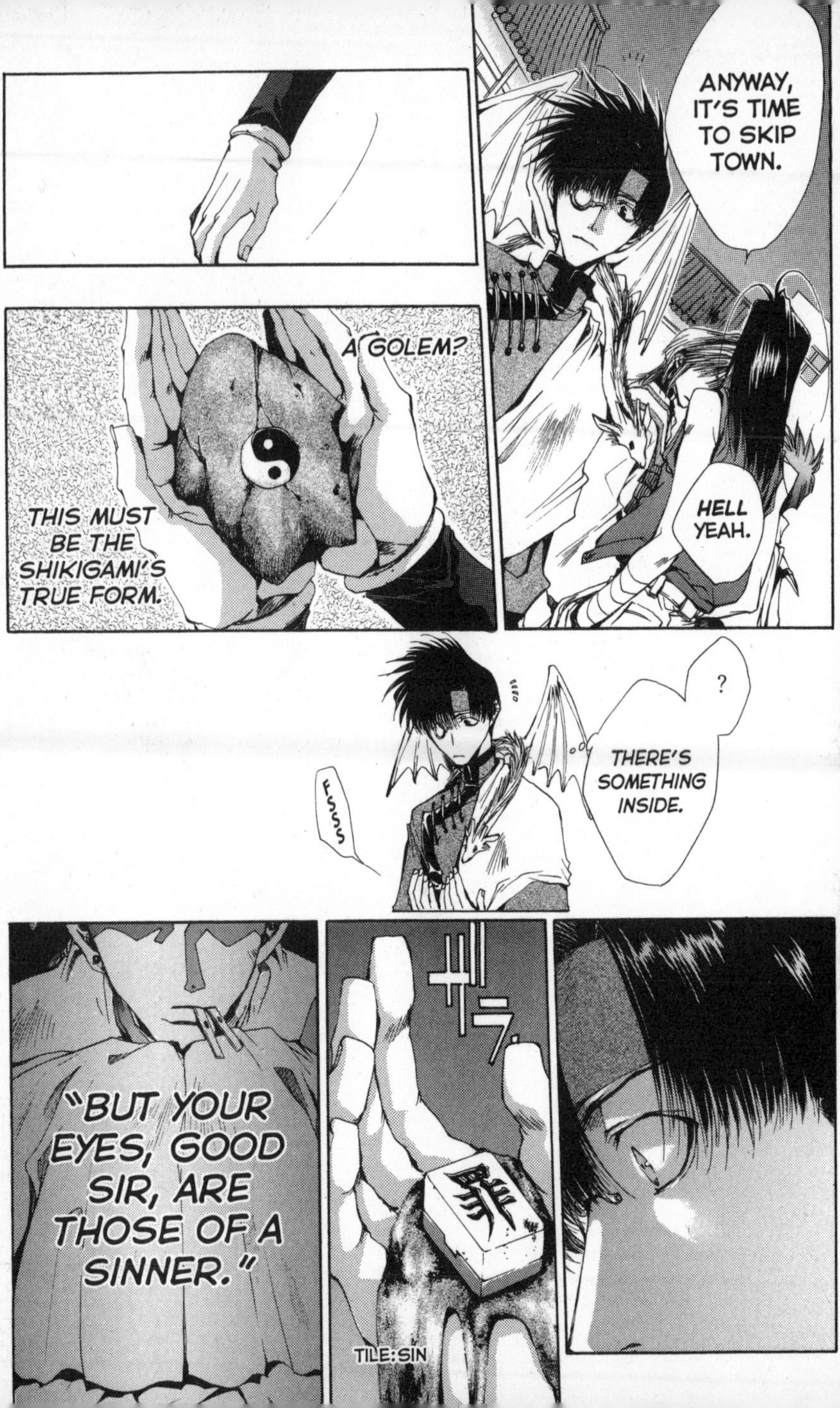
ANYWAY, IT'S TIME TO SKIP TOWN.
HELL YEAH.
A GOLEM?
THIS MUST BE THE SHIKIGAMI'S TRUE FORM.
?
THERE'S SOMETHING INSIDE.
FSSS
ピラ.
TILE: SIN
"BUT YOUR EYES, GOOD SIR, ARE THOSE OF A SINNER."

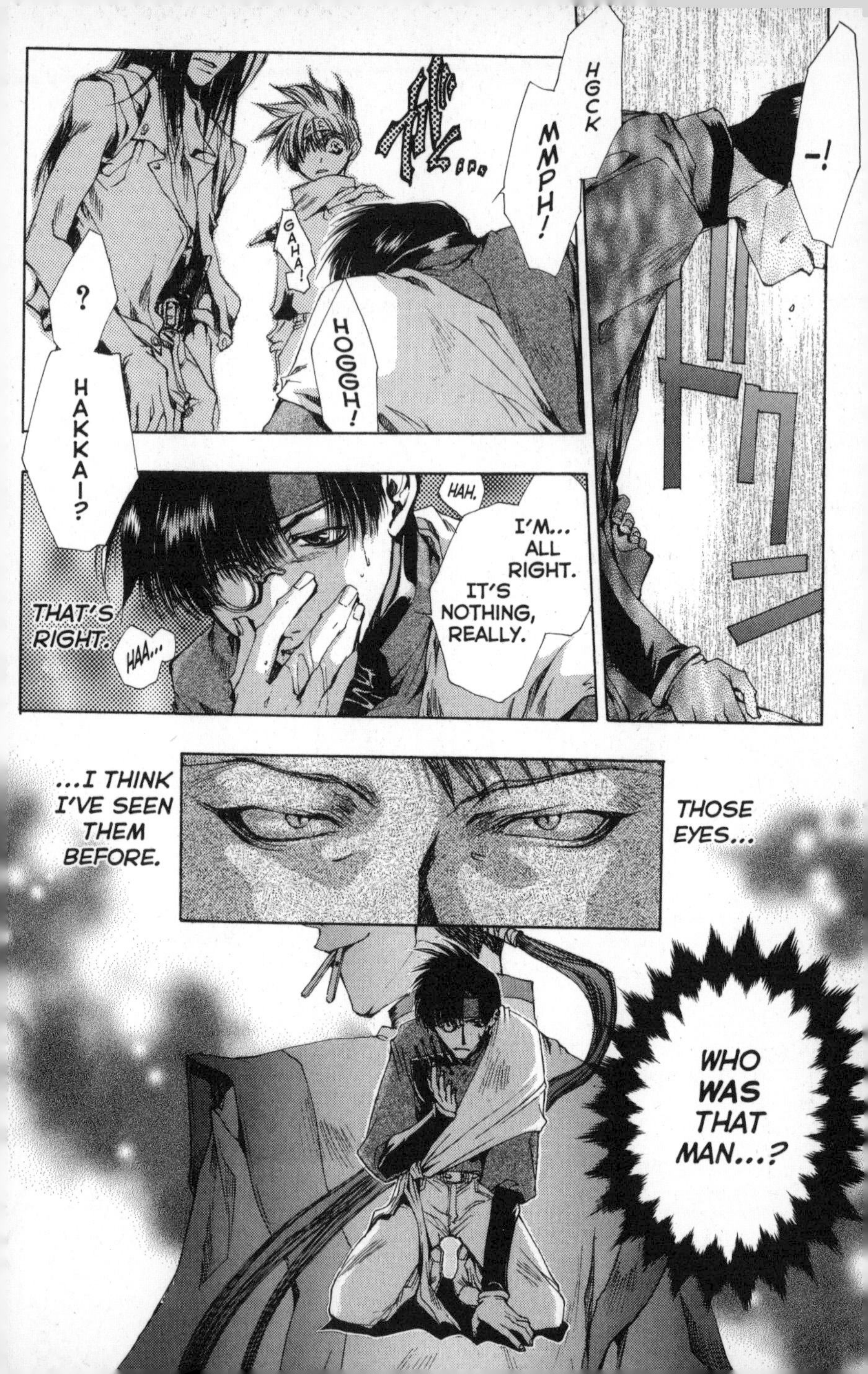
–!
HGCK MMPH!
GAHA!
HOGGH!
?
HAKKAI?
HAH.
I'M... ALL RIGHT. IT'S NOTHING, REALLY.
HAA...
THAT'S RIGHT.
THOSE EYES...
...I THINK I'VE SEEN THEM BEFORE.
WHO WAS THAT MAN...?

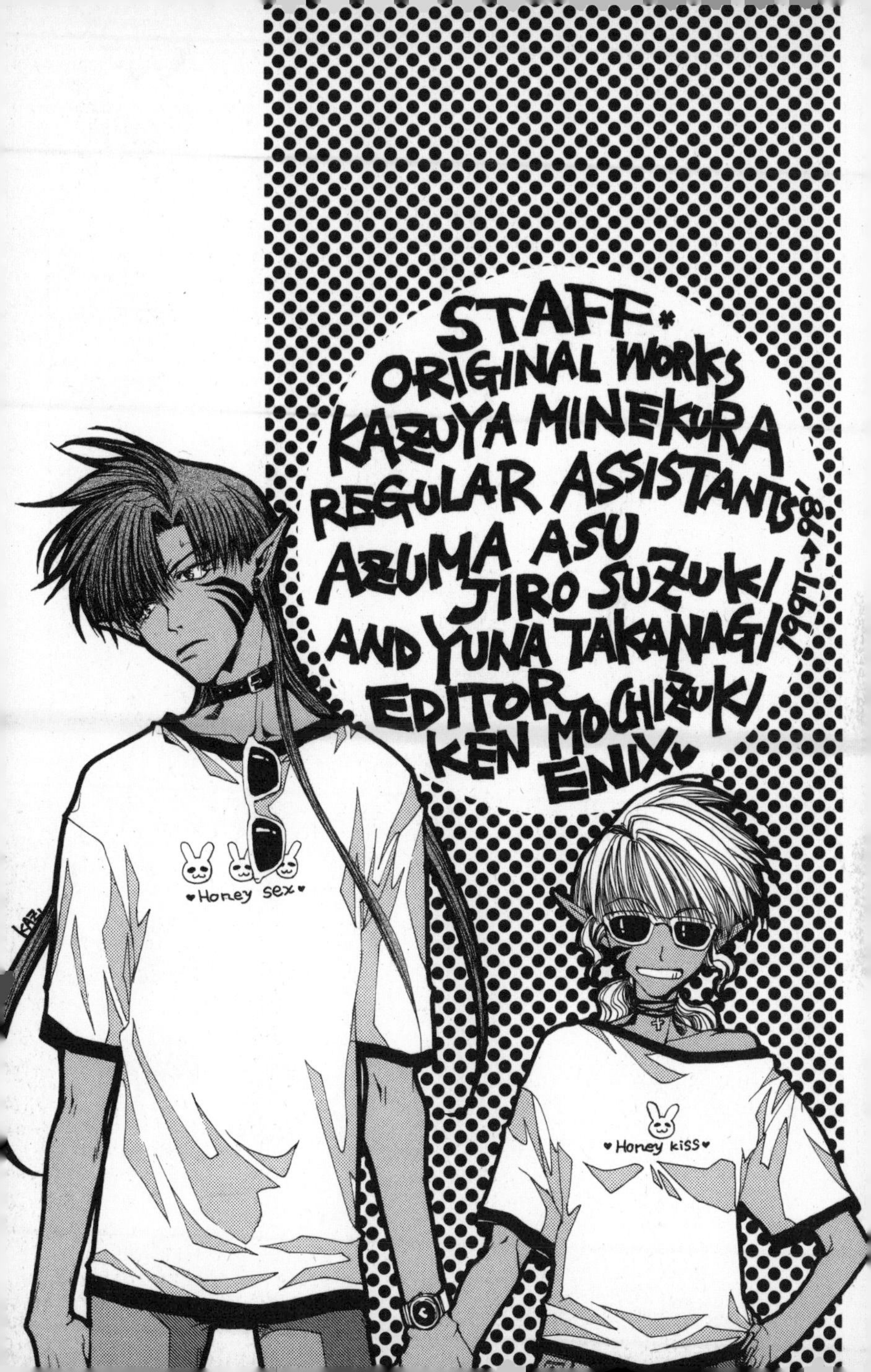
STAFF*
ORIGINAL WORKS
KAZUYA MINEKURA
REGULAR ASSISTANTS
AZUMA ASU
JIRO SUZUKI
AND YUNA TAKANAGI
EDITOR
KEN MOCHIZUKI
ENIX
Honey sex
Honey kiss

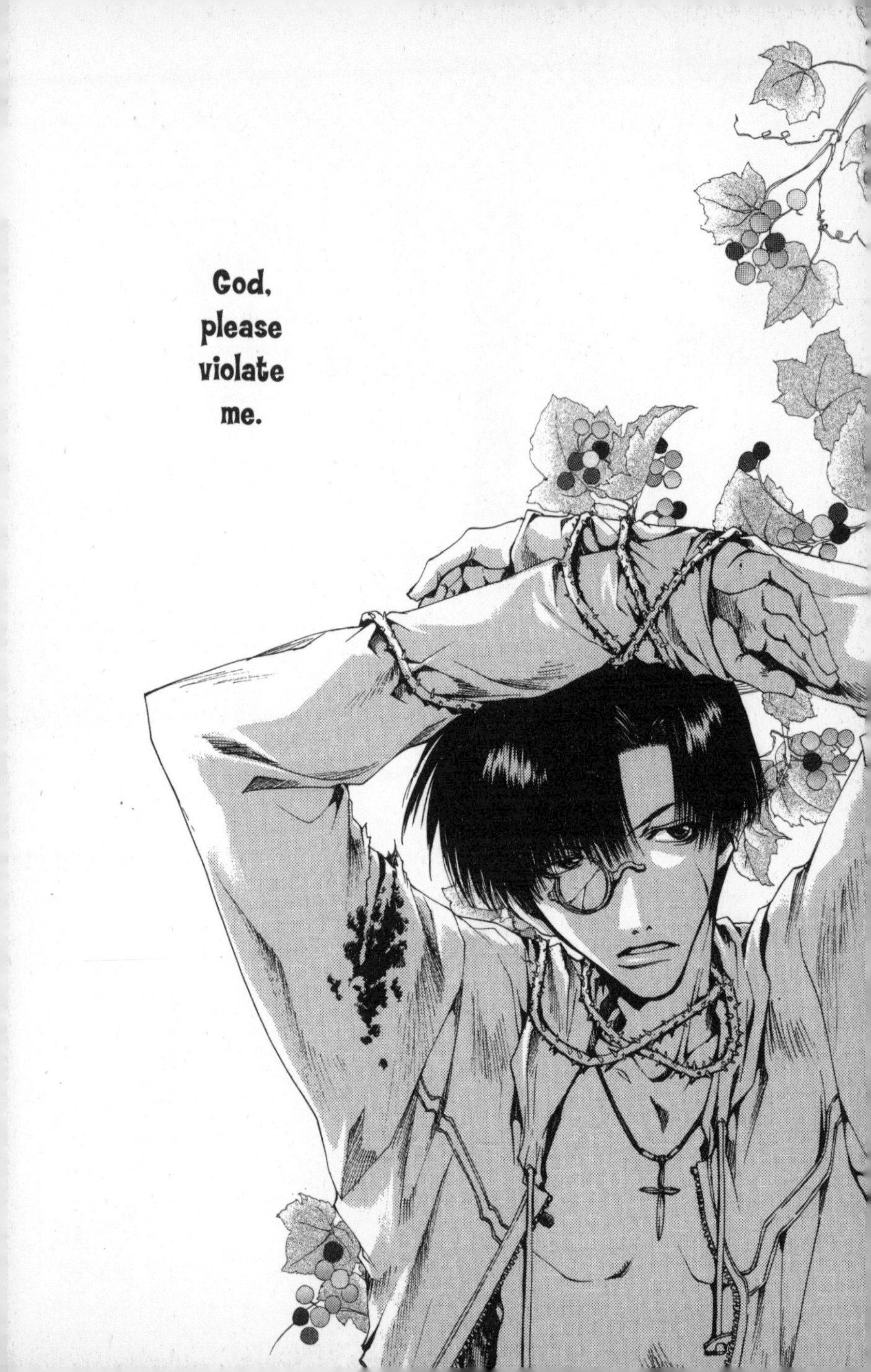
God, please violate me.

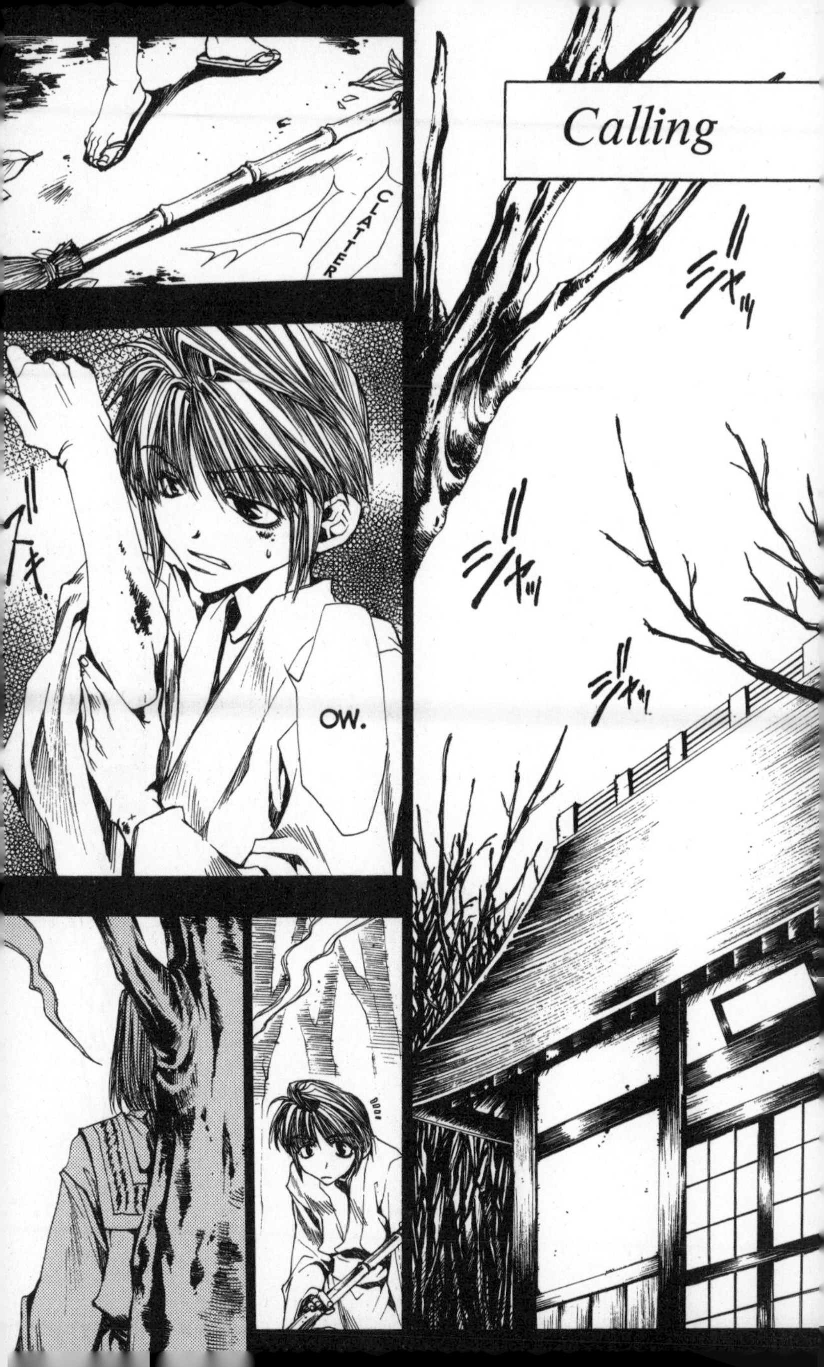

Calling
ジャッ
ジャッ
ジャッ
CLATTER
ズキ.
OW.

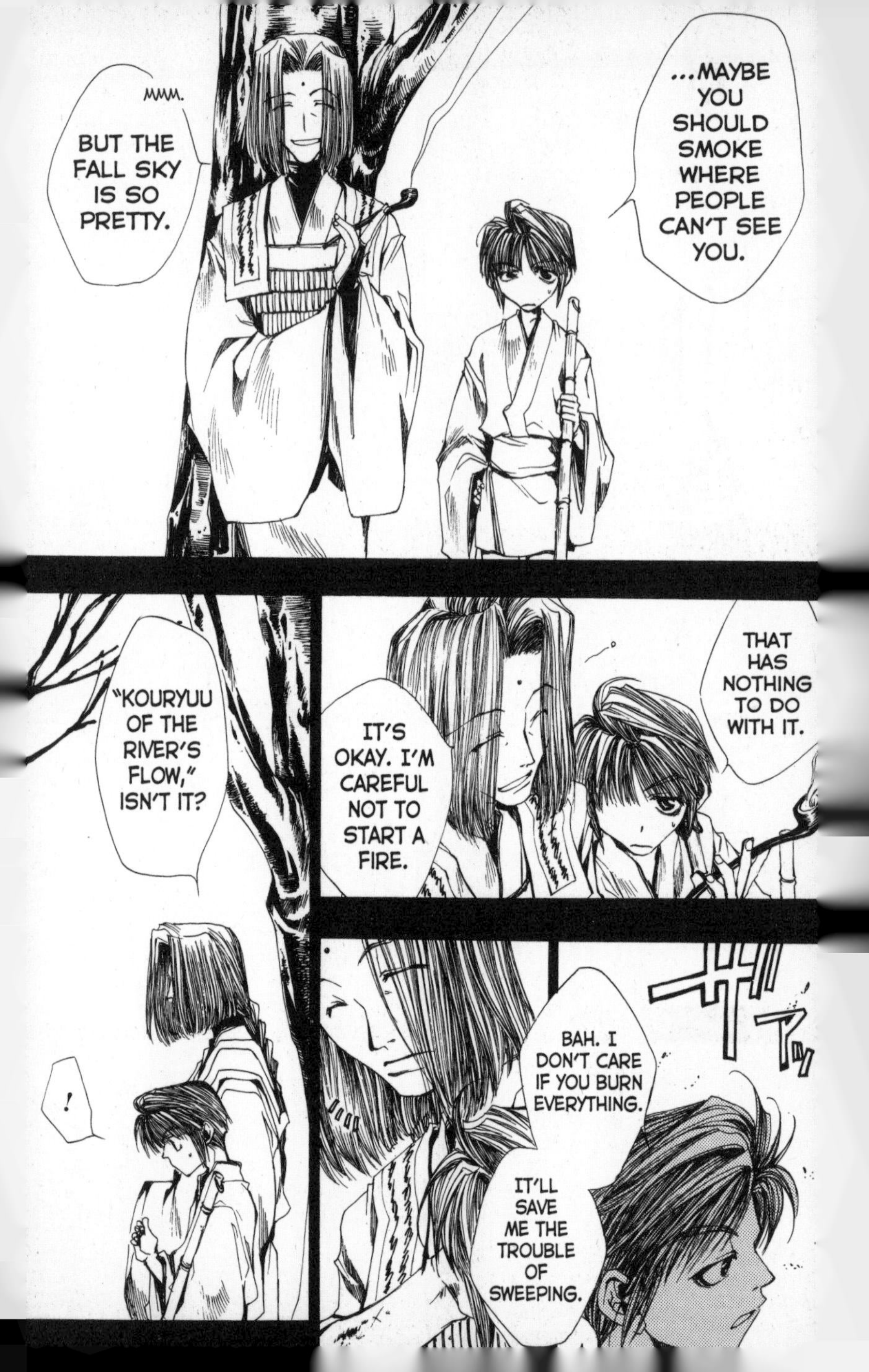
...MAYBE YOU SHOULD SMOKE WHERE PEOPLE CAN'T SEE YOU.
MMM.
BUT THE FALL SKY IS SO PRETTY.
THAT HAS NOTHING TO DO WITH IT.
IT'S OKAY. I'M CAREFUL NOT TO START A FIRE.
BAH. I DON'T CARE IF YOU BURN EVERYTHING.
IT'LL SAVE ME THE TROUBLE OF SWEEPING.
"KOURYUU OF THE RIVER'S FLOW," ISN'T IT?
!

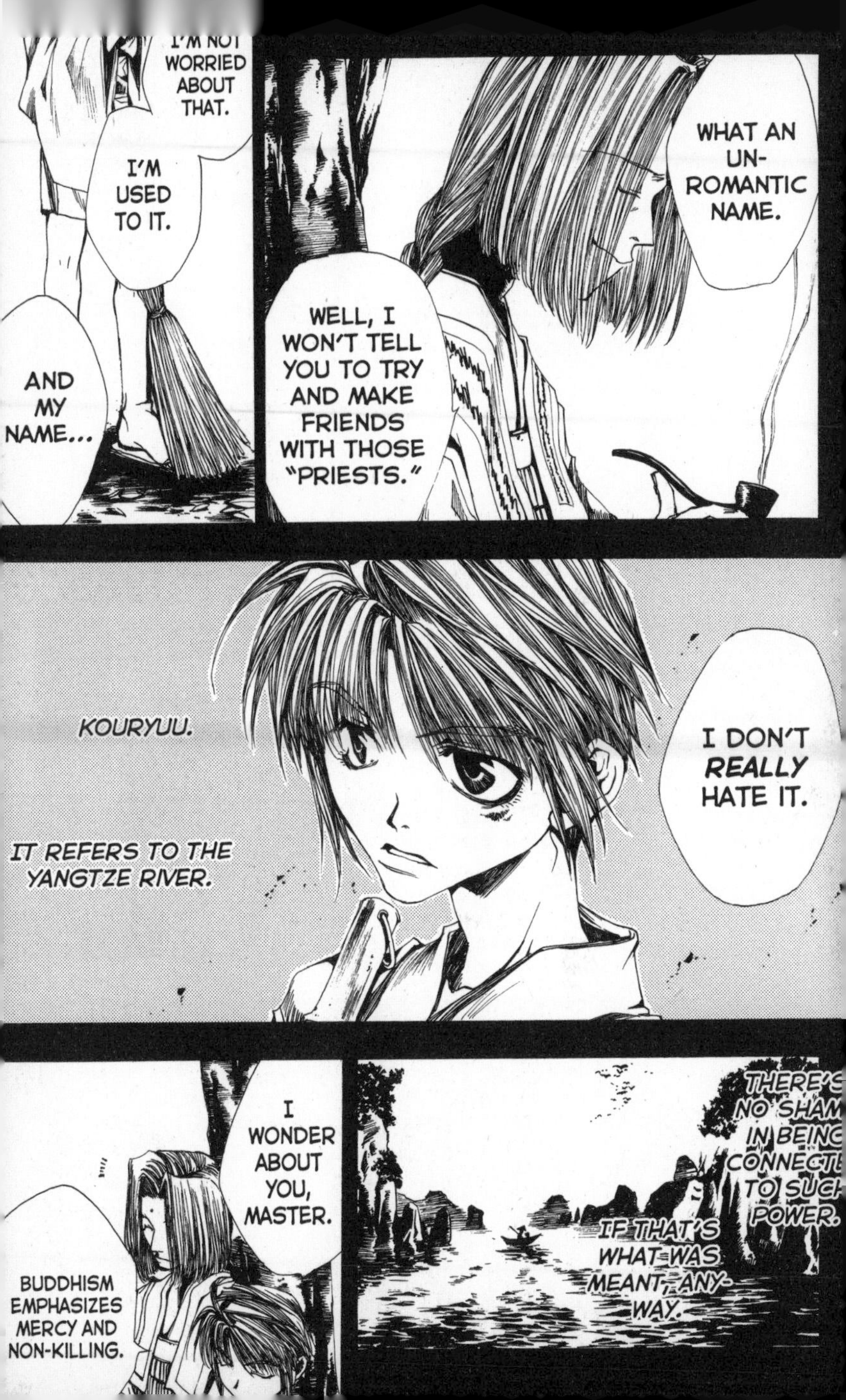
WHAT AN UN-ROMANTIC NAME.
WELL, I WON'T TELL YOU TO TRY AND MAKE FRIENDS WITH THOSE "PRIESTS."
I'M NOT WORRIED ABOUT THAT.
I'M USED TO IT.
AND MY NAME...
I DON'T *REALLY* HATE IT.
KOURYUU.
IT REFERS TO THE YANGTZE RIVER.
THERE'S NO SHAM IN BEING CONNECT TO SUCH POWER.
IF THAT'S WHAT WAS MEANT, ANYWAY.
I WONDER ABOUT YOU, MASTER.
BUDDHISM EMPHASIZES MERCY AND NON-KILLING.

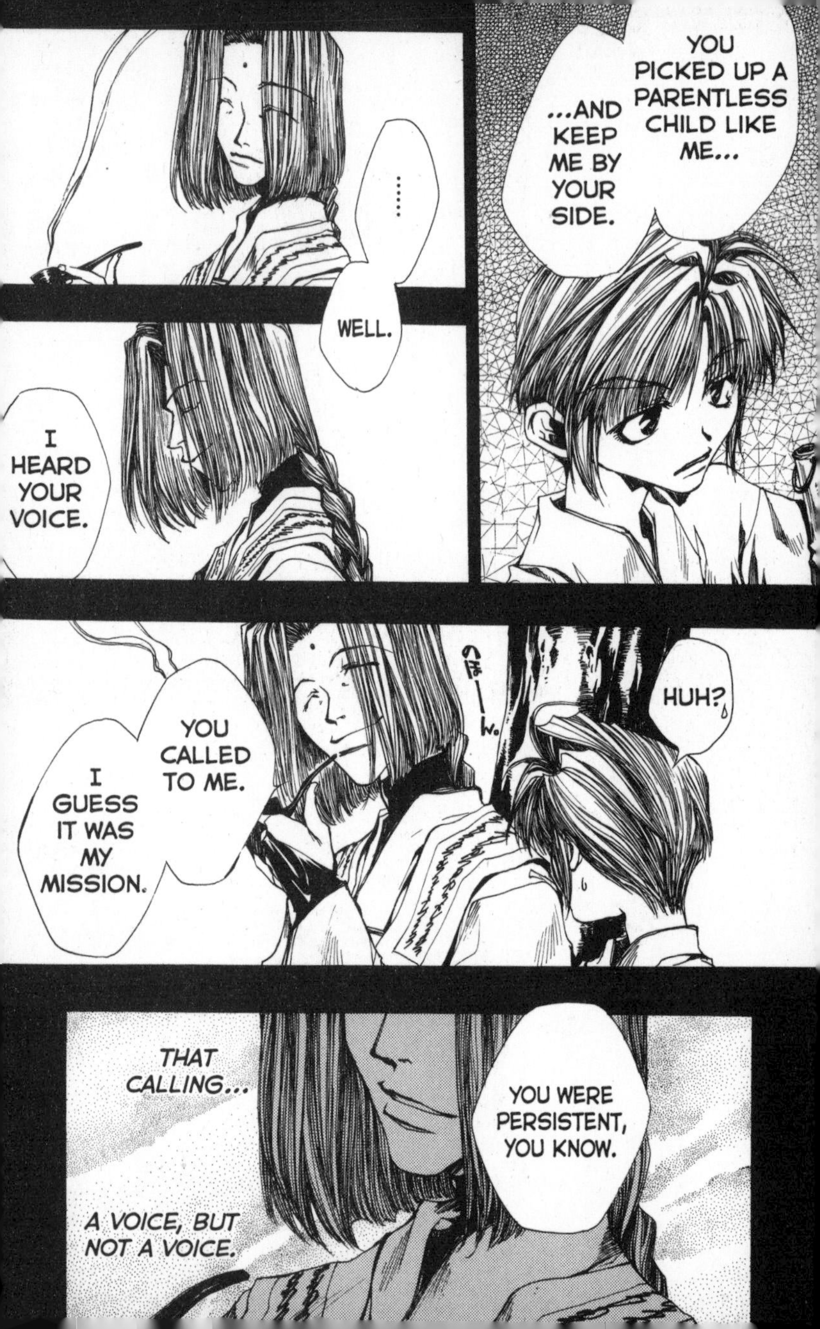
YOU PICKED UP A PARENTLESS CHILD LIKE ME...
...AND KEEP ME BY YOUR SIDE.
......
WELL.
I HEARD YOUR VOICE.
HUH?
のほーん
YOU CALLED TO ME.
I GUESS IT WAS MY MISSION.
YOU WERE PERSISTENT, YOU KNOW.
THAT CALLING...
A VOICE, BUT NOT A VOICE.

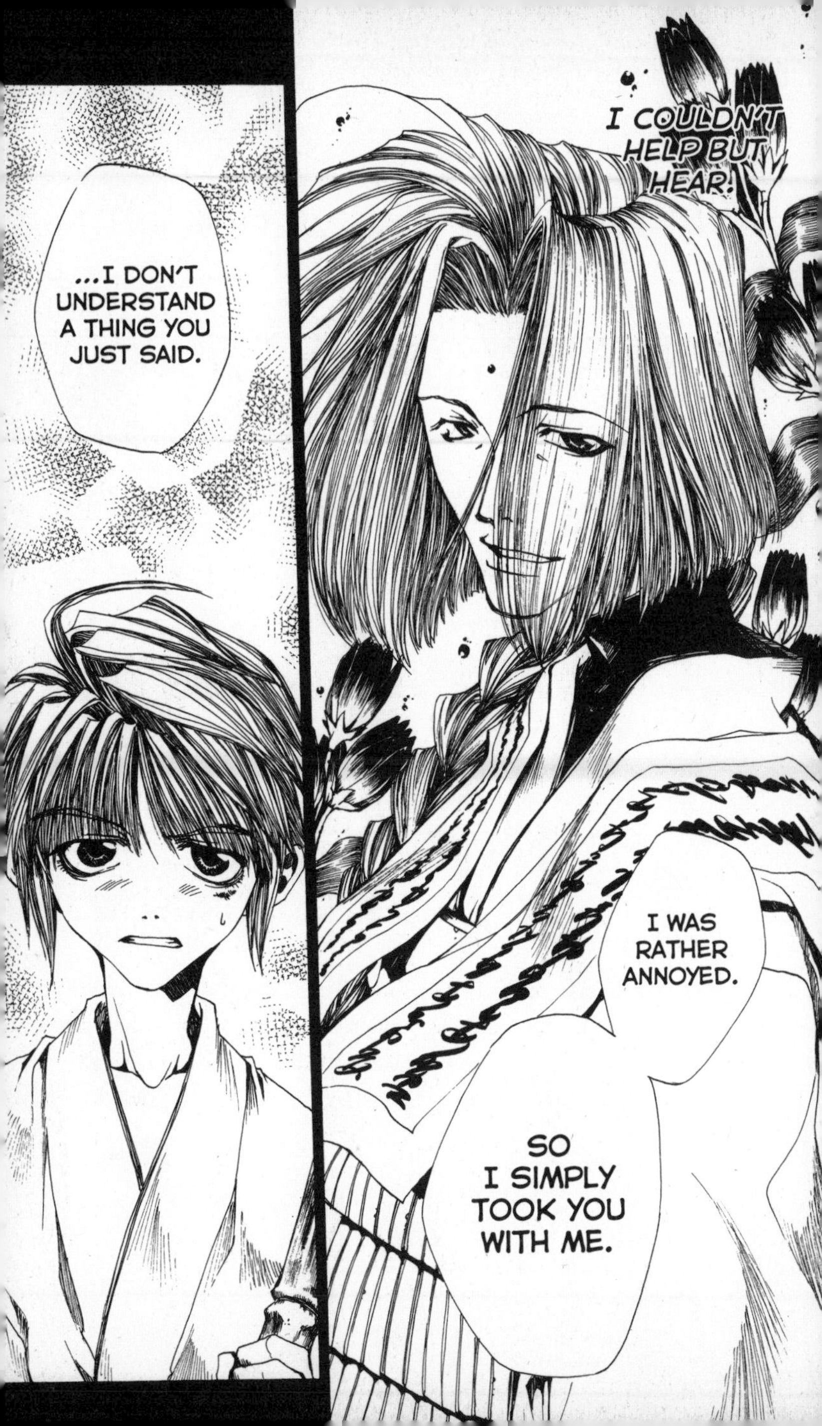
I COULDN'T HELP BUT HEAR!
I WAS RATHER ANNOYED.
SO I SIMPLY TOOK YOU WITH ME.
...I DON'T UNDERSTAND A THING YOU JUST SAID.

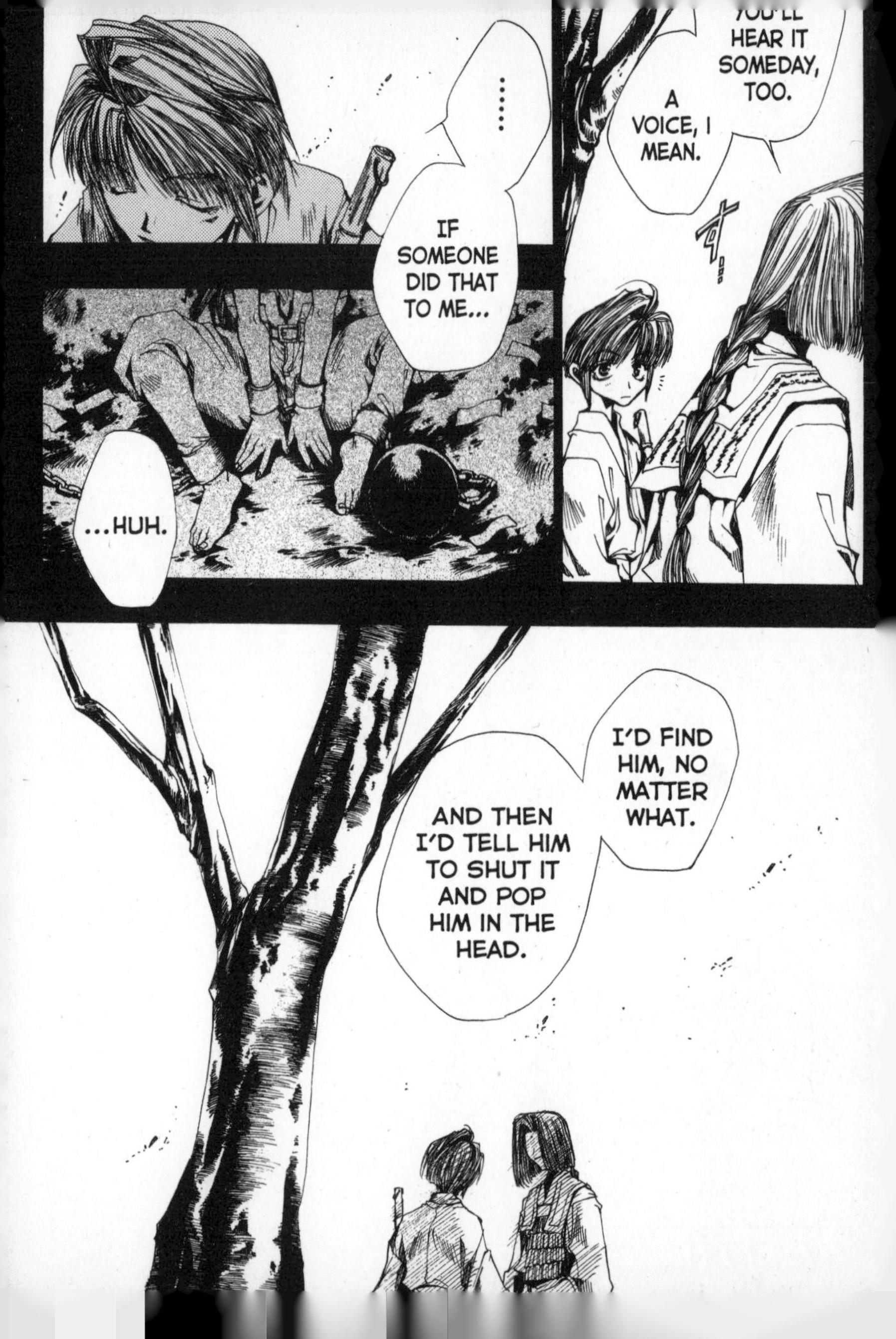
YOU'LL HEAR IT SOMEDAY, TOO.
A VOICE, I MEAN.
......
IF SOMEONE DID THAT TO ME...
...HUH.
I'D FIND HIM, NO MATTER WHAT.
AND THEN I'D TELL HIM TO SHUT IT AND POP HIM IN THE HEAD.

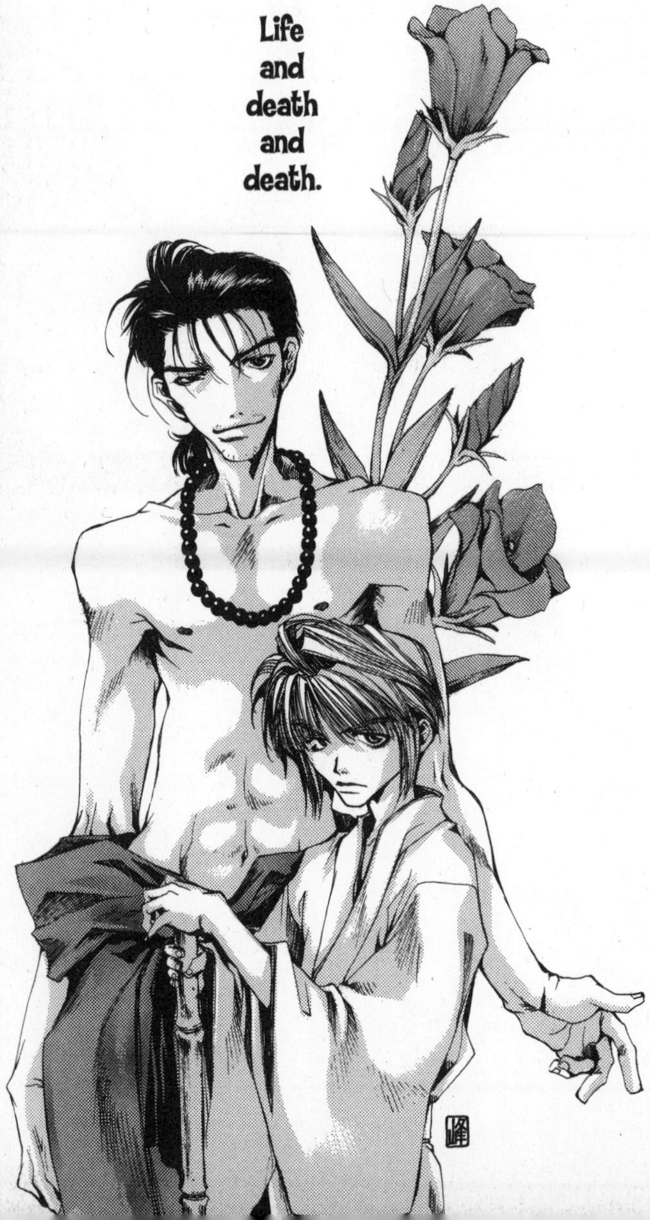
Life and death and death.

SOUND EFFECT CHART

THE FOLLOWING IS A LIST OF THE SOUND EFFECTS USED IN SAIYUKI. EACH SOUND IS LABELED BY PAGE AND PANEL NUMBER, SEPARATED BY A PERIOD. THE FIRST DESCRIPTION (IN BOLD) IS THE PHONETIC READING OF THE JAPANESE, AND IS FOLLOWED BY THE EQUIVALENT ENGLISH SOUND OR A DESCRIPTION.

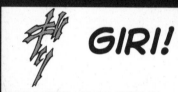

GIRI!

THIS USEFUL SOUND EFFECT HAS A COUPLE OF FUNCTIONS: IT CAN BE EITHER THE SOUND OF GRINDING TEETH OR TWO COMBATANTS STRUGGLING AGAINST EACH OTHER.

10.2	SHAAA: (RAIN)
10.4	SHAAA: (RAIN)
11.1-11.2	DOKUN X 3: (HEARTBEAT)
12.1	ZURU: SLIDE
12.3	GAKU X 2: TWITCH
12.5	GAKU X 2: TWITCH
13.1	GAKU: TWITCH
13.5	DOKUN: (HEARTBEAT)
14.1	PAKIIN: PASHING
14.2	KARAN: SHATTER
15.3	ZOZO: (GROWING EARS)
15.4	GIGIGI: (GROWING NAILS)
15.5	ZO: (GROWING HAIR)
15.6	SHUOOO:WHOOSH
15.7	ZAH: (SUDDEN APPEARANCE)
16-7	DON: (DRAMA!)
17.2	OOO: (WIND)
19.1	ZUN: LUNGE
19.2	GURI: GRIND
19.3	ZOKU: SHOCK
20.1	GIRI X3: (STRUGGLE)
20.2	SHUOOO:SHOOM
20.3	GUGU: STRAIN
20.4	GO: WHOOSH
20.5	ZUDOH: SLAM
21.1	ZAZAH: SKID
21.2	DAH: DASH
21.3	BYU: FWIP
21.4	BASHU X2: FIZZLE
22-23 TOP:	BAKII: POW
22-23 BOTTOM:	DOH: SLAM
23.3	JARI: CRUNCH
24.4	ZU: SLIDE
25.3	POU: GLOW
25.4	OOO: (EMANATE)
27.1	BERII: RIP
27.2	BOTA X 2: DRIP
27.4	POU: GLOW
28.2	KAH: BLAST
28.4	OOOO: SHIMMER
28.5	KURA: (HEADACHE)
28.6	BAH: FWIP
29.1	HYUN: (VANISH)
29.3	ZA: (TELEPATHY NOISE)
29.4	ZA X 2: (TELEPATHY NOISE)
30.6	GO: WHOOSH
31.1A	GOH: SWING

50.1	KURU: TURN
50.2	ZAAAH: FLASH
51.4	GACHA: CLACK (DOOR OPENING)
52.3	GATA: CLUNK
58.1	GATA: CLUNK
58.2	PAA: (BRIGHTEN)
58.3	TAH!: DASH
60.1	GORO: ROLL
61.2	ZUKIN: (SHARP PAIN)
61.3	GATA: CLUNK
61.5	HAH: GASP
65.3	OOO: (WIND)
65.4	ZA X 3: (TELEPATHY NOISE)
65.5	ZA: (TELEPATHY NOISE)
66.1	OOO: SHIMMER
66.2	ZA: (TELEPATHY NOISE)
66.4	ZA X 3: (TELEPATHY NOISE)
68.2	ZA: (DRAMATIC POSE)
68.3	ZAA: (DRAMATIC POSE)
73.1	ZAWAA: RUSTLE
73.2A	BAH: WHOOSH
73.2B	JAKI:CLICK (GUN COCKING)
73.3	ZA!!: (RECOIL)
73.4A	HYUN: (VANISH)
73.4B	GAN X 2: BANG
74.1	ZAAA: (SUDDEN APPEARANCE)
74.2	O: (EVIL AURA)
74.3	GAH: WHACK
74.5	GOH: SWING
75.1	GAKII: (PISTOL WHIP)
75.2	JAA:(RECOVER)
75.3	GAN X 2: BANG
75.4	SHIN: SILENCE
77.1	ZUKII: (SHARP PAIN)
77.2	ZAAAA: (RAIN)
79.2	ZAWA: RUSTLE
79.3	HAH: GASP
79.5	OOO: (EVIL AURA)
80.1	GISHII: FREEZE
80.3	OOOO: (EVIL AURA)
81.1	PAKII: (PARALYZE)
81.2	DOSAA: FWUMP

31.1B	BAH: BLOCK
31.3	ZAH: (DRAMATIC LOOK)
32.1	BASHI: GRAB
32.2	KAH!: (BARING FANGS)
32.3	GIRI: (STRUGGLE)
33.1	GOH: SWING
33.2	GAH: CHOMP
34.1	BUSHU: GUSH
34.2	GISHU: BITE
35.3	KIIII: (POWER)
35.4	BIKUN: (SNAP TO ATTENTION)
35.5	KIIII: (POWER)
36.1	KASHI: (DIVINE INTERVENTION...NOT TO BE CONFUSED WITH THE BREAKFAST CEREAL)
36.2	FUH: DAZE
36.3	DOSA: SLUMP
36.5	ZAH: (DRAMATIC FOOT)
38.1	DAN!: SLAM
38.2	YOO...: STAGGER
40-41	OOOO: SHIMMER
42.4	BAN!: (FANFARE)
44.4	KIRAN: SPARKLE
45.1	BISHI: POINT
45.3	GUII!!: GRAB!!
46.3	KURA: DAZE
46.4A	GAKUN: COLLAPSE
46.4B	BASHA: SPLASH
47.1	GUII: GRAB
48.1	OOOO: SHIMMER
48.2	PIKU: TWITCH
48.3	DON!: JOLT!

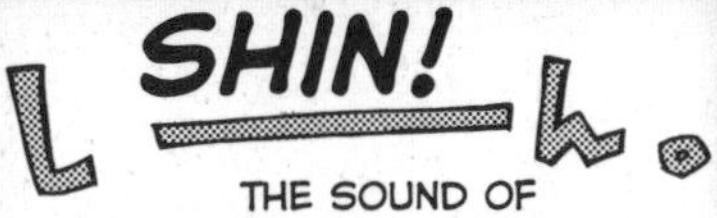
SHIN!

THE SOUND OF SILENCE. THE PERFECT "SOUND" EFFECT TO PUNCTUATE THOSE UNCOMFORTABLE MOMENTS WHERE JUST THE LACK OF ANY ACTUAL SOUNDS ISN'T SUFFICIENT. FOR EMPHASIS, YOU'LL USUALLY SEE A LONG LINE IN BETWEEN THE "SHI" AND THE "N," INDICATING PROLONGED SILENCE.

10.2	ZAAH: (DRAMA)
11.4	ZAWA X 2: CHATTER
11.5	KURU: TURN
12.1A	BII: (CRYING)
12.AB	FUUN: GRUNT
14.3	BIKU: TWITCH
15.1	BAN!: SLAM!
16.2	DOON: BOOM
17.2	GOBAN: KABOOM
18.1A	DOON: BOOM
18.1B	GICHICHI: (PINCERS CLICKING)
18.2	OO: (EVIL AURA)
19.1	BAH: WHOOSH
19.2	DOOON: BOOM
20.2	GARA X 2: RATTLE
20.3	BASHU: GUSH
20.4A	OOO: (EVIL AURA)
20.4B	DOOOON: BOOM
21.1	FUOOO: (MATERIALIZE)
21.2	HYUNN: WHOOSH
21.3	GOH: SWING
22.1	GAKII: CLANK
22.2	CHIIN!: CHING!
22.4	BUNN:WHUMP
22.5	HAH: GASP
23.1	DO: BOOM
23.3	GOH: TUMBLE
23.4	ZUSHA: CRASH
24.4A	ZAH: WHOOSH
24.4B	HYUOOO: (MATERIALIZE)
25.1	DAH: DASH
25.2	GOH: SWING
25.3	O: SWOOSH
25.4	DOUU: DOOM
26.3	TOH: POUNCE
26-127	DOGOO: SLAM
28.1	ZUSHA: CRASH
28.2	KYOTO: (DAZED AND CONFUSED)
28.5	BIKU X 2: TWITCH
81.4	JARI: CRUNCH
82.1	GAH: GAG!
82.2	GIRI: (STRUGGLE)
84.3	GII: SQUEEZE
84.4	GIRI X 2: (STRUGGLE)
84.5	DOKUN: (HEARTBEAT)
85.1	DOKUN: (HEARTBEAT)
85.2A	BIKI: SNAP
85.2B	GUKIKI: (VEINS POPPING)
85.3	GEHO: COUGH
85.4	PIKIN: CRACK
86-87	PAKIN:SHATTER
86.2	BIKU X 2: TWITCH
87.2	DOKUN X 3: (HEARTBEAT)
88.3	DOKUN: (HEARTBEAT)
88.4	BIKUU: X 2: TWITCH
89.1	GUII!: GRAB!
92.1A	PAN: BANG!
92.1B	BASA X 3: FLAP
93.4	ZAAA: (BREEZE)
94.3	GII: SLUMP
94.4	JARI: CRUNCH
96.3	TO: CATCH
96.4	DOSA: SLUMP
102.1	GOUN X 2: GONG

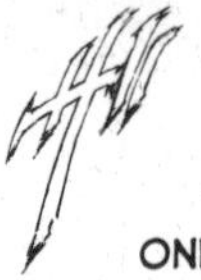

ZAA!

YOU'LL SEE THIS ONE A LOT IN *SAIYUKI*. "ZAA" INDICATES A DRAMATIC APPEARANCE. IF YOU WANT TO MAKE A LASTING IMPRESSION, ALWAYS COME IN WITH A COOL POSE AND A BIG "ZAA!"

152.4	GOPAA: SMACK!
153.1A	DAH: DASH
153.1B	DAN!: SLAM
153.3	DOKA X 3: PUNCH
153.4	GOH: WHAM
154.2	DA: DROP
154.3	GOH: WHAM
154.4	ZAZAH: SKID
155.1	BAKII: POW
156.1	DA DAH: DASH
157.2	GOH: WHAM
158.3	DOKAA: SLAM
159.2	BAH: BLOCK
159.3	ZAH: (DRAMA)
162.4	OOO: WHOOSH
162.5	DAH: DASH
163.7	BUCHII: RIP
164.1	DOH: TAP
164.5	DOKUN: (HEARTBEAT)
164.6	GARARA: CLATTER
165.4	GOH: WHOOSH
166.1	BAKII: POW
166.2	BUSHAA!: SKID
167.1	GOH: WHOOSH
167.2	BAH: WHOOSH
167.3	GAKII: CLANK
168.1	ZAN: SLICE
168.3	GOTO: THUNK
168.4	JUOOOO: (DEMATERIALIZE)
169.1	CHON: PLOP
169.2	OOO: (EVIL AURA)
170.2	DOSAA: FWUMP
170.4	OOO: (EVIL AURA)
170.6	BAH: WHOOSH
171.1	GOH: CRASH
173.4	OOO: SHIMMER
174.1	OOO: (EVIL AURA)
174.2	ZAZAH: CROUCH
174.4	DAN!: SLAM
175.3	OO: WHOOSH
175.5	DO: WHAM
176.2	GOH: WHOOSH
176-177	DON: (FANFARE)
178.1	GOON X 2: (MACHINERY)
178.3	PETAKO: SHUFFLE
179.6	KATA: TAP

137.5	DOGOO: SLAM
138.1	OOO: SMOLDER
138.4	ZAH: WHOOSH
138.5	GUH: GRAB
139.1	HAUA: (CONFUSED EXASPERATION)
139.3	PACHI X 2: CLAP
140.1	ZAH: (SUDDEN APPEARANCE)
141.3	SHITA: WAVE
141.4	POI: PLOP
142.5	ZAH X 2: ATTACK!
143.1	ZUGAH!: KICK!

ZAWA!

NO ONE REALLY CARES WHAT ALL THOSE EXTRAS IN THE BACKGROUND ARE SAYING, RIGHT? THAT'S WHY MANGA-KA USE THIS HANDY SOUND EFFECT TO INDICATE BACKGROUND CHATTER. YOU'LL SEE IT HOVERING OVER CROWDED CITY STREETS OR CLASSROOMS THROUGHOUT MANGA. IT CAN ALSO BE USED TO INDICATE THE SOUND OF WIND BLOWING THROUGH THE LEAVES OF A TREE. AIN'T THAT SWEET?

143.4A	GEHO X 2: COUGH
143.4B	BAH: HMPH
144.5	PEKO X 2: BOW
145.4	HYUN!: WHOOSH
146.1	GUN!: SNAG
147.5	DOH...: TAP
148.3	FUOOO: (MATERIALIZE)
148.4	O: (CONTINUATION OF ABOVE)
149.1	SHAKI: CLANK
149.2	SHARA: RATTLE
151.1	ZAZAH: SKID
151.3	FUOOO: (MATERIALIZE)
151.4	GOH: FOOM
151.5	GA X 2: CRACK
152.1	OO: SMOLDER
152.3	BAH: SHOCK

180.2	ZOKU: SHOCK
181.2	OO: SMOLDER
181.3	ZAH: (DRAMA)
183.5	ZUN: HOP
184-185	ZAAH: (DISAPPEAR)
187.6	ZARA: (DISINTIGRATE)
188.1	DOKUN: (HEARTBEAT)
188.2	GAKU: COLLAPSE
191.1	JAH X 3: SWEEP
191.3	ZUKI: (PAIN)
192.3	ZAAH: (BREEZE)
194.4	NOHON: SMIRK
196.1	SU: SLIDE

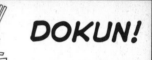

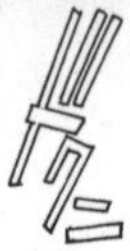

DOKUN!

IN MOST MANGA, A PLEASANT LITTLE "DOKI DOKI" IS THE PREFERRED SOUND FOR HEARTBEATS, BUT IN SAIYUKI, THEY NEEDED TO KICK IT UP A NOTCH. "DOKUN" IS THE SOUND OF A PARTICULARLY STRONG HEARTBEAT, USUALLY RESERVED FOR MOMENTS OF EXTREME SHOCK OR DEMONIC TRANSFORMATION.

SAIYUKI

最遊記

TOKYOPOP®

4

Kazuya Minekura

mysterious fortune-teller Chin Yisou takes great pleasure
ushing Hakkai's psychological boundaries, and Hakkai is
tened to find his bloody past nipping at his heels. When
Yisou starts targeting Sanzo and the others, our heroes
themselves not only fighting against him but against

Three warriors
with dragon blood
running through their veins

www.TOKYOPOP.com

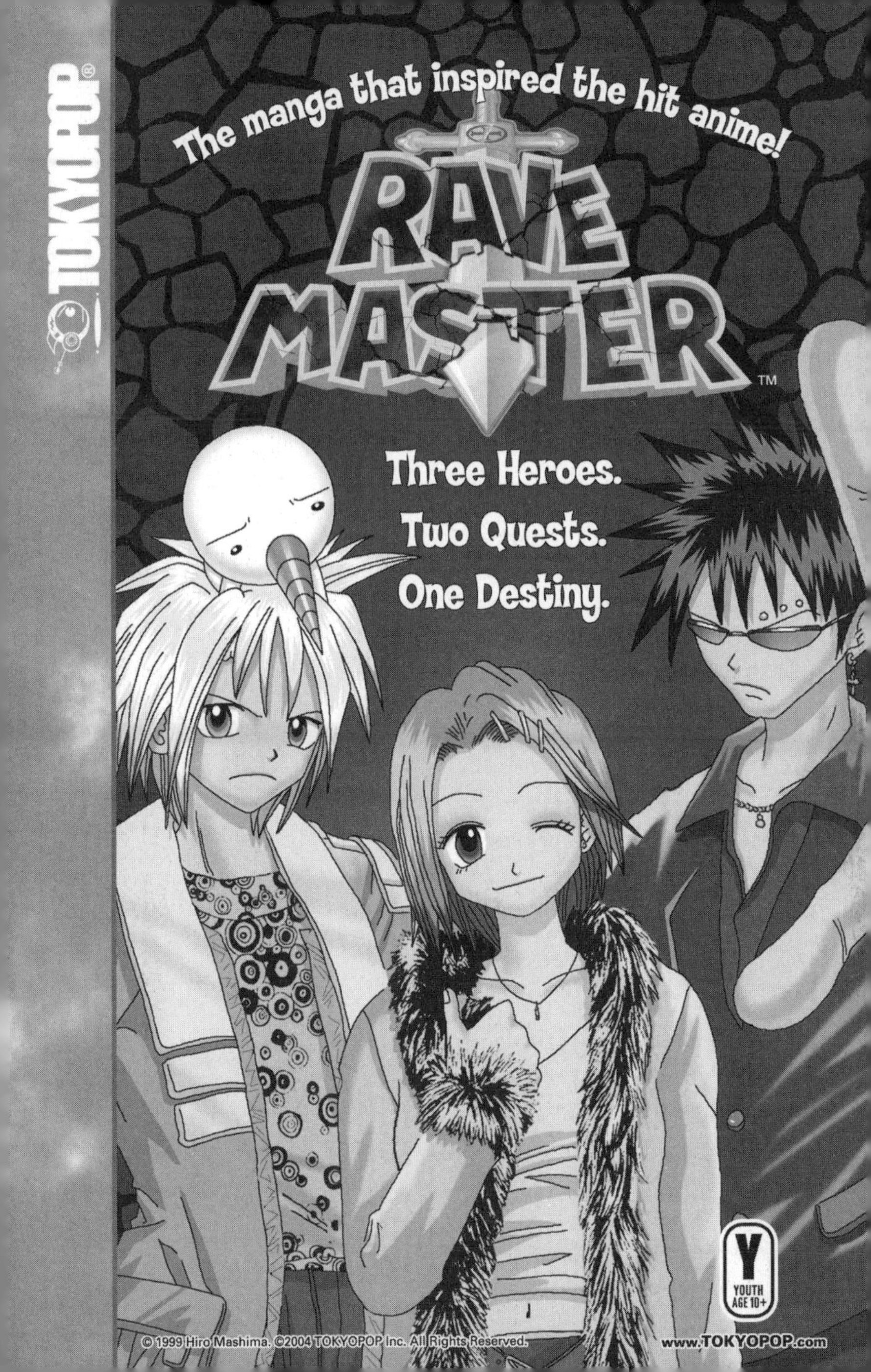
TOKYOPOP
The manga that inspired the hit anime!
RAVE MASTER™
Three Heroes.
Two Quests.
One Destiny.
Y YOUTH AGE 10+
© 1999 Hiro Mashima. ©2004 TOKYOPOP Inc. All Rights Reserved.
www.TOKYOPOP.com

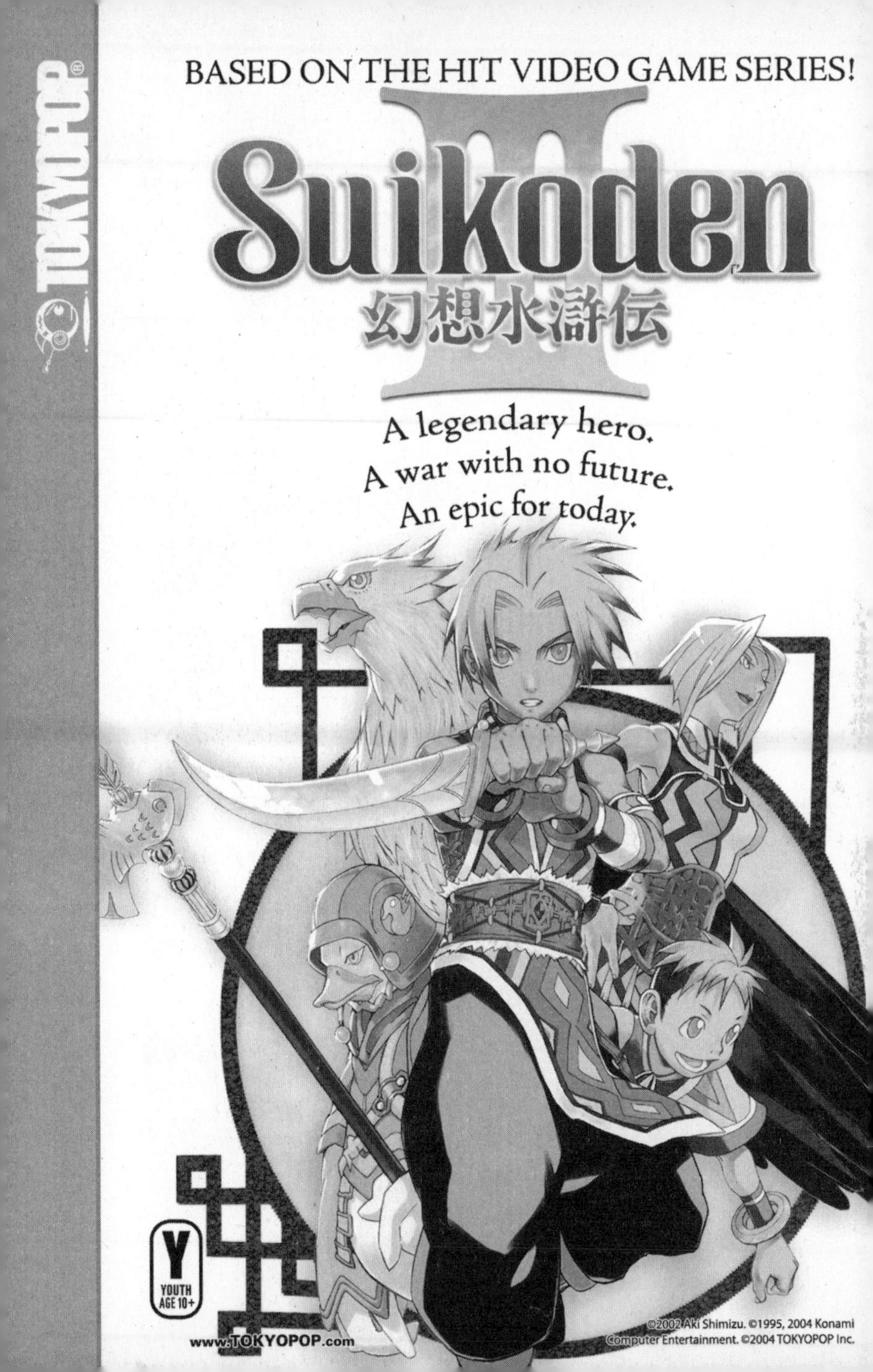
TOKYOPOP®
BASED ON THE HIT VIDEO GAME SERIES!
Suikoden
幻想水滸伝
III
A legendary hero.
A war with no future.
An epic for today.
Y
YOUTH AGE 10+
www.TOKYOPOP.com
©2002 Aki Shimizu. ©1995, 2004 Konami Computer Entertainment. ©2004 TOKYOPOP Inc.

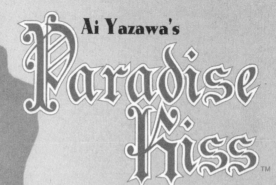

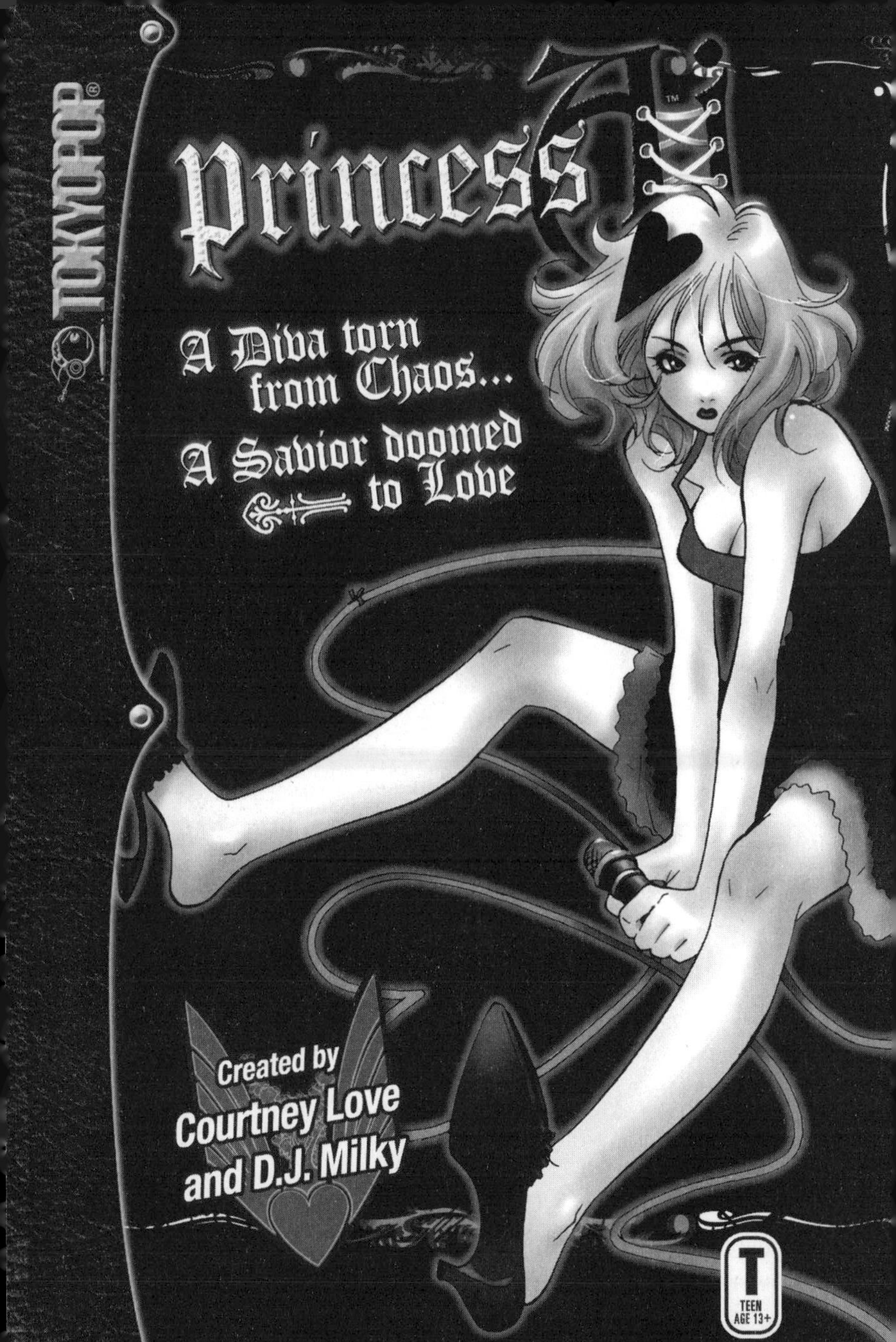
TOKYOPOP®
Princess Ai™
A Diva torn from Chaos...
A Savior doomed to Love
Created by
Courtney Love
and D.J. Milky
T
TEEN
AGE 13+

ALSO AVAILABLE FROM ☺TOKYOPOP®

ALSO AVAILABLE FROM TOKYOPOP

MANGA

.HACK//LEGEND OF THE TWILIGHT
@LARGE
ABENOBASHI: MAGICAL SHOPPING ARCADE
A.I. LOVE YOU
AI YORI AOSHI
ANGELIC LAYER
ARM OF KANNON
BABY BIRTH
BATTLE ROYALE
BATTLE VIXENS
BRAIN POWERED
BRIGADOON
B'TX
CANDIDATE FOR GODDESS, THE
CARDCAPTOR SAKURA
CARDCAPTOR SAKURA - MASTER OF THE CLOW
CHOBITS
CHRONICLES OF THE CURSED SWORD
CLAMP SCHOOL DETECTIVES
CLOVER
COMIC PARTY
CONFIDENTIAL CONFESSIONS
CORRECTOR YUI
COWBOY BEBOP
COWBOY BEBOP: SHOOTING STAR
CRAZY LOVE STORY
CRESCENT MOON
CROSS
CULDCEPT
CYBORG 009
D•N•ANGEL
DEMON DIARY
DEMON ORORON, THE
DEUS VITAE
DIABOLO
DIGIMON
DIGIMON TAMERS
DIGIMON ZERO TWO
DOLL
DRAGON HUNTER
DRAGON KNIGHTS
DRAGON VOICE
DREAM SAGA
DUKLYON: CLAMP SCHOOL DEFENDERS
EERIE QUEERIE!
ERICA SAKURAZAWA: COLLECTED WORKS
ET CETERA
ETERNITY
EVIL'S RETURN
FAERIES' LANDING
FAKE
FLCL
FLOWER OF THE DEEP SLEEP
FORBIDDEN DANCE
FRUITS BASKET
G GUNDAM

GATEKEEPERS
GETBACKERS
GIRL GOT GAME
GIRLS' EDUCATIONAL CHARTER
GRAVITATION
GTO
GUNDAM BLUE DESTINY
GUNDAM SEED ASTRAY
GUNDAM WING
GUNDAM WING: BATTLEFIELD OF PACIFISTS
GUNDAM WING: ENDLESS WALTZ
GUNDAM WING: THE LAST OUTPOST (G-UNIT)
GUYS' GUIDE TO GIRLS
HANDS OFF!
HAPPY MANIA
HARLEM BEAT
I.N.V.U.
IMMORTAL RAIN
INITIAL D
INSTANT TEEN: JUST ADD NUTS
ISLAND
JING: KING OF BANDITS
JING: KING OF BANDITS - TWILIGHT TALES
JULINE
KARE KANO
KILL ME, KISS ME
KINDAICHI CASE FILES, THE
KING OF HELL
KODOCHA: SANA'S STAGE
LAMENT OF THE LAMB
LEGAL DRUG
LEGEND OF CHUN HYANG, THE
LES BIJOUX
LOVE HINA
LUPIN III
LUPIN III: WORLD'S MOST WANTED
MAGIC KNIGHT RAYEARTH I
MAGIC KNIGHT RAYEARTH II
MAHOROMATIC: AUTOMATIC MAIDEN
MAN OF MANY FACES
MARMALADE BOY
MARS
MARS: HORSE WITH NO NAME
MINK
MIRACLE GIRLS
MIYUKI-CHAN IN WONDERLAND
MODEL
MY LOVE
NECK AND NECK
ONE
ONE I LOVE, THE
PARADISE KISS
PARASYTE
PASSION FRUIT
PEACH GIRL
PEACH GIRL: CHANGE OF HEART
PET SHOP OF HORRORS
PITA-TEN

04.23.04T

WITHDRAWN

STOP!

This is the back of the book.
You wouldn't want to spoil a great ending!

This book is printed "manga-style," in the authentic Japanese right-to-left format. Since none of the artwork has been flipped or altered, readers get to experience the story just as the creator intended. You've been asking for it, so TOKYOPOP® delivered: authentic, hot-off-the-press, and far more fun!

DIRECTIONS

If this is your first time reading manga-style, here's a quick guide to help you understand how it works.

It's easy... just start in the top right panel and follow the numbers. Have fun, and look for more 100% authentic manga from TOKYOPOP®!

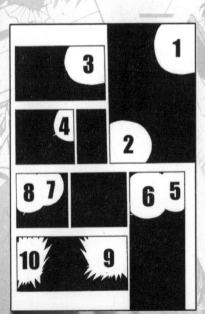